D1175848

Great Britain
and the
American Colonies,
1606–1763

edited by

JACK P. GREENE

HARPER PAPERBACKS

Harper & Row, Publishers
New York, Evanston, and London

GREAT BRITAIN AND THE AMERICAN
COLONIES, 1606–1763

Introduction, editorial notes, and compilation copyright
© 1970 by Jack P. Greene.

Printed in the United States of America.

First edition: HARPER PAPERBACKS, 1970, by
Harper & Row, Publishers, Inc., 49 East 33rd Street,
New York, N.Y. 10016.

A clothbound edition of this title is published by the
University of South Carolina Press.

Library of Congress Catalog Card Number: 78–95257

Contents

NOV 30 1970

V Reform, 1748–1763

Preface

THIS volume is largely devoted to an exploration of only two aspects of the relationship between Britain and the colonies—the economic and the political. It does not explicitly attempt to illustrate the much more subtle, much more elusive, and, ultimately, probably the much more important cultural connection. In doing the research necessary for the introductory essay, I was assisted by a grant-in-aid from the American Philosophical Society; I also wish to thank especially the staff of the William L. Clements Library for help in collecting documents, and the general editor of this series, Richard B. Morris, and my wife, Sue N. Greene, for helpful editorial advice.

Introduction*

I

"THE SETTLEMENT OF our colonies," Edmund Burke wrote in 1757, 150 years after the establishment of Jamestown, "was never pursued upon any regular plan; but they were formed, grew, and flourished, as accidents, the nature of the climate, or the dispositions of private men happened to operate." "Nothing of an enlarged and legislative spirit," he added, "appears in the planning of our colonies."[1] Burke's remarks accurately describe the process by which the English planted their colonies in America during the first three quarters of the seventeenth century. Undertaken almost entirely at their own expense by adventurers either singly or in proprietary or corporate groups, the colonies were not established according to any comprehensive design and during the early years received little direction and still less protection from the imperial government. Insofar as the colonies impinged upon imperial consciousness at all, English officials thought of them not as subordinate political communities, not as colonies of Englishmen organized into separate or auxiliary societies overseas, but rather as a series of economic units intended to contribute to the prosperity of England and to provide it with a solid claim to a portion of the vast riches of the New World.

Within the plantations, however, these broader purposes of colonization were submerged beneath a welter of personal and highly individual goals. To induce them to undertake so troublesome and expensive a work as the establishment of plantations, the Crown gave the sponsors of the several colonial enterprises exclusive title to vast areas of land, extensive governing powers, and, in many cases, special economic privileges. The sponsors in turn

* An abbreviated version of this introduction was presented at the American Historical Association meeting in San Francisco, December 29, 1965.
1. *An Account of the European Settlements in America* (2 vols., London, 1757), II, 288.

found it necessary to make generous concessions in the form of access to land, guarantees of self-governing rights, and, occasionally, temporary exemption from taxation to recruit settlers. Thus, on both levels—between the Crown and the sponsors on one hand and between the sponsors and individual colonists on the other—the English colonizing process depended initially upon contractual arrangements. These assured the sponsors and the individual colonists a generous amount of political freedom and the widest possible latitude to pursue their own personal objectives, with a minimum of reciprocal obligations either to the various governing agencies within the colonies or to the imperial government at home.

The result was the accentuation and acceleration of certain tendencies already present in English social and economic life. Already well on its way to becoming what C. B. MacPherson has recently and appropriately termed a "possessive market society," English society in the early seventeenth century was organized around and operated on a series of assumptions that MacPherson has called "possessive individualism." Among these assumptions, three were so extraordinarily congenial to conditions of settlement in the English colonies that they quickly came to govern in practice, if not in theory, most social relationships within the colonies and to determine the attitudes of the colonists toward the role of the home government in their affairs. The first of these assumptions was that all men are free from dependence upon the wills of others; the second, that freedom from dependence on others meant freedom from any relationships with others not entered into voluntarily by an individual with a view to his own interest; and the third, that the function of government was to protect the individual's property in his person and goods and to maintain orderly relations of exchange between the various individuals in society so that each could pursue his own interest.[2] Everywhere, even in colonies like Massachusetts Bay, where it was ostensibly subordinated to broader social and religious goals, individual enterprise was the dominant note. The belief that every individual should be free to seek his own interest, and that the Crown as well as the governments of the individual plantations was obligated by con-

2. C. B. MacPherson, *The Political Theory of Possessive Individualism* (Oxford: Clarendon Press, 1962), especially pp. 263–271.

tract to protect him in that search, was integral to English colonial life.

Prior to 1660, the imperial government made no sustained attempt to subordinate this individual enterprise to its own broader purposes, to counteract the centrifugal forces inherent in the conditions of settlement. When the Crown assumed control over Virginia in 1625 after the courts had vacated the charter of the Virginia Company, it asserted its jurisdiction over all the English plantations in America and declared its intention to provide "one uniforme Course of Government" for them all.[3] In developing an effective administration for Virginia, imperial officials did indeed work out an institutional framework for the internal administration of the colonies. And they articulated a series of policy objectives that explicitly asserted the right of the home government to regulate in its own interests all aspects of the internal government of the colonies. But the failure to develop any central agency in England for colonial administration, the distractions of the Civil War, the refusal of the colonists to abide by regulations they opposed, and the lack of adequate enforcement machinery prevented either Crown or Parliament from establishing effective controls over the colonies, despite sporadic attempts by one or the other to do so.

II

As the colonies increased in extent and population through the middle decades of the seventeenth century, however, and as their value both as sources of raw materials and as markets for English manufactures became more apparent, English commercial and political leaders alike began to fear lest the benefits of such valuable possessions be lost in the colonists' reckless pursuit of their several corporate and individual interests, lest they enter into destructive economic competition with each other or with England. They feared that the colonists might even take advantage of their extensive political privileges to set themselves up as autonomous polities or semi-independent allies of the Dutch, who had already successfully engrossed a large part of their carrying trade during the early years of the English Civil War. It was in response to these

3. "A Proclamation for Settlinge the Plantations of Virginia," May 13, 1625, Thomas Rymer (ed.), *Foedera, Conventiones, Literal, Acta Publica, Regis Anglicae* (2nd ed., 20 vols., London, 1726), XVIII, 72–73.

several fears that Parliament enacted the system of commercial regulations known as the navigation acts between 1650 and 1673. The first comprehensive attempt to define the economic relationship between England and the colonies, these measures gave expression to the mercantilist assumption that the economic interests of the colonies should be subordinated to those of the mother country; they also theoretically established a national monopoly of colonial trade and served as the basis for imperial economic policy toward the colonies for the remainder of the colonial period.

Although the navigation acts contained significant concessions to colonial interests, they proved exceedingly difficult to enforce, especially in the private colonies. The extensive powers conferred by the royal charters on the proprietors and governing corporations of those colonies made it possible for them to disregard and, in many cases, openly to flout the acts. When Edward Randolph, sent by imperial authorities in 1676 to investigate conditions in Massachusetts Bay, insisted that its leaders enforce the navigation acts, he was told that "laws made by your Majesty and your Parliament obligeth" Massachusetts residents "in nothing but what consists with the interests of that colony; that the legislative power is and abides in them solely to act and make laws by virtue" of their royal charter.[4] A simultaneous effort to persuade the colonies to remodel their political systems in such a way as to make them correspond as closely as possible to the English system was only somewhat more successful, encountering especially strenuous opposition in Massachusetts Bay.[5]

Reinforced by the pronounced tendency of both Charles II and James II to regard the colonies not simply as units for economic production but also, in the words of A. P. Thornton, as "adjuncts of the royal power, jewels in His Majesty's Crown,"[6] the realization

4. As quoted by A. Berriedale Keith, *Constitutional History of the First British Empire* (Oxford: Clarendon Press, 1930), pp. 104–105.

5. The most important attempt was by the Royal Commission of 1664–66 charged with capturing the New Netherlands from the Dutch and regulating the affairs of the New England colonies. Its success in both conquering and pacifying the New Netherlands and securing considerable cooperation from Connecticut and Rhode Island contrasted markedly with its failure in Massachusetts, where colonial leaders obstructed the commission in every way possible.

6. A. P. Thornton, *West-India Policy under the Restoration* (Oxford: Clarendon Press, 1956), p. 18.

grew that the movement for strict economic control and political uniformity would have to be accompanied by closer supervision in England if the navigation acts and the royal authority were ever to be fully obeyed in the private colonies. This realization resulted during the half century after 1675 in a sporadic attempt to reconstruct the political relationship between England and the colonies, by substituting for the traditional contractual arrangement (in which both colonists and Crown had been bound by certain mutual obligations set down in the charters) a new relationship in which the authority of the Crown would be unlimited and pre-eminent, if also benign and just. This movement proceeded in two phases, the first phase lasting from the mid-1670's until the Glorious Revolution of 1688, and the second from the establishment of new commercial regulations and new agencies of administration in 1696 until the early 1720's, when, under the long ministry of Sir Robert Walpole, imperial officials adopted a more casual attitude toward the colonies.

The first phase began with the creation in 1675 of the Lords of Trade, a permanent committee of the Privy Council responsible for overseeing the colonies. For ten years, until it lost its power to the Privy Council under James II, this body, assisted by a permanent staff and a flock of new Crown officers in the colonies, provided, for the first time since the beginning of English colonization nearly three quarters of a century earlier, vigorous and systematic supervision. In a concerted effort to secure colonial obedience to royal authority and the navigation acts, the Lords developed a comprehensive program that may be divided into three parts. The first part was simply to strengthen the Crown's hand in the four existing royal colonies: Virginia; Jamaica, which had been captured from the Spanish during the Interregnum; and Barbados and the Leeward Islands, which had passed from proprietary to royal control in 1663. In pursuit of this objective, the Lords sought to bring the royal governors themselves under closer supervision. Not only did they insist upon more frequent and fuller reports from all governors, but they also placed the governors under much more detailed and rigid regulations than ever before by greatly expanding both in scope and specificity the royal instructions given to governors to direct them in the conduct of their administrations.

Equally important in trying to establish effective imperial control over the royal colonies were the Lords' efforts to curtail the extensive powers of the elected legislative assemblies, the bastions of colonial opposition to imperial policy. Derived in large part from the dependence of the governors upon the assemblies for money, both for their own personal support and for all normal expenses of government, the power of the assemblies extended over virtually every aspect of colonial government; and the assumption of such full and complete legislative authority had already led colonial legislators to the heady conclusion that each assembly was the "epitome of the [English] House of Commons."[7] To render royal governors less dependent upon the assemblies, the Lords of Trade sought to persuade the assemblies of Virginia and Jamaica to follow the example of the legislatures of Barbados and the Leeward Islands; these, in 1663 and 1664, respectively, had voted a permanent revenue from which the salaries of the governor and other royal officials as well as many other ordinary expenses of government were drawn. The campaign, which was successful in Virginia and unsuccessful in Jamaica, was accompanied by a direct assault upon the legislative powers of the assemblies, in which the Lords not only attempted unsuccessfully to apply Poynings' Law—which required the Crown's prior approval of all laws passed by the Irish Parliament—to Jamaica and Virginia, but also ruled that the assemblies existed only by the favor of the Crown and not as a matter of right, as the assemblies claimed.

The second part of the Lords' program was to prevent the creation of any more private colonies and to convert those already in existence into royal colonies. Upon its recommendation, the New Hampshire towns were separated from Massachusetts Bay in 1679 and made a royal colony; and, although the Lords was unable to block the grant of Pennsylvania to William Penn in 1681, it did secure the insertion in the Pennsylvania Charter of a series of limitations and restrictions that subjected Penn to much stricter controls than any of his predecessors. Beginning in 1684, the Lords also engineered the general assault upon the charters of the private colonies in the courts that resulted in the forfeiture of the charter of Massachusetts Bay.

The third part of the program, a logical extension of the previous two, was the consolidation of the colonies into three general governments, presided over by vice-regal representatives of the King and unhampered by representative assemblies. This objective—evi-

7. The quotation is from Agnes M. Whitson, *The Constitutional Development of Jamaica 1660 to 1729* (Manchester: Manchester University Press, 1929), p. 162.

dently inspired at least in part by Colbert's reforms in the French colonial system—was in the air as early as 1678. In 1686, after the accession of James II, who shared with the Lords of Trade an antipathy to private colonies and colonial representative institutions, it led to the establishment of the Dominion of New England, intended to include all of the colonies from Maine south to Pennsylvania.

The second phase in the imperial attempt to reconstruct the political relationship between England and the colonies and to strengthen the navigation system was inaugurated in 1696—first, with the passage of a new navigation act to provide for stricter enforcement of the old measures and to declare null and void all colonial laws violating any of the navigation acts; and, second, with the creation of the Board of Trade, to take over the chores formerly handled by the then defunct Lords of Trade. For some time after the Glorious Revolution of 1688–89 it appeared that imperial officials might adopt a more permissive policy toward the colonies. Neither William III, the new king, nor his advisers showed any disposition to revive the Dominion of New England, which had been overthrown by the New Englanders in the wake of the revolution, or to govern without representative assemblies. In 1691 they granted a new charter to Massachusetts Bay, albeit one embodying severe limitations upon the colony's self-governing powers; and in 1694, Pennsylvania, which had been taken over by the Crown in 1692, was restored to William Penn.

But it soon became clear after 1696 that the new Board of Trade would pursue policies which bore a remarkable resemblance to those of its predecessor. Established in the midst of the first of the four major intercolonial wars between England and the Latin powers between 1689 and 1763, it was beseiged during its first months with complaints from royal officials and private individuals in the continental colonies about the failure of the colonies to unite in common defense against the French and Indians. The cause of the difficulty, the complainants agreed, was "the number and independency of so many small governments" which by "reason of their several interests" regarded each other "in a manner . . . as foreigners, so that, whatsoever mischiefs happen in one part the rest . . . remain unconcerned."[8] Reprehensible enough in peace-

8. The quotation is from John Nelson, Memorial to Board of Trade [Sept. 23, 1696] in William Noel Sainsbury, et al., (eds.), Calendar of State Papers, Colonial (43 vols., London, 1860–   ), 1696–97, 134–138.

time, such patent parochialism could be disastrous in the face of a unified enemy. And so, because experience seemed to indicate—as the Board declared in one of its first major reports—that the colonies "in their present state" would "always . . . refuse each other mutual assistance, minding more their present profit than the common defence,"[9] the Board, like the Lords of Trade a decade earlier, quickly concluded that the only remedy was consolidation of the colonies adjacent to the French. The Board was careful, however, not to repeat the mistakes of its predecessor. It deliberately sought to avoid offending local interests and raising a political storm by establishing only a military, rather than a civil union, securing the appointment in early 1697 of the Earl of Bellomont as governor of the three northern royal colonies—Massachusetts, New Hampshire, and New York—and commander-in-chief of the forces of all of the colonies north of Pennsylvania.

Resistance to Bellomont in the charter colonies of Rhode Island and Connecticut, and continued reports of their violation of the laws of trade, convinced the Board of Trade that the old Lords of Trade had been right in another of its objectives: the private colonies had to be brought under the direct supervision of the Crown if they were ever to be properly subordinated to the imperial government. Nor did the Board expect to have to use the costly and time-consuming process of going through the courts to accomplish this objective; it had a weapon unavailable to its predecessor: the authority of Parliament. Parliament's competence in this area would have been denied by Charles II or James II, but after 1688 imperial administrators counted on the assistance of Parliament in handling difficult colonial situations. When the Board began to consider recalling the colonial charters, it automatically assumed that the recall would be handled by parliamentary statute. In a stinging indictment of the private colonies, presented to the King in March, 1701, the Board declared that these colonies had in no way answered the design "for which such large tracts of land, and such privileges and immunities were granted"; charged them with disobeying the navigation acts, failing to defend themselves, and passing laws repugnant to those of the mother country; and recommended that they be "put into the same state and dependency as those of your Majestie's other

9. Board of Trade to Lords Justices, Sept. 30, 1696, in *ibid.*, 165–167.

Plantations . . . by the Legislative power of this Kingdom."[10] To
this end bills were brought into Parliament in 1701, 1702, and
1706, but because of the opposition of the proprietors, a genuine
reluctance by many members of Parliament to tamper with private
property, the vagaries of party politics, and, after the beginning of
Queen Anne's War in 1702, an uncertain international situation
that made any measure likely to produce discontent in the colonies
seem highly imprudent, none of the bills got a full hearing, all
failed to pass, and the Board temporarily abandoned the project.

But it was not only the private colonies that caused difficulties
for the Board of Trade. Governors of the royal colonies complained
of continued violations of the navigation acts and of their inability
to enforce their instructions from the Crown or to cope with the
representative assemblies, whose devotion to the protection of local
interests and pretensions to the status of colonial Houses of Commons seemed to have increased dramatically since the Glorious
Revolution. From Jamaica, Governor Sir William Beeston wrote in
1701 that the members of the lower house believed "that what a
House of Commons could do in England, they could do here, and
that during their sitting all power and authority was only in their
hands."[11] Similar reports came from Lord Cornbury and Robert
Hunter in New York and New Jersey, and from Robert Lowther in
Barbados, Cornbury remarking that "as the Country increases they
grow saucy, and noe doubt but if they were allowed to goe on, they
will improve upon it."[12] Such behavior, so obviously patterned
after the "various and dissonant models in the Charter and Pro-
priet[ar]y Governments," could only be interpreted, the governors universally agreed, as nothing less than a design among the
colonists "to make themselves an independent people, and to that
end . . . to divest the administration . . . [in the colonies] of
all the Queen's power and authority and to lodge it in the Assembly." "This project hath been a long time on foot and a great
progress hath been made in it," Lowther wrote in 1712, "for they
have extorted so many powers from my predecessors, that there is

10. Board of Trade to Queen, March 26, 1701, in *ibid.*, *1701*, 141–143;
italics added. The Board first suggested the possibility of calling on Parliament in a report of Feb. 26, 1698, in *ibid.*, *1697–98*, 121–122.
11. Beeston to Board of Trade, Aug. 19, 1701, in *ibid.*, *1701*, 424–425.
12. Cornbury to Board of Trade, Nov. 6, 1704, Feb. 19, 1705, in *ibid.*,
1704–5, 386.

now hardly enough left to keep the peace, much less to maintain the decent respect and regard that is due to the Queen's servant."[13] Resolved to prevent them from ever obtaining "the independency they thirst after," the Board of Trade rigidly adhered to the position laid down by the Lords of Trade a quarter of a century earlier, insisting that the lower houses existed not as a matter of right but only by the favor of the Crown, and would never be permitted to assume "all the priviledges of the House of Commons in England."[14] But, no matter how strong its resolution the Board, as a body with only advisory authority, was powerless either to check the growing pretensions of the lower houses or to provide effective support for the governors in carrying out their instructions against the opposition of local colonial interests.

Such obvious impotence, combined with the colonists' frequent defiance even of executive orders direct from the King and Privy Council, caused imperial officials to think more and more in terms of parliamentary intervention. How far they were willing to go in involving Parliament in the administration of the colonies was revealed in 1711–13 by their attempts to force the New York Lower House to settle a salary upon Robert Hunter, who became governor of the colony in 1710. When the Assembly failed to vote as large a salary as stipulated by Hunter's instructions or to provide for other executive officials, the Privy Council, upon the recommendation of the Board, took the unprecedented step in March, 1711 of threatening to bring before Parliament a bill "for Enacting a Standing Revenue . . . within the Province of New York for the Support of the Governor there, and the necessary Expences of the Government" if the Assembly continued to refuse to provide the "Necessary Support" itself.[15] Although the Board repeated this threat on several occasions and the Privy Council twice ordered bills to be brought before the House of Commons, the Assembly

13. Hunter to St. John, Jan. 1, 1712, in *ibid.*, *1711–12*, 189–190; Lowther to Board of Trade, Aug. 16, 1712, in *ibid.*, *1712–14*, 29.
14. Board of Trade to Bellomont, April 29, 1701, in *ibid.*, *1701*, 180; to Cornbury, Feb. 4, 1706, in *ibid.*, *1706–8*, 45; to St. John, April 23, 1712, in *ibid.*, *1711–12*, 267–268; to Hunter, June 12, 1712, in *ibid.*, *298–299*; and to Lowther, July 20, 1713, in *ibid.*, *1712–14*, 207–209.
15. Board of Trade to Privy Council, March 1, 1711, and Order in Council, March 1, 1711, in W. L. Grant and J. Munro (eds.), *Acts of the Privy Council, Colonial Series*, (6 vols., London: His Majesty's Stationary Office, 1908–12), II, 641–642.

stood firm for over two years. Finally, Hunter, despairing of getting any effective backing from London, agreed to a compromise solution in the summer of 1713 that led ultimately to the resolution of the conflict and the abandonment by imperial authorities of any plans to turn to Parliament. That no bill was actually brought into Parliament during this long controversy casts considerable doubt upon the sincerity of the threats and upon the ultimate willingness of Crown officials to take such a radical departure from traditional practice by admitting Parliament into the actual administration of the internal political affairs of the colonies. But both the statements and the behavior of the Board of Trade strongly indicate that its members did indeed want Parliament to intervene, hoping thereby to establish a precedent that would serve as a standing example to the "other Governments in America" of what might happen to them if they persisted in assuming "pretended rights tending to an independency on the Crown of Great Britain."[16] Whatever the real motives and intentions of either the members of the Board or higher Crown officials, this incident illustrates the extent to which they had come both to realize that executive power alone was insufficient to force the colonies to comply with royal commands and to expect that Parliament could and would be called upon whenever its assistance seemed necessary to handle any unusual emergency within the colonies.

Although the Board of Trade was unsuccessful in its efforts to enlist Parliament's aid in its campaigns to resume the charters of the private colonies and to enforce the royal instructions, it had no trouble in securing parliamentary legislation on the internal economic life of the colonies. In the decades following the Restoration, the initial enthusiasm for colonies among English commercial groups had waned somewhat; many of them began to argue that the colonies, by drawing people out of England and thereby reducing the size of the labor pool, retarded the development of manufacturing and slowed economic growth. After the Glorious Revolution, economic writers such as Sir Josiah Child and Charles Davenant tried to counter these arguments by pointing out that the colonies supplied England with commodities that would otherwise have to be purchased from foreign competitors, created additional

16. Board of Trade to Dartmouth, April 1, 1713, in Sainsbury, *et al.* (eds.), *Cal. St. Papers, Col.*, *1712–14*, 168; to Lowther, July 20, 1713, and to Lord Archibald Hamilton, March 22, June 21, 1714, in *ibid.*, 207–209, 322, 359–360.

"domestic" markets for English manufactured goods, encouraged the growth of English shipping and overseas trade, and otherwise stimulated the English economy. This counterargument was convincing enough when applied to the sugar colonies in the West Indies and the tobacco colonies of the Chesapeake—colonies whose economies obviously supplemented that of England, whose exports to England yielded large customs revenues, and whose labor requirements had been responsible for the development of the lucrative traffic in African slaves. But it was not so persuasive in regard to the northern continental colonies, whose economies were so similar to that of England as to be potentially competitive. In canvassing this question, economic thinkers and imperial officials gradually came to the conclusion that the northern colonies must be discouraged from embarking upon competitive manufactures and that, if possible, their economies should be reshaped so that they might complement the parent economy. This fear of future competition was behind the extension to the colonies of the Woolen Act of 1699, which, though primarily aimed at Ireland, limited the sale of finished woolens produced in the colonies to strictly local markets. And the desire to divert the northern colonies from trade and encourage them to produce naval stores, for which England was otherwise dependent upon the Baltic, was an important consideration in Parliament's decision to establish bounties for colonial naval stores by an act in 1705. Although it did indeed stimulate the development of a thriving naval stores industry in the Carolinas, the last statute failed to achieve the desired results in the northern colonies, and in New England the colonists openly violated a provision reserving all pine trees suitable for the production of masts for the Royal Navy. During Queen Anne's War, it became apparent that at least in wartime the northern colonies performed a vital function by supplying the West Indian colonies with provisions, lumber, work animals, and other necessaries which they could not then obtain directly from England. But there was still considerable sentiment among imperial officials for a legislative program that would, by operating directly upon the internal economic life of the northern colonies, make them fit more closely the prevailing concept of what an ideal colony should be.

This sentiment, plus the obvious difficulties encountered in trying to enforce imperial policies in both private and royal colonies, made it extremely likely that as soon as Queen Anne's War was over the Board of Trade would seek some major revisions in the existing colonial system. No sooner had the Board been created than it began to receive reform proposals from individuals concerned about the diversities and anomalies in the system and anxious to play the role of imperial statesmen. In the years following the Treaty of Utrecht in 1713, the number of such proposals increased sharply. The details of these proposals varied greatly. Some wanted to take colonial administration out of politics entirely and place it in the hands of a board of experts with full power to make and enforce decisions; others wanted a more elaborate structure of government in the colonies; and still others wanted to reorganize the colonies on the continent into one or more general governments. Whatever the differences in means, however, the basic objective of these proposals was the same: establishment of closer imperial controls. Yet, few advocated any drastic curtailment of colonial liberties. Most agreed with Charles Davenant that "nothing but such an arbitrary power as shall make them desparate, can bring them to rebel."[17]

Although the Board of Trade was obviously sympathetic with the central aim of these proposals, the uncertainty of the internal domestic situation arising out of the Hanoverian accession in 1714 and the Jacobite uprising in 1715 prevented the adoption of the comprehensive reforms it had long hoped for. In 1715, the Board's campaign to convert the private colonies into royal colonies received a major setback when Parliament failed for the fourth time to pass a bill for that purpose and the Privy Council decided to return Maryland, which had been taken over by the Crown in the wake of the Glorious Revolution, to the Calvert family. The Board did manage to make a few piecemeal changes, disallowing a number of laws that encroached upon the royal prerogative, inserting in the royal instructions several clauses intended to clamp down on the power of the colonial assemblies, and securing the appointment of its own special legal counsel to facilitate the review of colonial legislation. But continued reports of the lower houses' refusal to abide by the royal instructions, and the opposition of the charter governments to royal customs officials charged with enforcement of the navigation acts, seemed to indicate that major alterations were required.

17. The quotation is from Charles Davenant, "On the Plantation Trade," *Political and Commercial Works* (5 vols., London, 1771), II, 10–11.

The Board got its chance in August, 1720, when the advisers of the Crown, uncertain how to respond to the recent uprising against the proprietors in South Carolina, asked it to submit a report on the "state and condition" of the colonies, with recommendations for their "better government and security." The Board's response —"the most complete and illuminating of all the reports prepared by the office"[18]—took over a year to prepare and was of massive proportions. Finally submitted on September 8, 1721, the report, not surprisingly, called for a major renovation of colonial administration. Basically, it recommended the establishment of a more rational system that would permit the achievement of most of the specific objectives of British colonial policy as they had emerged since the Restoration. To remove the many ambiguities from the imperial-colonial relationship, achieve greater administrative unity, and secure more effective enforcement of the laws of trade were major priorities. The report also wished to divert the colonies from manufacturing, find some way to make the northern colonies fit more snugly into the mercantile system, give the Crown tighter control over the disposition of its lands and woods in the colonies, improve royal revenues through more systematic collection of quit rents, convert the proprietary and corporate colonies into royal colonies, check the extensive authority of colonial lower houses and the rampant particularism of the colonies, and render royal officials financially independent of the lower houses—all of these ancient goals of the Board and, in many cases, the Lords of Trade before it being important elements in the recommended program.

Although the Board's general objectives were not new, some of its proposals for achieving them were. Having by this date abandoned hope of securing parliamentary action on the recall of the charters of the private colonies, it now urged that the Crown resume the charters "by purchase, agreement or otherwise"—a procedure suggested by the recent offer from the proprietor of Pennsylvania to sell that colony to the Crown, and by the petition of the insurgents in South Carolina for royal government. Acting on proposals frequently made by colonial officials and other interested observers, the Board sought to secure more efficient administration in both London and the colonies by recommending that authority over the colonies be concentrated in one agency whose head

18. Charles M. Andrews, *The Colonial Period of American History* (4 vols., New Haven, Conn.: Yale University Press, 1935–38), IV, 389–390.

would have direct access to the King; that all colonial officeholders be required to discharge their duties "in person"; and that a general government be set up for the continental colonies, to be presided over by a lord lieutenant with absolute control over military affairs, supervisory power over governors of individual colonies, and, in conjunction wtih an advisory council of deputies from each colony, authority to set quotas of men and money in time of war.[19]

The fate of this report is instructive. A few of its specific proposals were eventually carried out. Although there was no intensive effort to redirect the economies of the northern colonies, Parliament did enact additional naval stores acts in 1722 and 1729 and, while there was no comprehensive program to purchase the private colonies, the imperial government did buy both Carolinas in 1719. Additional recommendations were implemented, at least in part, in the 1750's and 1760's. But the immediate failure of the imperial government to adopt a significant number of the proposals underlined the long-term failure of the Board of Trade. In twenty-five years it had been unable to gain sufficient support to enable it fully to carry out any of its projects for the political reconstruction of the empire, with the result that the colonists still refused to obey any trade laws that seemed, as one official in the colonies complained, to hinder "the growth and prosperity of their little commonwealths."[20] Imperial political authority within most colonies remained infinitely weaker and more uncertain than the members of the Board and officers in the colonies would have preferred.

Despite its failure to achieve many of its general policy objectives, the Board had, in the process of formulating them, articulated a cluster of working assumptions about the nature of the relationship between Britain and the colonies that had, at least within imperial circles, come to be so widely accepted that they had been elevated to the status of unchallengeable ideals. Two of the most important of these assumptions had been inherited from the Lords of Trade. The first and most fundamental was implied in the familiar parent-child metaphor employed increasingly to describe the imperial-colonial connection. If England was the mother

19. This report is in Sainsbury, et al. (eds.), Cal. St. Papers, Col., 1720–21, 408–449.
20. Caleb Heathcote to Board of Trade, Sept. 7, 1719, as quoted by Dixon Ryan Fox, Caleb Heathcote, Gentleman Colonist (New York: Scribner's, 1926), pp. 186–189.

country and the colonies were her offspring, it clearly followed that the colonies were dependents, who needed the protection of and who were obligated to yield obedience to their parent state. In any conflict of wills or judgment, the colonies had to defer to the superior strength and wisdom of the imperial government.

The second assumption held that the welfare of the whole empire had to take precedence over the good of any of the individual parts. It was "an unalterable Maxim," one writer declared, "that a lesser publick Good must give place to a greater; and that it is of more Moment to maintain a greater, than a lesser Number of Subjects, well employed to the Advantage of any State."[21] A hallowed political convention, this idea was a potentially useful counterbalance to the particularist and individualist inclinations of the colonists. As in most similar political associations, however, there was a strong tendency among governing officials to define the corporate welfare in terms of the interests of the dominant member, and to imperial officials in London the good of the whole empire meant the supremacy of the royal prerogative and the commercial interests of Great Britain. The worth of a colony, Sir Josiah Child wrote in 1693, was to be measured according to how it contributed to "the gain or loss of this Kingdom."[22] And it was an accepted principle, as economist Charles Davenant declared in 1698 in a passage copied into a number of later treatises on the colonies, that "Colonies are a strength to their mother kingdom, while they are under good discipline, while they are strictly made to observe the fundamental laws of their original country, and while they are kept dependent on it."[23]

This feeling that the colonies should be dependent gave rise to still a third assumption about the imperial-colonial relationship: that the colonial governments had to be and were subordinate to the imperial government; that, however similar they might be in appearance, structure, and function to the government of Britain, they were, in the final analysis, no more than "so many Incorporations at a Distance, invested with an Ability of making temporary By-Laws for themselves agreeable to their respective Situations and Climates, but no ways interfering with the legal Prerogative of the

21. Sir William Keith, "A short Discourse on the Present State of the Colonies in America with Respect to the Interest of Great Britain," November, 1728, in *Collection of Papers and Other Tracts* (London, 1740), p. 174.
22. *A New Discourse of Trade* (London, 1693), pp. 204–208.
23. *Political and Commercial Works*, II, 10.

Crown, or the true legislative Power of the Mother State." Thus, although the Board of Trade, in contrast to the Lords of Trade, accepted the representative assemblies as necessary and desirable elements in the constitutions of the colonies, it could never admit that those bodies, no matter what the aspirations and pretensions of their members, were in any way equal to the imperial House of Commons. To emphasize their subordinate status, imperial authorities always insisted that the assemblies existed not as a matter of right, not because they were necessary to provide for colonials their just rights as Englishmen, but only through the favor of the Crown.

Finally, if the primary reason for the existence of colonies was to contribute to the well-being of the parent state, and if colonial governments were necessarily "dependent" and "provincial," it followed that the colonies should be and were, in the phrase of Sir William Keith, onetime governor of Pennsylvania, "justly bound" by the laws of the mother country. Thus Parliament, as the supreme lawmaking power in Britain, obviously had jurisdiction over every aspect of colonial life, political and internal, as well as commercial and external. Ordinarily, colonial administration would be handled by the Crown and its officers, acting in their executive and judicial capacities; but, as the Board of Trade's proposals for parliamentary intervention to settle a permanent revenue in New York made clear, imperial authorities assumed after the Glorious Revolution that the authority of Parliament over the colonies was unlimited.[24]

Because there was no articulate opposition within imperial circles to any of these assumptions, and because all of the specific policy objectives of the Board of Trade were logical expressions of one or more of them, the Board's inability to achieve more of those objectives would seem, at least on the surface, almost incomprehensible. In some measure, the Board's failure may be traced to the vagaries of British politics and the preoccupation on the part of the men in power with other more immediate problems. The domestic political readjustments required by the Glorious Revolution, two major wars, the need to ensure the security of the Protestant and Hanoverian succession, and the constant and bitter churn of factional politics all combined between 1689 and 1721 to push all but the most pressing colonial questions well into the background of

24. Keith, "A Short Discourse," *Collection of Papers,* pp. 167–170, 175.

British public life. Yet the difficulties encountered by colonial officials at all levels in enforcing measures they could implement on their own, or that did have ministerial and/or parliamentary support, strongly suggest that, in a larger sense, the failures of British colonial policy between 1660 and 1721 derived ultimately from a deeper source, from the very nature of the empire itself.

For both that policy and the assumptions behind it were essentially foreign to the commercial traditions on which the empire had originally been based and to the spirit of individual enterprise in which the colonies had been founded. The colonists did not dispute the notion that their behavior should contribute to the welfare of the whole empire, but they saw that welfare from a very different perspective than did imperial officials. To them the common good seemed to require that they be able to pursue their own interests; and any restraints by the imperial government were a breach of the original contract, by which the colonists had been granted the right to pursue those goals in return for risking their lives to plant colonies in the wilderness and tropics of America. "In former daies," declared Edward Littleton, a planter of Barbados, in *The Groans of the Plantations* (a remarkable pamphlet published in London in 1689 in objection to certain features of the navigation acts he considered injurious to the sugar islands), "we were under the pleasing sound of Priviledges and Immunities, of which a free Trade was one, though we counted That, a Right and not a Priviledge . . . without such Encouragements, the Plantations had been still wild Woods. Now those things are vanisht and forgotten. . . . All the Care now is, to pare us close, and keep us low. We dread to be mention'd in an Act of Parliament; because it is alwaies to do us Mischief." What Littleton found most objectionable was that measures injurious to the colonies had been passed under "fair Pretences" that they were "for the common Good and Benefit of the *English* Nation." He did not go so far as Sir Dalby Thomas, another West Indian, who argued in 1690 that the "Colonies themselves are proper Judges of what they suffer, want, and would have," that "their minds must best appear in [their several] generall Assemblies," and that no "*Laws* or *Designs*" affecting the colonies should be undertaken "untill the Colonies by their Assembly[s] were consulted." But Littleton did insist that it was unfair always to improve one part of the empire to the disadvantage of the rest, unjust for the colonists to be "*commanded as Subjects, and . . . crusht as Aliens*. Which Condition is the most dismal and horrid, that people can be under." Did not the colonists "have as good *English* Bloud in our Veins, as some of those that we left behind us?" he inquired. "How came we to lose our Countrey, and the Priviledges of it? Why will you cast us out?" "No Society of Men," he wrote, "can stand without equal Justice, which is the Lady and Queen of all the Vertues. If the equal dividing the common Booties, be necessary to Pirates and *Buccaneers;* the equal distribution of publique Burdens, is much more to a State."[25]

The thrust of Littleton's argument was that the colonists ought to enjoy the same rights as those Englishmen who stayed at home, and that the interests of the colonies were entitled to equal consideration with those of England. This demand that the colonists be placed upon an equal footing with other Englishmen was implicit in such documents as the Bill of Privileges drawn up by the Jamaica Assembly in 1677, the Charter of Liberties enacted by the first New York Assembly in 1683, and the rash of attempts by the legislatures of Virginia, New York, Massachusetts, South Carolina, and Maryland—inspired by Parliament's example in passing the Declaration of Rights in 1689—to secure formal legal guarantees of their rights to English liberties between 1691 and 1696.[26] Such attempts revealed a markedly different conception of the imperial-colonial relationship from that held by English officials, a conception that involved a considerably greater measure of colonial equality than imperial theory allowed.

The tension between these two opposing views was intensified in the older settlements as early as the closing decades of the seventeenth century by the ambitions of emergent political elites within the colonies. However much they may have fought among themselves for wealth, status, and power, members of these elites all manifested a common desire to reproduce in the colonies a society and a political system that resembled as closely as possible that of Britain itself. Because the primary outlet for the political ambitions of the vast majority of them was through the elected lower houses,

25. Edward Littleton, *The Groans of the Plantations* (London, 1689), pp. 16, 20, 22–24; Sir Dalby Thomas, *An Historical Account of the Rise and Growth of the West-India Colonies* (London, 1690), pp. iii, 32.
26. Thornton, *West-India Policy*, pp. 171–172; David S. Lovejoy, "Equality and Empire: The New York Charter of Libertyes, 1683," *William and Mary Quarterly*, 3rd ser., XXI (1964), 493–515; Keith, *Constitutional History*, pp. 141–142.

they were especially intent upon making those bodies the equiva-
lents on the provincial level of the English House of Commons.
They wanted full legislative powers over their respective jurisdictions, by virtue of their constituents' inherited English right not to
be subject to any laws passed without the consent of their representatives. Although they were remarkably successful in their
efforts, the persistent refusal of imperial authorities to admit in
theory what had been achieved in fact made the status of the lower
house extremely uncertain.

The ambiguous status of the lower houses was a matter of continual concern to colonial legislators and other political leaders. To
have removed the ambiguity would have required, as Charles
Davenant once suggested, that the "bounds between the chief
power and the people" be somehow clearly delineated. What he
proposed was passage of a declaratory law guaranteeing to all Englishmen the "right to all the laws of England, while they remain in
countries subject to the dominion of the kingdom."[27] But colonials wanted something more: in the words of Jeremiah Dummer,
agent for the New England colonies and author of the celebrated
Defence of the New-England Charters, "a free Government, where
the Laws are sacred, Property secure, and Justice not only impartially, but expeditiously distributed." Assuming that "the Benefit
which *Great-Britain* receives from the Plantations, arises from their
Commerce" and that "Oppression is the most opposite Thing in
the World to Commerce," they wanted, as Dummer inferred, *freedom to* pursue their own individual and corporate interests under
conditions such as those agreed to by all parties in the original
charters and *freedom from* the oppression, the "direct plundering
[of the] . . . People, and [the many] . . . other Acts of Mis-
rule and lawless Power" that had sometimes marked the behavior
of governors in the plantations and that rendered both the property
of the colonists and their liberty to pursue it extremely precarious.
But the full achievement of these goals required something far
more than simply a jealous guarding of the original "Liberties of
the People" by the lower houses in the colonies and additional
curbs on potentially imperious or corrupt governors by imperial
authorities in Britain.[28] It demanded, as an anonymous Virginian

27. *Political and Commercial Works*, II, 35–36, 55.
28. Jeremiah Dummer, *Defence of the New-England Charters* (London,
1721), pp. 68–69, 73.

perceived in 1701, no less than "a Just and Equal Government" based on a "free Constitution," which would remove all ambiguity from the imperial-colonial relationship by defining "what is law, and what is not" in the colonies and specifying "how far the Legislative Authority is in the Assemblies."[29] In the absence of such an arrangement, the lower houses and the people and interests they represented could never be entirely secure, could never enjoy the same degree of protection of their liberties and properties as their fellow Englishmen did at home, and could never fully satisfy their mimetic impulses to reproduce in the colonies a complete English society.

III

Ironically, the very ambiguity that had been responsible for much of the tension between the home government and the colonies between 1689 and 1721 provided the basis for the development over the next thirty years of a remarkably stable political relationship. This development coincided and was closely associated with the rise to political hegemony of Sir Robert Walpole, who was First Minister from 1721 until 1742, and derived largely from the application to colonial matters of many of the underlying principles and techniques he had employed with such brilliant success in managing domestic affairs. To avoid any issues involving fundamentals and all debates over basic principles, to restrict the active role of government as much as possible and act only when it was expedient or necessary to do so, to attempt to bind potentially disruptive groups to the administration by catering to their interests, to seek to adjust all disputes by compromise and manipulation, and, if a choice had to be made between competing interests, always to align the government with the strongest—each of these characteristically Walpolean modes of procedure inevitably spilled over into and affected the handling of the colonies. Based on a clear recognition that the continued prosperity of the colonies—which had been such an important "Cause of enriching this Nation"—depended to some considerable degree upon their having, as one writer put it, "a Government . . . as Easy & Mild as possible to invite people to Settle under it" and to keep them happy

29. Louis B. Wright (ed.), *An Essay Upon the Government of the Plantations on the Continent of America* (San Marino, Calif.: Huntington Library, 1945), pp. 15–17, 23.

once they were there, the new imperial posture toward the colonies was succinctly characterized by Charles Delafaye, one of Walpole's subordinates. "One would not Strain any Point," Delafaye warned Governor Francis Nicholson of South Carolina early in Walpole's administration, "where it can be of no Service to our King and Country, and will Create Enemys to ones Self."[30] To promote the economic well-being of the empire in general and, not incidentally, to avoid political difficulties for the administration at home, the traditional goals of British colonial policy as they had been worked out since the Restoration were, whenever expedient, thus to give way to immediate political advantage. In practice, if not in theory, there was to be a partial return to something resembling the old contractual relationship between mother country and colonies as it had existed during the first half century of English colonization.

But this more relaxed attitude toward the colonies was not immediately copied by those most directly concerned with colonial administration. The Board of Trade at home and governors and other members of the official bureaucracy in the colonies still evaluated the colonial situation in terms of the old imperatives. Governors continued to complain that the colonists paid "little or no defference to any opinion or orders . . . from the Ministry at Home" and to rail at the lower houses for "making attempts upon the few Prerogatives" still "reserv'd to ye Crown."[31] Customs officials and others in the colonies bitterly denounced the colonists for flagrantly violating the navigation acts, wantonly turning the timber reserved for the Royal Navy to their own uses, and openly attempting to frustrate attempts to enforce the acts of trade through the vice-admiralty courts. For its part, the Board of Trade persisted in its attempts to hold royal governors to a rigid enforcement of their instructions, to achieve a more centralized and regular system of colonial control in London, to consolidate the colonies for more effective administration and defense, to try to bring the charter colonies under closer supervision, to secure permanent revenues from the colonies for the support of Crown

---

30. The quotations are from Joshua Gee, *The Trade and Navigation of Great-Britain* (London, 1729), p. 98, and Charles Delafaye to Francis Nicholson, Jan. 26, 1722, in Jack P. Greene (ed.), *Settlements to Society, 1584–1763,* (New York: McGraw-Hill, 1966), pp. 231–232.

31. Samuel Shute to Board of Trade, Oct. 29, 1722, and Shute to Crown [Aug. 16, 1723], in Sainsbury, *et al.* (eds.), *Cal. St. Papers, Col.,* 1722–23, 157–158, 324–330.

officials, and, on occasion, to threaten parliamentary intervention if its recommendations were not complied with.

But the Board regularly failed to get full ministerial support for its recommendations after 1721. Two cases, both involving the Board's efforts to deal with the refractory Massachusetts House of Representatives, may be cited as examples. The first grew out of a long series of charges levied against the House in August, 1723 by Governor Samuel Shute who, after several years of bitter wrangling with that body, had come to England to seek direct help from his superiors. The Board reported favorably on Shute's complaints and urged the "interposition of the British Legislature" to restrain the House "within the due bounds of obedience to the Crown." But the administration would not go that far. Although it agreed that each of the charges was valid, and strongly censured the House for having "unlawfully assumed . . . Powers which [did] not belong to [it]," it would do no more than issue an explanatory charter confirming the governor's position on only two of seven original charges and threaten that any resistance to the new charter might result in referral of the whole matter to Parliament.[32]

The Board's inability to obtain administration support for its directives in the colonies was even more dramatically revealed over the following decade by its failure to force the Massachusetts House of Representatives to establish a permanent revenue to provide salaries for Crown officers. After repeated instructions and entreaties had failed to move the House, the Board, in desperation, threatened in early 1729 to turn to Parliament. But the administration, as the Duke of Newcastle—who as Secretary of State for the Southern Department from 1724 until 1746 had primary responsibility for colonial decisions—admitted to Governor William Burnett, was not eager to bring "things to that extremity." The result was that the Massachusetts House stood firm, and the Board, unable to carry through on its threats, had first to give in temporarily while disclaiming that its concession could be "construed to enervate the Validity of . . . [the] former Instructions," and finally in 1736 to abandon the cause altogether and

32. Shute to Crown [Aug. 16, 1723], and Board of Trade to Lords Justices, Sept. 23, 1723, in *ibid.*, 324–330, 339–340; Shute to Dartmouth, March 5, 1724, and Newcastle to William Dummer, Sept. 30, 1725, in *ibid.*, 1724–25, 50–52, 442; Grant and Munro (eds.), *Acts of the Privy Council, Colonial*, III, 92–104

permit the governor (by then, Jonathan Belcher) to accept annual grants from the House.[33]

The Board's gradual retreat on this issue coincided with and symbolized a general decline in its activity and effectiveness, a decline that began in the early years of Walpole's administration and accelerated during the presidency of Lord Monson between 1737 and 1748. The Board never explicitly abandoned the program for which it had pressed so hard before 1721, but it was repeatedly forced, by a combination of the reluctance of the ministry to support it and the intransigence of the colonists, to bow before the practical necessity of getting on with day-to-day government within the colonies. Apparently because of "neglect and distraction," Newcastle was during much of his tenure as secretary similarly ineffective.[34] Royal officials in the colonies thus had to resign themselves to the fact that it was difficult to get anyone in Britain "to think of Plantation affairs," that the ministers were simply "too busily employ'd another way to mind Such Trifles."[35] With such "small countenance" from their "superiors in England,"[36] governors and other Crown officers were thus forced to rely largely upon their own resources in handling the domestic political affairs of the colonies.

The reluctance of the administration to give close attention to

---

33. Leonard Woods Labaree (ed.), *Royal Instructions to British Colonial Governors, 1670–1776* (2 vols., New York: Appleton-Century-Crofts, 1935), I, 257–265; Mass. House of Representatives to Crown, Nov. 22, 1728, Board of Trade to Newcastle, March 27, 1729, and Newcastle to Burnett, June 26, 1729 (two letters), all in Sainsbury, *et al.* (eds.), *Cal. of St. Papers, Col.*, 1728–29, 311–313, 339–340, 412–414; Belcher to Newcastle, June 11, 1734, and Board of Trade to King, Aug. 29, 1734, in *ibid.*, *1734–35*, 130–131, 194–195; and Grant and Munro (eds.), *Acts of the Privy Council, Colonial*, III, 259–264.

34. Philip Haffenden, "Colonial Appointments and Patronage under the Duke of Newcastle, 1724–1739," *English Historical Review*, CCCVIII (1963), 417–435.

35. The quotations are from Cadwallader Colden to George Clinton, Dec. 8, 1748, Clinton Papers, William L. Clements Library, Ann Arbor, Mich., Box VIII, and James Logan to William Logan, Dec. 1733, as quoted in Joseph E. Johnson, "A Quaker Imperialist's View of the British Colonies in America: 1732," *Pennsylvania Magazine of History and Biography*, LX (1936), 100.

36. Governor Gabriel Johnston to Lord Wilmington, Feb. 10, 1737, Historical Manuscripts Commission, *The Manuscripts of the Marquess of Townshend* (London, 1887), pp. 262–264.

the political administration of the colonies did not carry over into the economic realm. Extraordinarily sensitive to the demands of powerful interest groups within Britain, both the administration and Parliament regularly responded to their requests for new economic regulations concerning the colonies. Whenever colonial interests coincided with those of some influential group in Britain, the colonies could count on a favorable response to their requests. Thus, the rice growers of Carolina combined with rice traders in Britain in 1730 to persuade Parliament to permit the direct exportation of rice from Carolina to southern Europe, and South Carolina indigo planters joined with woolen manufacturers in 1748 to secure a bounty to encourage the production of Carolina indigo. The prevailing ideal, in fact, was still, as James Oglethorpe declared in the House of Commons in 1732, that

> in all cases that come before this House, where there seems to be a clashing of interests between one part of the country and another . . . we ought to have no regard to the particular interest of any country or set of people; the good of the whole is what we ought only to have under our consideration: our colonies are all a part of our own dominions; the people in every one of them are our own people, and we ought to shew an equal respect to all.[37]

Yet, whenever there actually was "a clashing of interests" between British and colonial groups, it was the British group that invariably came out best in Parliament. In 1732, British hatmakers had no difficulty in obtaining legislation designed to cramp a budding colonial hat industry and British merchants a law to make it easier for them to secure payment of colonial debts. Because the subjects were more complicated and rival British groups disagreed about what should be done, it required a long campaign by British iron producers and British merchants to secure regulation, respectively, of colonial iron manufacturing and colonial paper currency. Eventually both succeeded, but each had to accept some concessions to colonial interests. Even when they had the backing of the administration, no colonial interest group could hope for success in any proposal opposed by a major British lobby. To their great disappointment, the Virginia tobacco planters discovered this stark political fact in 1733, when they unsuccessfully joined with Wal-

37. Jan. 28, 1732, in Leo Francis Stock (ed.), *Proceedings and Debates of the British Parliaments Respecting North America* (5 vols., Washington, D.C.: Carnegie Institution, 1924–41), IV, 125.

pole in his excise scheme in the hope of remedying some aspects of the tobacco trade they found objectionable.

Moreover, whenever there was a collision of interests among colonials, the North American colonists had to reconcile themselves to the existence of a strong preference within Britain for the West Indies. The imperial valuation of the continental colonies increased enormously through the middle decades of the eighteenth century as their importance as markets for British manufactures became more and more obvious. The most dramatic measure of this development was Parliament's willingness—for the first time in the history of English colonization—to vote funds for the establishment of a new colony. Largely for strategic considerations, to strengthen the defenses of the southern colonies on the continent, beginning in 1732 it contributed an annual grant to defray the costs of the entire civil establishment and other expenses of Georgia: in the first twenty years alone, Parliament appropriated £136,608 for the colony. But if imperial authorities were ever more disposed to believe that it was "the true Interest of *Great Britain* to . . . encourage and nourish its Northern as well as Southern Colonies,"[38] they could not, when the choice was thrust upon them, yet overcome their traditional partiality for the sugar colonies. This preference was clearly revealed between 1731 and 1733, when the West Indian and mainland colonies clashed over West Indian demands for protection from competition by the foreign islands. During the first decades of the eighteenth century, the foreign islands, especially the French, began to produce sugar more cheaply than the British and to undersell them on the world market, with the result that New England merchants developed a brisk trade with the foreign islands after the Treaty of Utrecht in 1713. The economic fortunes of the British islands began to decline, and West Indian interests in London pressed Parliament to exclude the New Englanders from trading with the foreign islands. After a long and vigorous debate, Parliament responded in 1733 by passing the Molasses Act, which sought to discourage the trade with the foreign islands by placing prohibitive duties on their sugar products. The edge of this potentially grievous regulation for the northern continental colonies was only blunted by the failure of customs officials to enforce it strictly.

38. John Ashley, *Memoirs and Considerations Concerning the Trade and Revenues of the British Colonies in America* (London, 1740).

Parliament's willingness to act upon such a wide range of economic problems pointedly contrasted with its refusal on three occasions during the 1730's and 1740's to intervene to strengthen royal political authority in the colonies. Thus, in 1734 a House of Lords committee proposed a bill to prevent any colonial laws from taking effect until they had been approved by the Crown; but the Lords never formulated the proposal into a bill.[39] Similarly, two bills to regulate colonial paper currencies considered by the Commons in 1744 and 1749 contained clauses that would have given royal instructions the force of law in the colonies; but the Commons did not pass either, and the currency law finally enacted in 1751 included no such provision. The net effect of this inaction was to create the impression among the colonists that Parliament's undefined colonial authority did not include the right to intervene in the internal political life of the colonies.

Along with Walpole's tendency to let the colonies proceed on their own without interference by the administration except in such matters as were of serious and pressing concern to powerful interest groups in Britain, Parliament's inaction in the colonial domestic sphere gave the local governors more room for political maneuver than they had had at any time since the Restoration. For those governors operating from an actual or potential position of political strength, this relaxation of pressure meant that they could pursue the "real Advantage" of the parent state without having to be constantly on guard against reprimands from home for failing to enforce the "long established Maxims" of the Board of Trade.[40] Thus, in Massachusetts, the abandonment in 1736 of the attempt to force the House of Representatives to vote a permanent revenue provided the basis for an extraordinary extension of the influence of the royal governor over the next twenty years. William Shirley, who became Massachusetts governor in 1741, combined a remarkable talent for political management, powerful connections in Britain, and adroit use of a growing system of patronage in order to command the loyalty and secure the cooperation of the colony's elite, to make himself "the dominant figure" in Massachusetts politics, and to put an end to the battles between governors and legislatures that had characterized the political life of the colony

39. Laws relating to emergencies and defense were to be excepted.
40. The quotations are from William Gooch, "Some Remarks on a Paper transmitted into America . . .", *Journey to the Land of Eden and Other Tracts by William Byrd* (Richmond, Va., 1866), pp. 228, 248.

for almost all of its first half century under the Crown.[41] In Virginia, Lieutenant Governor William Gooch, who administered the colony from 1727 to 1749, was similarly successful, though for somewhat different reasons. With almost no patronage at his disposal, he could not employ Shirley's techniques of management. But by joining with local political leaders to stress the baneful effects of factionalism in politics, the desirability of disinterested behavior by magistrates and legislators, and, in the manner of Walpole, the necessity of institutional cooperation, Gooch managed to extirpate old factions and achieve a remarkable amount of political peace and stability.

Elsewhere, however, governors were neither so fortunate nor so successful in promoting the interests of the Crown. The kind of well-integrated society and polity that made possible Gooch's success in Virginia existed in no other royal colony, and no other governor had at his command the extensive patronage available to Shirley. Had governors been able to give each of the growing number of royal offices in the colonies to influential members of local elites, they could, like Shirley, have gone a long way toward parrying the opposition to British policy and securing the support of a critical segment of colonial society. Instead, authorities in Britain weakened the governors by taking most of the patronage out of their hands and appointing needy placeseekers from England to many of the offices, without pausing to consider "how despicable the Governor of a Province must be when stript of the Power of disposing of the few places that fall within his Government, and how little serviceable to the Crown, when deprived of the only means of rewarding Merit and creating and [exerting] Influence."[42] Indeed, for those colonies whose governors had little influence at home there was a marked tendency through the middle decades of the eighteenth century for Crown officials to do the same with colonial council seats, which had formerly been reserved for wealthy and well-affected colonials.

41. The quotation is from John M. Murrin, "From Corporate Empire to Revolutionary Republic: The Transformation of the Structure of the Concept of Federalism," an unpublished paper delivered at the annual meeting of the American Historical Association, December, 1966.
42. Gooch, "Some Remarks . . . ," Journey to the Land of Eden, pp. 243–244. On the general point about the Crown's assumption of patronage see Haffenden, "Colonial Appointments . . .", 417–435, and Bernard Bailyn, The Origins of American Politics (New York: Knopf, 1968), pp. 72–80.

In this situation, many governors chose simply not to "consider any Thing further than how to sit easy," and to be careful "to do nothing, which upon a fair hearing . . . can be blamed."[43] Because the surest way to "sit easy" was to reach a political accomodation with local interests, they very frequently aligned themselves with dominant political factions in the colonies. Such governors sought to avoid disputes with the lower houses by taking especial care not to challenge their customary privileges and, if necessary, even quietly giving way before their demands. As a consequence, the royal governors in many colonies were fully integrated into the local political community and came to identify and to be identified as much with the interests of the colonies as with those of the imperial government. This domestication of the governors eased tensions significantly as their personal prestige and sometimes even their political influence actually increased, while the lower houses contented themselves with the rather large amount of de facto power they could wield whenever it became necessary to do so. In this situation, the lower houses virtually ceased to demand the kind of explicit recognition of colonial rights they had so often sought during the years from 1660 to 1721. The effort of the Jamaica House in 1723 to obtain the Crown's specific acknowledgment that Jamaicans were entitled to all the rights of Englishmen in return for voting a perpetual revenue to the Crown was notable because it was the last such attempt by any assembly prior to the disturbances that immediately preceded the American Revolution.

The primary difficulty with this informal and pragmatic political arrangement was its extraordinary fragility. A loss of political influence in Britain, or a volatile economic or social situation within a colony, could suddenly bring a governor to total ruin. Similarly, a governor who refused to abide by the conditions of the arrangement—who, for whatever reason, was either intent upon making "a mighty change in the face of affairs" or reluctant to accept a status of equal or subordinate partner with the assembly—could easily revive old fears among legislators and powerful local interests and throw a colony into political deadlock or even chaos. The insecurity that derived from the possibility of getting a governor who was

43. The quotations are from Johnson, "A Quaker Imperialist's View," 114, and Johnston to Wilmington, Feb. 10, 1737, *Manuscripts of . . . Townshend*, pp. 262–264.

determined either to "suck up the Treasure of the Land, and to devour the Fruit of their honest Labours" or to turn "Topsy Turvy long established Constitutions in [the] Colonies" was intensified by the uncertain relationship of Parliament to the colonies.[44] That Parliament, whether or not it had the right, might exert its awesome power was ever a potentially disturbing possibility. Although there was some hope that "so great" a body would do nothing that by "preparing Slavery to us would give a presedent and hand it against themselves," there was always the unsettling prospect that it might act to bolster up prerogative power in the colonies and thereby strike "Emediately at the Liberty, of the Subject and Establish arbetrary pour to all the Contenant and Islands in American and Else where under the Kings Dominions."[45]

Notwithstanding these uncertainties, the relationship between the mother country and most of the colonies was, for the time being at least, a viable one. Reinforced by the mutual prosperity of most parts of the empire, and reflecting the phenomenal economic and social growth of the colonies in the decades following the end of Queen Anne's War, there was a growing pride among the colonists in their connection with Britain and a conscious cultivation of traditional English social and political values. The largely unarticulated and unacknowledged *quid pro quo* between imperial and colonial leaders that emerged in the decades after 1721 permitted the colonists a considerable amount of self-government and economic freedom, without requiring imperial officials explicitly to abandon any of the traditional ideals and assumptions of British colonial policy. The many ambiguities in this arrangement were thus not only its central weakness—the source of its latent insecurities and its extreme fragility—but also its primary strength. As long as British officials could believe in the old ideals without feeling compelled to try to achieve them, as long as they could assume that Parliament had the power and authority to set things right in the colonies without ever becoming convinced that it was

44. The questions are from Johnston to Wilmington, Feb. 10, 1737, *Manuscripts of . . . Townshend*, pp. 262–264; [Henry St. John, 1st Viscount Bolingbroke], *The Craftsman*, IX (London, 1727), p. 267; and Gooch, "Some Remarks . . . ", *Journey to the Land of Eden*, p. 231.

45. Henry Beekman to Henry Livingston, Jan. 7, 1745, as quoted by Philip L. White, *The Beekmans of New York in Politics and Commerce 1674–1877* (New York: The New-York Historical Society, 1956), p. 190.

neccssary for it to do so, as long as the lower houses in the colonies did not demand positive imperial recognition of all the privileges and powers they actually exercised and believed were rightfully theirs, as long as potentially grievous features of the navigation system were only loosely enforced—as long, in sum, as all parties were content to leave the wide divergence between imperial ideals and colonial practice implicit, this arrangement was functional.

IV

What finally undermined the system and prepared the way for its total collapse after 1763 was the simultaneous outbreak of severe political disturbances in most of the colonies in the late 1740's and early 1750's. During the last stages of King George's War, which lasted from 1744 to 1748, there were so many problems in so many colonies that the empire seemed to people in London to be on the verge of distintegration. Violent factional disputes had thrown New Jersey into civil war, put an end to all legislative activity in New Hampshire and North Carolina, and seriously undermined the position of the royal governors in Jamaica and New York. From New York, South Carolina, New Jersey, Bermuda, Jamaica, North Carolina, and New Hampshire—from all of the royal colonies except Massachusetts, Virginia, Barbados, and some of the smaller islands—governors complained that they were impotent to carry out either imperial directions or their own projects against the exorbitant power of the lower houses. The ultimate message in this rising chorus of laments came through with resounding clarity: they needed help from the imperial government. "The too great and unwarrantable encroachments of the Assemblies," declared Governor Lewis Morris of New Jersey, "make it necessary that a stop some way or other should be put to them, and they reduced to such propper and legall bounds as is consistent with his majestie's Prerogative and their dependence."[46] Drastic measures were required, echoed George Clinton from New York, "to put a stop to these perpetually growing Incroachments of the Assemblies . . . on the executive Powers."[47] What

46. To Board of Trade, Jan. 28, 1744, in *New Jersey Historical Society Collections* (Newark, 1852), IV, 225.
47. To the Board of Trade, Oct. 20, 1748, in Edmund B. O'Callaghan and Berthold Fernow (eds.), *Documents Relating to the Colonial History of the State of New-York* (15 vols., Albany, N.Y.: 1853–87), VI, 456–457.

was the more alarming was that the decay of executive authority seemed to be matched by a decline in public respect for governors —the chief symbol of imperial authority in the colonies—and from Bermuda there came reports that the status of the governor had sunk so low that one member of the Assembly had even offered a reward for his assassination. So desperate was the situation all over the colonies that nothing less than a complete remodeling of their constitutions seemed necessary.

The urgency of these appeals could scarcely be ignored by the imperial government. The Board of Trade had responded by showing some signs of its earlier vigor during the last three years of the presidency of Lord Monson, but it was not until 1748, when Monson died and the war was concluded, that an opportunity presented itself for the major overhaul in the colonial system that governors had been calling for. When the Duke of Newcastle proposed to replace the casual Monson with his brother-in-law, the Duke of Leeds, who wanted "some office which required little attendance and less application,"[48] the Duke of Bedford, then Secretary of State for the Southern Department, reminded Newcastle in a classic piece of understatement that it would have been "Highly improper, considering the present Situation of things, to have a nonefficient Man at the head of that Board."[49] What was needed, obviously, was an energetic man with a turn for business, and such a man was found in the person of the ambitious and indefatigable George Dunk, Earl of Halifax, who was president of the Board of Trade from 1748 to 1761 during what were to be its most active years.

Halifax performed as expected. Under his guidance, the Board presided over a major enterprise to strengthen the defenses of the English colonies against French Canada by turning Nova Scotia— hitherto only a nominal English colony inhabited almost entirely by neutral and even hostile French—into a full-fledged English colony. Equally important, it prepared a series of reports on the difficulties in most of the major trouble spots in the colonies. The recommendations contained in these reports revealed that, despite the long era of accommodation and easy administration since the advent of Walpole, the members of the Board and other colonial

48. Oliver M. Dickerson, *American Colonial Government 1696–1765* (Cleveland, Ohio: Arthur H. Clark, 1912), p. 39.
49. Bedford to Newcastle, Aug. 11, 1748, Additional Manuscripts, British Museum, London, 32716, f. 38.

officials had altered their notions about the proper relationship between the parent state and the colonies but slightly. Underlying all the recommendations was the assumption that it was absolutely "necessary to revise the Constitutions of the Settlements abroad" and "to regulate them, that they may be usefull to, & not rival in Power and Trade their Mother Kingdom,"[50] and it was rumored in both London and the colonies that the ministry was at last "determined to settle a general plan for establishing the Kings Authority in all the plantations."[51] Except for the Nova Scotia enterprise, which received strong backing from the administration and, like the Georgia venture, large sums of money from Parliament, the Board's recommendations were, however, virtually ignored by the administration. As James Abercromby, colonial agent for Virginia and North Carolina, later lamented, "matters of moment" were sometimes "delayed for years . . . after [Halifax] . . . had done his part."[52] Tired of waiting on the "Great Men," who "never want a pretence to protract the dispatch of Business,"[53] Halifax pushed very hard to have himself appointed a separate secretary of state with broad jurisdiction and full responsibility for the colonies. Although he failed in this effort because of the opposition of the King and the two older Secretaries of State, he did succeed in securing enlarged powers for the Board of Trade in April, 1752.

With its new powers, the Board embarked upon a vigorous campaign to enforce the traditional ideals of British colonial policy and, especially, to reduce the authority and influence of the lower houses. It established a packet boat system to provide more regular communication with the colonies, urged each of the royal governors to secure a comprehensive revisal of the laws in his colony and to send home copies of all public papers promptly, and enjoined the governors "strictly to adhere to your instructions and not to deviate from them in any point but upon evident necessity

50. "Some Considerations relating to the present Conditions of the Plantations . . ." [ca. 1748–51], Colonial Office Papers, Class 5, Public Record Office, London, ff. 313–318.
51. Cadwallader Colden to George Clinton, Feb. 12, 1756, Clinton Papers, William L. Clements Library, Ann Arbor, Mich., Box X.
52. Abercromby to William Pitt, Nov. 25, 1756, Chatham Papers, Public Record Office, London, 30/8: 95, ff. 197–208.
53. See John Catherwood to George Clinton, March 1, 1751, Clinton Papers, William L. Clements Library, Ann Arbor, Mich., Box XI.

justified by the particular Circumstances of the case."[54] Although the Board's programs were greeted in many places with enthusiasm by royal officeholders and others who had long been alarmed by the imbalance of the colonial constitutions caused by the lower houses' constant "nibbling at the Prerogative of the Crown,"[55] they were, in general, adamantly opposed by the lower houses, whose members considered them attacks upon the established constitutions of the colonies. Because of "the great lenity shewn them these 50 Years past," one writer penetratingly observed, it seemed to be impossible to bring the colonies "under any other Dominion" than the one to which they had become accustomed; [56] and even with its enlarged authority, the Board could not deal effectively with the opposition from the lower houses. The Board could and did intimidate the governors into a strict observance of their instructions, but that only reduced their room for political maneuver when they needed all the latitude possible to accomplish the impossible tasks assigned to them. Thus, the Board succeeded in its objectives only in New Hampshire, where Governor Benning Wentworth had put together a powerful political combination that monopolized all political power and stifled opposition, and in the new civil governments in Nova Scotia and Georgia, where the Board took extraordinary pains "to check all Irregularities and unnecessary Deviations from the Constitution of the Mother Country in their Infancy."[57] By the time the outbreak of the Seven Years' War forced it to suspend its reform activities in 1756, the Board had realized that its general campaign was a failure. Increasingly, it had been driven to threaten the intervention of Parliament, and in 1757, the House of Commons actually did intervene for the first time in the domestic affairs of a colony when it censured the Jamaica Assembly for making extravagant constitutional claims while resisting instructions issued from the Board.

There was a sharp contrast between the colonial and imperial reactions to the experience of the Seven Years' War. The aggres-

54. Board of Trade to Governors, June 3, 1752, Colonial Office Papers, Public Record Office, London, 324/15, pp. 318–323.
55. [Archibald Kennedy], A Speech said to have been Delivered . . . (New York, 1755), p. 5.
56. W. M. to Halifax, March 10, 1756, Chatham Papers, Public Record Office, London, 30/8: 95, ff. 157–160.
57. [John Pownall], "General Propositions . . ." Shelburne Papers, William L. Clements Library, Ann Arbor, Mich., IXL, 559–566.

sive tactics of the lower houses, which used the need for defense funds to extort still more power from the governors, and the open violation of the navigation acts by merchants in the northern colonies, left no doubt in the minds of officials in London that some major reconstruction of colonial administration would have to be undertaken at the end of the war to put a stop, once and for all, to the extreme particularism of the colonies. The experience of Halifax in the prewar years made it clear, as a number of new proposals for imperial reform emphasized, that much of that reconstruction would have to be undertaken by Parliament, because "no other Authority than that of the British Parliament" would "be regarded in the colonys or be able to awe them into acquiescence."[58] Among the colonists, on the other hand, the conviction that the colonies had played a major part in the "glorious" British victory and a genuine appreciation of the extraordinary military effort made by the British in the colonies produced at once an expanded sense of self-importance and a surge of British nationalism. In the glow of the great British victories of 1758 and 1759 and the Treaty of Paris in 1763, few colonists even noted that in 1759, as soon as the victory over the French in Canada had been won and colonial support for the war effort was no longer vital, imperial authorities had renewed the campaign to bring the colonies under closer supervision. Proud to be a part of the most extensive empire in the world since the Roman Empire, they looked forward to a bright new era of peace and prosperity in which they would, because of the elimination of the French in North America, be freer than ever to pursue their several interests.

V

This euphoric state depended, of course, upon a considerable amount of imperial permissiveness, upon a lax enforcement of the navigation acts on the one hand and the continued ability of dominant colonial interests to exercise a major voice in colonial government through the lower houses on the other; and it was tempered by the same anxieties about their relations with the imperial government that had gnawed at colonials for the past century. What they needed to complete their happiness and to

58. "Hints Respecting the Civil Establishment in Our American Colonies," [1763], Shelburne Papers, William L. Clements Library, Ann Arbor, Mich., LXIX, p. 508.

enable them to make their potential contribution to the future greatness of the empire were some assurances that their interests would not be sacrificed to those of the home islands, that they would not, as a New Yorker wrote, be deprived "of making use of those Means which Providence has been pleased to put into our Hands for the Ease and Comfort of Life, from what we raise and manufacture from our own Produce and Labour."[59] They needed as well some guarantee, as the Virginia Committee of Correspondence declared in July, 1764 in objecting to Parliament's proposed stamp duties, that their "just Liberties & Privileges as free born British Subjects" would be protected and that they would not be arbitrarily subjected by the British government to the full "Plenitude of its Power."[60] That the constitutions of the colonies were "so imperfect, in numberless instances, that the rights of the people lie, even now, at the mere mercy of their governours" was a source of major concern.[61] And it was clear, as one colonial had predicted a decade earlier, that the colonists would regard any parliamentary or ministerial restraints upon the free pursuit of their own interests as "oppression; especially such Laws, as according to the Conceptions . . . [they] have of English Liberty, they have no Hand in the contriving or making."[62]

Increasingly aware that the colonies were "certainly the greatest part of the Riches and Glory of these Kingdoms" and tormented— as they had been since the 1690's—by the possibility that their extensive self-governing powers would inevitably lead to "Notions of Indepen[den]cy of their Mother Kingdom,"[63] imperial officials tried with the full assistance of Parliament to impose just such restraints in the years after 1763. They attempted to confine the restless striving of the colonists into channels acceptable to British economic interests, to establish a stricter system of colonial admin-

59. [Archibald Kennedy], Observations on the Importance of the Northern Colonies Under Proper Regulations (New York, 1750), pp. 30–31.

60. Virginia Committee of Correspondence to Edward Montagu, July 28, 1764, "Proceedings of the Virginia Committee of Correspondence," Virginia Magazine of History and Biography, XII (1905), 8–14.

61. William Smith, History of New-York . . . (Albany, N.Y., 1814), p. 371.

62. [Kennedy], Observations on the Importance of the Northern Colonies . . . , p. 10.

63. W. M. to Pitt, Nov. 16, 1756, Chatham Papers, Public Record Office, London, 30/8: 95, ff. 194–195; "Some Considerations . . . , [1748–51], Colonial Office Papers, Public Record Office, London, 5/5, ff. 313–318.

istration, and to restrain the long-established self-governing powers of the colonists. The response of the leaders of the continental colonies, at least, was reluctantly to conclude that protection of their economic interests and security for their liberties could never be achieved within the British Empire. The removal of the tensions that had underlain the relationship between the colonies and the mother country ever since 1660 came only with separation. In revolution and independence, the individualistic tendencies which had been manifest in colonial life from the first establishment of the colonies in America and which had been at the heart of imperial administrative difficulties were finally given free rein. Tentatively elevated to the status of a right by the pursuit-of-happiness clause in the Declaration of Independence, these tendencies were to be transformed in the half century after 1776 into one of the central ideals of American life.

I

Foundations, 1606–1660

1. The Promise and Function of Plantations

A. The Case for Colonization

ONE OF the most comprehensive, detailed, and lucid summaries of the arguments for English colonization was set down by Richard Eburne—vicar of the parish church of Hentsridge in the county of Somerset—in A Plain Pathway to Plantations, published in 1624 before it was clear that any of the early English colonizing attempts were going to succeed. Set in the form of a dialogue between Enrubie, a merchant persuaded of the value of colonies, and Respire, a doubting farmer, this work is especially revealing of the economic and social roots of the colonizing impulse in England because it places so much emphasis upon the possible role of the colonies in helping to cure the many social ills—overpopulation, lack of opportunity, depressed economic conditions, moral decay—that so concerned Jacobean Englishmen.

SOURCE: Richard Eburne, A Plain Pathway to Plantations [1624], ed. Louis B. Wright (Ithaca, N.Y.: Cornell University Press, 1962), pp. 23–26, 30–37.

ENRUBIE. Without any dislike or disparagement to any other men's wits or understandings be it spoken: for mine own part, I do profess I estimate and account the actions themselves to be very good and godly, honorable, commendable, and necessary, such as it were much to be wished might be, and much to be lamented they be not, in far better sort than hitherto any of them are, followed and furthered, as which tend highly, first, to the honor and glory of Almighty God; secondly, to the dignity and renown of the King's most excellent Majesty; and, thirdly, to the infinite good and benefit of this our commonwealth—three things than which none weightier or worthier can in any design or project be leveled or aimed at.

RESPIRE. You make me even amazed to hear of you that so great good may be effected or expected out of those courses which of many are so much contemned and dispraised. Wherefore, for my better satisfaction therein, I pray you, let me hear of you in particular somewhat how these notable effects might be produced, and, namely, first, the glory and honor of God.

FIRSTLY, BY THEM THE CHURCH OF CHRIST
MAY NOTABLY BE ENLARGED

ENRUBIE. The glory of God cannot but be much furthered thereby, were it but only that the Gospel of Christ should thereby be professed and published in such places and countries by those alone that shall remove from hence to inhabit there, where before, since the beginning of the Gospel, for aught we know or is likely, it was never heard, at least professed, as it is now of late come to pass, God be praised, and we hope will be shortly in Newfoundland.

RESPIRE. Will be, say you? Methinks you should rather have reckoned that among the first because that for fifty or threescore years before ever the Summer Islands or Virginia were heard of our people did yearly go thither a-fishing, and so the name of Christ was there long since honored among them.

ENRUBIE. But for all that, till there be Christians inhabiting there we cannot say properly that the Gospel of Christ is planted there or that it is any part of Christendom. It must therefore in that respect give place to the other before named, as which indeed were Christian before it.

BY THE ADDITION OF OTHER COUNTRIES TO CHRISTENDOM

RESPIRE. I cannot dislike that you say. And indeed any man may see that this must needs be a great advancement to the honor of God whenas the scepter of His son is extended so much farther than it was as if from hence to those remote and unknown regions. Christendom will then be so much the larger. And it seems to me it will be in a goodly order, seeing that, as I understand, from England to Newfoundland, and so to the Summer Islands, and thence to Virginia, all is in one tract—no Turkish, no heathen country, lying between. But proceed, I pray you.

AND BY THE CONVERSION
OF INFINITE HEATHENS TO CHRISTIANITY

ENRUBIE. This is, as you see, greatly to the honor of God, but it will be much more if, when and where our people do plant themselves in such countries where already are an infinite number of other people, all savages, heathens, infidels, idolaters, etc., this in the plantation may principally and speedily be labored and intended: that by learning their languages and teaching them ours, by training up of their children, and by continual and familiar converse and commerce with them, they may be drawn and induced, persuaded and brought to relinquish and renounce their own heathenisms, idolatries, blasphemies, and devil worships.

The Papists Have Much Endeavored This Way

And if, for that I take it cannot be denied, the papists have done much good that way by spreading the name of Christ, though but after their corrupt and superstitious manner, into so many unknown nations that lived before altogether in the service and captivity of the devil—for better it is that God be served a bad way than no way at all—how much more good must it needs be if the name of the true God in a true and sound manner might there be published and spread abroad?

To which purpose, I would to God there were among us, us Protestants that profess and have a better religion than they the papists, one-half of that zeal and desire to further and disperse our good and sound religion as seems to be among them for furthering and dispersing theirs. Which not found—for our zeal is coldness and our forwardness backwardness in that behalf in respect of theirs—I need not say, "we may fear," but rather, "we may assure ourselves," that they shall rise against us in the day of judgment and condemn us. . . .

Respire. That these courses tend to the glory of God I plainly see and acknowledge. But how may they be to the renown and benefit of the King's most excellent Majesty?

Secondly, by Them the Majesty
and Renown of the Kings of England
May Be Much Augmented

Enrubie. These could not but much augment and increase the majesty and renown of our dread sovereign if thereby his dominion be extended, as it were, into another world, into those remote parts of the earth, and his kingdoms be increased into many mo[re] in number by the addition and access of so many, so spacious, so goodly, so rich, and some so populous countries and provinces as are by these beginnings offered unto his hands.

We see the evidence and certainty of this assumption as clear as the sunshine at high noon in the person of the King of Spain, whose predecessors and progenitors accepting that which others did refuse, and making better use of such opportunities than any else have done, he is thereby become lord not only of territories almost innumerable but also of treasures and riches in them inestimable.

Whose right thereto and to the rest of that continent, be it what it may be, cannot, I suppose, in any equity or reason be any sufficient bar to any Christian prince why he should not yet, by any lawful and good means, seize into his hands and hold as in his own right whatsoever countries and islands are not before actually inhabited or possessed by him the Spaniard or some other Christian prince or state. Of which sort, since yet there are many, it were much to be wished that his Majesty might in time, while opportunities serve, take notice and possession of some of them, whereunto these courses of plantation, being rightly prosecuted, are a singular if not the only means.

RESPIRE. All this is most apparent; but may the like be said for your third point, the good of this land likewise?

THIRDLY, BY THEM THE GOOD OF THIS LAND MAY NOTABLY BE PROCURED

ENRUBIE. Yes, verily. Whosoever shall but lightly consider the estate thereof as now it stands shall plainly see and will be enforced to confess that the prosecuting, and that in an ample measure, of those worthy attempts is an enterprise for our land and common good most expedient and necessary. For:

FIRSTLY, IN THE EASIER SUPPORTATION OF THE REGAL STATE

First of all, whereas toward the supportation of their regal estate for many and urgent necessities the kings of this land are oft occasioned to demand and take of their subjects great sums of money by subsidies and otherlike ways, which to many of the subjects . . . is somewhat hard and heavy to endure; this burden would be more easily borne and could not but become much the lighter if by the accession of more kingdoms to their crown, store of treasures being brought into their coffers, the same were borne by divers other lands and subjects as well as of this and the rest yet under their subjection.

SECONDLY, IN RIDDING OUT OF THE LAND THE GREAT AND SUPERFLUOUS MULTITUDE THEREOF

Secondly, whereas our land at this present, by means of our long-continued both peace and health freed from any notable either war or pestilence—the two great devourers of mankind to both which in former ages it was much subject—even swarmeth with multitude and plenty of people, it is time, and high time, that, like stalls that are overfull of bees or orchards overgrown with young sets, no small number of them should be transplanted into some other soil and removed hence into new hives and homes.

Truly, it is a thing almost incredible to relate and intolerable to behold what a number in every town and city, yea, in every parish and village, do abound, which for want of commodious and ordinary places to dwell in do build up cottages by the highwayside and thrust their heads into every corner, to the grievous overcharging of the places of their abode for the present and to the very ruin of the whole land within a while if it be not looked unto, which if they were transported into other regions might both richly increase their own estates and notably ease and disburden ours. . . .

THIRDLY, IN ABATING THE EXCESSIVE HIGH PRICES OF ALL THINGS TO LIVE BY

Next, thirdly, whereas at this present the prices of all things are grown to such an unreasonable height that the common, that is, the meaner sort of people, are even undone and do live, in respect of that they did for thirty or forty years past, in great neediness and extremity, that there is neither hope nor possibility of amending this evil but in the diminution of the number of people in the land. Which if men will not, by departing hence, elsewhere effect, we must expect that God, they having first eaten out one another, by war or pestilence [will] do it for them. . . .

FOURTHLY, IN ENRICHING THE POORER SORT HENCE REMOVED

Consider also the great riches, wealth, and good estate which such who here live, and cannot but live, *parce & duriter*, poor and hardly, might by transportation within a while rise unto; whileas they may have otherwise for their bad cottages good houses, for their little gardens great grounds, and for their small backsides large fields, pastures, meadows, woods, and otherlike plenty to live upon.

FIFTHLY, IN AMENDING THE TRADE AND TRAFFIC OF MERCHANTS

The benefit that might that way accrue unto merchants and all kind of adventurers by sea is infinite. For traffic and merchandise cannot but by means thereof wonderfully be bettered and increased. And withal, which is not the least point in observation, most commodious and delightful must merchandising and traffic needs be while it shall be exercised for the most part between one and the same people, though distant in region yet united in religion, in nation, in language and dominion. Which surely is a thing likely to prove so material and beneficial as may turn the greater part of our merchants' voyages that way and free them from many of those dangerous passages which now they are fain to make by the Straits and Narrow Seas; may find them out their rich and much-desired commodities, and greater store and at a better hand than now they have them otherwhere, and vent them many a thing which now do seldom or not at all pass their hands. . . .

SIXTHLY, IN ROOTING OUT IDLENESS OUT OF THIS LAND

The last benefit to our land, but not the least, is the curing of that evil disease of this land, which, if it be not looked unto and cured the sooner, will be the destruction of this land, I mean, idleness, the mother of many mischiefs, which is to be cured and may be rooted out of the land by this means, yea, by this only and by none other, viz., by plantation.

RESPIRE. Idleness is a naughty vice indeed, but commonly it doth hurt none but them in whom it is, and yet except that fault many that be idle be honest men and have in them divers good qualities; and therefore methinks you speak too hardly of it to call it "the mother of mischiefs." There be worse vices a great many in the land, as this drunkenness and unthrifty spending of their goods which are everywhere so common.

ENRUBIE. I perceive by you it is a very bad cause that cannot get a proctor. That which I have spoken against idleness is but little to that I could speak and which writers both human and divine have spoken of it, to whom I will refer you lest we protract this our conference over long. But for the vices you speak of, if they be, as you say, worse than idleness, yet—as sometimes of a bad mother there may come worse daughters—I assure you, they and many more, as filching and stealing, robbery and cozenage, adultery and incest, fornication and all kind of wantonness and uncleanness, beggary and roguery, profaneness and idolatry, and a number more that upon the sudden I cannot call to mind and with which this land of ours is defiled and filled, be none other, for the most part, than the fruits and offspring, the brood and increase of idleness, which alone taken away and weeded out these all would fall away and vanish with her. . . .

RESPIRE. A happy work indeed were the doing thereof. But do you think, or is there any probability, that this might be done by so speedy and easy a means as plantation?

ENRUBIE. Questionless. The best and the only cure thereof by the hand of man is this way and none other. The diminution of the people of the land unto a due and competent number will do it. This is apparent by experience. For look we back to the state of our land for forty, fifty, or sixty years ago, before it did thus exceed in multitude, and we shall see that few or none of these vices did then abound—nothing in comparison of that they do now—as which have since sprung up out of idleness, that since that time, together with the multitude and increase of the people, is risen and increased.

RESPIRE. Indeed, I remember well when I was a young man there were no such swaggering youths, potting companions, and idle gamesters as be now in the country; little fornication, bastardy, quarreling and stabbing, and otherlike wicked facts, in respect of those that be now, howsoever it be that the world is so much altered. But that these evils may be amended by plantations yet I see not.

ENRUBIE. I will make you see it and confess it too. You have yourself a great many of children. If you should keep them all at home and have not wherewith to set them to work, nothing to employ them in—for all the work you have to do ordinarily is not enough for above two or three of them—must they not needs fall to idleness? What will most of them prove but idlers and loiterers? Now, to prevent and avoid this what other remedy have you but either to get work for them into your own house from other men, if you can have it, or else perforce to place them forth of your own house into other men's, one to this trade or occupation, another to that, where they may be set awork and kept from idleness?

RESPIRE. This is true. But what is this to our purpose?

ENRUBIE. Very much. For the cases are very like. Thereby you may plainly perceive that, as the only way to rid idleness out of your house, having no work for them at home, is to place abroad your children into other houses, as it were into colonies, where they may be set awork; so the only way to rid idleness out of a whole parish, town, county, or country, the same being not able to set those that are idle therein awork—and it is a thing so evident, that for the idle people of our land, what by the great number of them, which is almost infinite, and what by the present damp and decay of all trades and employments, the land is not any way able to set them awork, that it needs no proof—is to place abroad the inhabitants thereof which therein be not nor can be set awork into other parishes, towns, counties, and countries.

RESPIRE. If this course should be taken, it would touch very near a great many of the best livers in the country, who both themselves and their children be as idle as any can be and yet would be loath, having so good means here to live by, to be removed into plantations abroad.

ENRUBIE. These might be brought from idleness and yet abide at home too. For, if the superfluous multitude of our land were removed, those which you speak of would for their own need fall to work and leave idleness, because, that multitude removed, they should have none to do their work for them as now they have while they go to playing, potting, and otherlike vain and idle courses. . . .

2. The Legal Instruments of Settlement

A. A Trading Company Charter

THE AUTHORITY to plant colonies in America derived from royal charters. Given by the Crown to an individual or group, these charters defined the relationships between the colonies and the Crown, and between the sponsors of the colonies and the men who actually settled them. To encourage the sponsors to undertake such risky and expensive enterprises, the charters gave them exclusive title to a specific area of land, broad economic privileges, and extensive governing powers. Both to protect the colonists from the sponsors and to preserve the dependence of the colonies upon the Crown, the charters also placed strict limitations upon the ways in which the sponsors could exercise their powers. There were two kinds of charters: trading company and proprietary. The trading company charter, represented by the Third Virginia Charter (March 12, 1612) reprinted below, was simply an adaptation of the usual charter of incorporation given to the many joint stock companies involved in overseas trade after 1550.

SOURCE: Francis Newton Thorpe (ed.), *The Federal and State Constitutions, Colonial Charters, and Other Organic Laws* (7 vols., Washington, D.C.: United States Government Printing Office, 1909), VII, 3802–3810.

JAMES, by the Grace of God, King of *England, Scotland, France,* and *Ireland,* Defender of the Faith; To all to whom these Presents shall come, Greeting. WHEREAS at the humble Suit of divers and sundry our loving Subjects, as well Adventurers as Planters of the first Colony in Virginia, and for the Propagation of *Christian* Religion, and Reclaiming of People barbarous, to Civility and Humanity, We have, by our Letters-Patents, bearing Date at *Westminster,* the three-and-twentieth Day of May, in the seventh Year of our Reign of *England, France,* and *Ireland,* and the two-and-fortieth of *Scotland,* GIVEN AND GRANTED unto them that they and all such and so many of our loving Subjects as should from time to time, for ever after, be joined with them as Planters or Adventurers in the said Plantation, and their Successors, for ever, should be one Body politick, incorporated by the Name of *The Treasurer and Company of Adventurers and Planters of the City of London for the first Colony in Virginia;*

And whereas also for the greater Good and Benefit of the said Company, and for the better Furtherance, Strengthening, and Establishing of the said Plantation, we did further GIVE, GRANT and CONFIRM, by our Letters-Patents unto the said Company and their Successors, for ever, all those Lands, Countries or Territories, situate, lying and being in that Part of *America* called *Virginia*, from the Point of Land called *Cape* or *Point Comfort* all along the Sea Coasts to the Northward two hundred Miles; and from the said Point of *Cape Comfort* all along the Sea Coast to the Southward two hundred Miles; and all that Space and Circuit of Land lying from the Sea Coast of the Precinct aforesaid, up into the Land throughout from Sea to Sea West and North-west; and also all the Islands lying within one hundred Miles along the Coast of both the Seas of the Precinct aforesaid; with divers other Grants, Liberties, Franchises and Preheminences, Privileges, Profits, Benefits, and Commodities granted in and by our said Letters-patents to the said Treasurer and Company and their Successors for ever.

Now foreasmuch as we are given to understand, that in those Seas adjoining to the said Coasts of *Virginia*, and without the Compass of those two hundred Miles by Us so granted unto the said Treasurer and Company as aforesaid, and yet not far distant from the said Colony in *Virginia*, there are or may be divers Islands lying desolate and uninhabited, some of which are already made known and discovered by the Industry, Travel, and Expences of the said Company, and others also are supposed to be and remain as yet unknown and undiscovered, all and every of which it may import the said Colony both in Safety and Policy of Trade to populate and plant; in Regard whereof, as well for the preventing of Peril, as for the better Commodity of the said Colony, they have been humble suitors unto Us, that We would be pleased to grant unto them an Enlargement of our said former Letters-patents, as well for a more ample Extent of their Limits and Territories into the Seas adjoining to and upon the Coast of *Virginia*, as also for some other Matters and Articles concerning the better government of the said Company and Colony, in which Point our said former Letters-Patents do not extend so far as Time and Experience hath found to be needful and convenient:

We therefore tendering the good and happy Success of the said Plantation, both in Regard of the General Weal of human Society, as in Respect of the Good of our own Estate and Kingdom, and being willing to give Furtherance unto all good Means that may

advance the Benefit of the said Company, and which may secure
the Safety of our loving Subjects planted in our said Colony, under
the Favour and Protection of God Almighty, and of our Royal
Power and Authority, have therefore of our especial Grace, certain
Knowledge, and mere Motion, given, granted, and confirmed, and
for Us, our Heirs and Successors, we do by these Presents give,
grant, and confirm to the said Treasurer and Company of Adventurers and Planters of the city of London for the first Colony in
Virginia, and to their Heirs and Successors for ever, all and singular
those Islands whatsoever situate and being in any Part of the
Ocean Seas bordering upon the Coast of our said first Colony in
Virginia, and being within three Hundred Leagues of any of the
Parts heretofore granted to the said Treasurer and Company in our
said former Letters-Patents as aforesaid, and being within or between the one-and-fortieth and thirtieth Degrees of Northerly
Latitude; together with all and singular Soils, Lands, Grounds,
Havens, Ports, Rivers, Waters, Fishings, Mines and Minerals, as
well Royal Mines of Gold and Silver, as other Mines and Minerals,
Pearls, precious Stones, Quarries, and all and singular other Commodities, Jurisdictions, Royalties, Privileges, Franchises, and Preheminences, both within the said Tract of Land upon the Main,
and also within the said Islands and Seas adjoining whatsoever and
thereunto or thereabouts, both by Sea and Land being or situate;
And which, by our Letters-Patents we may or can grant, and in as
ample Manner as We or any our noble Progenitors have heretofore
granted to any Person or Persons, or to any Company, Body
Politick or corporate, or to any Adventurer or Adventurers, Under-
taker or Undertakers of any Discoveries, Plantations, or Traffick,
of, in, or into any foreign Parts whatsoever, and in as large and
ample Manner as if the same were herein particularly named,
mentioned, and expressed. Provided always, that the said Islands or
any Premises herein mentioned, or by these Presents intended or
meant to be granted, be not actually possessed or inhabited by any
other Christian Prince or Estate, nor be within the Bounds, Limits,
or Territories of the Northern Colony heretofore by Us granted to
be planted by divers of our loving Subjects in the North Parts of
Virginia. To HAVE AND TO HOLD, possess and enjoy, all and singular
the said Islands in the said Ocean Seas so lying and bordering upon
the Coast and Coasts of the Territories of the said first Colony in
Virginia, as aforesaid. With all and singular the said Soils, Lands,
Grounds, and all and singular other the Premises heretofore by

these Presents granted or mentioned to be granted to them, the said Treasurer and Company of Adventurers and Planters of the City of London for the first Colony in Virginia, and to their Heirs, Successors, and Assigns, for ever, to the sole and proper Use and Behoof of them the said Treasurer and Company, and their Heirs and Successors and Assigns, for ever; TO BE HOLDEN OF US, our Heirs and Successors, as of our Manor of East-Greenwich, in Free and common Soccage, and not in Capite; YIELDING AND PAYING therefore to Us, our Heirs and Successors, the fifth Part of the Ore of all Gold and Silver which shall be there gotten, had, or obtained for all Manner of Services whatsoever. . . .

And we do hereby ordain and grant by these Presents, that the said Treasurer and Company of Adventurers and Planters aforesaid, shall and may, once every week, or oftener, at their Pleasure, hold, and keep a Court and Assembly for the better Order and Government of the said Plantation, and such Things as shall concern the same; And that any five Persons of our Council for the said first Colony in Virginia, for the Time being, of which Company the Treasurer, or his Deputy, to be always one, and the Number of fifteen others, at the least, of the Generality of the said Company, assembled together in such Manner, as is and hath been heretofore used and accustomed, shall be said, taken, held, and reputed to be, and shall be a sufficient Court of the said Company, for the handling and ordering, and dispatching of all such casual and particular Occurrences, and accidental Matters, of less Consequence and Weight, as shall from Time to Time happen, touching and concerning the said Plantation.

And that nevertheless, for the handling, ordering, and disposing of Matters and Affairs of greater Weight and Importance, and such as shall or may, in any Sort, concern the Weal Publick and general Good of the said Company and Plantation, as namely, the Manner of Government from Time to Time to be used, the ordering and Disposing of the Lands and Possessions, and the settling and establishing of a Trade there, or such like, there shall be held and kept every Year, upon the last Wednesday, save one, of Hillary Term, Easter, Trinity, and Michaelmas Terms, for ever, one great, general, and solemn Assembly, which four Assemblies shall be stiled and called, The four Great and General Courts of the Council and Company of Adventurers for Virginia; In all and every of which said Great and General Courts, so assembled, our Will and Pleasure is, and we do, for Us, our Heirs and Successors, for ever, Give and Grant to the said Treasurer and Company, and their Successors for ever, by these Presents, that they, the said Treasurer and Company, or the greater Number of them, so assembled, shall and may have full Power and Authority, from Time to Time, and at all Times hereafter, to elect and chuse discreet Persons, to be of our said Council for the said first Colony in *Virginia*, and to nominate and appoint such Officers as they shall think fit and requisite, for the Government, managing, ordering, and dispatching of the Affairs of the said Company; And shall likewise have full Power and Authority, to ordain and make such Laws and Ordinances, for the Good and Welfare of the said Plantation, as to them from Time to Time, shall be thought requisite and meet: So always, as the same be not contrary to the Laws and Statutes of this our Realm of *England*; And shall, in like Manner, have Power and Authority, to expulse, disfranchise, and put out of and from their said Company and Society for ever, all and every such Person and Persons, as having either promised or subscribed their Names to become Adventurers to the said Plantation, of the said first Colony in *Virginia*, or having been nominated for Adventurers in these or any other our Letters-Patents, or having been otherwise admitted and nominated to be of the said Company, have nevertheless either not put in any adventure at all for and towards the said Plantation, or else have refused or neglected, or shall refuse and neglect to bring in his or their Adventure, by Word or Writing, promised within six Months after the same shall be so payable and due. And whereas, the Failing and not Payment of such Monies as have been promised in Adventure, for the Advancement of the said Plantation, hath been often by Experience found to be dangerous and prejudicial to the same, and much to have hindered the Progress and Proceeding of the said Plantation, and for that it seemeth unto Us a Thing reasonable, that such Persons, as by their Hand Writing have engaged themselves for the Payment of their Adventures, and afterwards neglecting their Faith and Promise, should be compelled to make good and keep the same: Therefore, Our Will and Pleasure is, that in any Suit or Suits commenced, or to be commenced in any of our Courts at *Westminister*, or elsewhere, by the said Treasurer and Company, or otherwise against any such persons, that our Judges for the Time being, both in our Court of Chancery, and at the Common Pleas do favour and further the said Suits so far forth as Law and Equity will in any wise further and permit. And We do, for Us, our Heirs and Successors, further give and grant to the said Treasurer and Company, or their Successors forever, that the said Treasurer and Company, or the greater Part of them for the Time being, so in a full and general Court assembled as aforesaid, shall and may from Time to Time, and at all times forever hereafter, elect, choose and admit into their Company, and Society, any Person or Persons, as well Strangers and Aliens born in any Part beyond the Seas wheresoever, being in Amity with us, as our natural Liege Subjects born in any our Realms and Dominions: And that all such Persons so elected, choose, and admitted to be of the said Company as aforesaid, shall thereupon be taken, reputed, and held, and shall be free Members of the said Company, and shall have, hold, and enjoy all and singular Freedoms, Liberties, Franchises, Privileges, Immunities, Benefits, Profits, and Commodities whatsoever, to the said Company in any Sort belonging or appertaining, as fully, freely and amply as any other Adventurers now being, or which hereafter at any Time shall be of the said Company, hath, have, shall, may, might, or ought to have and enjoy the same to all Intents and Purposes whatsoever. And We do further of our especial Grace, certain Knowledge, and mere Motion, for Us, our Heirs and Successors, give and grant unto the said Treasurer and Company, and their Successors for ever, by these Presents, that it shall be lawful and free for them and their Assigns, at all and every Time and Times hereafter, out of any our Realms and Dominions whatsoever, to take, lead, carry, and transport in and into the said Voyage, and for and towards the said Plantation of our said first Colony in *Virginia*, all such and so many of our loving Subjects, or any other Strangers that will become our loving Subjects, and live under our Allegiance, as shall willingly accompany them in the said Voyages and Plantation, with Shipping, Armour, Weapons, Ordnance, Munition, Powder, Shot, Victuals, and all Manner of Merchandises and Wares, and all Manner of Clothing, Implements, Furniture, Beasts, Cattle, Horses, Mares, and all other Things necessary for the said Plantation, and for their Use and Defence, and for Trade with the People there, and in passing and returning to and from, without paying or yielding any Subsidy, Custom, or Imposition, either inward or outward, or any other Duty to Us, our Heirs and Successors, for the same, for the Space of Seven Years from the Date of these Presents.

And We do further, for Us, our Heirs and Successors, give and grant to the said Treasurer and Company, and their Successors forever, by these Presents, that the said Treasurer of that Company, or his Deputy for the Time being, or any two other of the said Council, for the said first Colony in Virginia, for the Time being, or any two other at all Times hereafter, and from Time to Time, have full Power and authority to minister and give the Oath and Oaths of Supremacy and Allegiance, or either of them, to all and every Person and Persons, which shall at any Time or Times hereafter, go or pass to the said Colony in Virginia:

And further, that it shall be lawful likewise for the said Treasurer, or his Deputy for the Time being, or any two or others of our said Council, for the said first Colony in Virginia, for the Time being, from Time to Time, and at all Times hereafter to minister such a formal Oath, as by their discretion shall be reasonably devised, as well unto any Person or Persons employed in, for, or touching the said Plantation, for their honest, faithful and just Discharge of their Service in all such Matters as shall be committed unto them, for the Good and Benefit of the said Company, Colony and Plantation; As also unto such other Person or Persons as the said Treasurer, or his Deputy, with two others of the said Council shall think meet, for the Examination or clearing of the Truth, in any Cause whatsoever, concerning the said Plantation, or any Business from thence proceeding, or thereunto belonging.

And furthermore, whereas We have been certified, That divers lewd and ill disposed Persons, both Sailors, Soldiers, Artificers, Husbandmen, Labourers and others, having received Wages, Apparel and other Entertainment, from the said Company, or having contracted and agreed with the said Company to go, or to serve, or to be employed in the said Plantation of the said first Colony in Virginia, have afterwards either withdrawn, hid, or concealed themselves, or have refused to go thither, after they have been so entertained and agreed withal: And that divers and sundry Persons also, which have been sent and employed in the said Plantation of the said first Colony in Virginia, at and upon the Charge of the said Company, and having there misbehaved themselves by Mutinies, Sedition, or other notorious Misdemeanors, or having been employed or sent abroad by the Governor of Virginia, or his Deputy, with some Ship or Pinnace, for our Provision of the said Colony, or for some Discovery, or other Business and Affairs concerning the same, have from thence most treacherously either come back again, and returned into our Realm of England, by Stealth, or without Licence of our Governor of our said Colony in Virginia, for the

Time being, or have been sent thither as Misdoers and Offenders: And that many also of those Persons after their Return from thence, having been questioned by our Council here, for such their Misbehaviors and Offences, by their Insolent and Contemptuous Carriage in the Presence of our said Council, have shewed little Respect and Reverence either to the Place or Authority in which we have placed and appointed them; And others for the colouring of their Lewdness and Misdemeanors committed in Virginia, have endeavoured by most vile and slanderous Reports made and divulged, as well of the Country of Virginia, as also of the Government and Estate of the said Plantation and Colony, as much as in them lay, to bring the said Voyage and Plantation into Disgrace and Contempt: By Means whereof, not only the Adventurers and Planters already engaged in the said Plantation, have been exceedingly abused and hindered, and a great Number of other, our loving and well-disposed Subjects, otherwise well affected and inclined to join and adventure in so noble, Christian, and worthy an Action, have been discouraged from the same; but also the utter overthrow and Ruin of the said Enterprise hath been greatly endangered, which cannot miscarry without some Dishonour to Us, and our Kingdom.

Now, forasmuch as it appeareth unto us, that these Insolences, Misdemeanors, and Abuses, not to be tolerated in any civil Government, have, for the most part, grown and proceeded, in regard our said Council have not any direct Power and Authority, by any express Words in our former Letters-patents, to correct and chastise such Offenders; We therefore, for more speedy Reformation of so great and enormous Abuses and Misdemeanors heretofore practised and committed, and for the preventing of the like hereafter, do by these Presents for Us, our Heirs, and Successors, GIVE and GRANT, to the said Treasurer and Company, and their Successors for ever, that it shall, and may be lawful for our said Council for the first Colony in Virginia, or any two of them (whereof the said Treasurer or his Deputy for the Time being, to be always one) by Warrant under their Hands, to send for, or cause to be apprehended, all, and every such Person or Persons, who shall be noted, or accused, or found at any Time or Times hereafter, to offend or misbehave themselves, in any the Offences before mentioned and expressed, and upon the Examination of any such Offender or Offenders, and just Proof made by Oath, taken before the said

Council, of any such notorious Misdemeanors by them committed as aforesaid; And also upon any insolent and contemptuous, or indecent Carriage and Misbehaviour, to, or against, any our said Council, shewed or used by any such Person or Persons so called, convented, and appearing before them as aforesaid; That in all such cases, they our said Council, or any two of them for the time being, shall, and may have full Power and Authority, either here to bind them over with good Sureties for their good Behaviour, and further therein, to proceed to all Intents and Purposes, as it is used in other like Cases, within our Realm of *England*; Or else, at their Discretions, to remand and send back the said Offenders, or any of them, unto the said Colony in *Virginia*, there to be proceeded against and punished, as the Governor, Deputy or Council there, for the Time being, shall think meet; Or otherwise, according to such Laws and Ordinances, as are and shall be in Use there, for the well-ordering and good Government of the said Colony.

And for the more effectual Advancing of the said Plantation, We do further, for Us, our Heirs, and Successors, of our especial Grace and Favour, by Virtue of our Prerogative Royal, and by the Assent and Consent of the Lords and others of our Privy Council, GIVE and GRANT, unto the said Treasurer and Company, full Power and Authority, free Leave, Liberty, and Licence, to set forth, erect, and publish, one or more Lottery or Lotteries, to have Continuance, and to endure and be held, for the Space of one whole Year, next after the opening of the same; And after the End and Expiration of the said Term, the said Lottery or Lotteries to continue and be further kept, during our Will and Pleasure only, and not otherwise. And yet nevertheless, we are contented and pleased, for the Good and Welfare of the said Plantation, that the said Treasurer and Company shall, for the Dispatch and Finishing of the said Lottery or Lotteries, have six Months Warning after the said Year ended, before our Will and Pleasure shall, for and on that Behalf, be construed, deemed, and adjudged, to be in any wise altered and determined.

And our further Will and Pleasure is, that the said Lottery and Lotteries shall and may be opened and held, within our City of *London*, or in any other City or Town, or elsewhere, within this our Realm of *England*, with such Prizes, Articles, Conditions, and Limitations, as to them, the said Treasurer and Company, in their Discretions, shall seem convenient:

And it shall and may be lawful, to and for the said Treasurer and Company, to elect and choose Receivers, Surveyors, Auditors, Commissioners, or any other Officers whatsoever, at their Will and Pleasure, for the better marshalling, disposing, guiding, and governing of the said Lottery and Lotteries; And that it shall likewise be lawful, to and for the said Treasurer and any two of the said Council, to minister to all and every such Person, so elected and chosen for Offices, as aforesaid, one or more Oaths, for their good Behaviour, just and true Dealing, in and about the said Lottery or Lotteries, to the Intent and Purpose, that none of our loving Subjects, putting in their Names, or otherwise adventuring in the said general Lottery or Lotteries, may be, in any wise, defrauded and deceived of their said Monies, or evil and indirectly dealt withal in their said Adventures.

And we further GRANT, in Manner and Form aforesaid, that it shall and may be lawful, to and for the said Treasurer and Company, under the Seal of our said Council for the Plantation, to publish, or to cause and procure to be published by Proclamation, or otherwise (the said Proclamation to be made in their Name, by Virtue of these Presents) the said Lottery or Lotteries, in all Cities, Towns, Burroughs, and other Places, within our said Realm of *England*; And we Will and Command all Mayors, Justices of the Peace, Sheriffs, Bailiffs, Constables, and other Officers and loving Subjects, whatsoever, that in no wise, they hinder or delay the Progress and Proceedings of the said Lottery or Lotteries, but be therein, touching the Premises, aiding and assisting, by all honest, good, and lawful Means and Endeavours.

And further, our Will and Pleasure is, that in all Questions and Doubts, that shall arise, upon any Difficulty of Construction or Interpretation of any Thing, contained in these, or any other our former Letters-patent, the same shall be taken and interpreted, in most ample and beneficial Manner for the said Treasurer and Company, and their Successors, and every Member thereof. . . .

B. A Proprietary Charter

THE PROPRIETARY charter, exemplified by the Maryland Charter (June 30, 1632), was similar in nature to earlier feudal grants. It is notable for requiring the proprietor to obtain the consent of the freemen to all laws. Subsequently included in all proprietary charters except the one issued to the Duke of York for New York in 1664, this stipulation assured the colonies of participation in the governing process.

SOURCE: Thorpe (ed.), *Federal and State Constitutions*, III, 1677–1681, 1684–1685.

Whereas our well beloved and right trusty Subject Caecilius Calvert, Baron of Baltimore, in our Kingdom of Ireland, Son and Heir of George Calvert, Knight, late Baron of Baltimore, in our said Kingdom of Ireland, treading in the steps of his Father, being animated with a laudable, and pious Zeal for extending the Christian Religion, and also the Territories of our Empire, hath humbly besought Leave of us, that he may transport, by his own Industry, and Expense, a numerous Colony of the English Nation, to a certain Region, herein after described, in a Country hitherto uncultivated, in the Parts of America, and partly occupied by Savages, having no knowledge of the Divine Being, and that all that Region, with some certain Privileges, and Jurisdiction, appertaining unto the wholesome Government, and State of his Colony and Region aforesaid, may by our Royal Highness be given, granted and confirmed unto him, and his Heirs.

Know Ye therefore, that We . . . by this our present Charter . . . do Give, Grant and Confirm, unto the aforesaid Caecilius, now Baron of Baltimore, his Heirs, and Assigns, all that Part of the Peninsula, or Chersonese, lying in the Parts of America, between the Ocean on the East and the Bay of Chesapeake on the West, divided from the Residue thereof by a Right Line drawn from the Promontory, or Head-Land, called Watkin's Point, situate upon the Bay aforesaid, near the river Wigloo, on the West, unto the main Ocean on the East; and between that Boundary on the South, unto that Part of the Bay of Delaware on the North, which lieth under the Fortieth Degree of North Latitude from the Equinoctial, where New England is terminated; And all that Tract of Land within the Metes underwritten (that is to say) passing from the said Bay, called Delaware Bay, in a right Line, by the Degree aforesaid, unto the true meridian of the first Fountain of the River of Pattowmack, thence verging toward the South, unto the further Bank of the said River, and following the same on the West and South, unto a certain Place, called Cinquack, situate near the mouth of the said River, where it disembogues into the aforesaid Bay of Chesapeake, and thence by the shortest Line unto the aforesaid Promontory or Place, called Watkin's Point; so that the whole tract of land, divided by the Line aforesaid, between the main Ocean and Watkin's Point, unto the Promontory called Cape

Charles, and every the Appendages thereof, may entirely remain excepted for ever to Us, our Heirs and Successors.

Also We do grant . . . all Islands and Inlets within the Limits aforesaid, all and singular the Islands, and Islets, from the Eastern Shore of the aforesaid Region, towards the East, which had been, or shall be formed in the Sea, situate within Ten marine Leagues from the said shore; with all and singular the Ports, Harbours, Bays, Rivers, and Straits belonging to the Region or Islands aforesaid, and all the Soil, Plains, Woods, Marshes, Lakes, Rivers, Bays, and Straits, situate, or being within the Metes, Bounds, and Limits aforesaid, with the Fishings of every kind of Fish, as well of Whales, Sturgeons, and other royal Fish, as of other Fish, in the Sea, Bays, Straits, or Rivers, within the Premises, and the fish there taken; And moreover all Veins, Mines, and Quarries, as well opened as hidden, already found, or that shall be found within the Region, Islands, or Limits aforesaid, of Gold, Silver, Gems, and precious Stones, and any other whatsoever, whether they be of Stones, or Metals, or of any other Thing, or Matter whatsoever; And furthermore the Patronages, and Advowsons of all Churches which (with the increasing Worship and Religion of Christ) within the said Region, Islands, Islets, and Limits aforesaid, hereafter shall happen to be built, together with License and Faculty of erecting and founding Churches, Chapels, and Places of Worship, in convenient and suitable places, within the Premises, and of causing the same to be dedicated and consecrated according to the Ecclesiastical Laws of our Kingdom of England, with all, and singular such, and as ample Rights, Jurisdictions, Privileges, Prerogatives, Royalties, Liberties, Immunities, and royal Rights, and temporal Franchises whatsoever, as well by Sea as by Land, within the Region, Islands, Islets, and Limits aforesaid, to be had, exercised, used, and enjoyed, as any Bishop of Durham, within the Bishoprick or County Palatine of Durham, in our Kingdom of England, ever heretofore hath had, held, used, or enjoyed, or of right could, or ought to have, hold, use, or enjoy.

And we do by these Presents . . . Constitute Him, the now Baron of Baltimore, and his Heirs, the true and absolute Lords and Proprietaries of the Region aforesaid, and of all other Premises (except the before excepted) saving always the Faith and Allegiance and Sovereign Dominion due to Us. . . . To Hold of Us . . . as of our Castle of Windsor, in our County of Berks, in free and common Soccage, by Fealty only for all Services, and not in Capite, nor by Knight's Service, Yielding therefore unto Us . . . Two Indian Arrows of these Parts, to be delivered at the said Castle of Windsor, every Year, on Tuesday in Easter Week: And also the fifth Part of all Gold and Silver Ore, which shall happen from Time to Time, to be found within the aforesaid Limits. . . .

And . . . We . . . do grant unto the said now Baron . . . free, full, and absolute Power, by the Tenor of these Presents, to Ordain, Make, and Enact Laws, of what Kind soever, according to their sound Discretions, whether relating to the Public State of the said Province, or the private Utility of Individuals, of and with the Advice, Assent, and Approbation of the Free-Men of the same Province, or the greater Part of them, or of their Delegates or Deputies, whom We will shall be called together for the framing of Laws, when, and as often as Need shall require . . . in the Form which shall seem best to him or them, and the same to publish under the Seal of the aforesaid now Baron of Baltimore, and his Heirs, and duly to execute the same upon all Persons, for the time being, within the aforesaid Province, and the Limits thereof, or under his or their Government and Power . . . by the Imposition of Fines, Imprisonment, and other Punishment whatsoever; even if it be necessary, and the Quality of the Offence require it, by Privation of Member, or Life. . . . So, nevertheless, that the Laws aforesaid be consonant to Reason, and be not repugnant or contrary, but (so far as conveniently may be) agreeable to the Laws, Statutes, Customs, and Rights of this Our Kingdom of England.

And forasmuch as, in the Government of so great a Province, sudden accidents may frequently happen, to which it will be necessary to apply a Remedy, before the Freeholders of the said Province, their Delegates, or Deputies, can be called together for the framing of Laws; neither will it be fit that so great a Number of People should immediately, on such emergent Occasion, be called together, We therefore, for the better Government of so great a Province, do Will and Ordain . . . that the . . . Baron of Baltimore . . . may, and can make and constitute fit and Wholesome Ordinances from Time to Time, to be Kept and observed within the Province aforesaid, as well for the Conservation of the Peace, as for the better Government of the People inhabiting therein, and publicly to notify the same to all Persons whom the same in any wise do or may affect. . . . So that the said Ordinances be consonant to Reason and be not repugnant nor contrary, but (so far as conveniently may be done) agreeable to the Laws, Statutes, or

Rights of our Kingdom of England: And so that the same Ordinances do not, in any Sort, extend to oblige, bind, charge, or take away the Right or Interest of any Person or Persons, of, or in Member, Life, Freehold, Goods or Chattels. . . .

We will also, and of our more abundant Grace, for Us, our Heirs and Successors, do firmly charge, constitute, ordain, and command, that the said Province be of our Allegiance . . . and in all Things shall be held, treated, reputed, and esteemed as the faithful Liege-Men of Us . . . born within our Kingdom of England; also Lands, Tenements, Revenues, Services, and other Hereditaments whatsoever, within our Kingdom of England, and other our Dominions, to inherit, or otherwise purchase, receive, take, have, hold, buy, and possess, and the same to use and enjoy, and the same to give, sell, alien and bequeath; and likewise all Privileges, Franchises and Liberties of this our Kingdom of England, freely, quietly, and peaceably to have and possess, and the same may use and enjoy in the same manner as our Liege-Men born, or to be born within our said Kingdom of England, without Impediment, Molestation, Vexation, Impeachment, or Grievance of Us. . . .

Moreover, We will, appoint, and ordain . . . that the same Baron of Baltimore . . . shall have, and enjoy the Taxes and Subsidies payable, or arising within the Ports, Harbors, and other Creeks and Places aforesaid, within the Province aforesaid, for Wares bought and sold, and Things there to be laden, or unladen, to be reasonably assessed by them, and the People there as aforesaid, on emergent Occasion; to whom We grant Power by these Presents, for Us, our Heirs and Successors, to assess and impose the said Taxes and Subsidies there, upon just Cause and in due Proportion.

And furthermore . . . We . . . do give, grant and confirm, unto the said now Baron of Baltimore . . . full and absolute License, Power, and Authority . . . [to] assign, alien, grant, demise, or enfeoff so many, such, and proportionate Parts and Parcels of the Premises, to any Person or Persons willing to purchase the same, as they shall think convenient, to have and to hold to the same Person or Persons willing to take or purchase the same, and his and their Heirs and Assigns, in Fee-simple, or Fee-tail, or for Term of Life, Lives or Years; to hold of the aforesaid now Baron of Baltimore, his Heirs and Assigns, by so many, such, and so great Services, Customs and Rents of this Kind, as to the same now

Baron of Baltimore, his Heirs, and Assigns, shall seem fit and agreeable . . .

We also . . . do give and grant License to the same Baron of Baltimore, and to his Heirs, to erect any Parcels of Land within the Province aforesaid, into Manors, and in every of those Manors, to have and to hold a Court-Baron, and all Things which to a Court Baron do belong; and to have and to Keep View of Frank-Pledge, for the Conservation of the Peace and better Government of those Parts, by themselves and their Stewards, or by the Lords, for the Time being to be deputed, of other of those Manors when they shall be constituted, and in the same to exercise all Things to the View of Frank Pledge belong.

And further We will, and do, by these Presents, for Us, our Heirs and Successors, covenant and grant to, and with the aforesaid now Baron of Baltimore, His Heirs and Assigns, that We, our Heirs, and Successors, at no Time hereafter, will impose, or make or cause to be imposed, any Impositions, Customs, or other Taxations, Quotas, or Contributions whatsoever, in or upon the Residents or Inhabitants of the Province aforesaid for their Goods, Lands, or Tenements within the same Province, or upon any Tenements, Lands, Goods or Chattels within the Province aforesaid, or in or upon any Goods or Merchandizes within the Province aforesaid, or within the Ports or Harbors of the said Province, to be laden or unladen . . .

C. A Plantation Covenant

GROUPS OF colony founders who had failed or neglected to obtain a royal charter sought to legitimatize their enterprises and provide a basis for maintaining social order by entering into written covenants among themselves, in which they agreed to bind themselves into a body politic and to obey its laws. The Mayflower Compact, adopted by the Pilgrims at Plymouth on November 11, 1620, was the first and most famous of these "plantation covenants."

SOURCE: Thorpe (ed.), Federal and State Constitutions III, 1841.

IN THE NAME OF GOD, AMEN. We, whose names are underwritten, the Loyal Subjects of our dread Sovereign Lord King James, by the Grace of God, of Great Britain, France, and Ireland, King, Defender of the Faith, &c. Having undertaken for the Glory of God, and Advancement of the Christian Faith, and the Honour of our King and Country, a Voyage to plant the first Colony in the northern Parts of *Virginia;* Do by these Presents, solemnly and mutually, in the Presence of God and one another, covenant and combine ourselves together into a civil Body Politick, for our better Ordering and Preservation, and Furtherance of the Ends aforesaid: And by Virtue hereof do enact, constitute, and frame, such just and equal Laws, Ordinances, Acts, Constitutions, and Officers, from time to time, as shall be thought most meet and convenient for the general Good of the Colony; unto which we promise all due Submission and Obedience. In Witness whereof we have hereunto subscribed our names at *Cape-Cod* the eleventh of *November,* in the Reign of our Sovereign Lord King *James,* of *England, France,* and *Ireland,* the eighteenth, and of *Scotland,* the fifty-fourth, *Anno Domini,* 1620.

Mr. John Carver,	Mr. Samuel Fuller,	Edward Tilly,
Mr. William Bradford,	Mr. Christopher Martin,	John Tilly,
Mr. Edward Winslow,	Mr. William Mullins,	Francis Cooke,
Mr. William Brewster,	Mr. William White,	Thomas Rogers,
Isaac Allerton,	Mr. Richard Warren,	Thomas Tinker,
Myles Standish,	John Howland,	John Ridgdale,
John Alden,	Mr. Steven Hopkins,	Edward Fuller,
John Turner,	Digery Priest,	Richard Clark,
Francis Eaton,	Thomas Williams,	Richard Gardiner,
James Chilton,	Gilbert Winslow,	Mr. John Allerton,
John Craxton,	Edmund Margesson,	Thomas English,
John Billington,	Peter Brown,	Edward Doten,
Joses Fletcher,	Richard Britteridge,	Edward Liester.
John Goodman,	George Soule,	

3. Origins of Colonial Self-Government

A. *Establishment of Representative Government in Virginia*

To ATTRACT new settlers to the colonies and keep them happy, sponsors had to offer very favorable conditions of settlement. Early in the history of Virginia, the Virginia Company found it necessary to offer easy access to land and a share in government. By the so-called Great Charter of November, 1618, the Company authorized the calling of an assembly of representatives of the inhabitants of the colony, an action that led to the beginnings of representative government in the English overseas colonies. Although the Great Charter is no longer extant, it was probably similar to the Ordinance of July 24, 1621, which is reprinted below.

SOURCE: William Waller Hening (ed.), *The Statutes at Large* (13 vols., Richmond, Va., 1809–23, I, 110–113.

I. To all people, to whom these presents shall come, be seen, or heard, the treasurer, council, and company of adventurers and planters for the city of London for the first colony of Virginia, send greeting. Know ye, that we, the said treasurer, council, and company, taking into our careful consideration the present state of the said colony of Virginia, and intending by the divine assistance, to settle such a form of government there, as may be to the greatest benefit and comfort of the people, and whereby all injustice, grievances, and oppression may be prevented and kept off as much as possible, from the said colony, have thought fit to make our entrance, by ordering and establishing such supreme councils, as may not only be assisting to the governor for the time being, in the administration of justice, and the executing of other duties to this office belonging, but also, by their vigilant care and prudence, may provide, as well for a remedy of all inconveniences, growing from time to time, as also for advancing of increase, strength, stability, and prosperity of the said colony:

II. We therefore, the said treasurer, council, and company, by authority directed to us from his majesty under the great seal, upon mature deliberation, do hereby order and declare, that, from hence forward, there shall be two supreme councils in Virginia, for the better government of the said colony aforesaid.

III. The one of which councils, to be called the council of state, (and whose office shall chiefly be assisting, with their care, advice, and circumspection, to the said governor) shall be chosen, nominated, placed, and displaced, from time to time, by us the said treasurer, council and company, and our successors: which council of state shall consist, for the present only of . . . persons . . . here inserted. . . . Which said counsellors and council we earnestly pray and desire, and in his majesty's name strictly charge and command, that (all factions, partialities, and sinister respect laid aside) they bend their care and endeavours to assist the said governor; first and principally, in the advancement of the honour and service of God, and the enlargement of his kingdom against the heathen people; and next, in erecting of the said colony in due obedience to his majesty, and all lawful authority from his majesty's directions; and lastly, in maintaining the said people in justice and christian conversation amongst themselves, and in strength and ability to withstand their enemies. And this council, to be always, or for the most part, residing about or near the governor.

IV. The other council, more generally to be called by the governor, once yearly, and no oftener, but for very extraordinary and important occasions, shall consist for the present, of the said council of state, and of two burgesses out of every town, hundred, or other particular plantation, to be respectively chosen by the inhabitants: which council shall be called The General Assembly, wherein (as also in the said council of state) all matters shall be decided, determined, and ordered by the greater part of the voices then present; reserving to the governor always a negative voice. And this general assembly shall have free power, to treat, consult, and conclude, as well of all emergent occasions concerning the publick weal of the said colony and every part thereof, as also to make, ordain, and enact such general laws and orders, for the behoof of the said colony, and the good government thereof, as shall, from time to time, appear necessary or requisite;

V. Whereas in all other things, we require the said general assembly, as also the said council of state, to imitate and follow the policy of the form of government, laws, customs, and manner of trial; and other administration of justice, used in the realm of England, as near as may be even as ourselves, by his majesty's letters patent, are required.

VI. Provided, that no law or ordinance, made in the said general assembly, shall be or continue in force or validity, unless the same shall be solemnly ratified and confirmed, in a general quarter court of the said company here in England, and so ratified, be returned to them under our seal; it being our intent to afford the like measure also unto the said colony, that after the government of the said colony shall once have been well framed, and settled accordingly, which is to be done by us, as by authority derived from his majesty, and the same shall have been so by us declared, no orders of court afterwards, shall bind the said colony, unless they be ratified in like manner in the general assemblies. . . .

B. The Character of Early Colonial Representative Government

THE CHARACTER and concerns of the early legislatures may be surmised from the following laws passed by the Virginia Assembly in March, 1624. Virtually every aspect of the life of the colony came under the purview of the Assembly, which, as paragraphs 8 and 11 suggest, was already beginning to define its role in Virginia society in terms similar to those used by Parliament in England.

SOURCE: Hening (ed.), Statutes at Large, I, 122–128.

1. That there shall be in every plantation, where the people use to meete for the worship of God, a house or roome sequestred for that purpose, and not to be for any temporal use whatsoever, and a place empaled in, sequestered only to the buryal of the dead.
2. That whosoever shall absent himselfe from divine service any Sunday without an allowable excuse shall forfeite a pound of tobacco, and he that absenteth himselfe a month shall forfeit 50lb. of tobacco.
3. That there be an uniformity in our church as neere as may be to the canons in England; both in substance and circumstance, and that all persons yeild readie obedience unto them under paine of censure.
4. That the 22d of March be yeerly solemnized as holliday, and all other hollidays (except when they fall two together) betwixt the feast of the annunciation of the blessed virgin and St. Michael the archangell, then only the first to be observed by reason of our necessities.
5. That no minister be absent from his church above two months in all the yeare upon penalty of forfeiting halfe his

means, and whosoever shall absent above fowre months in the year shall forfeit his whole means and cure.

6.   That whosoever shall disparage a minister without bringing sufficient proofe to justify his reports whereby the mindes of his parishioners may be alienated from him, and his ministry prove the less effectual by their prejudication, shall not only pay 500lb. waight of tobacco but also aske the minister so wronged forgiveness publickly in the congregation.

7.   That no man dispose of any of his tobacco before the minister be satisfied, upon pain of forfeiture double his part of the minister's means, and one man of every plantation to collect his means out of the first and best tobacco and corn.

8.   That the Governor shall not lay any taxes or ympositions upon the colony their lands or comodities other way than by the authority of the General Assembly, to be levyed and ymployed as the said Assembly shall appoynt.

9.   The governor shall not withdraw the inhabitants from their private labors to any service of his own upon any colour whatsoever and in case the publick service require ymployments of many hands before the holding a General Assemblie to give order for the same, in that case the levying of men shall be done by order of the governor and whole body of the counsell and that in such sorte as to be least burthensome to the people and most free from partiality.

10.   That all the old planters that were here before or came in at the last coming of sir Thomas Gates they and their posterity shall be exempted from their personal service to the warrs and any publick charge (church duties excepted) that belong particularly to their persons (not exempting their families) except such as shall be ymployd to command in chief.

11.   That no burgesses of the General Assembly shall be arrested during the time of the assembly, a week before and a week after upon pain of the creditors forfeiture of his debt and such punishment upon the officer as the court shall award.

12.   That there shall be courts kept once a month in the corporations of Charles City and Elizabeth Citty for the decyding of suits and controversies not exceeding the value of one hundred pounds of tobacco and for punishing of petty offences, That the commanders of the places and such others as the governor and council shall appoint by commission shall be the judges,

with reservation of apeal after sentence to the governor and counsell and whosoever shall appeal yf he be there cast in suit shall pay duble damages, The commanders to be of the quorum and sentence to be given by the major parties.

13. That every privatt planters devident shall be surveyed and laid out in several and the bounds recorded by the survey; yf there be any pettie differences betwixt neighbours about their devidents to be divided by the surveyor if of much importance to be referred to the governor and counsell: the surveyor to have 10 lbs. of tobacco upon every hundred acres.

14. For the encouragement of men to plant store of corne, the prise shall not be stinted, but it shall be free for every man to sell it as deere as he can.

15. That there shall be in every parish a publik granary unto which there shall be contributed for every planter exceeding the adge of 18 years alive at the crop after he hath been heere a year a bushel of corne, the which shall be disposed for the publique uses of every parish by the major part of the freemen, the remainder yearly to be taken out by the owners at St. Tho's his day and the new bushell to be putt in the roome.

16. That three sufficient men of every parish shall be sworne to see that every man shall plant and tende sufficient of corne for his family. Those men that have neglected so to do are to be by the said three men presented to be censured by the governor and counsell.

17. That all trade for corne with the salvages as well publick as private after June next shall be prohibited.

18. That every freeman shall fence in a quarter of an acre of ground before Whitsuntide next to make a garden for planting of vines, herbs, roots, &c. subpoena ten pounds of tobacco a man, but that no man for his own family shall be tyed to fence above an acre of land and that whosoever hath fenced a garden and   of the land shall be paid for it by the owner of the soyle; they shall also plant Mulberry trees.

19. The proclamations for swearing and drunkenness sett out by the governor and counsell are confirmed by this Assembly; and it is further ordered that the churchwardens shall be sworne to present them to the commanders of every plantation and that the forfeitures shall be collected by them to be for publique uses.

20.   That a proclamation be read aboard every ship and afterwards fixed to the maste of such   in, prohibiting them to break boulke or make privatt sales of any commodity until   James City, without special order from the governor and counsell.

21.   That the proclamation for the rates of commodities be still in force and that there be some men in every plantation to censure the tobacco.

22.   That there be no weights nor measures used but such as shall be sealed by officers appointed for that purpose.

23.   That every dwelling house shall be pallizaded in for defence against the Indians.

24.   That no man go or send abroad without a sufficient partie will armed.

25.   That men go not to worke in the ground without their arms (and a centinell upon them.)

26.   That the inhabitants go not aboard ships or upon any other occasions in such numbers, as thereby to weaken and endanger the plantations.

27.   That the commander of every plantation take care that there be sufficient of powder and amunition within the plantation under his command and their pieces fixt and their arms compleate.

28.   That there be dew watch kept by night.

29.   That no commander of any plantation do either himselfe or suffer others to spend powder unnecessarily in drinking or entertainments, &c.

30.   That such persons of quality as shall be founde delinquent in their duties being not fitt to undergoe corporal punishment may notwithstanding be ymprisoned at the discretione of the commander & for greater offences to be subject to a ffine inflicted by the monthlie court, so that it exceed not the value aforesaid.

31.   That every man that hath not contributed to the finding a man at the castell shall pay for himself and servants five pounds of tobacco a head, towards the discharge of such as had their servants there.

32.   That at the beginning of July next the inhabitants of every corporation shall fall upon their adjoyning salvages as we did the last yeare, those that shall be hurte upon service to be cured

at the publique charge; in case any be lamed to be maintained by the country according to his person and quality.

33.   That for defraying of such publique debts our troubles have brought upon us. There shall be levied 10 pounds of tobacco upon every male head above sixteen years of adge now living (not including such as arrived since the beginning of July last.)

34.   That no person within this colony upon the rumur of supposed change and alteration, presume to be disobedient to the present government, nor servants to their private officers, masters or overseers at their uttermost perills.

35.   That Mr. John Pountis, counsellor of state, going to England, (being willing by our intreatie to accept of that imployment,) to solicite the general cause of the country to his majesty and the counsell, towards the charges of which voyage, the country consente to pay for every male head above sixteen years of adge then living, which have been here a yeare four pounds of the best merchantable tobacco, in leafe, at or before the last of October next.

4. Beginnings of Imperial Control

A. Regulating Tobacco

THE FIRST efforts of the imperial government to develop a commercial policy for the Colonies involved the regulation of tobacco. As early as October 24, 1621, the Crown required that any tobacco bound from the colonies to foreign ports first pass through England. A few years later, the Crown tried to encourage colonial tobacco producers by giving them a monopoly of the English market, excluding Spanish and Portuguese tobacco, and forbidding tobacco growing in England. On May 24, 1625, these regulations were combined in one general order of the King in Privy Council. That order is printed below.

SOURCE: W. L. Grant and James Munro (eds.), Acts of the Privy Council of England, Colonial Series (6 vols., London, 1908–12), I, 89–90.

Upon severall petitions presented to the Board by divers Planters and Marryners lately come from Verginia wherein they were humble Suitors, for the obtayning of leave to utter and sell for their best proffitt and advantage such quantities of Tobacco of the groath of Virginia, as they or any of them had brought over with them. In the venting whereof they were now hindred and restrayned, to the great damage and almost undoing of most of them as was alledged, the same being their whole meanes and lyvelyhood. Their lordshipps upon full Debate and Consideration had thereof have in favour of the petitioners for their present releif and Comfort, thought fitt and hereby ordered, that they and every of them, shalbe at libertie to utter and sell, all such quantities of Tobacco, as they have brought over of the groath of the foresaid Plantation, they first satisfying and paying for the same to the Collecter or Collecters of his Majesties imposts upon Tobacco— 9d.—upon each pound for Impost, and to the Farmors of his Majesties Customes 3d. upon the pound, for Custome, And for the better encouragement of all English planters to goe on Chearfully in the advancing of any the English plantations Their lordshipps have lykewise thought fitt and ordered, that thease Instructions following be strictly observed and putt in Execution viezt

That all Tobacco whatsoever, which shall not be of the groath of the English Plantations, be utterly prohibited to bee imported into this Kingdome

That noe Tobacco be suffered to be planted within this Kingdome

That all Tobacco of the groath of any English Plantations whatsoever be brought into this Kingdome

Lastly whereas it was now informed, by some of the Planters that Spanish Tobacco was frequently vented in divers shopps, and other places under the name of Virginia and Bermoodos Tobacco to the great prejudice of those Plantations, and defrauding of his Majesties Proclamation prohibiting the same. Their lordshipps for the better discovery and reforming of the said abuse doe hereby Declare and Order, that the discoverer shalbe well rewarded, and every such Offendor severely punished, upon information thereof at any tyme given, and prooved before this Board.

B. Establishment of Royal Government in Virginia

THE CROWN first took over direct responsibility for administering a colony in 1625, when the courts in London vacated the charter of the Virginia Company. The formal proclamation converting Virginia into a royal colony, reprinted here, was issued on May 13, 1625. It specified the general form of government and the broad objectives of royal policy in the colony.

SOURCE: Thomas Rymer (ed.), Foedera, Conventiones, Literae, Acta Publica, Regis Anglicae (2nd ed., 20 vols., London, 1726), XVIII, 72–73.

Whereas the Collonie of Virginia, planted by the handes of Our most deere Father of blessed Memorie, for the Propagation of Christian Religion, the Increase of Trade, and the inlarging of his Royall Empire, hath not hetherto prospered soe happiely as was hoped and desired, a great Occasion whereof his late Majestie conceived to bee, for that the Governement of that Collonie was comytted to the Companie of Virginia, incorporated of a Multitude of Persons of severall Dispositions, amongst whome the Affaires of greatest Moment were and must be ruled by the greater Number of Votes, and Voyces, and therefore his late Majestie, out of his greate Wisedome and Depth of Judgment, did desire to resume that Popular Government, and accordingly the Letters Patentes of that Incorporation were, by his Highnes Direction, in a legal Course questioned, and thereuppon judicially repealed and adjudged to be voyd, wherein his Majestyes ayme was onlie to reduce that Government into such a right Course as might best agree with that Forme which was held in the rest of his Royall Monarchie, and was not intended by him to take awaie or ympeach the particuler Interest of anie private Planter or Adventurer, nor to alter the same otherwise then should be of Necessitie for the Good of the Publique;

And whereas Wee contynue the like Care of those Collonies and Plantations as Our late deere Father did, and upon deliberate Advise and Consideration, are of the same Judgment that Our said Father was of for the Government of that Collonie of Virginia; Nowe, least the Apprehension of former personall Differences which have heretofore happened, (the receivinge and contynuing whereof Wee utterly disallowe and strictly forbid) might distracte the Myndes of the Planters and Adventurers, or the Opynion that Wee would neglect those Plantations might discourage Men to goe or send thither, and soe hinder the perfectinge of that Worke, wherein Wee hould the Honor of Our deere Father deceased and Our owne Honor to be deepely ingaged;

Wee have thought fitt to declare, and by Our Royall Proclamation to publishe Our owne Judgment and Resolution in these things, which by Godes Assistance Wee purpose constantly to pursue, And therefore Wee doe by these Presents publish and declare to all Our lovinge Subjectes, and to the whole World, that Wee hould those Territories of Virginia and the Summer Islandes, as alsoe that of Newe England, where Our Collonies are alreadie planted, and within the Lymittes and Boundes where of Our late deere Father, by his Letters Patents under his Greate Seale of England remayninge of Record, hath given Leave and Libertie to his Subjects to plant and inhabite, to be a parte of Our Royall Empire discended uppon Us and undoubtedlie belonginge and apperteyninge unto Us, And that Wee hould Our Selfe as well bound by Our Royall Office to protecte, maynteyne and supporte the same, and are soe resolved to doe, as anie other Parte of Our Domynions; And that Our full Resolution is, that there maie be one uniforme Course of Governement in and through all Our whole Monarchie; That the Goverment of the Collonie of Virginia shall ymediately depend uppon Our Selfe, and not be commytted to anie Companie or Corporation, to whome itt maie be proper to trust Matters of Trade and Commerce, but cannot bee fitt or safe to communicate the ordering of State Affaires be they of never soe meane Consequence, And that therefore We have determyned that Our Commissioners for those Affaires shall proceede according to the Tenor of Our Commission directed unto them, untill Wee shall declare Our further Pleasure therein; Nevertheless We doe hereby declare that We are resolved, with as much convenyent Expedition as Our Affaires of greater Importance will give leave, to establish a Counsell consistinge of a fewe Persons of Understandinge and Quallitie, to whome Wee will give Trust for the ymmediate Care of the Affaires of that Collonie, and whoe shall be answerable to Us for their Proceedings, and in Matters of greater Moment shall be subordinate and attendant unto Our Privie Counsell heere; And that Wee will alsoe establish an other Counsell to be resident in Virginia, whoe shalbe subordinate to Our Counsell here for that Collonie; and that att Our owne Charge We will maynteyne those publique Officers and Mynisters, and that Strength of Men, Munition and Fortification as shalbe fitt and necessarie for the Defence of that Plantation, and will, by anie course that shalbe desired of Us, settle and assure the perticuler Rights and Interests of every Planter and Adventurer in anie of those Territories which shall desire the same, to give them full Satisfaction for their quiet and assured enjoying thereof. . . .

C. Emergence of Crown Policy Toward the Colonies

CROWN OFFICIALS *early began to give specific written instructions to each of the governors in Virginia at the beginning of their tenures, directing them in the exercise of all of their duties. These documents, exemplified by the instructions given to Sir William Berkeley at the time of his appointment as governor of Virginia in the summer of 1641, represented the Crown's attempt to establish closer supervision over governors and to enlarge its role in the internal administration of the colony. As they were extended to governors of other royal colonies, and as they grew more and more elaborate after the Restoration, they came to constitute the most comprehensive statement of the policy of the Crown toward the colonies.*

SOURCE: "Instructions to Berkeley, 1642," *Virginia Magazine of History and Biography*, II (1894–95), 281–288.

That in the first place you be carefull Almighty God may be duly and daily served according to the Form of Religion established in the church of England both by yourself and all the people under your charge, which may draw down a blessing on all your endeavours. . . . Suffer no invasion in matters of Religion and be careful to appoint sufficient and conformable Ministers to each congregation, that you chatechise and instruct them in the grounds and principles of Religion.

2.   That you administer the Oaths of Allegiance and Supremacy to all such as come thither with intention to plant themselves in the country, which if he shall refuse he is to be returned and shipped from thence home and certificate made to the Lords of the Councill, the same oath is to be administered to all other persons when you shall see it fitt as Mariners, Merchants &c. to prevent any danger of spyes.

3.   That Justice be equally administered to all his Majesty's subjects there residing and as neere as may bee after the forme of this Realm of England and vigilant care to be had to prevent corruption in officers tending to the delay or perverting of Justice.

4.   That you and the Councellors as formerly once a year or oftener, if urgent occasion shall require, Do summon the Burgesses of all and singler Plantations there, which together with the Governor and Councill makes the Grand Assembly, and shall have Power to make Acts and Laws for the Government of that Plantation correspondent, as near as may be, to the Laws of England, in which assembly the Governor is to have a negative voice, as formerly.

That you and the Councill assembled are to sett down the fittest Months of the Quarterly meeting of the Council of State, whereas they are to give their attendance for one and consult upon matter of Councill and State and to decide and determine such Causes as shall come before them, and that free access be admitted to all Suitors to make known their particular grievances, being against what persons So ever wherein the Governor for the time being, as formerly, is to have but a casting voyce if the number of the councellors should be equally divided in opinion, besides the Quarterly Meeting of the Council it shall be lawful for you to summon, from time to time, Extraordinary meetings of the Councill according to emergent occasions.

6.   In case there shall be necessary cause to proceed against any of the Councill for their own persons they are in such cases to be summoned by you, the Governor, to appear at the next Sessions of the Councill, holden there to abide their Sensure or otherwise, if you shall think it may concern either the Safety or

quiet of that State to proceed more speedily with such an offender. It shall be lawful to summon a councill extraordinary where at six of the councill at least are to be present with you, and by the Major part if their voyces comit my councillors to safe custody or upon Bayle to abide the order of the next quarter councill.

7.   For the ease of the Country and quicker despatch of Business you, the Governor and Councill, may appoint in places convenient Inferior Courts of Justice and Commissioners for the Same, to determine of suits not exceeding the value of Ten Pounds and for the punishments of such offences as you and the Councill shall think fitt to give them the power to hear and determine.

8.   The Governor shall appoint officers of sealing of writts and subpoenas and such officers as shall be thought necessary for the execution orders.

And—also the acts and Laws of the Generall Assembly and for punishing any neglect or contempt of the Said Orders, Acts or Laws respectively. And shall nominate and appoint all other publique officers under the degree of the councill, the Captain of the Fort, Master and Surveyor Generall excepted. . . .

11.   To the end the country may be the better served against all Hostil Invasions it is requisite that all persons from the age of 16 to 60 be armed with arms, both offensive and defensive. And if any person be defective in this kind, wee strictly charge you to command them to provide themselves of sufficient arms within one year or sooner if possible it may be done, and if any shall faill to be armed at the end of the Term limited we will that you punish them severely. . . .

14.   That new Comers be exempted the 1st yeare from going in p'son or contributing to the wars Save only in defence of the place where they shall inhabit and that only when the enemies shall assail them, but all others in the Colony shall go or be rated to the maintenance of the war proportionately to their abilitys, neither shall any man be priviledged for going to the warr that is above 16 years old and under 60, respect being had to the quality of the person, that officers be not forced to go as private soldiers or in places inferior to their Degrees, unless in case of supreme necessity.

15.   That you may better avoid and prevent the treachery of the savages we strictly forbid all persons whatsoever to receive into

their houses the person of any Indian or to converse or trade with them without the especiall license and warrant given to that purpose according to the commissioner inflicting severe punishment upon the offenders. . . .

17. That for raising of towns every one ye have and shall have a grant of 500 acres of land, shall, within a convenient time, build a convenient house of brick of 24 feet long and 16 feet broad with a cellar to it and so proportionately for Grants of larger or lesser quantity. And the grounds and platforms for the towns to be laid out in such form and order as the Governor and Councill shall appoint. And that you cause at ye publick charge of ye country a convenient house to be built where you and the councill may meet and sitt for the dispatching of publick affairs and hearing of causes. And because the buildings at Jamestown are for the most part decayed and the place found to be unhealthy and inconvenient in many respects. It shall be in the power of you and the council, with the advice of ye Generall Assembly, to choose such other seate for your chiefe Town and Residence of the Governor as by them shall be judged most convenient, retaining the ancient name of James Town.

18. That you shall have power to grant Patents and to assign such Proportion of Land to all adventurers and Planters as have been useful heretofore in the like cases, either for adventurers of money, Transportation of people thither according to the orders of the late company and since allowed by his Majesty.

And that there likewise be the same proportion of Fifty acres of land granted and assigned for every p'son transported thither since Midsummer, 1625. And that you continue ye same course to all persons transported thither untill it shall be otherwise determined by his Majesty.

19. Whereas the greatest part of the Land on James River hath been formerly granted unto particular persons or public society but being by them either not planted at all or for many years deserted, divers planters have by orders and leave of the Governor and Councill of Virginia set down upon these lands or some part of them which was absolutely necessary for the defence and security of the Colony against the Indians, that the Governor confirm those Lands unto the present Planters and Possessors thereof. And that the like course be taken for Planting new Patents in any other places so unplanted and deserted

as aforesaid where it shall be found necessary. And in case former proprietors make their claims thereunto that there be assigned to them the like quantities in any other part of the Colony not actually possessed where they shall make choice. . . .

21. That in regard you may daily expect the coming of a Foraign enemy, Wee require you soon after the first landing that you publish by proclamation throughout the Colony that no person whatsoever upon the arrival of any ships shall dare to go on board without ye express warrant from you the Governor and councill, least by the means they be surprized to the great prejudice if not the overthrow of the Plantation. . . .

24. That especiall care be taken for ye preservacion of neat cattle and that the Females be not killed up as formerly, whereby the Colony will in short time have such plenty of victualls, yt much people may come thither for the setting up of iron works and other staple commodities. That you cause the People to plant great store of corne, as there may be one whole years provision before hand in the Colony least in relying upon one single Harvest, Drought, Blasting or otherwise they fall into such wants or Famine as formerly they have endured. And that the Plow may go and English be sowed in all places convenient. And that no Corne nor Cattle be sold out of the Plantation without leave from the Governor and Councill.

25. That they apply themselves to the Impaling of Orchards and gardens for Roots and Fruits which that country is so proper for, & that every Planter be compelled for every 500 acres granted unto him to Inclose and sufficiently ffence either with Pales or Quicksett and Dikes, and so from time to time to preserve, enclosed and ffenced a quarter of an acre of Ground in ye most convenient place near his Dwelling House for Orchards and gardens.

26. That whereas your Tobacco falleth every day more and more unto a baser price, that it be stinted into a far less proportion then hath been made in ye last year 1637, not only to be accounted by the plants but by the quantity when 'tis cured. And because of Great Debts of the Planter in Tobacco, occasioned by the excessive rates of commodities have been the stinting thereof, so hard to be put into execution that the course commanded by his Majesty in his letter of the 22nd of April, in ye 13th year of His Reign for regulating ye debts of ye Colony be

duly observed. And also not to suffer men to build slight cottages as heretofore hath been there used. And to remove from place to place, only to plant Tobacco. That Trademen and Handy Crafts be compelled to follow their severall Trades and occupations, and that ye draw you into Towns.

27.   We require you to use your best endeavor to cause ye people there to apply themselves to the raising of more staple commodities as Hemp and Flax, Rope, Seed and Madder, Pitch & Tarr for Tanning of Hides and Leather. Likewise every Plantation to plant a proportion of Vines, answerable to their numbers, and to plant white Mulberry Trees, and attend Silk Worms.

28.   That the Merchant be not constrained to take Tobacco at any Price, in Exchange for his wares. But that it be lawfull for him to make his own Bargain for his goods he so changeth notwithstanding any Proclamation here published to the contrary.
. . .

30.   That whereas many ships laden with Tobacco and other merchandize from thence, carry ye same immediately into Forraine countries, whereby his Majesty loseth ye custom and Duties thereupon due, nothing being answered in Virginia, You bee very carefull that no ship or other vessell whatsoever depart from thence, fraighted with Tobacco or other commodities which that country shall afford, before Bond which sufficient sureties be taken to Majesties use to bring the same directly unto his Majesties Dominions and not else where, and to bring a Bill of Lading from home that the staple of those comodities may be made here, whereby his Majestie, after so great expence upon that Plantation and so many of his subjects Transported thither, may not be defrauded of what shall be justly due unto him for custom and other duties upon those goods. These Bonds to be transmitted to ye Councill here, and from thence to ye Exchequer, that ye Delinquent may be proceeded with according to due course of Law.

31.   Next that you strictly and resolutely forbid all Trade or Trucking for any Merchandize whatsoever which any ship other then His Majesties subjects, that shall either purposely or casually come to any of your plantations. And that if, upon some unexpected occasions and necessity, the Governor and Councill shall think fitt to admitt such intercourse, which we admitt not but upon some extremity, That good caution and

Bond be taken, both of the Master and also the owner of the said Tobacco or other comodities so laden that they shall (Damages of the Sea Excepted) be brought to our Port of London, there to pay unto us such duties as are due upon the same.

And to conclude, That in all things accordingly to your best understanding ye endeavour the extirpation of vice and encouragement of Religion, virtue and goodness.

D. Parliament Asserts Its Jurisdiction over the Colonies

ALTHOUGH Sir Edward Coke asserted Parliament's authority over Virginia as early as April, 1621, and the Long Parliament tried to establish its jurisdiction over all of the colonies in the early 1640's, it was not until the Interregnum that Parliament gained an active role in colonial affairs. On October 3, 1650, Parliament reacted to reports of strong royalist sympathy in Virginia, Barbados, Antigua, and Bermuda by passing an act to prohibit trade with those colonies. Reprinted here, this act explicitly asserted the colonists' obligation to obey all acts of Parliament and, by implication, the corollary of that obligation: Parliament's right to legislate for the colonies. Further, the measure acted upon that assertation by declaring any colonist who opposed Parliament's will a traitor, prohibiting him from engaging in any form of commerce, and authorizing the appointment of commissioners to make the colonies obey.

SOURCE: C. H. Firth and R. S. Rait (eds.), *Acts and Ordinances of the Interregnum, 1642–1660* (3 vols., London: His Majesty's Stationary Office, 1911), II, 425–429.

Whereas in Virginia, and in the Islands of Barbada's, Antego, St. Christophers, Mevias, Mounsirat, Bermuda's, and divers other Islands and places in America, there hath been and are Colonies and Plantations, which were planted at the Cost, and setled by the People, and by Authority of this Nation, which are and ought to be subordinate to, and dependent upon England; and hath ever since the Planting thereof been, and ought to be subject to such Laws, Orders and Regulations as are or shall be made by the Parliament of England; And whereas divers acts of Rebellion have been committed by many persons inhabiting in Barbada's, Antego, Bermuda's and Virginia, whereby they have most Trayterously, by Force and Subtilty, usurped a Power of Government, and seized the Estates of many well-affected persons into their hands, and banished others, and have set up themselves in opposition to, and distinct from this State and Commonwealth, many of the chief Actors in, and Promoters of these Rebellions, having been transported and carried over to the said Plantations in Forein Ships, without leave, license or consent of the Parliament of England; the Parliament of England taking the premises into consideration, and finding themselves obliged to use all speedy, lawful and just means for the Suppression of the said Rebellion in the said Plantations, and reducing the same to fidelity and due obedience, so as all peaceable and well-affected people, who have been Robbed, Spoiled, Imprisoned or Banished through the said Treasonable practices, may be restored to the freedom of their persons, and possession of their own Lands and Goods, and due punishment inflicted upon the said Delinquents, do Declare all and every the said persons in Barbada's, Antego, Bermuda's and Virginia, that have contrived, abetted, aided or assisted those horrid Rebellions, or have since willingly joyned with them, to be notorious Robbers and Traitors, and such as by the Law of Nations are not to be permitted any maner of Commerce or Traffique with any people whatsoever; and do forbid to all maner of persons, Foreiners, and others, all maner of Commerce, Traffique and Correspondency whatsoever, to be used or held with the said Rebels in the Barbada's, Bermuda's, Virginia and Antego, or either of them.

And be it Enacted by this present Parliament, and by the authority of the same, That after due publication of this Act made, to the end that none may justly pretend ignorance, it shall and may be lawful to any the Fleet or Ships sent forth or imployed by the Parliament, or any private Men of War or Ships to be allowed or approved in that behalf by the immediate Power of Parliament, or the Council of State established by Parliament, to seize, surprize and take all and all maner of Ships, Vessels and Goods, of what nature or kinde soever, belonging to all persons whatsoever whether Foreiners or others, or of what Nation soever, that shall be found or met withal, Trading or going to Trade, or coming from Trading with the said Rebels, or in or at the said Island of Barbada's, Bermudas, Virginia, or Antego aforesaid, or any part or parts thereof, or that shall hold any Correspondency with the said Rebels, or yield them any assistance or relief for the supporting their said Rebellion: And the same Ships and Goods so surprized, to send in to be proceeded against in the Court of Admiralty by vertue of this Act; and the Judges of that Court finding the same to be within the tenor and true meaning of this Act, to adjudge the same to be well taken, and to be good and lawful Prize. . . .

And to prevent for the time to come, and to hinder the carrying over of any such persons as are Enemies to this Commonwealth, or that may prove dangerous to any of the English Plantations in America, the Parliament doth forbid and prohibit all Ships of any Forein Nation whatsoever, to come to, or Trade in, or Traffique with any of the English Plantations in America, or any Islands, Ports or places thereof, which are planted by, and in possession of the People of this Commonwealth, without License first had and obtained from the Parliament or Council of State.

And be it further Enacted, Ordained and Declared by the Authority aforesaid, That from and after the Twentieth day of November, One thousand six hundred and fifty, It shall and may be lawful for any Ship or Ships set forth by the Parliament, or allowed of by the Parliament or Council of State, to seize, take and surprize any Ship or Ships of any Forein Nation whatsoever, that shall be outward bound to any of the said Plantations, Ports or places, without such License as aforesaid; and from and after the first of January, One thousand six hundred and fifty, It shall and may be lawful for such Ships set forth and allowed as aforesaid, to seize, take and surprize any Forein Ships that shall be found Trading at any of the Plantations, Islands and places aforesaid, without such License as aforesaid; and from and after the Twentieth day of March, One thousand six hundred and fifty, It shall and may be lawful for any of the Parliaments Ships, or private Men of War, allowed of by the Parliament or Council of State for the time being, to seize, take and surprize any Ship or Ships that are coming from, or have Traded at any of the Plantations as aforesaid, without such License as aforesaid. . . .

Provided nevertheless, and it is further Enacted, That the Council of State for the time being have hereby Power to grant License and Leave to any of the Ships of this Nation to go to, and Trade at Barbada's, Antego, Bermuda's, Virginia, or any of them, without prejudice or damage, Any thing in this Act to the contrary notwithstanding.

And it is further Enacted by the Authority aforesaid, That the said Council of State have hereby Power and Authority to send Ships to any of the Plantations aforesaid, and to grant Commission or Commissions to such person or persons as they shall think fit, with power to enforce all such to obedience as do or shall stand in opposition to the Parliament or their Authority; and to grant Pardons, and to setle Governors in all or any the said Islands, Plantations and places, and to do all just things, and use all lawful means to setle and preserve them in peace and safety, until the Parliament shall take further or other order therein, Any Letters Patents, or other Authority formerly granted or given to the contrary notwithstanding. . . .

5. Colonial Resistance to Imperial Control

A. *In Defense of Their "Ould Liberties and Privileges"*

BECAUSE THE colonies were distant from England and widely dispersed, and because the Crown had no means to control them, they enjoyed a remarkably wide latitude in both economic and political matters. The regulations concerning the tobacco trade, for instance, were virtually unenforceable, and throughout the middle decades of the seventeenth century, the tobacco colonies carried on a brisk trade with the Dutch. Accustomed to such extraordinary freedom, these colonies reacted defiantly to the news that Parliament had proscribed its royalist enemies in the colonies, interdicted their trade, and was sending an armed force to subdue them. This defiance was partly attributable, especially in Virginia and Barbados, to the groups in power being largely royalist. More importantly, however, it came from the recognition that Parliament's action seemed, by bringing the might of the home islands directly to bear upon the colonies, to strike at their very "freedom, safety, and well-being" and to threaten to bring them into complete "contempt and slavery." The most explicit and boldest denunciation of Parliament's action was the Declaration of the Barbados Assembly on February 18, 1651. Justifying its resistance as a defense of the islanders' rights as Englishmen, the Assembly called upon its constituents to "chuse a noble death" rather "than forsake their ould liberties and privileges." Although the defiance of the Barbadians and other colonists quickly wilted upon the appearance of the parliamentary commissioners during the next year, the Barbados Declaration revealed how powerful were the centrifugal tendencies that had developed within the English Empire during the first few decades of its existence and how intense was the colonial commitment to the many privileges and freedoms they considered essential elements of the contractual agreements between them and the Crown that had formed the basis of original settlement.

SOURCE: N. Darnell Davis, *The Cavaliers and Roundheads of Barbados, 1650–1652* (Georgetown, British Guiana, 1883), pp. 197–200.

A Declaration of my Lord Willoughby, Lieutenant-General, and Governor of Barbados, and other Carabis Islands; and also the Council of the Island belonging to it; serving in answer to a certaine Act formerly put forth by the Parliament of England, the 3rd of October 1650.

A Declaration, published by Order of my Lord Lieutenant-General, the 18th of February 1651, the Lords of the Council, and of the Assemblie, being occasioned at the sight of certaine printed Papers, intituled, an Act forbidding Commerce and Traffic with the Barbados, Virginia, Bermudas, and Antego.

The Lord Lieutenant-General, together with the Lords of this Council and Assembly, having carefully read over the said printed Papers, and finding them to oppose the freedom, safety, and well-being of this island, have thought themselves bound to communicate the same to all the inhabitants of this island; as also their observation and resolution concerning it, and to proceed therein after the best manner, wherefore they have ordered the same to be read publicly.

Concerning the abovesaid Act, by which the least capacity may comprehend how much the inhabitants of this island would be brought into contempt and slavery, if the same be not timely prevented:

First—They alledge that this island was first settled and inhabited at the charges, and by the esspecial order of the people of England, and therefore ought to be subject to the same nation. It is certain, that we all of us know very well, that wee, the present inhabitants of this island, were and still be that people of England, who with great danger to our persons, and with great charge and trouble, have settled this island in its condition, and inhabited the same, and shall wee therefore be subjected to the will and command of those that stay at home? Shall we be bound to the Government and Lordship of a Parliament in which we have no Representatives, or persons chosen by us, for there to propound and consent to what might be needful to us, as also to oppose and dispute all what should tend to our disadvantage and harm? In truth, this would be a slavery far exceeding all that the English nation hath yet suffered. And we doubt not but the courage which hath brought us thus far out of our own country, to seek our beings and livelihoods in this wild country, will maintaine us in our freedoms; without which our lives will be uncomfortable to us.

Secondly—It is alledged that the inhabitants of this island have, by cunning and force, usurped a power and Government.

If we, the inhabitants of this island, had been heard what we could have said for ourselves, this allegation had never been printed; but those who are destined to be slaves may not enjoy those privileges; otherwise we might have said and testified with a truth, that the Government now used among us, is the same that hath always been ratified, and doth every way agree with the first settlement and Government in these places; and was given us by the same power and authority that New England hold theirs; against whom the Act makes no objection.

And the Government here in subjection, is the nearest model of conformity to that under which our predecessors of the English nation have lived and flourished for above a thousand years. Therefore we conclude, that the rule of reason and discourse is most strangely mistaken, if the continuation and submission to a right well-settled Government be judged to be an usurping of a new power, and to the contrarie, the usurpation of a new Government be held a continuation of the old.

Thirdly—By the abovesaid Act all outlandish nations are forbidden to hold any correspondency or traffick with the inhabitants of this island; although all the antient inhabitants know very well, how greatly they have been obliged to those of the Low Countries for their subsistence, and how difficult it would have been for us, without their assistance, ever to have inhabited these places, or to have brought them into order: and we are yet dayly sensible, what necessary comfort they bring us dayly, and that they do sell their commodities a great deal cheaper than our own nation will doe: But this comfort must be taken from us by those whose will must be a Law to us: But we declare, that we will never be so unthankful to the Netherlanders for their former help and assistance, as to deny or forbid them, or any other nation, the freedom of our harbours, and the protection of our Laws, by which they may continue, if they please, all freedom of commerce and traffick with us.

Fourthly—for to perfect and accomplish our intended slavery, and to make our necks pliable for to undergo the yoake, they got and forbid to our own countrymen, to hold any correspondency, commerce, or traffick with us, nor to suffer any to come at us, but such who have obtained particular licences from some persons, who are expressly ordered for that purpose, by whose means it might be brought about, that none other goods or merchandizes shall be brought hither, than such as the licensed persons shall think fit to give way to; and that they are to sell the same at such a price, as they shall please to impose on them; and suffer no other ships to come hither but their own: As likewise that no inhabitants of this Island may send home upon their own account any island goods of this place, but shall be as slaves to the Companie, who shall have the abovesaid licenses, and submit to them the whole advantage of our labour and industry.

Wherefore, having rightly considered, we declare, that as we would not be wanting to use all honest means for the obtaining of a continuance of commerce, trade, and good correspondence with our country, soe wee will not alienate ourselves from those old heroick virtues of true English men, to prostitute our freedom and privileges, to which we are borne, to the will and opinion of any one; neither do we think our number so contemptible, nor our resolution so weake, to be forced or persuaded to so ignoble a submission, and we cannot think, that there are any amongst us, who are soe simple, and soe unworthily minded, that they would not rather chuse a noble death, than forsake their ould liberties and privileges."

II

Reconstruction, 1660–1689

II

Reconstruction, 1660–1685

6. Defining the Economic Relationship

A. Monopolizing the Colonial Carrying Trade

THE ENGROSSMENT of a significant amount of the carrying trade of the English colonies by the Dutch during the English Civil War and Interregnum led to the demand by substantial overseas merchants in England for parliamentary measures to establish an English monopoly over that trade. Parliament responded by passing the first navigation acts in 1650 and 1651, the first comprehensive effort to define the economic relationship between England and the colonies. Although these acts were voided at the Restoration, Parliament included their main provisions in the still more elaborate Navigation Act of September 13, 1660, which restricted the carrying trade of the colonies to English (including colonial) ships and required that certain designated "enumerated articles" be exported only to England or to other English colonies.

SOURCE: Danby Pickering (ed.), *The Statutes at Large* (46 vols., London, 1762–1807), VII, 452–455, 459–460.

For the increase of shipping and encouragement of the navigation of this nation, wherein, under the good providence and protection of God, the wealth, safety and strength of this kingdom is so much concerned; (2) be it enacted by the King's most excellent majesty, and by the lords and commons in this present parliament assembled, and by the authority thereof, That from and after the first day of December one thousand six hundred and sixty, and from thenceforward, no goods or commodities whatsoever shall be imported into or exported out of any lands, islands, plantations or territories to his Majesty belonging or in his possession, or which may hereafter belong unto or be in the possession of his Majesty, his heirs and successors, in Asia, Africa or America, in any other ship or ships, vessel or vessels whatsoever, but in such ships or vessels as do truly and without fraud belong only to the people of England or Ireland, dominion of Wales or town of Berwick upon Tweed, or are of the built of and belonging to any of said lands, islands, plantations or territories, as the proprietors and right owners thereof, and whereof the master and three fourths of the mariners at least are English; (3) under the penalty of the forfeiture and loss of all the goods and commodities which shall be imported into or exported out of any the aforesaid places in any other ship or vessel, as also of the ship or vessel . . . (4) and all admirals and other commanders at sea of any the ships of war or other ship having commission from his Majesty or from his heirs or successors, are hereby authorized and strictly required to seize and bring in as prize all such ships or vessels as shall have offended contrary hereunto, and deliver them to the court of admiralty, there to be proceeded against. . . .

II. And be it enacted, That no alien or person not born within the allegiance of our sovereign lord the King, his heirs and successors, or naturalized, or made a free denizen, shall from and after the first day of February, which will be in the year of our Lord one thousand six hundred sixty-one, exercise the trade or occupation of a merchant or factor in any the said places; (2) upon pain of the forfeiture and loss of all his goods and chattels, or which are in his possession . . . (3) and all governors of the said lands, islands, plantations or territories, and every of them, are hereby strictly required and commanded, and all who hereafter shall be made governors of any such islands, plantations or territories, by his Majesty, his heirs or successors, shall before their entrance into their government take a solemn oath, to do their utmost, that every the aforementioned clauses, and all the matters and things therein contained, shall be punctually and *bona fide* observed according to the true intent and meaning thereof: (4) and upon complaint and proof made before his Majesty, his heirs or successors, or such as shall be by him or them thereunto authorized and appointed, that any the said governors have been willingly and wittingly negligent in doing their duty accordingly, that the said governor so offending shall be removed from his government.

III. And it is further enacted by the authority aforesaid, That no goods or commodities whatsoever, of the growth, production or manufacture of *Africa, Asia* or *America*, or of any part thereof, or which are described or laid down in the usual maps or cards of those places, be imported into *England, Ireland* or *Wales*, islands of *Guernsey* and *Jersey*, or town of *Berwick* upon *Tweed*, in any other ship or ships, vessel or vessels whatsoever, but in such as do truly and without fraud belong only to the people of *England* or *Ireland*, dominion of *Wales*, or town of *Berwick* upon *Tweed*, or of the lands, islands, plantations or territories in *Asia, Africa* or *America*, to his Majesty belonging, as the proprietors and right owners thereof, and whereof the master, and three fourths at least of the mariners are *English*; (2) under the penalty of the forfeiture of all such goods and commodities, and of the ship or vessel in which they were imported, with all her guns, tackle, furniture, ammunition and apparel. . . .

IV. And it is further enacted by the authority aforesaid, That no goods or commodities that are of foreign growth, production or manufacture, and which are to be brought into *England, Ireland, Wales,* the islands of *Guernsey* and *Jersey,* or town of *Berwick* upon *Tweed,* in *English*-built shipping, or other shipping belonging to some of the aforesaid places, and navigated by *English* mariners, as aforesaid, shall be shipped or brought from any other place or places, country or countries, but only from those of the said growth, production or manufacture, or from those ports where the said goods and commodities can only, or are, or usually have been, first shipped for transportation, and from none other places or countries. . . .

VII. And it is further enacted by the authority aforesaid, That where any ease, abatement or privilege is given in the book of rates to goods or commodities imported or exported in *English*-built shipping, that is to say, shipping built in *England, Ireland, Wales,* islands of *Guernsey* or *Jersey,* or town of *Berwick* upon *Tweed,* or in any the lands, islands, dominions and territories to his Majesty in *Africa, Asia,* or *America,* belonging, or in his possession, that it is always to be understood and provided, that the master and three fourths of the mariners of the said ships at least be also *English;* (2) and that where it is required that the master and three fourths of the mariners be *English,* that the true intent and meaning thereof is, that they should be such during the whole voyage, unless in case of sickness, death, or being taken prisoners in the voyage, to be proved by the oath of the master or other chief officer of such ships. . . .

XVIII. And it is further enacted by the authority aforesaid, That from and after the first day of *April,* which shall be in the year of our Lord one thousand six hundred sixty-one, no sugars, tobacco, cotton-wool, indicoes, ginger, fustick, or other dying wood, of the growth, production or manufacture of any *English* plantations in *America, Asia* or *Africa,* shall be shipped, carried, conveyed or transported from any of the said *English* plantations to any land, island, territory, dominion, port or place whatsoever, other than to such other *English* plantations as do belong to his Majesty, his heirs and successors, or to the kingdom of *England* or *Ireland,* or principality of *Wales,* or town of *Berwick* upon *Tweed,* there to be laid on shore, (2) under the penalty of the forfeiture of the said goods, or the full value thereof, as also of the ship, with all her guns, tackle, apparel, ammunition and furniture. . . .

XIX. And be it further enacted by the authority aforesaid, That for every ship or vessel, which from and after the five and twentieth day of *December* in the year of our Lord one thousand six hundred and sixty shall set sail out of or from *England, Ireland, Wales,* or town of *Berwick* upon *Tweed,* for any *English* plantation in *America, Asia* or *Africa,* sufficient bond shall be given with one surety to the chief officers of the custom-house of such port or place from whence the said ship shall set sail, to the value of one thousand pounds, if the ship be of less burthen than one hundred tons; and of the sum of two thousand pounds, if the ship shall be of greater burthen; that in case the said ship or vessel shall load any of the said commodities at any of the said *English* plantations, that the same commodities shall be by the said ship brought to some port of *England, Ireland, Wales,* or to the port or town of *Berwick* upon *Tweed,* and shall there unload and put on shore the same, the danger of the seas only excepted: (2) And for all ships coming from any other port or place to any of the aforesaid plantations, who by this act are permitted to trade there, that the governor of such *English* plantations shall before the said ship or vessel be permitted to load on board any of the said commodities, take bond in manner and to the value aforesaid, for each respective ship or vessel, that such ship or vessel shall carry all the aforesaid goods that shall be laden on board in the said ship to some other of his Majesty's *English* plantations, or to *England, Ireland, Wales,* or town of *Berwick* upon *Tweed* (3) And that every ship or vessel which shall load or take on board any of the aforesaid goods, until such bond given to the said governor, or certificate produced from the officers of any custom-house of *England, Ireland, Wales,* or of the town of *Berwick,* that such bonds have been there duly given, shall be forfeited with all her guns, tackle, apparel and furniture, to be imployed and recovered in manner as aforesaid; and the said governors and every of them shall twice in every year after the first day of *January* one thousand six hundred and sixty, return true copies of all such bonds by him so taken, to the chief officers of the custom in *London.*

B. Monopolizing the Export Trade to the Colonies

By THE Staple Act of July 27, 1663, Parliament sought to establish a national monopoly over the export trade to the colonies. That act required that all goods shipped from any European country to the colonies —except salt for New England fisheries; wine from the Madeiras and the Azores; and servants, horses, and provisions from Ireland—had first to pass through England.

SOURCE: Pickering (ed.), *Statutes at Large*, VIII, 163–164.

. . . V. And in regard his Majesty's plantations beyond the seas are inhabited and peopled by his subjects of this his kingdom of England; for the maintaining a greater correspondence and kindness between them, and keeping them in a firmer dependance upon it, and rendring them yet more beneficial and advantageous unto it in the further imployment and increase of English shipping and seamen, vent of English woolen and other manufactures and commodities, rendring the navigation to and from the same more safe and cheap, and making this kingdom a staple, not only of the commodities of those plantations, but also of the commodities of other countries and places, for the supplying of them; and it being the usage of other nations to keep their plantations trade to themselves.

VI. Be it enacted, and it is hereby enacted, That from and after the five and twentieth day of *March* one thousand six hundred sixty-four, no commodity of the growth, production or manufacture of *Europe*, shall be imported into any land, island, plantation, colony, territory or place to his Majesty belonging, or which shall hereafter belong unto or be in the possession of his Majesty, his heirs and successors, in *Asia, Africa* or *America* (*Tangier* only excepted) but what shall be *bona fide*, and without fraud, laden and shipped in *England, Wales*, or the town of *Berwick* upon *Tweed*, and in *English* built shipping, or which were *bona fide* bought before the first day of *October* one thousand six hundred sixty and two, and had such certificate thereof as is directed in one act passed the last sessions of this present parliament, intituled, *An act for preventing frauds, and regulating abuses in his Majesty's customs*; and whereof the master and three fourths of the mariners at least are *English*, and which shall be carried directly thence to the said lands, islands, plantations, colonies, territories or places, and from no other place or places whatsoever; any law, statute or usage to the contrary notwithstanding; (2) under the penalty of the loss of all such commodities of the growth, production or manufacture of *Europe*, as shall be imported into any of them from any other place whatsoever, by land or water; and if by water, of the ship or vessel also in which they were imported, with all her guns, tackle, furniture, ammunition and apparel. . . .

VII. Provided always, and be it hereby enacted by the authority aforesaid, That it shall and may be lawful to ship and lade in such ships, and so navigated, as in the foregoing clause is set down and expressed, in any part of *Europe*, salt for the fisheries of *New-England* and *Newfoundland*, and to ship and lade in the *Madera's* wines of the growth thereof, and to ship and lade in the Western islands of *Azores* wines of the growth of the said islands, and to ship and take in servants or horses in *Scotland* or *Ireland*, and to ship or lade in *Scotland* all sorts of victual of the growth or production of *Scotland*, and to ship or lade in *Ireland* all sorts of victual of the growth or production of *Ireland*, and the same to transport into any of the said lands, islands, plantations, colonies, territories or places: any thing in the foregoing clause to the contrary in any wise notwithstanding.

VIII. And for the better prevention of frauds, be it enacted, and it is hereby enacted, That from and after the five and twentyieth day of *March* one thousand six hundred sixty and four, every person or persons importing by land any goods or commodities whatsoever into any the said lands, islands, plantations, colonies, territories or places, shall deliver to the governor of such land, island, plantation, colony, territory or place, or to such person or officer as shall be by him thereunto authorized and appointed, within four and twenty hours after such importation, his and their names and surnames, and a true inventory and particular of all such goods or commodities: (2) and no ship or vessel coming to any such land, island, plantation, colony, territory or place, shall lade or unlade any goods or commodities whatsoever, until the master or commander of such ship or vessel shall first have made known to the governor of such land, island, plantation, colony, territory or place, or such other person or officer as shall be by him thereunto authorized and appointed, the arrival of the said ship or vessel, with her name, and the name and surname of her master or commander, and have shewn to him that she is an *English-built* ship, or made good by producing such certificate, as abovesaid, that she is a ship or vessel *bona fide* belonging to *England*, *Wales*, or the town of *Berwick*, and navigated with an *English* master, and three fourth parts of the mariners at least *Englishmen*, and have delivered to such governor or other person or officer a true and perfect inventory or invoice of her lading, together with the place or places in which the said goods were laden or taken into the said ship or vessel; (3) under the pain of the loss of the ship or vessel, with all her guns, ammunition, tackle, furniture and apparel, and of all such goods of the growth, production or manufacture of *Europe*, as were not *bona fide* laden and taken in *England*, *Wales*, or the town of *Berwick*, to be recovered and divided in manner aforesaid; (4) and all such as are governors or commanders of any the said lands, islands, plantations, colonies, territories or places (*Tangier* only excepted) shall before the five and twentieth day of *March* one thousand six hundred sixty and four, and all such as shall hereafter be made governors or commanders of any of them, shall before their entrance upon the execution of such trust or charge, take a solemn oath before such person or persons as shall be authorized by his Majesty, his heirs and successors, to administer the same, to do their utmost within their respective governments or commands, to cause to be well and truly observed what is in this act enacted, in relation to the trade of such lands, islands, plantations, colonies, territories and places, under the penalty of being removed out of their respective governments and commands: (5) and if any of them shall be found, after the taking of such oath, to have wittingly and willingly offended contrary to what is by this act required of them, that they shall for such offence be turned out of their governments, and be uncapable of the government of any other land, island, plantation or colony; and moreover, forfeit the sum of one thousand pounds of lawful money of *England*; the one moiety to his Majesty, his heirs and successors; and the other moiety to him or them that shall inform or sue for the same in any of his Majesty's courts in any of the said plantations, or in any court of record in *England*, wherein no essoin, protection or wager of law shall be allowed.

IX. And it is hereby further enacted, That if any officer of the customs in *England*, *Wales*, or town of *Berwick* upon *Tweed*, shall give any warrant for, or suffer any sugar, tobacco, ginger, cotton-wool, indigo, speckle-wood or *Jamaica*-wood, fustick or other dying-wood of the growth of any of the said lands, islands, colonies, plantations, territories or places, to be carried into any other country or place whatsoever, until they have been first unladen *bona fide* and put on shore in some port or haven in *England* or *Wales*, or in the town of *Berwick*; that every such officer for such offence shall forfeit his place, and the value of such of the said goods as he shall give warrant for, or suffer to pass into any other country or place; the one moiety to his Majesty, his heirs and successors; and the other moiety to him or them that shall inform or sue for the same in any court of record in England or Wales, wherein no essoin, protection or wager in law shall be allowed. . . .

C. Plugging Loopholes in the Act of 1660

PARLIAMENT completed its basic navigation system with the Plantation Duties Act of March 29, 1673. By levying duties on enumerated articles imported into England but not on those sent from one colony to another, the Navigation Act of 1660 had unintentionally favored the colonists—making it possible for them to buy enumerated goods more cheaply than people could in the home islands. In addition, that act had not prohibited the transshipment of such goods directly to Europe where, because they had not had duties levied upon them, they could be sold more cheaply by colonial merchants than similar goods which had come through England sold by English merchants. The Plantation Duties Act sought to eliminate these loopholes by levying duties to be collected in the colonies on all enumerated goods not bound for England.

SOURCE: Pickering (ed.), Statutes at Large, VIII, 398–399.

. . . And whereas by one act passed in this present parliament in the twelfth year of your Majesty's reign, intituled, An act for encouragement of shipping and navigation, and by several other laws passed since that time, it is permitted to ship, carry, convey and transport sugar, tobacco, cotton-wool, indico, ginger, fustick and all other dying-wood of the growth, production and manufacture of any of your Majesty's plantations in America, Asia or Africa, from the places of their growth, production and manufacture, to any of your Majesty's plantations in those parts, (Tangier only excepted) and that without paying of custom for the same, either at the lading or unlading of the said commodities, by means whereof the trade and navigation in those commodities, from one plantation to another is greatly increased; (3) and the inhabitants of divers of those colonies, not contenting themselves with being supplied with those commodities for their own use, free from all customs, (while the subjects of this your kingdom of England have paid great customs and impositions for what of them hath been spent here) but contrary to the express letter of the aforesaid laws, have brought into divers parts of Europe great quantities thereof, and do also daily vend great quantities thereof, to the shipping of other nations who bring them into divers parts of Europe, to the great hurt and diminution of your Majesty's customs, and of the trade and navigation of this your kingdom; (4) for the prevention thereof, we your Majesty's commons in parliament assembled, do pray that it may be enacted; and be it enacted by the King's most excellent majesty, by and with the advice and consent of the lords spiritual and temporal, and commons, in this present parliament assembled, and by authority of the same, That from and after the first day of *September* which shall be in the year of our Lord one thousand six hundred seventy and three, if any ship or vessel which by law may trade in any of your Majesty's plantations, shall come to any of them to ship and take on board any of the aforesaid commodities, and that bond shall not be first given with one sufficient surety to bring the same to *England* or *Wales*, or the town of *Berwick* upon *Tweed*, and to no other place, and there to unload and put the same on shore, (the danger of the seas only excepted) that there shall be answered and paid to your Majesty, your heirs and successors, for so much of the said commodities as shall be laded and put on board such ship or vessel, these following rates or duties: that is to say, for sugar white, the hundred weight containing one hundred and twelve pounds, five shillings; and brown sugar and muscovadoes, the hundred weight containing one hundred and twelve pounds, one shilling and six pence; (5) for tobacco, the pound one peny; for cotton-wool, the pound one half-peny; for indico, the pound two pence; for ginger, the hundred weight containing one hundred and twelve pounds, one shilling; (6) for logwood, the hundred weight containing one hundred and twelve pounds, five pounds; for fustick and all other dying-wood, the hundred weight containing one hundred and twelve pounds, six pence: and also for every pound of cocoa-nuts, one peny; (7) to be levied, collected and paid at such places and to such collectors and other officers as shall be appointed in their respective plantations to collect, levy and receive the same, before the lading thereof, and under such penalties both to the officers and upon the goods, as for nonpayment of or defrauding his Majesty of his customs in *England*. . . .

7. Obstacles to Enforcing Imperial Policy

A. Massachusetts Defies the Commissioners of the King

BESET WITH complaints from a variety of sources that the New Englanders and, especially, the settlers of Massachusetts Bay had "transgressed their grants and powers by enacting laws . . . repugnant to the laws of England" and claimed "an exemption to the payment of customs" duties imposed by the navigation acts, Crown officials in April, 1664 set up a commission. Colonel Richard Nicolls—leader of the expedition that had seized New Netherlands from the Dutch for the Duke of York in 1664—and three other men were to investigate conditions in New England, settle existing boundary disputes among the colonies, and, most controversial, make sure that the colonists obeyed the Crown and the laws of Parliament. The commissioners were largely successful in every colony except Massachusetts, where they failed in their task almost completely. Interpreting the commission as an attempt to subject them "to the arbitrary power of strangers," the leaders of Massachusetts explained and tried to justify their opposition to the commissioners in a letter to Charles II of October 19, 1664. Like the Barbados Declaration of 1651, this letter revealed how tenaciously colonists would resist any attempt that seemed in any way to encroach upon the privileges confirmed to them by charter, and how liberally those privileges had come to be interpreted in Massachusetts Bay. Crown officials withdrew the commission but ordered Massachusetts to answer the charges brought against it by the commissioners. Bay Colony leaders refused, however, to comply with this order, an indication of just how little control the Crown actually had over the colony.

SOURCE: Nathaniel B. Shurtleff (ed.), Records of the Governor and Company of Massachusetts Bay in New England (Boston, 5 vols., 1853–54), IV, Part II, 129–133.

To the Kings most Excellent Majesty

The humble supplication of the Generall Court of the Massachusets colony in New England.

DREAD SOVERAIGNE:—

If your poore subjects, who have remooved themselves into a remote corner of the earth to enjoy peace with God & man, doe in this day of theire trouble prostrate themselves at your royal feete, &

begg your favor, wee hope it will be graciously accepted by your
majestie, and that as the high place you susteine on earth doeth
number you here among the gods, so you will imitate the God of
heaven, in being ready to mainteyne the cause of the afflicted & the
right of the poore, & to receive their cries & addresses to that end.
And wee humbly beseech your majesty with princely patience &
clemency to heare & accept our plaine discourse, though of somewhat greater length then would be comely in other or lesser cases.
Wee are remote, & can speake but seldome, & therefore crave leave
to speake the more at once. Wee shall not largely repeate how that
the first undertakers for this plantation, having by considerable
summes purchased the right thereof, granted to the counsell established at Plymouth by King James, your royal grandfather, did after
obteine a pattent given & confirmed to themselves by your royall
Father, King Charles the First, wherein is granted unto them,
theire heires, assignes, & associates forever, not onely the absolute
use & propriety of the tract of land therein mentioned, but also full
& absolute power of governing all the people of this place, by men
chosen from among themselves, & according to such lawes as they
shall from time to time see meete to make & establish, being not
repugnant to the lawes of England, (they paying only the fifth
parte of the oare of gold & silver that shall heere be found for & in
respect of all duties, demands, exactions, & services whatsoever,) as
in the said pattent is at large declared; under the encouragement &
security of which royall charter this people did at theire oune
charges transport themselves, their wives, & families over the
ocean, purchase the lands of the natives, & plant this colony with
great labour, hazards, costs, & difficulties; for a long time wrestling
with the wants of a wildernes, & the burdens of a new plantation.
Having also now above thirty yeares enjoyed the aforesaid power &
priviledge of government within themselves, as their undoubted
right in the sight of God & man, and having had moreover this
further favor from God & from your majesty, that wee have received severall gracious letters from your royall selfe, full of expressions tending to confirme us in our enjoyments, vizt: in your
majesties letter bearing date the 15th day of February, 1660, you
are pleased to consider New England as one of the cheifest of your
colonies & plantations abroad, having enjoyed & groune up in a
long & orderly establishment, adding this royall promise, 'Wee
shall not come behind any of our royall predecessors in a just encouragement & protection of all our loving subjects there.' In your

majesties letter of the 28th of June, 1662, sent us by our messengers, besides many other gracious expressions, there is this: 'Wee will preserve & doe heereby comfirme the pattent & charter heeretofore granted unto them by our royall Father, of blessed memory, & they shall freely enjoy all the privileges & liberties granted unto them in & by the same.' As for such particculars of a civill & religious nature, which are subjoined in the said letter, wee have applyed ourselves to the utmost to sattisfy your majesty, so farr as doth consist with conscience of our duty towards God, & the just liberties & priviledges of our patent. Wee are further bound with humble thankfulnes to acknowledge your majesties gracious expressions in the last letter wee have received, dated Aprill 23^d, 1664, as, (besides other instances thereof,) that your majesty hath not the least intention or thought of violateing or in the least degree infringing the charter heretofore granted by your royall Father with great wisdome & upon full deliberation, &c. But now what afliction of heart must it needs be unto us, that our sinnes have provoked God to permitt our adversaries to sett themselves against us, by their misinformations, complaints, & solicitations, (as some of them have made that their worke for many yeares,) & thereby to procure a commission under the great seale, wherein fower persons (one of them our knoune & proffessed ennemy) are empowred to heare, receive, examine, & determine all complaints & appeales in all causes & matters, as well military as criminall & civil, & to proceede in all things for setling this country according to their good & sound discretions, &c, whereby, instead of being governd by rulers of our oune choosing, (which is the fundamentall priviledge of our patent,) & by lawes of our oune, wee are like to be subjected to the arbitrary power of strangers, proceeding not by any established lawe, but by their oune discretions! And whereas our patent gives a sufficient royall warrant & dischardge to all officers & persons for executing & observing the lawes here made & published, as is therein directed, wee shall now not be discharged & at rest from further molestation when wee have so executed & observed our lawes, but be lyable to complaints & appeales, & to the determinations of new judges, whereby our government & administrations willbe made voyd & of none effect. And though wee have yet had but a litle tast of the words or actings of these gentlemen that are come over hither in this capacity of commissioners, yett wee have had enough to confirme us in our feares, that their improovement of this power, in pursuance of their commission, (should the same proceede,) will end in the subvertion of our all. Wee should be glad to hope that your majesties instructions (which they have not yet been pleased to impart unto us) may put such limitations to their buisnes heere as will take of much of our Feare; but according to the present appearance of things we thus speake.

In this case (dread soveraigne) our refuge under God is your royall selfe, whom wee humbly addresse ourselves unto; & are the rather emboldened therein, because your majesties last gracious letter doth encourage us to suggest what, upon the experience wee have had & observation wee have made, wee judge necessary or convenient for the good & bennefit of this your plantation, & because wee are well perswaded that had your majesty a full & right information of the state of things heere, you would finde apparent reason to put a stop to these proceedings, which are certainly disservient to your majesties interest, & to the prosperity & welfare of this place.

If these things goe on, (according to their present appearance,) your subjects heere will either be forced to seeke new dwellings or sinck & faint under burdens that will be to them intollerable; the vigour of all mens indeavors in their severall callings & occupations (either for merchandise abroad or further subduing this wilderness at home) will be enfeebled, as wee perceive it already beginns to be; the good worke of converting the natives obstructed; the inhabitants driven to wee know not what extremities; & this hopefull plantation in the issue ruined. But whatever become of us, wee are suer the adversary cannot countervaile the kings damage. It is indeede a griefe to our hearts to see your majesty put upon this extraordinary charge & cost about a business the products whereof can never reimburse the one half of what will be expended upon it. Imposed rulers officers will have occasion to expend more then can be raised heere, so as nothing will returne to your majesties exchecquer; but instead thereof the wonted bennefit by customes of goods exported & imported into England from hence willbe diminished by the discouragement & diminution of mens endeavors in theire severall occupations, or if the aime should be to grattify some particcular gentlemen by livings & revenues heere, that will also faile; where nothing is to be had, the king himself will be a looser; & so will the case be found to be heere; for such is the poverty & meanesse of the people of this country, (by reason of the length & coldnes of the winters, the difficulty of subduing a wildernesse, defect of a staple commodity, the want of money, &c,)

that if with hard labour men gett a subsistance for theire families, it is as much as the generality are able to doe, paying but very smale rates towards the publicke charges; & yet if all that the country hath ordinarily raised by the yeare for all the charges of the whole government were put together, & then doubled or trebled, it would not be counted for one of these gentlmen a considerable accommodation. It is true that the estates men have in conjunction with hard labour & vigorous indeavors in their severall places, doe bring in a comfortable subsistance for such a meane people, (wee dare not diminish our thankfulnes to God that he provides for us in a wildernesse as he doeth,) yet neither will the former stand if the latter be discouraged, nor will both ever answer the ends of those that seeke or neede great things. Wee perceive there have been great expectations of what is to be had heere, raised by some mens informations; but those informations will proove fallacious, disapointing them that have relyed upon them. And if the taking of this course should drive this people out of the country, (for to a coalition therein they will never come,) it willbe hard to finde another people that will stay long or stand under any considerable burden in it, seeing it is not a country where men can subsist without hard labor & great frugallity. There have also been high representations of great divissions & discontents amongst us, & of a necessity of sending commissioners to releive the agreived, &c; whereas it plainly appeares that the body of this people are unanimously sattisfied in the present government, & abhorrent from change, and that what is now offered will, instead of releiving, raise up such greivances as are intollerable. Wee supose there is no government under Heaven wherein some discontented persons may not be found, and if it be a sufficient accusation against a government, that there are some such who will be innocent, yet, through the favour of God, there are but few amongst us that are malcontent, & fewer that have cause to be so.

Sir: The allknowing God he knowes our greatest ambition is to live a poore & a quiet life in a corner of the world, without offence to God or man. Wee came not into this wildernes to seek great things to ourselves; & if any come after us to seeke them heere, they will be disapointed. Wee keepe ourselves within our line, & medle not with matters abroad. A just dependance upon & subjection to your majesty, according to our charter, it is farr from our hearts to dissacknowledge. Wee so highly prize your favorable aspect (though at this great distance) as wee would gladly doe anything that is within our power to purchase the continuance of it. Wee were willing to testify our affection to your majesties services by answering the proposalls of your honorable commissioners, of which wee doubt not but they have already given your majesty an account. Wee are carefully studious of all due subjection to your majesty, & that not only for wrath, but for conscience sakes; and should divine Providence ever offer an oppertunity wherein wee might, in any righteous way, according to our poore & meane capacity, testify our dutifull affection to your majesty, wee hope we should most gladly embrace it. But it is a great unhappines to be reduced to so hard a case as to have no other testimony of our subjection & loyalty offered us but this, vizt, to destroy our oune being, which nature teacheth us to preserve, or to yeild up our liberties, which are farr dearer to us then our lives, & which had wee had any feare of being deprived of, wee had never wandered from our fathers houses into these ends of the earth, nor layd out our labors & estates therein, besides engaging in a most hazardous & difficult warre with the most warlike of the natives, to our great charge & the losse of some of the lives of our deare freinds; neither can the deepest invention of man find out a more certeine way of consistence then to obteyne a royall donation from so great a prince, under his great seale, which is the greatest security that may be had in humaine affaires.

Royall Sir: It is in your power to say of your poore people in New England, they shall not dye. If wee have found favour in the sight of our king, let our life be given us at our petition, (or rather that which is dearer than life, that wee have ventured our lives, & willingly passed through many deaths to obteyne, & our all;) at our request let our government live, our patent live, our magistrates live, our lawes & liberties live, our religious enjoyments live; so shall wee all have yet further cause to say from our heart, 'Let the king live forever'; and the blessing of them that were ready to perish shall come upon your majesty, having delivered the poore that cryed, & such as had none to help them. It was an honor to one of your royall ancestors that he was called the poore mans king. It was Jobs excellency, when he sate as king among his people, that he was a father to the poore. They are a poore people (destitute of outward succor, wealth, or power) who now cry unto the lord the king. May your majesty please to regard theire cause, & maintain their right; it will stand among the markes of lasting honor to after generations; and wee and ours shall have lasting cause to rejoyce that wee have been numbered among

Your majesties most humble

Servants & suplyants

By order of the Generall Court

JOHN ENDECOTT, Governor

B. The Transgressions of New England

THE CONTINUED defiance of New England led in 1676 to the sending of Edward Randolph (ca. 1632–1703) by the recently created Lords of Trade to report on conditions in Massachusetts. Although he won the cooperation of certain dissident elements in the colony, especially merchants who were dependent upon the maintenance of close commercial ties with England, Randolph, like the earlier commissioners, met with strong opposition from Bay Colony leaders. His many adverse reports on Massachusetts, including the report of May 6, 1677, reprinted below, helped to persuade the Lords of Trade that tighter political controls would be required to ensure the enforcement of the navigation acts and obedience to royal authority.

SOURCE: Robert Noxon Toppan (ed.), Edward Randolph, Including His Letters and Official Papers (7 vols., Boston, 1898–1909), II, 265–268.

REPRESENTATION OF THE AFFAIRES
OF N. ENGLAND BY MR. RANDOLPH

The present State of the affaires of New England depending before the Lords of the Committee for Plantations are reduced to Two heads Vizt. matter of Law and Fact.

Matter of Law ariseth from the Title of Lands and Government claimed by Mr Mason and Mr Gorges in their Several provinces of New Hampshire and Main, and also what right and Title the Massachusets have to either Land or Government in any part of New England; these are referred to the Lords Cheif Justices of the Kings Bench and Common Pleas for their Opinion.

Matters of Fact concerne as well his Majestie as Mr Mason and Mr Gorges, and against the Government of the Massachusets these following Articles will be proved.

1. That they have noe right either to Land or Government in any part of New England and have allwayes been Usurpers.

2.   That they have formed themselves into a Common Wealth, deneying any Appeals to England, and contrary to other Plantations doe not take the Oath of Allegiance.

3.   They have protected the Late Kings Murtherers, directly contrary to his Majesties Royall Proclamation of the 6th of June 1660 and of his Letters of 28th June 1662.

4.   They Coine money with their owne Impress.

5.   They have put his Majesties Subjects to death for opinion in matters of Religion.

6.   In the yeare 1665 they did violently oppose his Majesties Commissioners in the Settlement of New Hampshire and in 1668 by Armed Forces turned out his Majesties Justices of the peace in the Province of Main in Contempt of his Majesties Authority and Declaration of the 10th of Aprill 1666.

7.   They impose an Oath of Fidelity upon all that inhabit within their Territoryes To be true and Faithfull to their Government.

8.   They violate all the Acts of Trade and navigation, by which they have ingrossed the greatest part of the West India Trade whereby his Majestie is damaged in his Customs above £100,000 yearely and this Kingdome much more.

Reasons induceing a Speedy hearing and Determination.

1.   His Majestie hath an oppertunity to Settle that Country under his Royall Authority with Little charge Sir John Berry being now at Virginia not farr distance from New England, and it Lyes in his way home, where are many good harbours free from the worms, convenient Townes for Quartering of Souldiers, and plentifull Accomidation for men and shipping.

2.   The Earnest desire of most and best of the Inhabitants (wearied out with the Arbitrary proceedings of those in the present Government) to be under his Majesties Governement and Laws.

3.   The Indians upon the Settlement of that Country it is presumed would unanimously Submitt and become very Servicable and usefull for improveing that Country there being upward of Three hundred Thousand English inhabiting therein.

Proposals for the Setling of that Country.

1.   His Majesties Gratious and General pardon upon their conviction of haveing acted without and in Contempt of his Maj-

esties Authority will make the most refractory to comply to save their Estates.

2.   His Majesties declaration of confirming unto the Inhabitants the Lands and houses they now possess upon payment of an Easie Quit rent and granting Libertie of Conscience in matters of Religion.

3.   His Majesties Commission directed to the most Eminent persons for Estates and Loyalty in every Colony to meet consult and act for the present peace and Safety of that Country dureing his Majesties pleasure, and that Such of the present Magistrates be of the Councill as shall readily comply with his Majesties Commands in the Setleing of the Country and a pention to be allowed them out of the publicque Revenue of the Country with Some Title of Honour to be conferred upon the most deserveing of them, will cause a generall Submission. . . .

EDWARD RANDOLPH.

8. Reconstructing the Political Relationship

A. The Attempt to Apply the Principles of Poynings' Law to the Colonies

PRIVATE COLONIES like Massachusetts Bay were not the only sources of opposition to the efforts by imperial authorities to tighten up the economic and political bonds between the mother country and her colonies after the Restoration. Through the elected lower houses of assembly in the royal colonies, local groups seemed to oppose imperial authority whenever it appeared to be in their best interests to do so. To curb the extensive power of these assemblies and to weaken the centrifugal forces they represented, the Lords of Trade tried with the instruction reprinted below to apply the principles of Poynings' Law to Jamaica in 1678 and Virginia in 1679. By that law, the Irish Parliament had been forbidden to pass any legislation which did not have the prior approval of the Crown. But this attempt, which would have drastically limited the legislative authority of the colonial lower houses, was so strongly opposed in both colonies that the Lords quickly abandoned it.

SOURCE: Leonard Woods Labaree (ed.), *Royal Instructions to British Colonial Governors, 1670–1776* (2 vols., New York: Appleton-Century-Crofts, 1935), I, 125.

AND whereas by our commission we have directed that for the future no general assembly be called without our special directions, but that upon occasion you do acquaint us by letter with the necessity of calling such an assembly and pray our consent and direction for their meeting, you shall at the same time transmit unto us with the advice and consent of the council a draught of such acts as you shall think fit and necessary to be passed that we may take the same into our consideration and return them in the form we shall think fit they be enacted in. And upon receipt of our commands you shall then summon an assembly and propose the said laws for their consent. AND accordingly we have ordered to be delivered unto you herewith a certain body of laws for the use of our said island framed in pursuance of those laws transmitted unto us by former governors with such alterations and amendments as we have thought fit with the advice of our Privy Council here; which, upon your arrival in our said [colony, island] you shall offer unto the next assembly that they may be consented to and enacted to as laws originally coming from us.

B. Articulating an Imperial Conception
of the Colonial Lower Houses

That imperial officials did not willingly abandon the attempt to apply the principles of Poynings' Law to the royal colonies is revealed by the following document, a report of a Privy Council committee on the Jamaica Assembly's rejection of a set of laws drawn up in England for passage in Jamaica. Dated May 28, 1679, the report attacked the proceedings of the Assembly as "irregular violent and unwarrantable" and presented the imperial case against the Assembly. More important, the report defined more fully than had any previous document the imperial conception of the role and position of the colonial assembly. This definition—that the assembly was a subordinate body, with a limited purpose—dominated imperial thinking for the rest of the colonial period.

SOURCE: Grant and Munro (eds.), *Acts of the Privy Council, Colonial*, I, 827–833.

. . . Wee have in Obedience to your Majestys Commands entred into the Consideration of the present state of your Majestys Island of Jamaica in order to propose such means as may put an End to the great Discouragements your Majestys good Subjects there lye under by the unsetled Condition thereof, occasioned by the Refusal of the Laws lately offered by the Earl of Carlisle to the Assembly for their Consent. All which Proceedings and Dissatisfactions appear to have arisen in the manner following By the Commission granted by Your Majesty unto the Lord Vaughan and several preceding Governors It was Your Royal Pleasure to entrust the Assembly of Jamaica with a Power to frame and enact Laws by the Advice and Consent of the Governor and Council, Which Laws were to continue in force for the Space of two Years and no longer. But so it hath hapened that your Majesty finding the Inconveniencies which did attend that Power and manner of making Laws by the irregular violent and unwarrantable Proceedings of the Assembly, was pleased with the Advice of your Privy Council, to provide by the Earl of Carlisle's Commission that no Laws should be Enacted in Jamaica but such as being framed by the Governor and Council and transmitted unto your Majesty for your Royal Approbation were afterwards remitted to Jamaica and consented unto by the Assembly there. And in Pursuance hereof, the Earl of

Carlisle carried over a Body of Laws under the Great Seal of England; Which Laws upon his Lordships Arrival there, have been rejected by the General Assembly upon Grounds and reasons contained in an Address to your Majesty's Governor, and in divers Letters received from his Lordship in that behalf.

1. In the first Place we find they are unsatisfyed with a Clause in the Militia Bill, whereby it is provided that the Governor may, upon all Occasions or Emergencies, act as Governor in Chief according to and in Pursuance of all the Powers and Authorities given unto him by your Majesty's Commission, fearing that thereby they shall make it legal to execute all Instructions that either are or shall be sent to your Majesty's Governor.

   2ly: They have likewise rejected the Bill for raising a Publick Revenue as being perpetual and lyable (as they say) to be diverted.

   3ly: It is objected that the said Laws contain divers fundamental Errors.

   4ly: That they were not compared with and amended by the last Laws sent over by the Lord Vaughan.

   5ly: That the Distance of the Place renders the present Method of passing Laws wholly impracticable.

   6ly: That the nature of all Colonies is changeable, and consequently the Laws must be adapted to the Interest of the Place and must alter with it.

   7ly: That hereby they lose the Satisfaction of a Deliberative Power in making Laws.

   8ly: That the Form of Government renders your Governor absolute.

   9ly: That by the former Method of enacting Laws your Majesty's Prerogative was better secured.

These being the Objections and Pretences upon which the Assembly has, with so much animosity, proceeded to reject those Bills transmitted by your Majesty, Wee cannot but offer for your Majesty's information and Satisfaction, such a short Answer thereunto as may not only give a Testimony of the unreasonableness of their Proceedings, but also furnish your Governor, when occasion shall serve with such Arguments as may be fit to be used in Justification of your Majesty's Commission and Powers granted unto him.

1.   It is not without the greatest Presumption that they go about to question your Majesty's Power over the Militia in that Island, since it has been allowed and declared, even by the Laws of this your Kingdom, that the sole supreme Government, Command and Disposition of the Militia, and of all Forces by Sea and Land, and of all Forts and Places of Strength, is residing in your Majesty within all your Majesty's Realms and Dominions.

2.   The Objection made against the Bill for the Publick Revenue hath as little Ground, since it being perpetual is no more than what was formerly offered by them unto your Majesty during the Government of Sir Thomas Lynch, in the same Measure and Proportion as is now proposed: nor can it be diverted, since Provision is thereby expressly made that the same shall be for the better Support of that Government. Besides that it is not suitable to the Duty and Modesty of Subjects to suspect Your Majesty's Justice or Care for the Government of that Colony whose Settlement and Preservation has been most particularly carried on by your Majesty's tender regard and by the great Expence of your own Treasure.

3.   It cannot, with any Truth be said that these Laws contain many and great Errors, nothing having been done therein but in pursuance of former Laws at divers times Enacted by the Assembly and with the Advice of your Majesty's Privy Council as well as the Opinion and Approbation of Your Attorney General upon Perusal of the same.

4.   To the fourth Objection it may be answered that if anything had been found of moment or Importance in the last Parcel of Laws transmitted by the Lord Vaughan, your Majesty's tender Care of your Subjects Welfare would have been such as not to have sent those Bills imperfect or defective in any necessary matter.

5.   As to the Distance of the place which renders as they say, the present Method of making Laws altogether impracticable, Your Majesty having been pleased to regulate the same by Advice of your Privy Council, according to the usage of Ireland, such Care was then taken so that no Law might be wanting which might Conduce to the Welbeing of the Plantation, and that nothing might be omitted which in all former Governments had been thought necessary. Nor is it likely that this Colony is subject to greater Accidents than your Kingdom of Ireland so as to require a more frequent and sudden Change of Laws in other Cases

than such as are already provided for upon Emergencies or in other manner than is directed by your Majesty's Commission, Whereby the Inhabitants have free Access to make Complaints to your Governor and Council of any Defect in any old Law, or to give reasons for any new one which being modelled by the Governor and Council into form of Law and transmitted unto your Majesty if by your Majesty and Council found reasonable, may be transmitted back thither to be enacted accordingly.

6.   It was sufficiently apparent unto your Majesty that Laws must alter with the Interest of the Place, when you were graciously pleased to Lodge such a Power in that Government as might not only from time to time with your Majesty's Approbation and by Advice both of your Privy Council here and of the Governor and Council there enable the Assembly to Enact new Laws answerable to their growing Necessities, but even upon urgent occasions to provide by raising money for the Security of the Island, without attending your Majesty's Orders or Consent.

7.   It is not to be doubted but the Assembly have endeavoured to grasp all Power as well as that of a Deliberative Voice in making Laws; but how far they have thereby intrenched upon your Majesty's Prerogative and exceeded the Bounds of their Duty and Loyalty upon this Pretence, may appear by their late exorbitant and unwarrantable Proceedings during the Government of the Lord Vaughan, in ordering and signing a Warrant unto the Marshal of the Island your Majesty's Officer of Justice, for the stopping and preventing the Execution of a Sentence passed according to the ordinary Forms of Law, upon a notorious Pyrate and Disturber of your Majesty's Peace. And they have farther taken upon them, by vertue of this Deliberative Power, to make Laws contrary to those of England, and to imprison your Majesty's subjects. Nor have they forborn to raise mony by Publick Acts, and to dispose of the same according to their Will and Pleasure, without any mention made of Your Majesty which has never in like case been practised in any of your Majesty's Kingdoms. How far therefore it is fit to entrust them with a Power which they have thus abused and to which they have no Pretension of Right, was the Subject of your Majesty's Royal Consideration when you were pleased to put a Restraint upon these Enormities, and to take the Reins of Government into your own hands, which they in express words against their Duty and Allegiance, have challenged and refused to part withe.

8.   It cannot with any truth be supposed that by the present Form of Government, the Governor is rendered Absolute since he is now more than ever become accountable unto your Majesty of all his most important Deliberations and Actions, and is not warranted to do anything but according to Law and your Majesty's Commission and Instructions given by Advice of your Privy Council.

9.   And whether your Majesty's Prerogative is prejudiced by the present Constitution is more the Concernment of Your Majesty and subject of your own Care, than of their Consideration.

Lastly and in the General, We humbly Conceive that it would be a great Satisfaction to your Subjects there inhabiting and an Invitation to Strangers when they shall know what Laws they are to be governed by, and a great Ease to the Planters not to be continually obliged to attend the Assemblies to re-enact old Laws which his Majesty has now thought fit, in a proper form to ascertain and establish: Whereas the late Power of making Temporary Laws could be understood to be of no longer continuance than until such wholsome Laws, founded upon so many Years Experience should be agreed on by the People and finally Enacted by your Majesty in such manner as hath been practised in other of your Majesty's Dominions, to which your English Subjects have transplanted themselves. For as they cannot pretend to farther Priviledges than have been granted to them either by Charter or some solemn Act under your Great Seal; so having, from the first beginning of that Plantation been governed by such Instructions as were given by your Majesty unto your Governor, according to the Power your Majesty had originally over them, and which you have by no one Authentic Act ever yet parted with; and having never had any other right to Assemblies than from the Permission of the Governors and that only Temporary and for Probation It is to be wondered how they should presume to provoke Your Majesty by pretending a right to that which hath been allowed them meerly out of favour, and discourage Your Majesty from future Favors of that kind; when what your Majesty ordered for a Temporary Experiment, to see what Form would best sute with the Safety and Interest of the Island shall be construed to be a total Resignation of the Power inherent in your Majesty and a Devolution of it to themselves and their Wills without which neither Law nor Government, the essential Incidents of their Subsistance and welbeing, may take place among them.

Since therefore it is evident that the Assembly of Jamaica, have, without any just Grounds and with so much Animosity and Undutifulness, proceeded to reject the marks of your Majesty's Favour towards them and that your Majesty's Resolutions in this Case are like to be the measure of Respect and Obedience to your Royal Commands in other Colonies; We can only offer as a Cure for Irregularities past and a Remedy against all farther Inconveniencies, That Your Majesty would be pleased to Authorize and Impower Your Governor to call another Assembly and to represent unto them the great Convenience and Expediency of accepting and consenting unto such Laws as your Majesty has, under Your Great Seal, transmitted unto them. And that in case of Refusal, his Lordship be furnisht with such Powers as were formerly given unto Colonell Doyley your first Governor of Jamaica, and since unto other Governors, whereby his Lordship may be enabled to govern according to the Laws of England, where the different nature and Constitution of that Colony may conveniently permit the same, and in other Cases to act with the Advice of the Council in such manner as shall be held necessary and proper for the good Government of that Plantation, untill your Majesty's further Orders. And that by all Opportunities of Conveyance, the Governor do give your Majesty a constant and particular Account of all his Proceedings in pursuance of your Instructions herein.

C. Tightening the Reins on the Private Colonies

THE LORDS of Trade had so much difficulty in exerting royal authority and enforcing the navigation acts in the private colonies that it vigorously opposed the creation of more such colonies. Although unable to prevent William Penn from securing a charter for Pennsylvania on March 4, 1681, because of the close relationship between Charles II and Penn's father, it did succeed in inserting several limitations and requirements in the charter that subjected Penn to much tighter controls by the imperial government than any previous proprietor.

SOURCE: Thorpe (ed.), Federal and State Constitutions, V, 3039–3041, 3043.

AND to the End the said William Penn, or his heires, or other the Planters, Owners, or Inhabitants of the said Province, may not att any time hereafter by misconstruction of the powers aforesaid through inadvertencie or designe depart from that Faith and due allegiance, which by the lawes of this our Kingdom of *England*, they and all our subjects, in our Dominions and Territories, alwayes owe unto us, Our heires and Successors, by colour of any Extent or largnesse of powers hereby given, or pretended to bee given, or by force or colour of any lawes hereafter to bee made in the said Province, by vertue of any such Powers; Our further will and Pleasure is, that a transcript or Duplicate of all Lawes, which shall bee soe as aforesaid made and published within the said Province, shall within five yeares after the makeing thereof, be transmitted and delivered to the Privy Councell, for the time being, of us, our heires and successors: And if any of the said Lawes, within the space of six moneths after that they shall be soe transmitted and delivered, bee declared by us, Our heires or Successors, in Our or their Privy Councell, inconsistent with the Sovereigntey or lawful Prerogative of us, our heires or Successors, or contrary to the Faith and Allegiance due by the legall government of this Realme, from the said *William Penn*, or his heires, or of the Planters and Inhabitants of the said Province, and that thereupon any of the said Lawes shall bee adjudged and declared to bee void by us, our heires or Successors, under our or their Privy Seale, that then and from thenceforth, such Lawes, concerning which such Judgement and declaration shall bee made, shall become voyd: Otherwise the said Lawes soe transmitted, shall remaine, and stand in full force, according to the true intent and meaneing thereof. . . .

WE Will alsoe, and by these presents, for us, our heires and Successors, Wee doe Give and grant Licence by this our Charter, unto the said *William Penn*, his heires and assignes, and to all the inhabitants and dwellers in the Province aforesaid, both present and to come, to import or unlade, by themselves or theire Servants, ffactors or assignes, all merchandizes and goods whatsoever, that shall arise of the fruites and comodities of the said Province, either by Land or Sea, into any of the ports of us, our heires and successors, in our Kingdome of *England*, and not into any other Countrey whatsoever: And wee give him full power to dispose of the said goods in the said ports; and if need bee, within one yeare next after the unladeing of the same, to lade the said Merchandizes and Goods again into the same or other shipps, and to export the same into any other Countreys, either of our Dominions or fforeigne, according to Lawe: Provided alwayes, that they pay such customes and impositions, subsidies and duties for the same, to us, our heires and Successors, as the rest of our Subjects of our Kingdome of *England*, for the time being, shall be bound to pay, and doe observe the Acts of Navigation, and other Lawes in that behalfe made. . . .

AND WEE doe further appoint and ordaine, and by these presents, for us, our heires and Successors, Wee doe grant unto the said *William Penn*, his heires and assignes, That he, the said *William Penn*, his heires and assignes, may from time to time for ever, have and enjoy the Customes and Subsidies, in the Portes, Harbours, and other Creeks and Places aforesaid, within the Province aforesaid, payable or due for merchandizes and wares there to be laded and unladed, the said Customes and Subsidies to be reasonably assessed upon any occasion, by themselves and the People there as aforesaid to be assembled, to whom wee give power by these presents, for us, our heires and Successors, upon just cause and in due p'portion, to assesse and impose the same; Saveing unto us, our heires and Successors, such impositions and Customes, as by Act of Parliament are and shall be appointed.

AND it is Our further Will and plasure, that the said *William Penn*, his heires and assignes, shall from time to time constitute and appoint an Attorney or Agent, to Reside in or neare our City of *London*, who shall make knowne the place where he shall dwell or may be found, unto the Clerks of our Privy Counsell for the time being, or one of them, and shall be ready to appeare in any of our Courts att *Westminster*, to Answer for any Misdemeanors that shall be committed, or by any wilful default or neglect permitted by the said *William Penn*, his heires or assignes, against our Lawes of Trade or Navigation; and after it shall be ascertained in any of our said Courts, what damages Wee or our heires or Successors shall have sustained by such default or neglect, the said *William Penn*, his heires and assignes shall pay the same within one yeare after such taxation, and demand thereof from such Attorney: or in case there shall be noe such Attorney by the space of a yeare, or such Attorney shall not make payment of such damages within the space of one yeare, and answer such other forfeitures and penalties within the said time, as by the Acts of Parliament in *England* are or shall be provided, according to the true intent and meaneing of these presents; then it shall be lawfull for us, our heires and Successors, to seize and Resume the government of the said Province or Countrey, and the same to retaine untill payment shall be made thereof: But notwithstanding any such Seizure or resumption of the government, nothing concerneing the propriety or ownership of any Lands, tenements, or other hereditaments, or goods or chattels of any the Adventurers, Planters, or owners, other then the respective Offenders there, shall be any way be affected or molested thereby. . . .

AND FURTHER our pleasure is, and by these presents, for us, our heires and Successors, Wee doe covenant and grant to and with the said *William Penn*, and his heires and assignes, That Wee, our heires and Successors, shall at no time thereafter sett or make, or cause to be sett, any impossition, custome or other taxation, rate or contribution whatsoever, in and upon the dwellers and inhabitants of the aforesaid Province, for their Lands, tenements, goods or chattells within the said Province, or in and upon any goods or merchandize within the said Province, or to be laden or unladen within the ports or harbours of the said Province, unless the same be with the consent of the Proprietary, or chiefe governor, or assembly, or by act of Parliament in *England*. . . .

AND Our further pleasure is, and wee doe hereby, for us, our heires and Successors, charge and require, that if any of the inhabitants of the said Province, to the number of Twenty, shall at any time hereafter be desirous, and shall by any writeing, or by any person deputed for them, signify such their desire to the Bishop of *London* for the time being that any preacher or preachers, to be approved of by the said Bishiop, may be sent unto them for their instruction, that then such preacher or preachers shall and may be and reside within the said Province, without any deniall or molestation whatsoever. . . .

D. An Experiment in Consolidation

IN THEIR efforts to bring the private colonies under close supervision, Crown officials requested in 1683 that Massachusetts Bay permit the revision of its charter. When the colony refused, they initiated legal proceedings that led to the total revocation of the charter in 1684. Shortly thereafter, in 1685, the accession to the throne of James II set the stage for a revolutionary experiment in colonial administration. Believing that the Crown should exercise the dominant role in all political affairs, and impressed by the highly centralized colonial administration of the French, James and his advisers moved to place all of the colonies north of Pennsylvania under one general government with no representative assembly. The theory behind this action was that the colonies had *lost all of their traditional rights and privileges with the forfeiture of their charters, and that the Crown subsequently had unlimited authority over them. The governor of this new Dominion of New England was to be Sir Edmund Andros (1637–1714), a favorite of James's, who had previously served him as governor of New York. The commission to Andros, dated April 7, 1688, excerpts from which are given below, reveals the objectives and character of the Dominion experiment.*

SOURCE: Thorpe (ed.), *Federal and State Constitutions*, III, 1863–1868.

James the Second by the Grace of God King of England, Scotland France and Ireland Defender of the Faith &c. To our trusty and welbeloved Sr Edmund Andros Knt Greeting: Whereas by our Commission under our Great Seal of England, bearing date the third day of June in the second year of our reign wee have constituted and appointed you to be our Captain Generall and Governor in Chief in and over all that part of our territory and dominion of New England in America known by the names of our Colony of the Massachusetts Bay, our Colony of New Plymouth, our Provinces of New Hampshire and Main and the Narraganset Country or King's Province. And whereas since that time Wee have thought it necessary for our service and the better protection and security of our subjects in those parts to join and annex to our said Government the neighboring Colonies of Road Island and Connecticutt, our Province of New York and East and West Jersey, with the territories thereunto belonging, as wee do hereby join annex and unite the same to our said government and dominion of New England. Wee therefore reposing especiall trust and confidence in the prudence courage and loyalty of you the said Sir Edmund Andros, out of our especiall grace certain knowledge and meer motion, have thought fit to constitute and appoint as wee do by these presents constitute and appoint you the said Sr Edmund Andros to be our Captain Generall and Governor in Cheif in and over our Colonies of the Massachusetts Bay and New Plymouth, our Provinces of New Hampshire and Main, the Narraganset country or King's Province, our Colonys of Road Island and Connecticutt, our Province of New York and East and West Jersey, and of all that tract of land circuit continent precincts and limits in America lying and being in breadth from forty degrees of Northern latitude from the Equinoctiall Line to the River of St. Croix Eastward, and from thence directly Northward to the river of

Canada, and in length and longitude by all the breadth aforesaid and throughout the main land from the Atlantick or Western Sea or Ocean on the East part, to the South Sea on the West part, with all the Islands, Seas, Rivers, waters, rights, members, and appurtenances, thereunto belonging (our province of Pensilvania and country of Delaware only excepted), to be called and known as formerly by the name and title of our territory and dominion of New England in America. . . .

And Wee do hereby give and grant unto you full power and authority to suspend any member of our Councill from sitting voting and assisting therein, as you shall find just cause for so doing. . . .

And Wee do hereby give and grant unto you full power and authority, by and with the advise and consent of our said Councill or the major part of them, to make constitute and ordain lawes statutes and ordinances for the public peace welfare and good governmt of our said territory & dominion and of the people and inhabitants thereof, and such others as shall resort thereto, and for the benefit of us, our heires and successors. Which said lawes statutes and ordinances, are to be, as near as conveniently may be, aggreeable to the lawes & statutes of this our kingdom of England: Provided that all such lawes statutes and ordinances of what nature or duration soever, be within three months, or sooner, after the making of the same, transmitted unto Us, under our Seal of New England, for our allowance or disapprobation of them, as also duplicates thereof by the next conveyance.

And Wee do by these presents give and grant unto you full power and authority by and with the advise and consent of our said Councill, or the major part of them, to impose assess and raise and levy rates and taxes as you shall find necessary for the support of the government within our territory and dominion of New England, to be collected and leveyed and to be imployed to the uses aforesaid in such manner as to you & our said Councill or the major part of them shall seem most equall and reasonable.

And for the better supporting the charge of the governmt of our said Territory and Dominion, our will and pleasure is and wee do by these presents authorize and impower you the sd Sr Edmund Andros and our Councill, to continue such taxes and impositions as are now laid and imposed upon the Inhabitants thereof; and to levy and distribute or cause the same to be levyed and distrubuted to those ends in the best and most equall manner, untill you shall by

& with the advise and consent of our Councill agree on and settle such other taxes as shall be sufficient for the support of our government there, which are to be applied to that use and no other.

And our further will and pleasure is, that all publick money raised or to be raised or appointed for the support of the government within our said territory and dominion be issued out by warrant or order from you by & with the advise and consent of our Council as aforesaid. . . .

And Wee do further hereby give and grant unto you full power and authority with the advise and consent of our said Councill to erect constitute and establish such and so many Courts of Judicature and public Justice within our said Territory and Dominion as you and they shall think fitt and necessary for the determining of all causes as well Criminall as Civill according to law and equity, and for awarding of execution thereupon, with all reasonable and necessary powers authorities fees and privileges belonging unto them.

And Wee do hereby give and grant unto you full power and authority to constitute and appoint Judges and in cases requisite Commissioners of Oyer and Terminer, Justices of the Peace, Sheriffs, & all other necessary Officers and Ministers within our said Territory, for the better administration of Justice and putting the lawes in execution, & to administer such oath and oaths as are usually given for the due execution and performance of offices and places and for the cleering of truth in judiciall causes. . . .

And Wee do hereby give and grant unto you full power where you shall see cause and shall judge any offender or offenders in capitall and criminall matters, or for any fines or forfeitures due unto us, fit objects of our mercy, to pardon such offenders and to remit such fines & forfeitures, treason and wilfull murder only excepted, in which case you shall likewise have power upon extraordinary occasions to grant reprieves to the offenders therein untill and to the intent our pleasure may be further known.

And Wee do hereby give and grant unto you the said Sr Edmd Andros by your self your Captains and Commanders, by you to be authorized, full power and authority to levy arme muster command or employ, all persons whatsoever residing within our said Territory and Dominion of New England, and, as occasion shall serve, them to transferr from one place to another for the resisting and withstanding all enemies pyrats and rebells, both at land and sea, and to transferr such forces to any of our Plantations in America or the

Territories thereunto belonging, as occasion shall require for the defence of the same against the invasion or attempt of any of our enemies, and then, if occasion shall require to pursue and prosecute in or out of the limits of our said Territories and Plantations or any of them, And if it shall so please God, them to vanquish; and, being taken, according to the law of arms to put to death or keep and preserve alive, at your discretion. And also to execute martiall law in time of invasion insurrection or warr, and during the continuance of the same, and upon soldiers in pay, and to do and execute all and every other thing which to a Captain Generall doth or ought of right to belong, as fully and amply as any our Captain Generall doth or hath usually don. . . .

And Wee do hereby give and grant unto you the said Sr Edmund Andros full power and authority to erect one or more Court or Courts Admirall within our said Territory and Dominion, for the hearing and determining of all marine and other causes and matters proper therein to be heard & determined, with all reasonable and necessary powers, authorities fees and priviledges.

And you are to execute all powers belonging to the place and office of Vice Admirall of and in all the seas and coasts about your Government; according to such commission authority and instructions as you shall receive from ourself under the Seal of our Admiralty or from High Admirall of our Foreign Plantations for the time being. . . .

And Wee do likewise give and grant unto you full power and authority by and with the advice and consent of our said Council to agree with the planters and inhabitants of our said Territory and Dominion concerning such lands, tenements & hereditaments as now are or hereafter shall be in our power to dispose of, and them to grant unto any person or persons for such terms and under such moderat Quit Rents, Services and acknowledgements to be thereupon reserved unto us as shall be appointed by us. Which said grants are to pass and be sealed by our Seal of New England and (being entred upon record by such officer or officers as you shall appoint thereunto, shall be good and effectual in law against us, our heires and successors. . . .

9. Centrifugal Forces in the Colonies

A. *The Quest for Charter Protection*

WHILE IMPERIAL authorities in London were attempting to tighten their control over the empire, the colonists in the older colonies were showing a marked determination to retain and, if possible, even to strengthen their claim to the extensive self-governing rights and economic privileges they had enjoyed throughout the period before the Restoration. In Massachusetts, this took the form of resistance to Edmund Randolph and to any attempt to modify its charter. In Virginia, it was manifested in the effort to obtain a new charter in 1675–76, a direct response to Charles II's grant of Virginia to the Earl of Arlington and Thomas Lord Culpeper in early 1673. Alarmed by the comprehensive powers given to these two proprietors, the Virginia Assembly had sent three agents to London in 1674 to lobby for the revocation of the grant. They wished to secure a charter that would protect the colony against any similar grant in the future, guarantee its existing property and self-governing rights, and give it the maximum amount of control over its own affairs. The proprietary grant was eventually withdrawn, and the agents failed in their efforts only because news of Bacon's rising against the royal government in Virginia caused Charles II not to approve a charter in early 1676 after it had already been prepared. The specific proposals of the Virginians, most of which were included in the final version, may be seen in the following document, which was submitted by the agents in 1675 as the basis for the charter.

SOURCE: John Daly Burk, *The History of Virginia* (4 vols., Petersburg, Va., 1804–16), II, Appendix XLV–1.

Heads, which we are commanded in our instructions to present unto his majesty, and humbly to petition him, that, by his gracious concession, they may be drawn up into a charter for Virginia, with explanatory notes on each head, as presented.

The first head. . . . That Virginia may be enabled, by his majesty's letters patent, by the name of governor, council, and burgesses, to purchase the lands contained in the northern grant of all the lands between the rivers of Rappahannock and Potomack, granted to the earl of St. Albans, lord Culpepper, &c. and that, when the patentees of that grant have assigned over the right and interest of that patent, that then as full and ample power may be in the governor, council, and burgesses, as was formerly in the patentee, before such assignment.

THAT we may the better understand, as well by his majesty's learned council, (who are by the order of the references to report) as by the right honorable the committee (who, by the same order, are to receive and consider it) we have thought it a necessary duty to explain each head presented whereby we may take off all suspicion that we intend not (whilst we humbly petition his majesty, for a confirmation, of our just rights and privileges) to obtain such a power from him as may hereafter justle with the royal prerogative, which we have (and shall always) to our utmost endeavors assert.

FOR the clause of the first head, of incorporating governor, council, and burgesses, we do hereby declare, that no more is meant or intended by it, but that the country may be made capable of purchasing two grants, which his majesty has been pleased to grant, which otherwise are (and will be) very uneasy to the country. But if it may be otherwise eased by a compensation from the honorable patentees, and that the grants may be revoked, we shall then most willingly acquiesce, and no further insist upon that for an incorporation.

AND clearer to demonstrate, that his majesty's interest is as well aimed at by this purchase as the country's ease and quiet, (which is his majesty's interest too) we shall not desire so great benefits and privileges by our assignment as the honorable patentees do and may by their patents claim; but shall most willingly assent, and do most humbly desire, that all those regalities divested from his majesty, may be again invested in him, (the quit-rents excepted) which, we humbly conceive, cannot be reckoned in that number, since they are no other than the fee farm rents, (which have been granted here) as those of Virginia, which are transferred to their lordships by their patent.

FOR the power of granting land, as well in the Northern Neck, which we are to purchase, as in the rest of the country, we desire may be in his majesty's governor and council, as formerly impowered thereunto by royal instructions, and that the composition for escheats may be there (as it is in the rest of the country) left to the governor and council, as ordered by his majesty's last instructions to sir William Berkley.

THAT if there can be no other way found out to enable a community of men to purchase, but (incorporating) a word we are by no means in love with, then we humbly desire, that it may be so limited and circumscribed as to be only effectual for purchasing, (the end that we have expressed, and intended for it) without which the country must be either forced to lie under a burthen, how uneasy soever, or never hope to be reimbursed with any part of the money they are to give (with the whole we are sure they cannot) since the interest of it is much more than the annual rents, which they are to purchase.

To conclude, all we have to add to this first head is, that we humbly hope it will not be thought unreasonable, that the country should enjoy the quit-rents and compositions for escheats of all lands granted between the rivers of Potomac and Rappahannock for ever, as it was granted the said lords and their heirs, &c. at the same value as they have been formerly paid, or shall hereafter be paid by the rest of the country, since the country must pay so great a sum for the purchase of them, and without which they cannot part with their money, having no other way to be reimbursed. Wherefore, we shall desire, that after the surrender of the grant by the said patentees, that that part only, which concerns the quit-rents and escheats, may be granted by his majesty to the country.

THE second head. . . . That his majesty will be pleased, in his royal grant, to assure the people, that it is his majesty's intention (as it has been all his royal predecessors', as will appear by many gracious grants and concessions made to them) that Virginia shall have no other dependence, but only upon the crown of England, now, for the future, be cantonized by grant into parcels, made to particular persons; and for prevention of all surreptitious grants, that his majesty, for the time to come, will be graciously pleased so long to suspend the passing of such grants, until he be informed by his governor and council there (or some impowered from them here) of the fitness or unfitness of them.

EXPLANATION of the second head:

WE say, and do declare, that we do not intend, or hope for any unlimited power to be granted us, or such as may lessen his majesty's authority in that country; but on the contrary, that by the said charter we may be assured to depend only on the crown, under the protection whereof we have always esteemed ourselves most secure, and cannot be happy if any ways hereafter aliened from it.

THE third head. . . . That all land may be assured to the present possessors and owners of it.

EXPLANATION of the third head:

WE humbly conceive, that it will be thought reasonable and

necessary, for the peace and welfare of the country, that all lands granted by their majesty's governor, empowered thereunto by royal instructions, may be confirmed and assured to the present possessors and owners of it, since upon confidence of such grants the inhabitants have been encouraged to lay out their estates, and employ their industry upon the said several tracts of land, for the improvement and advancement of that country.

AND since by experience tis found, that the granting fifty acres of land for every person, hath, next to the blessing of God, (and the indulgent care of our most gracious princes) been the greatest means of promoting the settlement of that country, and bringing it to the present hopeful condition that now it is in, and from whence arises so great an emolument to the crown and kingdom: we therefore humbly pray, that the same encouragement may be continued (as before used) to all adventurers thither.

THE fourth head. . . . That all lands, which have been held in right of administration, acquisition, or other customary title, may be assured to the possessors; though, perhaps, by strictness of law, they may be found escheated to his majesty, which, if it shall so happen, that then his majesty's escheators shall take no more than two pounds of tobacco per acre, as is ordered by governor and council, empowered by his majesty's last instructions to make composition for escheats.

EXPLANATION to the fourth head:

THAT the governor, instructed by his majesty's last instructions to make compositions for escheats, and finding by enquiry thereinto, that many held their land by colorable titles, which, in every deed, for want of heirs, were, by law, escheated to his majesty; yet, upon due consideration of the disturbances that must of necessity arise, by ousting so many from their possessions, so long enjoyed and so much improved by their estates and industry, and that no emolument could any ways accrue to the crown by regranting such lands to strangers and new adventurers; he therefore, most prudently, with the advice of the grand assembly, (to avoid all such inconveniences) set and prefixed one general composition for all lands so held and so escheated, viz two pounds of tobacco per acre: which composition we most humbly desire, may be confirmed by his majesty, for the better settling and quieting of the minds of the present possessors.

THE fifth head. . . . Though we shall never presume to nominate to his majesty a governor and council, or refuse any that he shall please to send us, yet we humbly desire, that our governor, council, and chief officers may be resident in the country: and if it chances the governor's private occasions shall draw him thence, (which shall be thought necessary either by his majesty here, or four of the council there) that then the deputy governor may be one of the council, and such as has an estate and interest in the country.

EXPLANATION to the fifth head:

No more is intended, or can be, by this head, but that his majesty may have the better account of the country, when managed by a person principally entrusted with it; and that his subjects may not be left, in case of the governor's absence, to strangers, who have no interest in the country to be responsible for any misdemeanors or oppression committed there. Nor is this a new or groundless fear, since it hath been always thus carefully provided against; as will appear, not only by the commission of the present governor, but of all the former, since the foundation of the government.

THE sixth head. . . . That his majesty will be graciously pleased, in this his grant, fully to empower the governor and council for the time being; or a quorum of them, consisting of the governor, and as many of the council as his majesty shall think fit, to hear and determine all treasons, mis[   ] of treasons, murders, and felonies, since the government being so remote, ought to be armed with all authority and power, necessary for the suppressing and punishing offences of that nature.

EXPLANATION to the sixth head:

No more is desired by this, but that, instead of a commission of oyer and terminer, (which oath the governor now hath) there may be a standing power in the charter for the governor for the time being, and a quorum of the council, to hear and determine all criminal causes, and this to prevent a justi whereby such offences would go unpunished.

THE seventh head. . . . That there shall be no tax or imposition laid on the people of Virginia, but according to their former usage, by the grand assembly, and no otherwise.

EXPLANATION to the seventh head:

WE therefore, hope, that his majesty and most honorable council, with our learned referees, will not think us immodest in humbly petitioning for this; especially if they please to consider, that both the acquisition and defence of this country hath been, for the most part, at the country's charge: and that the whole support now, both of governor and government, is defrayed wholly at the people's charge, which occasions the annual taxes there to be very high, and will not only continue so, but must, with the growth of the country, every year be encreased.

THE eighth head. . . . His majesty is humbly desired to confirm, by his royal charter, the authority of the grand assembly, consisting of governor, council and burgesses.

EXPLANATION to the eighth head:

THIS in effect is to pray, that all laws made, or hereafter to be made for Virginia, may be of force and value, since the legislative power has ever resided in an assembly so qualified, and by fifty years' experience, has been found a government more easy to the people, and more advantageous to the crown; for, in all that time, there has not been one law complained of, as burthensome to the one, or prejudicial to the prerogative of the other. And though his majesty's governor has ever had a negative voice in the said assembly, yet, to express how far we are from desiring that his majesty should any ways be concluded by any laws made, we do humbly offer (that besides the negative voice there) his majesty shall reserve full power here to disannul any law, so that his dissent be signified to the governor and council within two years after the enacting of it. And to make this effectual, the laws shall annually be transmitted, and presented to one of the principal secretaries of state, to know his majesty's royal pleasure therein.

THUS, in all humility and duty, have we presented this paper, which contains not any thing in it but what we are particularly enjoined to offer by our instructions, and what we ourselves know, by long residence there, to be absolutely necessary for the peace and quiet of that country, which undoubtedly, is his majesty's chiefest interest to preserve.

B. The Demand for English Liberties

THE ULTIMATE objective of the colonists in pressing their claims for the sanctity of the old charters or the protection of new ones was explicit recognition by the governing authorities that they were in fact upon an equal footing with Englishmen who stayed at home and were therefore necessarily entitled to all liberties and privileges traditionally enjoyed by Englishmen. During the Restoration, the most comprehensive and pointed statement of what colonists considered those liberties and privileges to be was the New York "Charter of Libertyes and priv-

iledges," enacted on October 30, 1683, by the first New York Assembly and reprinted in full below. The only Restoration proprietor not specifically required by charter to obtain the consent of the colonists in passing laws, the then Duke of York—brother of Charles II and later James II—resisted the demands of disgruntled New Englanders and others for an assembly for fifteen years after his lieutenants had conquered the colony from the Dutch in 1664. With this document, the New York Assembly tried both to ensure the permanency of representative government in the colony and to define the fundamental rights of the colonists as Englishmen.

SOURCE: *The Colonial Laws of New York from the Year 1664 to the Revolution* (5 vols., Albany, N.Y., 1894–96), I, 111–116.

FOR The better Establishing the Government of this province of New Yorke and that Justice and Right may be Equally done to all persons within the same

BEE It Enacted by the Governour Councell and Representatives now in Generall Assembly mett and assembled and by the authority of the same.

THAT The Supreme Legislative Authority under his Majesty and Royall Highnesse James Duke of Yorke Albany &c Lord proprietor of the said province shall forever be and reside in a Governour, Councell, and the people mett in Generall Assembly.

THAT The Exercise of the Cheife Magistracy and Administration of the Government over the said province shall bee in the said Governour assisted by a Councell with whose advice and Consent or with at least four of them he is to rule and Governe the same according to the Lawes thereof.

THAT In Case the Governour shall dye or be absent out of the province and that there be noe person within the said province Comissionated by his Royal Highnesse his heires or Successours to be Governour or Comander in Cheife there That then the Councell for the time being or Soe many of them as are in the Said province doe take upon them the Administration of the Governour and the Execution of the Lawes thereof and powers and authorityes belonging to the Governour and Councell the first in nomination in which Councell is to preside untill the said Governour shall returne and arrive in the said province againe, or the pleasure of his Royall Highnesse his heires or Successours Shall be further knowne.

THAT According to the usage Custome and practice of the Realme of England a sessions of a Generall Assembly be held in this province once in three yeares at least.

THAT Every Freeholder within this province and Freeman in any Corporation Shall have his free Choise and Vote in the Electing of the Representatives without any manner of constraint or Imposition. And that in all Elections the Majority of Voices shall carry itt and by freeholders is understood every one who is Soe understood according to the Lawes of England.

THAT The persons to be Elected to sitt as representatives in the Generall Assembly from time to time for the severall Cittyes townes Countyes Shires or Divisions of this province and all places within the same shall be according to the proportion and number hereafter Expressed that is to say for the Citty and County of New Yorke four, for the County of Suffolke two, for Queens County two, for Kings County two, for the County of Richmond two for the County of West Chester two.

FOR The County of Ulster two for the County of Albany two and for Schenectade within the said County one for Dukes County two, for the County of Cornwall two and as many more as his Royall Highnesse shall think fitt to Establish.

THAT All persons Chosen and Assembled in manner aforesaid or the Major part of them shall be deemed and accounted the Representatives of this province which said Representatives together with the Governour and his Councell Shall forever be the Supreame and only Legislative power under his Royall Highnesse of the said province.

THAT The said Representatives may appoint their owne Times of meeting dureing their sessions and may adjourne their house from time to time to such time as to them shall seeme meet and convenient.

THAT The said Representatives are the sole Judges of the Qualifications of their owne members, and likewise of all undue Elections and may from time to time purge their house as they shall see occasion dureing the said sessions.

THAT Noe member of the general Assembly or their servants dureing the time of their Sessions and whilest they shall be goeing to and returning from the said Assembly shall be arrested sued imprisoned or any wayes molested or troubled nor be compelled to make answere to any suite, Bill, plaint, Declaration or otherwise, (Cases of High Treason and felony only Excepted) provided the number of the said servants shall not Exceed three.

THAT All bills agreed upon by the said Representatives or the Major part of them shall be presented unto the Governour and his Councell for their Approbation and Consent All and Every which Said Bills soe approved of Consented to by the Governour and his Councell shall be Esteemed and accounted the Lawes of the province, Which said Lawes shall continue and remaine of force untill they shall be repealed by the authority aforesaid that is to say the Governour Councell and Representatives in General Assembly by and with the Approbation of his Royal Highnesse or Expire by their owne Limittations.

THAT In all Cases of death or removall of any of the said Representatives The Governour shall issue out Sumons by Writt to the Respective Townes Cittyes Shires Countryes or Divisions for which he or they soe removed or deceased were Chosen willing and requireing the Freeholders of the Same to Elect others in their place and stead.

THAT Noe freeman shall be taken and imprisoned or be diseized of his Freehold or Libertye or Free Customes or be outlawed or Exiled or any other wayes destroyed nor shall be passed upon adjudged or condemned But by the Lawfull Judgment of his peers and by the Law of this province. Justice nor Right shall be neither sold denyed or deferred to any man within this province.

THAT Noe aid, Tax, Tallage, Assessment, Custome, Loane, Benevolence or Imposition whatsoever shall be layed assessed imposed or levyed on any of his Majestyes Subjects within this province or their Estates upon any manner of Colour or pretence but by the act and Consent of the Governour Councell and Representatives of the people in Generall Assembly mett and Assembled.

THAT Noe man of what Estate or Condition soever shall be putt out of his Lands or Tenements, nor taken, nor imprisoned, nor disherited, nor banished nor any wayes distroyed without being brought to Answere by due Course of Law.

THAT A Freeman Shall not be amerced for a small fault, but after the manner of his fault and for a great fault after the Greatnesse thereof Saveing to him his freehold, And a husbandman saveing to him his Wainage and a merchant likewise saveing to him his merchandize And none of the said Amerciaments shall be assessed but by the oath of twelve honest and Lawfull men of the Vicinage provided the faults and misdemeanours be not in Contempt of Courts of Judicature.

ALL Tryalls shall be by the verdict of twelve men, and as neer as may be peers or Equalls And of the neighbourhood and in the County Shire or Division where the fact Shall arise or grow Whether the Same be by Indictment Infermation Declaration or otherwise against the person Offender or Defendant.

THAT In all Cases Capitall or Criminall there shall be a grand Inquest who shall first present the offence and then twelve men of the neighbourhood to try the Offender who after his plea to the Indictment shall be allowed his reasonable Challenges.

THAT In all Cases whatsoever Bayle by sufficient Suretyes Shall be allowed and taken unlesse for treason or felony plainly and specially Expressed and mentioned in the Warrant of Committment provided Alwayes that nothing herein contained shall Extend to discharge out of prison upon bayle any person taken in Execution for debts or otherwise legally sentenced by the Judgment of any of the Courts of Record within the province.

THAT Noe Freeman shall be compelled to receive any Marriners or Souldiers into his house and there suffer them to Sojourne, against their willes provided Alwayes it be not in time of Actuall Warr within this province.

THAT Noe Comissions for proceeding by Marshall Law against any of his Majestyes Subjects within this province shall issue forth to any person or persons whatsoever Least by Colour of them any of his Majestyes Subjects bee destroyed or putt to death Except all such officers persons and Soldiers in pay throughout the Government.

THAT From hence forward Noe Lands Within this province shall be Esteemed or accounted a Chattle or personall Estate but an Estate of Inheritance according to the Custome and practice of his Majesties Realme of England.

THAT Noe Court or Courts within this province have or at any time hereafter Shall have any Jurisdiction power or authority to grant out any Execution or other writt whereby any mans Land may be sold or any other way disposed off without the owners Consent provided Alwayes That the issues or meane proffitts of any mans Lands shall or may be Extended by Execution or otherwise to satisfye just debts Any thing to the Contrary hereof in any wise Notwithstanding.

THAT Noe Estate of a feme Covert shall be sold or conveyed But by Deed acknowledged by her in Some Court of Record the Woman being secretly Examined if She doth it freely without threats or Compulsion of her husband.

THAT All Wills in writing attested by two Credible Witnesses shall be of the same force to convey Lands as other Conveyances being registered in the Secretaryes Office within forty dayes after the testators death.

THAT A Widdow after the death of her husband shall have her Dower And shall and may tarry in the Cheife house of her husband forty dayes after the death of her husband within which forty dayes her Dower shall be assigned her And for her Dower shall be assigned unto her the third part of all the Lands of her husband dureing Coverture, Except shee were Endowed of Lesse before Marriage.

THAT All Lands and Heritages within this province and Dependencyes shall be free from all fines and Lycences upon Alienations, and from all Herriotts Ward Shipps Liveryes primer Seizins yeare day and Wast Escheats and forfeitures upon the death of parents and Ancestors naturall unaturall casuall or Judiciall, and that forever; Cases of High treason only Excepted.

THAT Noe person or persons which professe Faith in God by Jesus Christ Shall at any time be any wayes molested punished disquieted or called in Question for any Difference in opinion or Matter of Religious Concernment, who doe not actually disturb the Civill peace of the province, But that all and Every such person or persons may from time to time and at all times freely have and fully enjoy his or their Judgments or Consciencyes in matters of Religion throughout all the province, they behaveing themselves peaceably and quietly and not useing this Liberty to Lycentiousnesse nor to the civill Injury or outward disturbance of others provided Always that this liberty or any thing contained therein to the Contrary shall never be Construed or improved to make void the Settlement of any publique Minister on Long Island Whether Such Settlement be by two thirds of the voices in any Towne thereon which shall alwayes include the Minor part Or by Subscriptions of perticuler Inhabitants in Said Townes provided they are the two thirds thereon Butt that all such agreements Covenants and Subscriptions that are there already made and had Or that hereafter shall bee in this Manner Consented to agreed and Subscribed shall at all time and times hereafter be firme and Stable And in Confirmation hereof It is Enacted by the Governour Councell and Representatives; That all Such Sumes of money soe agreed on Consented to or Subscribed as aforesaid for maintenance of said publick Ministers by the two thirds of any Towne on Long Island

Shall alwayes include the Minor part who shall be regulated thereby And also Such Subscriptions and agreements as are before mentioned are and Shall be alwayes ratified performed and paid, And if any Towne on said Island in their publick Capacity of agreement with any Such minister or any perticuler persons by their private Subscriptions as aforesaid Shall make default deny or withdraw from Such payment Soe Covenanted to agreed upon and Subscribed That in Such Case upon Complaint of any Collector appointed and Chosen by two thirds of Such Towne upon Long Island unto any Justice of that County Upon his hearing the Same he is here by authorized impowered and required to issue out his warrant unto the Constable or his Deputy or any other person appointed for the Collection of Said Rates or agreement to Levy upon the goods and Chattles of the Said Delinquent or Defaulter all such Sumes of money Soe convenanted and agreed to be paid by distresse with Costs and Charges without any further Suite in Law Any Lawe Custome or usage to the Contrary in any wise Notwithstanding.

PROVIDED Always the said sume or sumes be under forty shillings otherwise to be recovered as the Law directs.

AND WHEREAS All the Respective Christian Churches now in practice within the City of New Yorke and the other places of this province doe appeare to be priviledged Churches and have beene Soe Established and Confirmed by the former authority of this Government BE it hereby Enacted by this Generall Assembly and by the authority thereof That all the Said Respective Christian Churches be hereby Confirmed therein And that they and Every of them Shall from henceforth forever be held and reputed as priviledged Churches and Enjoy all their former freedomes of their Religion in Divine Worshipp and Church Discipline And that all former Contracts made and agreed upon for the maintenances of the severall ministers of the Said Churches shall stand and continue in full force and virtue And that all Contracts for the future to be made Shall bee of the same power And all persons that are unwilling to performe their part of the said Contract Shall be Constrained thereunto by a warrant from any Justice of the peace provided it be under forty Shillings Or otherwise as this Law directs provided allsoe that all Christian Churches that Shall hereafter come and settle within this province shall have the Same priviledges.

C. Protest Against Economic and Political Inequality

ONE OF the boldest, most moving, and most explicit denunciations during the seventeenth century of imperial attempts to subordinate the economic and political interests of the colonies to those of the mother country was the pamphlet The Groans of the Plantations (published in London in 1689) written by Edward Littleton, a Barbadian planter who had recently settled in England. The immediate object of Littleton's wrath was the heavy duties levied upon sugar in both England and the sugar colonies. But in developing his case against the duties, he gave vent to strong resentments against the unequal and, in his view, discriminatory treatment of the colonies by the imperial government and entered an eloquent plea for the importance of guaranteeing the colonists all of the basic rights of Englishmen and giving their interests equal attention with those of the home islands.

SOURCE: [Edward Littleton], The Groans of the Plantations (London, 1689), pp. 1–2, 8–9, 15–17, 20–32.

In former times we accounted our selves a part of England: and the Trade and Entercourse was open accordingly, so that Commodities came hither as freely from the Sugar Plantations, as from the Isles of Wight or Anglesey.

But upon the King's Restauration we were in effect made Forainers and Aliens: a Custom being laid upon our Sugars amongst other Forain Commodites. And this was in a higher Proportion than others; that is, above the common Poundage of Twelve Pence in the Pound. For eighteen pence a Hundred, was laid upon Muscovadoes, and five Shillings upon Whites: the common price of the Muscovado Hundred being little above twenty Shillings, and the Whites under fifty.

At the same time the Duty of four and a half per Cent. was extorted from us in Barbados, full sore against our Wills. For it may well be imagined, that we had no mind to burden our own Commodities. The use of this Duty were pretended and express'd to be; For support of the Government, and for the publick Services of the Island. But the Duty was soon farmed out for Money payable in England. Which Money hath been here paid, and none of the Uses performed, nor any thing allowed towards them. And all the Applications that we have made for it, have been without success. So that we make and repair our Forts and Brest-works, we build our Magazines, we buy our great Guns and Ammunition; and are forced to lay great Taxes upon our selves, for defraying these and all other publick Charges. Moreover this *four and a half* is collected in such manner, that in the Judgment of all that have tryed it, the Attendance and Slavery is a greater burden than the Duty.

Upon the laying these Impositions (the one in *England*, the other in *Barbados*) the price of Sugar continued the same: nor could we in the least advance it, either then or any time since. So that we find plainly, that we the poor Planters bear the whole burden of these Duties: and whatever we pay, year after year, by occasion of them; is the same thing in effect, as a Land-Tax upon our Estates. . . .

Upon the coming of King *James* to the Crown, a Parliament being called, We were preparing a Complaint against the Comissioners of the Customs. Who had taken a liberty of late, to our grievous prejudice, to call that *White* Sugar, which had never been accounted such before, and which was far from that Colour. And whatever They pleased to call *Whites*, must pay the Duty of five shillings the Hundred.

But we were soon forced to lay aside these Thoughts, to provide against a new Storm that threaten'd. For we were told, to our great Astonishment, that a Project was set on foot to lay more Load upon us: no less then seven Groats a Hundred more upon *Muscovado*, and seven shillings upon Sugars *fit for Use*. For that was now the word. We saw this tended plainly to our destruction. But the thing was driven on furiously by some *Empsons* and *Dudleys* about the late King; who did not care how many People they destroyed, so they might get Favour and Preferment for themselves.

Since we were put into the Heard of Forrainers, and paid Duties with them; we hoped we should fare no worse than other Forrainers did. But that the Plantations should be singled out, as the hunted Deer; and the burden upon their Commodities should be doubled and almost trebled, when all others were untoucht; was matter of Amazement and Consternation. We humbly moved, that if the whole Tax must be laid upon Trade, it might be laid upon all Commodities alike. We said that a small advance upon all the Customs, might serve every purpose, as well as a great one upon some and that this might be born with some ease, there being so many shoulders to bear it. But they would hearken to nothing of that kind: being resolved and fixt to lay the whole burden upon the Plantations. Which could not but seem very strange to us.

But here lay the Mystery. The Projectors consider'd, that if other Forrainers were hardly used in *England*, they would carry or send their Commodities to other Places. But we poor *English Forrainers* are compell'd to bring all Hither and therefore they thought they could hold Our Noses to the Grind stone, and make us pay what they pleased.

However they told us, that this new Duty should do us no hurt: in regard it was to be paid by the Buyer. But this we knew to be a meer Mockery. (the Mockery seem'd almost as bad as the Cruelty.) For if an Impost be laid upon the Sugar, who ever pays it, the Planter is sure to bear it. What avails it though the Buyer pays the Duty, if the Seller must presently allow it in the price?

The Brewer hath a certain price for his Beer: and he adds the Excise or Duty to his price: and the Customer pays it. But where the price is uncertain, and a bargain is to be driven, and a Duty yet to be paid; the first word of this bargain will be, who must pay the Duty? And 'tis not the Appointment of Law, but the Agreement of the Parties, that must decide the question. In Our case, the Buyer will naturally be at this lock: If you clear the Duty, I will give you so much for a Hundred of your White Sugar; if I must pay it, you must have seven shillings less. Which is as broad as long.

The Buyer, they say, must pay the Duty, but sure the Seller may pay it if he please. And he will please to pay it, rather then not sell his Sugar. If He will not, there are enow beside that will.

This Duty upon Sugar is the same thing in effect, as a Duty of twelve pence a Bushel would be upon Corn. Though it be said that the Buyer shall pay this, yet the Seller or the Farmer would be sure to feel it, and it would be a heavy Tax upon the Land.

. . . What have we done, or wherein have we offended, that we should be used in this manner? Or what strange Crime have we committed, to make us the Object of so great Severities? And how have we incurred the displeasure of *England*, our great and dear Mother? The very Sense of our dear Mothers displeasure (though the direful Effects had not followed), and the very Thought that we are grown hateful to her, is worse then death it self. Had we been in the hands of our Enemies, and They had set themselves to crush and oppress us; it had been in some measure to be born, because we could expect no better. But to be ruin'd by those, by whom we hoped to be cherish't and protected, is wholly unsupportable.

These things notwithstanding, our Hearts continue as firm to *England*, as if all were well with us. Nor can any Usage lessen our Obsequious Devotion to our dear and native Country. We renounce the Doctrine of *Grotius*, That Colonies owe an Observance to their Mother Country, but not an Obedience. It is Obedience as well as Observance, that we owe eternally to *England*; and though our dear Mother prove never so unkind, we cannot throw off our Affection and Duty to her. We had rather continue our Subjection to *England*, in the sad Condition we are in; then be under any others in the World, with the greatest Ease and Plenty. No Advantages can tempt us to hearken to any such thing: nor can move in the least our stedfast Loyalty. In this matter we shall stop our Ears, even to the wisest Charmers. Nor shall we only not affect such a Change, but we shall likewise oppose it to the uttermost of our power. Upon such an occasion, we shall cheerfully expose our selves to hardships and dangers of every kind; and fight for our Drudgery and Beggery, as freely as others do for their Liberties and Fortunes. Nay though it were represented to us, that our setting up for our selves were never so feasible and beneficial; yet we should loathe that Liberty, that would rob us of our dependence upon our dear native Country.

We, and those under whom we claim, have (without any Assistance from the Publick) settled these Plantations, with very great Expence and Charge, with infinite Labour, with Hazards innumerable. And with Hardships that cannot be exprest. And now when we thought to have had some fruit of our Industry, we find our selves most miserably disappointed. Our Measures are broken, and our Hopes are confounded, and our Fortunes are at once ruined, by Pressures and Taxes which we are not able to bear. Is all our Care and Pains come to this? and is this the End and Upshot of all our Adventures? Have we gone so many hundred Leagues, and hewed out our Fortunes in another World; to have the Marrow suck'd out of our Bones by Taxes and Impositions? Had these things been foreseen, it had cool'd the Courage of our most forward Adventurers. They would never have gone so far, to be made Rogues of by those that staid at home. They would have thought it more advisable to sit by the Fire side, and to sleep in a whole Skin.

Many of us have our Estates by purchase: and we thought we had purchased Estates, but now they prove just nothing though most commonly we laid out upon them all we had, and all that we could borrow.

Some of the Plantations, 'tis true, came to *England* by Conquest. But must the Conquerors themselves be look't upon as a conquered People? It were very strange, if those that bring Countries under the Dominion of *England*, and maintain the possession, should by so doing lose their own *English* Liberties.

In former daies we were under the pleasing sound of Priviledges and Immunities, of which a free Trade was one, though we counted That, a Right and not a Priviledge. But without such Encouragements, the Plantations had been still wild Woods. Now those things are vanisht and forgotten: and we hear of nothing but Taxes and Burdens. All the Care now is, to pare us close, and keep us low. We dread to be mention'd in an Act of Parliament; because it is alwaies to do us Mischief.

We hear that People of *Carolina* go upon the making of Silk: which surely is one of the best Commodities in the World, and the Design seems very hopeful. But it were but fair to let them know before hand, That when they have brought their matters to any perfection, there will be ways found to leave them not worth a Groat; and to make them miserable Drudges and Beggers, even as We are. It will then be time for them, to be improved to the advantage of *England*.

The Improvement of the Plantations to the advantage of *England* sounds so bravely, and seems to the Projectors a thing so plausible; that they would have it believed to be their chief Aim and End, in all that they do against us. And then they think they talk very wisely, when they talk of Improving the Plantations to the advantage of *England*. Just as a Landlord would improve his Mannor, by racking his Lands to the utmost Rent. Or as the Masters of Slaves, improve and contrive their Labour to their own best advantage. But it is our misery and ruin to be thus improved. And so it would be to the Counties of Wales, or any *English* Counties, to be improved to the advantage of the rest. . . .

If our *Empsons* and *Dudleys* had duly consider'd these things, they would have laid aside their inhumane Project against the poor Plantations. But they consider nothing, but how they may do most mischief.

These are the Men that will perswade Princes, that it is a more glorious Conquest to crush their own Subjects, then to subdue an Enemy.

These Men seem to be trying Conclusions, whether they can so far provoke us, as to make us desperate. And as much as in them lyes, they would make the very Name of *England* hatefull to us. But there is no danger. For we shall bear whatsoever is laid upon us, with the most submissive patience; and nothing can make us forget or lay down our love, to the *English* Name and Nation.

They would make our Great and Dear Mother, *England*, to be so cruel and unnatural, as to destroy and devour her own Children.

They would put us in the dismal Condition of those that said, being opprest by a hard Master; *Subjectos nos habuit tanquam suos, & viles ut alienos. We are commanded as Subjects, and we are crusht as Aliens.* Which Condition is the most dismall and horrid, that people can be under.

They would use us like Sponges: or like Sheep. They *think* us fit to be squeezed and fleeced; as soon as we have got any Moisture within us, or any Wooll upon us.

These *Egyptian* Tax masters would bring us into the State of *Villenage.* They would make us the Publique *Villeins.* They would have us work and labour, to pay the Publique Taxes, as far as it will go.

They would make meer *Gibeonites* of us: hewers of Wood, and drawers of Water. And tho these things must inevitably bring us to desolation and destruction, what do the Projectors care?

But although we are designed by the Projectors to be made perfect *Villeins,* yet they should remember, that even *Villeins* must not be misused too much. We are told out of old Law Books, that 'tis *Wast for the Tenant to misentreat the Villeins of the Mannor, so that they depart from the Mannor, and depart from their tenures.* And in another place; *Destruction of Villeins by tallage is adjudged Wast.* In which Cases the Writ says; *Quod fecit Vastum, destructionem, & exilium.* Surely in our Case, there is a plain destruction by Tallage.

The names of old *Empson* and *Dudley* are infamous and odious to this day. And they were hang'd for their Villianies. Yet they ruin'd men but singly, and one by one. How much higher Gibbets, and how much greater detestation, do these men deserve, that have destroyed whole Countreys?

A Quack pretending great Skill, makes a Woman give her Child

Arsenick: he facing her down, that Arsenick is not poyson. The Child is kill'd, and the Quack is hang'd. Even so our dear Mother hath seen a Cup of deadly Poyson, given to her Children the Plantations: these men (who would be thought great Quacks in Trade) giving the highest assurances that the Drench should do no harm: by which means the Plantations are murder'd and destroyed. And shall not these Men be hang'd? Some think they deserve it better, then all that have been hang'd at Tyburn this twice seven years.

The Projectors might think, in the Naughtiness of their hearts, that many would favour this Project against us, for their owne Ease: and would be willing, or at least content, to have the Plantatons bear the whole Burden. Not caring how heavy the burden lay upon others, so they could shift it off from themselves. But this is a thing of so great baseness, that we are very confident, it cannot enter into the heart of any English man, the Projectors themselves excepted. At least there is no English Parliament but will put it far from them. They know that they are entrusted to do equal and righteous Things. They know that the raising of Money is one of the most important things in a State. If it be done equally, though the burden be heavy, yet it is born with cheerfulness. If otherwise, it occasions furious Discontents, and at last brings all to Confusion. When a Government falls once to shifting and sharking, (pardon the expression, I hope we are not concern'd in it'); it is a great sign that that Government will not stand. No Society of Men can stand without equal Justice, which is the Lady and Queen of all the Vertues. If the equal dividing the common Booties, be necessary to Pirates and Buccaneers; the equal distribution of publique Burdens, is much more to a State.

But it is the Projectors base sharking Principle to make Inequality in these Matters: and to get Ease to themselves by laying the burden upon others. The Writer of these Papers heard one of them say (it was, after that the late Parliament had been so liberal: I forbear his Name, I would not put that Brand upon him): but he said Vauntingly in his drink; We have given the King several Millions of Money, and I shall not pay six pence towards it. And yet he was a great landed Man, which also made the saying the less become him.

The Projectors chief skill is to fall upon the weakest, and make Them pay all. But then why do not they persuade the Western men, since they can out-vote the Northern, to make them pay all the Taxes, themselves paying nothing? Or why do they not single out a few Counties, which by the combining of the rest against them, may be made to pay Taxes for all the rest? The six Western Counties (for now the Dice are turn'd against Them) are in value above two Millions yearly. So that a Tax of two thirds (such as the Plantations now bear) would amount yearly to thirteen hundred thousand pounds. And if this were kept constantly upon them, all the rest of the Kingdom needed to pay nothing. But perhaps these things might cost a great deal of Noise. They might therefore, to go a smoother way, direct their Projects against Widows and Orphans, and Heirs within age. If these were tax'd, well towards the value of their Estates, it would be a great Ease to the rest of the Kingdom.

But our Masters the Projectors think they have a great advantage over us, in regard we have none to represent us in Parliament. 'Tis true, we have not: but we hope we may have them. It is no disparagement to the Kingdome of Portugall, rather it is the only thing that looks great; that in the assembly of their Estates, the Deputies of the City of Goa have their place, among their other Cities. But at present we have them not, and what follows? Must we therefore be made meer Beasts of burden? It is not long, since the Bishoprick of Durham had any representatives in Parliament. But we do not find, that before they had this Priviledge, they were in the least over-laid with Taxes. Also there are now divers Counties that have but few Members in comparison. Essex hath but eight: whereas Cornwall, which is of much less value, hath above forty. But because they have not half their proportion of Members, must an advantage be taken against them, to make them pay double their proportion of Taxes?

They have a Saying Beyond Sea of Us English Men, that we will not let others live by us. The Saying is false: but if it were never so true, sure it would not hold among our selves, but is only in relation to Strangers. To be cruel to and among our selves, would be a Cruelty without Example. Even Wolves and Bears spare their own Kind; nor is there to be found so fell a Monster in Nature, as to deny his Brother Monsters their Means of living. What do the Projectors take us to be? Are we not of your own number? Are we not English Men? Some of us pretend to have as good English

Bloud in our Veins, as some of those that we left behind us. How came we to lose our Countrey, and the Priviledges of it? Why will you cast us out?

Suppose a Quantity of Land were gain'd here out of the Sea, by private Adventurers, as bigg as two or three Counties. (Never say that the thing is impossible; for we may suppose any thing.) Suppose also, that people went by degrees from all parts of *England*, to inhabit and cultivate this New Country. Would you now look upon these people as Forrainers and Aliens? Would you grudge at their Thriving and Prosperity, and ply them with all the methods of Squeezing and Fleecing? Would you forbid them all forrain Trade; and so burden their Trade to *England*, that their Estates should become worth nothing? Would you make them pay the full value of their Lands in Taxes and Impositions? It cannot be thought that you would do these things. Rather you would esteem the Country a part of *England*, and cherish the People as *English* Men. And why may not the Plantations expect the like Kindness and Favour? If the thing be duly weighed, They also are meer Additions and Accessions to *England*, and Enlargements of it. And our case is the very same with the case supposed. Only herein lies the difference, that there is a distance and space between *England* and the Plantations. So that we must lose our Country upon the account of Space; a thing little more then imaginary: a thing next neighbour to nothing.

The Citizens of *Rome*, though they lived in the remotest Parts of the World then known, were still *Roman* Citizens to all Intents. But we poor Citizens of *England*, as soon as our backs are turn'd, and we are gone a spit and a stride; are presently reputed Aliens, and used accordingly.

It is a great wonder that these Projectors never took *Ireland* to task. They might there have had a large Field for their squeezing and fleecing Projects. And they might have found out wayes, to skim the Cream of all the Estates in *Ireland*. But what is it they could have done in this Affair? the answer is, that they might have thought of several good things. In the first place, Nothing to be brought to *Ireland*, or carried thence, but in English Ships, navigated by English Men. The next thing had been, to consider, what things those People had most occasion for: and to put those Things under a severe Monopoly, which also must be in the Conduct and Management of a Company here in *England*. Then care should be taken, that what ever is carried out of *Ireland*, be brought directly to *England* and to no place else: and what ever that Country wants, be had only from *England*. By which means, *England* would be the Staple, of all the Commodities imported thither, or exported thence. There is also another thing, which is by no means to be forgotten: and that is, That the Commodities they send into *England* may be under such Impositions, as may drink up the whole Profit.

These are some of the Waies for Improving *Ireland* to the advantage of *England*. Nor can any thing hinder their Execution; in regard those People are in our power, as well as the Plantations, and subject to the Laws of *England* when we please to name them. But you will say; These things make up such a Devillish Oppression, as is not to be endured. Truly it must be confesst, that the things may seem something hard. But yet there is no Oppression in the case. For all these things, and divers more of the like nature, do the Plantations ly under.

The Projectors think they have been very merciful to us, in that the new Duties are to continue but eight years. They might tell a Man as well, that in pity and tenderness to him, they will hold his head under water but half an hour, or keep him but a Week without Victuals: that is, long enough to destroy him. For the Plantations will be certainly ruin'd within that time, if these Burdens ly upon them: some few perhaps excepted, who had Money beforehand, or have Estates in *England*. And these also must be involved in the general Ruine.

Hitherto we have given some account of our deplorable Condition. But to afflict us yet more, we are told that we deserve no better usage, in respect of the great hurt and damage we do to *England*: as all new Colonies do. But then it had been more prudent, and likewise more just and merciful, rather to prevent the settling of the Plantations, then to ruine them now they are settled. The least signification that they were not pleasing, would have kept people at home. People would never have ventured their Estates and Lives, and undergone such Labours; to get the ill will of those, whose Favour they valued. Had this been the opinion alwaies concerning Colonies, it might pass for a Mistake in Judgment. But when We, who had all encouragement at first, shall as soon as we have got something, be accounted pernicious to our Country; we have reason to doubt, that this is only a pretence to oppress us, and not a real belief or sentiment.

If a new Country should now offer, no question but free leave would be given to make a Settlement, and all due Encouragements granted. We must not say that the People in this case would be decoyed and trapann'd and chous'd and cheated; these are not fit words to be here used. But they would find, that they had miserably deceived themselves. For by that time they were warm in their Houses, and had got things about them; the Projectors would be upon their bones: and these new Favourites would be esteemed pernicious, and used accordingly, as well as the rest of the Plantations.

But we are very sure, that this Opinion concerning us (if any be really of it) is a great Mistake: and that the Plantations are not only not pernicious; but highly beneficial and of vast advantage to *England*.

We by our Labour, Hazards, and Industry, have enlarged the *English* Trade and Empire. The *English* Empire in *America*, what ever we think of it our selves, is by others esteemed greatly considerable.

We employ seven or eight hundred *English* Ships in a safe and healthy Navigation. They find less danger in a Voyage to our Parts, then in a Voyage to *Newcastle*. And as the Ships come safe, so the Men come sound. Whereas of those that go to the *East-Indies*, half the Ships Company (take one Ship with another) perish in the Voyage.

It did the Seamens hearts good, to think of a Plantation Voyage: where they might be merry amongst their Friends and Countrymen, and where they were sure of the kindest Reception. While we had it, we thought nothing too good for them. But now their beloved Navigation is gone. For by destroying the Plantations, it could not be, but that the Navigation to them must be destroyed likewise: or at least made good for nothing. Which, to them, is the same thing as destroying. We are so pinched our selves by the Impositions, that we are forced to pinch all those, with whom we are concern'd. And our Trade is become so hard and so bare a pasture, that it starves every thing that relates to it. And in particular, we cannot now afford the Seamen, that liberal Fraight which we did formerly. We would willingly do reason to our good Friends the Seamen, and give them a fair and full price for the transportation of our Goods; but we are not able.

The Seamen did well foresee, that they should feel the ill consequence of our new Burdens. And we have good Assurance, that while the thing was brewing, they had thoughts of making humble and earnest Addresses to keep them off. But the swiftness of the Projectors motion prevented their design.

And what followed upon the laying the new Taxes? Truly such a flight of the *English* Seamen in the late Reign, as never was known. They plainly deserted the *English* Service. Of which there was no cause so visible, as the spoiling that Navigation which was most dear to them. So that it plainly appears, that by the Sufferings of the Plantations, the Navigation doth highly suffer; whereas while they are permitted to be in a tolerable Condition, they are a great advance to the Navigation of *England*.

Let us now consider the further advantages of Trade, though the building, repairing, fitting and furnishing so many Ships, and the finding Cloths and Victuals for the Seamen, is a considerable Trade of it self. But moreover, there is hardly a Ship comes to us, but what is half loaden at least (many of them are deep loaden) with *English* Commodities.

Several Scores of Thousands are employed in *England*, in furnishing the Plantations with all sorts of Necessaries; and these must be supplied the while with Cloths and Victuals, which employs great numbers likewise. All which are paid, out of Our Industry and Labour.

We have yearly from *England* an infinite Quantity of Iron Wares ready wrought. Thousands of Dozens of Howes, and great numbers of Bills to cut our Canes; many Barrels of Nails; many Sets of Smiths, Carpenters, and Coopers Tools; all our Locks and Hinges; with Swords, Pistols, Carbines, Muskets, and Fowling Pieces.

We have also from *England* all sorts of Tin-ware, Earthen-ware, and Wooden-ware: and all our Brass and Pewter. And many a Serne of Sope, many a Quoyle of Rope, and of Lead many a Fodder, do the Plantations take from *England*.

Even *English* Cloth is much worn amongst us; but we have of Stuffs far greater Quantities. From *England* come all the Hats we weare; and of Shoos, thousands of Dozens yearly. The white Broad cloth that we use for Strainers, comes also to a great deal of Money. Our very Negro Caps, of Woollen-yarn knit, (of which also we have yearly thousands of Dozens) may pass for a Manufacture.

How many Spinners, Knitters, and Weavers are kept at work here in England, to make all the Stockings we wear? Woollen Stockings for the ordinary People, Silk Stockings when we could go to the price, Worsted Stockings in abundance, and Thread Stockings without number.

As we have our Horses from England; So all our Saddles and Bridles come from England likewise, which we desire should be good ones, and are not sparing in the price.

The Bread we eat, is of English Flower: we take great Quantities of English Beer, and of English Cheese and Butter: we sit by the light of English Candles; and the Wine we drink, is bought for the most part with English Commodities. Ships bound for the Plantations touch at Madera, and there sell their Goods, and invest the Produce in Wines.

Moreover we take yearly thousands of Barrels of Irish Beef: with the price whereof those people pay their Rents, to their Landlords that live and spend their Estates in England.

'Tis strange we should be thought to diminish the People of England, when we do so much increase the Employments. Where there are Employments, there will be People: you cannot keep them out, nor drive them away, with Pitchforks. On the other side, where the Employments faile or are wanting, the People will be gone; they will never stay there to starve, or to eat up one another. Great numbers of French Protestants that came lately to England, left us again upon this account. It was their Saying; We have been received with great Kindness and Charity, but here is no Imployment.

However it is charged upon the Plantations (and we can be charged with nothing else), that they take People from England. But doth not Ireland do the same? It may be truly said, that if the American Colonies have taken thousands, Ireland hath taken ten thousand. Yet we cannot find, that people were ever stopp'd from going thither, or that ever it was thought an Inconvenience. You will say the Cases are different: in regard the Plantations are remote; whereas Ireland is neer at hand, and our people that are in Ireland can give us ready Assistance. In answer hereunto it is confess'd, that where Colonies are neer, the Power is more united. But it must be confess'd likewise, that where the Colonies are remote, the Power is farther extended. So that These may be as useful one way, as Those are another way. It concerns a Generall to have his Army united; but may he not detach part of it, to possess a Post at some distance, though it be of never so great advantage? It is plainly an advantage, to have a Command and Influence upon remote Parts of the World. Moreover the remote Colonies of *America* are much more advantageous to *England* in point of Trade, then is this neer one of *Ireland*. For Ireland producing the same things, takes little from us, and also spoiles our Markets in other places. Nor doth it furnish us with any thing, which before we bought of Forrainers. But the *American* Plantations do both take off from *England* abundance of Commodities; and do likewise furnish *England* with divers Commodities of value, which formerly were imported from forrain Parts; which things are now become our owne: and are made Native. For you must know, and may please to consider, That the Sugar we make in the *American Plantations* (to instance only in that) is as much a native *English* Commodity, as if it were made and produced in *England*.

But still you will say, that we draw People from *England*. We confess we do, as a Man draws Water from a good Well. Who the more he draws in reason, the more he may: the Well being continually supplied. *Anglia puteus inexhaustus*, said a Pope of old in another sense, that is, in matter of Money. But in matter of People it is likewise true; That *England* is a Well or Spring inexhausted, which hath never the less Water in it, for having some drawn from it.

You will say yet further, that the Plantations dis-people *England*. But this we utterly deny. Why may not you say as well, that the *Roman* Colonies dispeopled *Rome*? which yet was never pretended or imagined. That wise and glorious State, when ever there was a convenience of settling a Colony, thought fit to send out thousands of people at a time, at the Publick Charge. And wise Men are of opinion, That as the *Roman* Empire was the greatest that the World hath yet seen; so it chiefly owed its Grandeur to its free emission of Colonies.

And whereas the Kingdoms of *Spain* may seem dispeopled and exhausted by their *American* Colonies; if the thing be well examin'd, their Sloth and not their Colonies hath been the true

Cause. To which may be added the Rigour of their Government, and their many Arts and Waies of destroying Trade.

But what will you say to the *Dutch?* for They, we know, have Colonies in the *East-Indies*. Do these exhaust and depopulate *Holland*, or at least are they a Burden and an Inconvenience? The *Dutch* themselves are so far from thinking so, that they justly esteem them the chief and main foundation of their Wealth and Trade. Their *East-Indy* Trade depends upon their *East-Indy* Colonies; and their whole State in effect, that is, the Greatness and Glory of it, depends upon their *East-Indy* Trade. Moreover as their Wealth and Trade increases, their People increase likewise.

They have also some Places in the *West-Indies:* which they prize not a little. How do they cherish *Suranam*, though it be one of the basest Countries in the World? And their Island of *Quaracoa* (*Carisaw* we pronounce it) they are as tender of, as any man can be of the apple of his Eye. Also their repeated Endeavours to settle *Tabago* do sufficiently evince, that they would very willingly spare some of their People, to increase their share in the Sugar Trade. But for a further proof of their Sentiment in these Matters; we may remember, that in the heat of their last War with *France*, they sent their Admiral *De Ruyter* with a great Force, to attempt the *French* Sugar-Islands in *America;* which they would not have done, had they not thought them highly valuable. But the *French* King was as mindful to keep his Islands, as they were to get them: and he took such order and had such Force to defend them, as render'd the *Dutch* Attempts ineffectual. Thus the *French* and *Dutch*, while all lay at stake at home, were contending in the *West-Indies* for Plantations; which our Politicians count worth nothing, or worse then nothing. You'll say, this same French Court, and these Dutch States, are meer ignorant Novices, and do not know the World. Perhaps not so well as our Politicians: But however something they know.

Many have observed that *France* is much dispeopled by Tyranny and Oppression. But that their Plantations have in the least dispeopled it, was never yet said nor thought. And That King sets such a value upon his Plantations, and is so far from thinking his People lost that are in his Plantations; that he payes a good part of the Fraight, of all those that will go to them to settle: giving them all fair Encouragements besides.

If Colonies be so pernicious to their Mother Country, it was a great happiness to *Portugal*, that the *Dutch* stripp'd them of their *East-India* Colonies. And surely they feel the difference: but it is much for the worse. *Lisbon* is not that *Lisbon* now, which it was in those days. And did not the recovery of *Brasile* (though that Trade be now low) in some measure support them, with the help of *Madera*, the *Western Islands*, and some other Colonies; *Portugal* would be one of the poorest places upon Earth.

But still you persist in the opinion, that the Plantations do more hurt then good, and are pernicious to *England*. Truly if it be so, it were your best way to shake them off, and cleerly to rid your hands of them. And you must not be averse to this motion. For if you cry out that the Plantations do hurt, and yet are not wlling to part with them, it cannot be thought that you are in earnest. You will say, this should have been done sooner. But if 'tis fit to be done, 'tis better done late then not at all. Have the Plantations robbed you of your People already? Let them rob you no more. A man will stop a leake in his Vessell, though some be run out.

We of the Plantations cannot hear the mention of being cast off by *England*, without regrett. Nevertheless if it must be so, we shall compose our Minds to bear it. And like Children truly dutifull, we shall be content to part with our dearest Mother, rather than be a burden to her. But though we must part with our Country, yet we would not willingly part with our King: and therefore, if you please, let us be made over to *Scotland*. We are confident that *Scotland* would be well pleased to supply us with People, to have the sweet Trade in Exchange. And we should agree well with them: for we know by Experience that they are honest Men and good Planters. They would now be as busy as Bees all *Scotland* over, working merrily for the Plantations. And *England* the while might keep her People at home: to pick strawes, or for some such other good work; though some of them, 'tis doubt, would make the Highway their way of Living. And now *Scotland* would be the Market for Sugar: where our Friends of *England* would be welcome with their Money. We should be glad to meet them there, and should use them well for old acquaintance. But what would be the Effect of these things? The Effect would be; that in a very few years, the value of Lands in *England* would fall a fourth part, if not a third: and the Land in *Scotland* would be more than doubled. . . .

III

Stalemate, 1689–1721

III

Stalemate, 1689–1721

10. Renewal of Reconstruction

A. Charter Reform for Massachusetts

THAT THE Glorious Revolution and the expulsion of James II did not herald the abandonment of imperial attempts to reconstruct the political and economic relationship between England and the colonies was indicated by a series of actions by the imperial government over the following decade and a half. Following the overthrow of the dominion of New England in the wake of the Revolution, Massachusetts leaders had tried to secure the restoration of their old charter. The best they could do, however, was to obtain a new charter that was considerably more restrictive than the older one. Although it confirmed the colony's right to a representative assembly, this second Massachusetts Charter, issued on October 7, 1691, and reprinted in part below, placed significant limitations upon the authority of that assembly. It provided for the appointment of a governor by the Crown, and in an attempt to weaken the political power of the Puritan leadership of the colony, substituted a property for a religious qualification for the franchise.

SOURCE: Thorpe (ed.), *Federal and State Constitutions*, III, 1877–1883.

. . . And Wee doe further for Us Our Heires and Successors Will Establish and ordeyne that from henceforth for ever there shall be one Governour One Leiutenant or Deputy Governour and One Secretary of Our said Province or Territory to be from time to time appointed and Commissionated by Us Our Heires and Successors and Eight and Twenty Assistants or Councillors to be advising and assisting to the Governour of Our said Province or Territory for the time being as by these presents is hereafter directed and appointed which said Councillors or Assistants are to be Constituted Elected and Chosen in such forme and manner as hereafter in these presents is expressed. . . . And Our Will and Pleasure is that the Governour of Our said Province from the time being shall have Authority from time to time at his discretion to assemble and call together the Councillors or Assistants of Our said Province for the time being and that the said Governour with the said Assistants or Councillors or Seaven of them at the least shall and may from time to time hold and keep a Councill for the ordering and directing the Affaires of Our said Province. And

further Wee Will and by these presents for Us Our Heires and
Successors doe ordeyne and Grant that there shall and may be
convened held and kept by the Governour for the time being upon
every last Wednesday in the Moneth of May every yeare for ever
and at all such other times as the Governour of Our said Province
shall think fitt and appoint a great and Generall Court of Assembly
Which said Great and Generall Court of Assembly shall consist of
the Governour and Councill or Assistants for the time being and of
such Freeholders of Our said Province or Territory as shall be from
time to time elected or deputed by the Major parte of the Freeholders and other Inhabitants of the respective Townes or Places
who shall be present at such Elections Each of the said Townes
and Places being hereby impowered to Elect and Depute Two
Persons and noe more to serve for and represent them respectively
in the said Great and Generall Court or Assembly To which Great
and Generall Court or Assembly to be held as aforesaid Wee doe
hereby for Us Our Heires and Successors give and grant full power
and authority from time to time to direct appoint and declare what
Number each County Towne and Place shall Elect and Depute to
serve for and represent them respectively in the said Great and
Generall Court or Assembly *Provided* always that noe Freeholder
or other Person shall have a Vote in the Election of Members to
serve in any Greate and Generall Court or Assembly to be held as
aforesaid who at the time of such Election shall not have an estate
of Freehold in Land within Our said Province or Territory to the
value of Forty Shillings per Annum at the least or other estate to
the value of Forty pounds Sterling And that every Person who shall
be soe elected shall before he sitt or Act in the said Great and
Generall Court or Assembly take the Oaths mentioned in an Act
of Parliament made in the first yeare of Our Reigne Entituled an
Act for abrogateing of the Oaths of Allegiance and Supremacy and
appointing other Oaths and thereby appointed to be taken instead
of the Oaths of Allegiance and Supremacy and shall make Repeat
and Subscribe the Declaration mentioned in the said Act before
the Governour and Lieutenant or Deputy Governour or any two of
the Assistants for the time being who shall be thereunto authorized and Appointed by Our said Governour and that the Govenour
for the time being shall have full power and Authority from time
to time as he shall Judge necessary to adjourne Prorogue and dissolve all Great and Generall Courts or Assemblyes met and convened as aforesaid. And Our Will and Pleasure is and Wee doe

hereby for Us Our Heires and Successors Grant Establish and Ordeyne that yearly once in every yeare for ever hereafter the aforesaid Number of Eight and Twenty Councillors or Assistants shall be by the Generall Court or Assembly newly chosen that is to say Eighteen at least of the Inhabitants of or Proprietors of Lands within the Territory formerly called the Colony of the Massachusetts Bay and four at the least of the Inhabitants of or Proprietors of Lands within the Territory formerly called New Plymouth and three at the least of the Inhabitants of or Proprietors of Land within the Territory formerly called the Province of Main and one at the least of the Inhabitants of or Proprietors of Land within the Territory lying between the River of Sagadahoc and Nova Scotia. And that the said Councillors or Assistants or any of them shall or may at any time hereafter be removed or displaced from their respective Places or Trust of Councillors or Assistants by any Great or Generall Court or Assembly. And that if any of the said Councillors or Assistants shall happen to dye or be removed as aforesaid before the Generall day of Election That then and in every such Case the Great and Generall Court or Assembly at their first sitting may proceed to a New Election of one or more Councillors or Assistants in the roome or place of such Councillors or Assistants soe dying or removed. And Wee doe further Grant and Ordeyne that it shall and may be lawfull for the said Governour with the advice and consent of the Council or Assistants from time to time to nominate and appoint Judges Commissioners of Oyer and Terminer Sheriffs Provosts Marshalls Justices of the Peace and other Officers to Our Councill and Courts of Justice belonging Provided always that noe such Nomination or Appointment of Officers be made without notice first given or summons yssued out seaven dayes before such Nomination or Appointment unto such of the said Councillors or Assistants as shall be at that time resideing within Our said Province. And Our Will and Pleasure is that the Governour and Leiutenant or Deputy Governour and Councillors or Assistants for the time being and all other Officers to be appointed or Chosen as aforesaid shall before the Undertaking the Execution of their Offices and Places respectively take their severall and respective Oaths for the due and faithfull performance of their duties in their severall and respective Offices and Places and alsoe the Oaths appointed by the said Act of Parliament made in the first yeare of Our Reigne to be taken instead of the Oaths of Allegiance and Supremacy and shall make

repeate and subscribe the Declaration mentioned in the said Act
before such Person or Persons as are by these presents herein after
appointed. . . . *And further* Our Will and Pleasure is and Wee
doe hereby for Us Our Heires and Successors Grant Establish and
Ordaine That all and every of the Subjects of Us Our Heires and
Successors which shall goe to and Inhabit within Our said Province
and Territory and every of their Children which shall happen to be
born there or on the Seas in goeing thither or returning from
thence shall have and enjoy all Libertyes and Immunities of Free
and naturall Subjects within any of the Dominions of Us Our
Heires and Successors to all Intents Constructions and purposes
whatsoever as if they and every of them were borne within this Our
Realme of England and for the greater Ease and Encouragement
of Our Loveing Subjects Inhabiting our said Province or Territory
of the Massachusetts Bay and of such as shall come to Inhabit
there Wee doe by these presents for us Our heires and Successors
Grant Establish and Ordaine that for ever hereafter there shall be a
liberty of Conscience allowed in the Worshipp of God to all
Christians (Except Papists) Inhabiting or which shall Inhabit or
be Resident within our said Province or Territory. . . . *And
whereas* Wee judge it necessary that all our Subjects should have
liberty to Appeale to us our heires and Successors in Cases that
may deserve the same Wee doe by these presents Ordaine that
incase either party shall not rest satisfied with the Judgement or
Sentence of any Judicatories or Courts within our said Province or
Territory in any Personall Action wherein the matter in difference
doth exceed the value of three hundred Pounds Sterling that then
he or they may appeale to us Our heires and Successors in our or
their Privy Councill Provided such Appeale be made within Four-
teen dayes after the Sentence or Judgement given and that before
such Appeale be allowed Security be given by the party or parties
appealing in the value of the matter in Difference to pay or Answer the Debt or Damages for the which Judgement or Sentence
is given With such Costs and Damages as shall be Awarded by
us Our Heires or Successors incase the Judgement or Sentence
be affirmed. . . . *And* we doe for us our Heires and Successors
Give and grant that the said Generall Court or Assembly shall
have full power and Authority to name and settle annually all
Civill Officers within the said Province such Officers Excepted the
Election and Constitution of whome wee have by these presents

reserved to us Our Heires and Successors or to the Governor of our said Province for the time being and to Settforth the severall Duties Powers and Lymitts of every such Officer to be appointed by the said Generall Court or Assembly and the formes of such Oathes not repugnant to the Lawes and Statutes of this our Realme of England as shall be respectively Administered unto them for the Execution of their severall Offices and places. And alsoe to impose Fines mulcts Imprisonments and other Punishments. And to impose and leavy proportionable and reasonable Assessments Rates and Taxes upon the Estates and Persons of all and every the Proprietors and Inhabitants of our said Province or Territory to be Issued and disposed of by Warrant under the hand of the Governor of our said Province for the time being with the advice and Consent of the Councill for Our service in the necessary defence and support of our Government of our said Province or Territory and the Protection and Preservation of the Inhabitants there according to such Acts as are or shall be in force within our said Province and to dispose of matters and things whereby our Subjects inhabitants of our said Province may be Religiously peaceably and Civilly Governed Protected and Defended soe as their good life and orderly Conversation may win the Indians Natives of the Country to the knowledge and obedience of the onely true God and Saviour of Mankinde and the Christian Faith which his Royall Majestie our Royall Grandfather king Charles the first in his said Letters Patents declared was his Royall Intentions And the Adventurers free Profession to be the Princepall end of the said Plantation. And for the better secureing and maintaining Liberty of Conscience hereby granted to all persons at any time being and resideing within our said Province or Territory as aforesaid. *Willing* Comanding and Requireing and by these presents for us Our heires and Successors Ordaining and appointing that all such Orders Lawes Statutes and Ordinances Instructions and Directions as shall be soe made and published under our Seale of our said Province or Territory shall be Carefully and duely observed kept and performed and put in Execution according to the true intent and meaning of these presents. *Provided* alwaies and Wee doe by these presents for us Our Heires and Successors Establish and Ordaine that in the frameing and passing of all such Orders Lawes Statutes and Ordinances and in all Elections and Acts of Government whatsoever to be passed made or done by the said Generall Court or Assembly or in Councill the Governor of our said Province or Territory of the Massachusetts Bay in New England for the time being shall have the Negative voice and that without his consent or Approbation signified and declared in Writeing no such Orders Laws Statutes Ordinances Elections or other Acts of Government whatsoever soe to be made passed or done by the said Generall Assembly or in Councill shall be of any Force effect or validity anything herein contained to the contrary in anywise notwithstanding. And wee doe for us Our Heires and Successors Establish and Ordaine that the said Orders Laws Statutes and Ordinances be by the first opportunity after the makeing thereof sent or Transmitted unto us Our Heires and Successors under the Publique Seale to be appointed by us for Our or their approbation or Disallowance And that incase all or any of them shall at any time within the space of three years next after the same shall have presented to us our Heires and Successors in Our or their Privy Councill be disallowed and rejected and soe signified by us Our Heires and Successors under our or their Signe Manuall and Signett or by or in our or their Privy Councill unto the Governor for the time being then such and soe many of them as shall be soe disallowed and rejected shall thenceforth cease and determine and become utterly void and of none effect. Provided alwais that incase Wee our Heires or Successors shall not within the Terme of Three Yeares after the presenting of such Orders Lawes Statutes or Ordinances as aforesaid signifie our or their Disallowance of the same Then the said orders Lawes Statutes or Ordinances shall be and continue in full force and effect according to the true Intent and meaneing of the same untill the Expiration thereof or that the same shall be Repealed by the Generall Assembly of our said Province for the time being. . . .

B. A New Navigation Act

IN RESPONSE to intense competition from the Scots for the trade of the colonies and continued complaints from the colonies about the difficulties of securing obedience to the navigation acts, Parliament passed a new Navigation Act on April 10, 1696. Intended to ensure the strict enforcement of the older acts rather than to introduce any major policy changes, the new act required all colonial governors to take an oath to uphold the navigation acts, reorganized the colonial customs service, attempted to tighten up the legal and judicial mechanisms for the enforcement of the acts and, most significantly, declared void all colonial laws in contravention of the navigation acts.

SOURCE: Pickering (ed.), *Statutes at Large*, IX, 428–437.

WHEREAS notwithstanding divers acts made for the encouragement of the navigation of this kingdom, and for the better securing and regulating the plantation trade . . . great abuses are daily committed to the prejudice of the English navigation, and the loss of a great part of the plantation trade to this kingdom, by the artifice and cunning of ill-disposed persons: For remedy whereof for the future,

II. Be it enacted, and it is hereby enacted and ordained by the King's most excellent majesty, by and with the advice and consent of the lords spiritual and temporal, and commons, in parliament assembled, and by the authority of the same, That after the five and twentieth day of *March*, one thousand six hundred ninety eight, no goods or merchandizes whatsoever shall be imported into, or exported out of, any colony or plantation to his Majesty, in *Asia*, *Africa* or *America*, belonging, or in his possession, or which may hereafter belong unto, or be in the possession of his Majesty, his heirs or successors, or shall be laden in, or carried from any one port or place in the said colonies or plantations to any other port or place in the same, the kingdom of *England*, dominion of *Wales*, or town of *Berwick* upon *Tweed*, in any ship or bottom, but what is or shall be of the built of *England*, or of the built of *Ireland*, or the said colonies or plantations, and wholly owned by the people thereof, or any of them, and navigated with the masters and three fourths of the mariners of the said places only (except such ships only as are or shall be taken as prize, and condemnation thereof made in one of the courts of admiralty in *England*, *Ireland*, or the said colonies or plantations, to be navigated by the master and three fourths of the mariners *English*, or of the said plantations as aforesaid, and whereof the property doth belong to *English* men; and also except for the space of three years, such foreign built ships as shall be employed by the commissioners of his Majesty's navy for the time being, or upon contract with them, in bringing only masts, timber, and other naval stores for the King's service from his Majesty's colonies or plantations to this kingdom, to be navigated as aforesaid, and whereof the property doth belong to *English* men) under pain of forfeiture of ship and goods. . . .

IV. And . . . That all the present governors and commanders in chief of any *English* colonies or plantations, shall, before the five and twentieth day of *March*, one thousand six hundred ninety seven, and all who hereafter shall be made governors or commanders in chief of the said colonies or plantations, or any of them, before their entrance into their government, shall take a solemn oath to do their utmost, that all the clauses, matters and things, contained in the before recited acts of parliament heretofore passed, and now in force, relating to the said colonies and plantations, and that all and every the clauses contained in this present act, be punctually and *bona fide* observed, according to the true intent and meaning thereof (which oath shall be taken before such person or persons as shall be appointed by his Majesty, his heirs and successors, who are hereby authorized to administer the same) so far as appertains unto the said governors or commanders in chief respectively; and upon complaint and proof made before his Majesty, his heirs and successors, or such as shall be by him or them thereunto authorized and appointed by the oath of two or more credible witnesses, that any of the said governors or commanders in chief have neglected to take the said oath at the times aforesaid, or have been wittingly or willingly negligent in doing their duty accordingly, the said governor so neglecting or offending shall be removed from his government, and forfeit the sum of one thousand pounds sterling.

V . . . That all and every the said [naval] officers already appointed shall, within two months after notice of this act in the respective plantations, or as soon as conveniently it may be, give security to the commissioners of the customs in *England* for the time being, or such as shall be appointed by them, for his Majesty's use, for the true and faithful performance of their duty; and all and every person or persons, who shall hereafter be appointed to the said office or employment, shall within two months, or as soon as conveniently it may be, after his or their entrance upon the said office or employment, give sufficient security to the commissioners of the customs as aforesaid, for his Majesty's use, for the true and faithful performance of his or their duty; and in default thereof, the person or persons neglecting or refusing to give such security, shall be disabled to execute the said office or employment; and until such security given, and the person appointed to the said office or employment be approved by the commissioners of the customs as aforesaid, the respective governor or governors shall be answerable for any the offences, neglects or misdemeanors, of the person or persons so by him or them appointed.

VI. And for the more effectual preventing of frauds, and regu-lating abuses in the plantation trade in *America*, be it further enacted by the authority aforesaid, That all ships coming into, or going out of, any of the said plantations, and lading or unlading any goods or commodities, whether the same be his Majesty's ships of war, or merchants ships, and the masters and commanders thereof, and their ladings, shall be subject and liable to the same rules, visitations, searches, penalties and forfeitures, as to the entring, lading or discharging their respective ships and ladings, as ships and their ladings, and the commanders and masters of ships, are subject and liable unto in this kingdom, by virtue of an act of parliament made in the fourteenth year of the reign of King *Charles* the Second, intituled, *An act for preventing frauds, and regulating abuses in his Majesty's customs*, and that the officers for collecting and managing his Majesty's revenue, and inspecting the plantation trade, in any of the said plantations, shall have the same powers and authorities, for visiting and searching of ships, and taking their entries, and for seizing and securing or bringing on shore any of the goods prohibited to be imported or exported into or out of any the said plantations, or for which any duties are payable, or ought to have been paid, by any of the before men-tioned acts, as are provided for the officers of the customs in *Eng-land* by the said last mentioned act made in the fourteenth year of the reign of King *Charles* the Second, and also to enter houses or warehouses, to search for and seize any such goods; and that all the wharfingers, and owners of keys and wharfs, or any lightermen, bargemen, watermen, porters, or other persons assisting in the con-veyance, concealment or rescue of any of the said goods, or in the hindring or resistance of any of the said officers in the performance of their duty, and the boats, barges, lighters or other vessels, em-ployed in the conveyance of such goods, shall be subject to the like pains and penalties as are provided by the same act made in the fourteenth year of the reign of King *Charles* the Second, in relation to prohibited or uncustomed goods in this kingdom; and that the like assistance shall be given to the said officers in the execution of their office, as by the said last mentioned act is provided for the officers in *England*; and also that the said officers shall be subject to the same penalties and forfeitures, for any corruptions, frauds, connivances, or concealments, in violation of any the before men-tioned laws, as any officers of the customs in *England* are liable to, by virtue of the said last mentioned act; and also that in case any officer or officers in the plantations shall be sued or molested for any thing done in the execution of their office, the said officer shall and may plead the general issue, and shall give this or other custom acts in evidence, and the judge to allow thereof, have and enjoy the like privileges and advantages, as are allowed by law to the officers of his Majesty's customs in *England*.

VII. And it is hereby further enacted, That all the penalties and forfeitures before mentioned, not in this act particularly disposed of, shall be one third part to the use of his Majesty, his heirs and successors, and one third part to the governor of the colony or plantation where the offence shall be committed, and the other third part to such person or persons as shall sue for the same, to be recovered in any of his Majesty's courts at *Westminster*, or in the kingdom of *Ireland*, or in the court of admiralty held in his Majesty's plantations respectively, where such offence shall be committed, at the pleasure of the officer or informer, or in any other plantation belonging to any subject of *England*, wherein no essoin, protection, or wager of law, shall be allowed; and that where any question shall arise concerning the importation or exportation of any goods into or out of the said plantations, in such case the proof shall lie upon the owner or claimer, and the claimer shall be reputed the importer or owner thereof.

VIII. *And whereas in some of his Majesty's American planta-tions, a doubt or misconstruction has arisen upon the before men-tioned act, made in the five and twentieth year of the reign of King Charles the Second, whereby certain duties are laid upon the commodities therein enumerated (which by law may be trans-ported from one plantation to another for the supply of each others wants) as if the same were by the payment of those duties in one plantation, discharged from giving the securities intended by the aforesaid acts, made in the twelfth, two and twentieth, and three and twentieth years of the reign of King Charles the Second, and consequently be at liberty to go to any foreign market in Europe, without coming to England, Wales, or Berwick: it is hereby further* enacted and declared, That notwithstanding the payment of the aforesaid duties in any of the said plantations, none of the said goods shall be shipped or laden on board, until such security shall be given as is required by the said acts, made in the twelfth, two and twentieth and three and twentieth years of the reign of King *Charles* the second, to carry the same to *England, Wales*, or *Berwick*, or to some other of his Majesty's plantations, and so *toties quoties,* as any of the said goods shall be brought to be re-shipped or laden in any of the said plantations, under the penalty and forfeiture of ship and goods, to be divided and disposed of as aforesaid.

IX. And it is further enacted and declared by the authority afore-said, That all laws, by-laws, usages or customs, at this time, or which hereafter shall be in practice, or endeavoured or pretended to be in force or practice, in any of the said plantations, which are in any wise repugnant to the before mentioned laws, or any of them, so far as they do relate to the said plantations, or any of them, or which are any ways repugnant to this present act, or to any other law hereafter to be made in this kingdom, so far as such law shall relate to and mention the said plantations, are illegal, null and void, to all intents and purposes whatsoever. . . .

XI. And for the better executing the several acts of parliament relating to the plantation trade, be it enacted by the authority aforesaid, That the lord treasurer, commissioners of the treasury, and the commissioners of the customs in *England* for the time being, shall and may constitute and appoint such and so many officers of the customs in any city, town, river, port, harbour or creek, of or belonging to any of the islands, tracts of land and proprieties, when and as often as to them shall seem needful; be it further also enacted, That upon any actions, suits, and informa-tions that shall be brought, commenced or entred in the said plantations, upon any law or statute concerning his Majesty's duties, or ships or goods to be forfeited by reason of any unlawful importations or exportations, there shall not be any jury, but of such only as are natives of *England* or *Ireland*, or are born in his Majesty's said plantations; and also that upon all such actions, suits and informations, the offences may be laid or alledged in any colony, province, county, precinct or division of any of the said plantations where such offences are alledged to be committed, at the pleasure of the officer or informer.

XII. Provided always, That all places of trust in the courts of law, or what relates to the treasury of the said islands, shall, from the making of this act, be in the hands of the native-born subjects of *England* or *Ireland*, or of the said islands. . . .

XIV. *And whereas several ships and vessels laden with tobacco, sugars, and other goods of the growth and product of his Majesty's plantations in America, have been discharged in several ports of the kingdoms of Scotland and Ireland, contrary to the laws and* statutes now in being, under pretence that the said ships and vessels were driven in thither by stress of weather, or for want of provisions, and other disabilities could not proceed on their voyage: for remedy whereof be it enacted by the authority aforesaid, That from and after the first day of December, one thousand six hundred ninety six, it shall not be lawful, on any pretence whatsoever, to put on shore in the said kingdoms of Scotland or Ireland, any goods or merchandize of the growth or product of any of his Majesty's plantations aforesaid, unless the same have been first landed in the kingdom of England, dominion of Wales, or town of Berwick upon Tweed, and paid the rates and duties wherewith they are chargeable by law, under the penalty of the forfeiture of the ship and goods; three fourths without composition to his Majesty, his heirs and successors, and the other fourth to him or them that shall sue for the same. . . .

XVI. And be it further enacted by the authority aforesaid, That all persons and their assignees, claiming any right or propriety in any islands or tracts of land upon the continent of America, by charter or letters patents, shall not at any time hereafter aliene, sell or dispose of any of the said islands, tracts of lands or proprieties, other than to the natural-born subjects of England, Ireland, dominion of Wales, and town of Berwick upon Tweed, without the licence and consent of his Majesty, his heirs and successors, signified by his or their order in council, first had and obtained; and all governors nominated and appointed by any such persons or proprietors, who shall be intitled to make such nomination, shall be allowed and approved of by his Majesty, his heirs and successors, as aforesaid, and shall take the oaths injoined by this or any other act to be taken by the governors or commanders in chief in other his Majesty's colonies and plantations, before their entring upon their respective governments, under the like penalty, as his Majesty's governors and commanders in chief are by the said acts liable to.

XVII. And for a more effectual prevention of frauds which may be used to elude the intention of this act, by colouring foreign ships under English names; be it further enacted by the authority aforesaid, That from and after the five and twentieth day of March, which shall be in the year of our Lord one thousand six hundred ninety eight, no ship or vessel whatsoever shall be deemed or pass as a ship of the built of England, Ireland, Wales, Berwick, Guernsey, Jersey, or any of his Majesty's plantations in America, so as to be qualified to trade to, from or in any of the plantations, until the person or persons claiming property in such ship or vessel shall register the same. . . .

XX. Provided also, That nothing in this act shall be construed to require the registring any fisher-boats, hoys, lighters, barges, or any open boats on other vessels (though of *English* or plantation built) whose navigation is confined to the rivers or coasts of the same plantation or place where they trade respectively, but only of such of them as cross the seas to or from any of the lands, islands, places or territories, in this act before recited, or from one plantation to another. . . .

C. A New Agency for Colonial Supervision

ALONG WITH the Navigation Act of 1696 came the establishment of the Board of Trade, the new agency charged with the supervision of the colonies and overseas trade. The assignments and function of the Board, which played a central—if usually only an advisory—role in colonial administration until its abolition in 1782, were elaborated in the commission that created it. Dated May 15, 1696, that commission is given in full below.

SOURCE: E. B. O'Callaghan and B. Farnow (eds.), *Documents Relative to the Colonial History of the State of New-York* (15 vols., Albany, N.Y., 1853–87), IV, 145–148.

William the Third by the Grace of God King of England, Scotland, France and Ireland, Defender of the Faith &a. To our Keeper of oure Great Seale of England or Chancellor of England for the time being, Our President of Our Privy Council for the time being, Our first Commissioner of Our Treasury And our Treasurer of England for the time being, Our first Commissioner of our Admiralty and Our Admirall of England for the time being, And our principall Secretarys of State for the time being, And the Chancellor of Our Exchequer for the time being, To Our Right Trusty and Right Well beloved Cousin and Councillor John Earl of Bridgewater, and Ford Earl of Tankerville, To our trusty and Well beloved Sir Philip Meadows, Knight, William Blaithwayte, John Pollexfen, John Locke, Abraham Hill, and John Methwen, Esquires, Greeting:

Whereas We are extreamly desirous that the Trade of Our Kingdom of England, upon which the strength and riches thereof do in a great measure depend, should by all proper means be promoted and advanced; And Whereas We are perswaded that nothing will more effectually contribute thereto than the appointing of knowing and fitt persons to inspect and examin into the general Trade of our said Kingdom and the severall parts thereof, and to enquire into the severall matters and things herein after mentioned relating thereunto, with such Powers and Directions as are herein after specified and contained.

Know yee therefor that We reposing espetiall Trust and Confidence in your Discretions, Abilityes and Integrities, Have nominated, authorized and constituted, and do by these presents nominate authorize and appoint the said Keeper of Our Great Seale or Chancellor for the time being, The President of Our Privy Council for the time being, The Keeper of our Privy Seale for the time being, The first Commissioner of Our Treasury or Treasurer for the time being, The First Commissioner for executing the Office of Admirall and Our Admirall for the time being, Our Principall Secretarys of State for the time being, And Our Chancellor of the Exchequer for the time being, And you John Earl of Bridgewater, Ford Earl of Tankerville, Sir Philip Meadows, William Blathwayte, John Pollexfen, John Locke, Abraham Hill, and John Methwen, or any other three or more of you, to be Our Commissioners during our Royal Pleasure, for promoting the Trade of our Kingdome, and for Inspecting and Improving our Plantations in America and elsewhere.

And to the end that Our Royall purpose and intention herein may the better take effect OUR WILL and PLEASURE is, and We do hereby order, direct and appoint, That you do diligently and constantly as the nature of the service may require, meet togeather at some convenient Place in Our Palace of Whitehall which we shall assigne for that purpose, or at any other place which we shall appoint for the execution of this Our Commission.

And We do by these presents authorize and impower you Our said Commissioners, or any Three or more of you, to enquire, examin into and take an Account of the state and condition of the general Trade of England, and also of the several particular Trades in all Forreigne parts, and how the same respectively are advanced or decayed, and the causes or occasions thereof; and to enquire into and examine what Trades are or may prove hurtfull, or are or may be made beneficiall to our Kingdom of England, and by what ways and means the profitable and advantageous Trades may be more improved and extended and such as are hurtfull and prejudiciall rectifyed or discouraged; and to enquire into the several obstructions of Trade and the means of removing the same. And also in what manner and by what proper methods the Trade of our said Kingdom may be most effectually protected, and secured, in all the parts thereof; And to consider by what means the severall usefull and profitable manufactures already settled in Our said Kingdom may be further improved, and how and in what manner new and profitable Manufactures may be introduced.

And we do further by these presents Authorize and require you Our said Commissioners, or any three or more of you, to consider of some proper methods for setting on worke and employing the Poore of Our said Kingdome, and makeing them usefull to the Publick, and thereby easeing Our Subjects of that Burthen; and by what ways and means such designe may be made most effectuall; and in generall, by all such methods and ways as you in your Discretions shall thinke best, to inform your selves of all things relating to Trade and the promoting and encouraging thereof; As also to consider of the best and most effectual means to regaine, encourage and establish the Fishery of this Kingdom.

AND OUR FURTHER WILL AND PLEASURE is, that you Our said Commissioners, or any Five or more of you, do from time to time make representations touching the Premisses to Us, or to Our Privy Council, as the nature of the Business shall require, which said Representations are to be in writing, and to be signed by Five or more of you.

And We do hereby further Impower and require you Our said Commissioners to take into your care all Records, Grants and Papers remaining in the Plantation Office or thereunto belonging.

And likewise to inform your selves of the present condition of Our respective Plantations, as well with regard to the Administration of the Government and Justice in those places, as in relation to the Commerce thereof; And also to inquire into the Limits of Soyle and Product of Our severall Plantations and how the same may be improved, and of the best means for easing and securing Our Colonies there, and how the same may be rendred most usefull and beneficiall to our said Kingdom of England.

And We do hereby further impower and require you Our said Commissioners, more particularly and in a principal manner to inform yourselves what Navall Stores may be furnished from Our Plantations, and in what Quantities, and by what methods Our

Royall purpose of having our Kingdom supplied with Navall Stores from thence may be made practicable and promoted; And also to inquire into and inform your selves of the best and most proper methods of settling and improving in Our Plantations, such other Staples and other Manufactures as Our subjects of England are now obliged to fetch and supply themselves withall from other Princes and States; And also what Staples and Manufactures may be best encouraged there, and what Trades are taken up and exercised there, which are or may prove prejudiciall to England, by furnishing themselves or other Our Colonies with what has been usually supplied from England; And to finde out proper means of diverting them from such Trades, and whatsoever else may turne to the hurt of Our Kingdom of England.

And to examin and looke into the usuall Instructions given to the Governors of Our Plantations, and to see if any thing may be added, omitted or changed therein to advantage; To take an Account yearly by way of Journall of the Administration of Our Governors there, and to draw out what is proper to be observed and represented unto Us; And as often as occasion shall require to consider of proper persons to be Governors or Deputy Governors, or to be of Our Councill or of Our Councill at Law, or Secretarys, in Our respective Plantations, in order to present their Names to Us in Councill.

And We do hereby further Authorize and impower you Our said Commissioners, to examin into and weigh such Acts of the Assemblies of the Plantations respectively as shall from time to time be sent or transmitted hither for Our Approbation; And to set down and represent as aforesaid the Usefulness or Mischeif thereof to Our Crown, and to Our said Kingdom of England, or to the Plantations themselves, in case the same should be established for Lawes there; And also to consider what matters may be recommended as fitt to be passed in the Assemblys there, To heare complaints of Oppressions and maleadministrations, in Our Plantations, in order to represent as aforesaid what you in your Discretions shall thinke proper; And also to require an Account of all Monies given for Publick uses by the Assemblies in Our Plantations, and how the same are and have been expended or laid out.

And We do by these Presents Authorize and impower you Our said Commissioners or any Three of you, to send for Persons and Papers, for your better Information in the Premisses; and as Occasion shall require to examin Witnesses upon Oath, which Oath you are hereby impowred to Administer in order to the matters aforesaid.

And We do declare Our further Will and Pleasure to be, That you Our said Commissioners do from time to time report all your doeings in relation to the Premisses in writing under the hands of any Five of you, as aforesaid, to Us, or to Our Privy Council, as the nature of the thing shall require.

And We do hereby further Authorize and impower you Our said Commissioners to execute and perform all other things necessary or proper for answering our Royall Intentions in the Premisses.

And We do further give power to you Our said Commissioners, or any three or more of you, as aforesaid, from time to time, and as occasion shall require, to send for and desire the advice and assistance of Our Atturney or Sollicitor Generall or other Our Councill at Law:

And We do hereby further declare Our Royall Will and Pleasure to be, that We do not hereby intend that Our Chancellor of England or Keeper of Our great Seale for the time being, The President of Our Privy Councill for the time being, The Keeper of Our Privy Seale for the time being, The Treasurer of first Commissioner of Our Treasury for the time being, Our Admirall or first Commissioner for executing the Office of Admirall for the time being, Our Principall Secretarys of State for the time being, or Our Chancellor of the Exchequer for the time being, should be obliged to give constant attendance at the meeting of Our said Commissioners, but only so often and when the presence of them or any of them shall be necessary and requisite, and as their other Publick service will permitt. . . .

D. Limiting Colonial Woolen Manufacturing

ON MAY 4, 1699, Parliament passed the Woolen Act, which was primarily intended to prevent the exportation of woolen products from Ireland to foreign markets. Paragraph XIX, which is reprinted below along with the Preamble, extended the act to the colonies. This was the first of several parliamentary attempts to discourage colonists from manufacturing items that competed with products of the home islands.

SOURCE: Pickering (ed.), Statutes at Large, X, 249–256.

FORASMUCH as wooll and the woollen manufactures of cloth, serge, bays, kerseys, and other stuffs made or mixed with wooll, are the greatest and most profitable commodities of this kingdom, on which the value of lands, and the trade of the nation do chiefly depend: and whereas great quantities of the like manufactures have of late been made, and are daily increasing in the kingdom of Ireland, and in the English plantations in America, and are exported from thence to foreign markets, heretofore supplied from England, which will inevitably sink the value of lands, and tend to the ruin of the trade, and the woollen manufactures of this realm: for the prevention whereof, and for the encouragement of the woollen manufactures within this kingdom, be it enacted . . .

XIX. And for the more effectual encouragement of the woollen manufacture of this kingdom: be it further enacted by the authority aforesaid, That from and after the first day of December, in the year of our Lord one thousand six hundred ninety nine, no wool, woolfells, shortlings, mortlings, woolflocks, worsted, bay, or woollen yarn, cloth, serge, bays, kerseys, says, frizes, druggets, cloth-serges, shalloons, or any other drapery stuffs or woollen manufactures whatsoever, made or mixed with wool or woolflocks, being of the product or manufacture of any of the English plantations in America, shall be loaden or laid on board in any ship or vessel, in any place or parts within any of the said English plantations, upon any pretence whatsoever; as likewise that no such wool, woolfells, shortlings, mortlings, woolflocks, worsted, bay, or woollen yarn, cloth, serge, bays, kerseys, says, frizes, druggets, cloth-serges, shalloons, or any other drapery stuffs, or woollen manufactures whatsoever, made up or mixt with wool or woolflocks, being of the product or manufacture of any of the English plantations in America as aforesaid, shall be loaden upon any horse, cart, or other carriage, to the intent and purpose to be exported, transported, carried or conveyed out of the said English plantations to any other of the said plantations, or to any other place whatsoever. . . .

E. Attempt to Redirect the Economy of New England

IN AN attempt to reorient the economy of New England away from commerce and manufacturing to the production of naval stores, for which England depended upon the Baltic countries, Parliament provided in the Naval Stores Act of March 14, 1705, for the establishment of bounties upon pitch, tar, rosin, turpentine, hemp, masts, yard, and bowsprits produced in the colonies. Although the act did not succeed in changing the New England economy, it did help to stimulate the growth of a large naval stores industry in the Carolinas, and the bounty system was extended to indigo in 1748 in an effort to stimulate its production in South Carolina.

SOURCE: Pickering (ed.), *Statutes at Large*, XI, 109–111.

WHEREAS the royal navy, and the navigation of England, wherein, under God, the wealth, safety and strength of this kingdom is so much concerned, depends on the due supply of stores necessary for the same, which being now brought in mostly from foreign parts, in foreign shipping, at exorbitant and arbitrary rates, to the great prejudice and discouragement of the trade and navigation of this kingdom, may be provided in a more certain and beneficial manner from her Majesty's own dominions: and whereas her Majesty's colonies and plantations in America were at first settled, and are still maintained and protected, at a great expence of the treasure of this kingdom, with a design to render them as useful as may be to England, and the labour and industry of the people there, profitable to themselves: and in regard the said colonies and plantations, by the vast tracts of land therein, lying near the sea, and upon navigable rivers, may commodiously afford great quantities of all sorts of naval stores, if due encouragement be given for carrying on so great and advantageous an undertaking, which will likewise tend, not only to the further imployment and increase of English shipping and seamen, but also to the enlarging, in a great measure, the trade and vent of the woollen and other manufactures and commodities of this kingdom, and of other her Majesty's dominions, in exchange for such naval stores, which are now purchased from foreign countries with money or bullion: and for enabling her Majesty's subjects, in the said colonies and plantations, to continue to make due and sufficient returns in the course of their trade; be it therefore enacted by the Queen's most excellent majesty, by and with the advice and consent of the lords spiritual and temporal, and commons, in this present parliament assembled, and by the authority of the same, That every person or persons that shall, within the time appointed by this act, import or cause to be imported into this kingdom, directly from any of her Majesty's English colonies or plantations in America, in any ship or ships that may lawfully trade to her Majesty's plantations, manned as by law is required, any of the naval stores, hereafter mentioned, shall have and enjoy, as a reward or *præmium* for such importation, after and according to the several rates for such naval stores, as follows, (viz.)

II. For good and merchantable tar per tun, containing eight barrels, and each barrel to gage thirty one gallons and an half, four pounds.

For good and merchantable pitch per tun, each tun containing twenty gross hundreds (net pitch) to be brought in eight barrels, four pounds.

For good and merchantable rozin or turpentine per tun, each tun containing twenty gross hundreds (net rozin or turpentine) to be brought in eight barrels, three pounds.

For hemp, water rotted, bright and clean, per tun, each tun containing twenty gross hundreds, six pounds.

For all masts, yards, and bowsprights, per tun, allowing forty foot to each tun, girt measure, according to the customary way of measuring round bodies, one pound.

III. Which several rewards or præmiums, for each species afore-mentioned, shall be paid and answered by the commissioners or principal officers of her Majesty's navy, who are hereby impowered and required to make out bill or bills, to be paid in course for the same, upon certificate of the respective chief officer or officers of the customs, in any port of this kingdom, where such naval stores shall be imported, as aforesaid; such bill or bills to be made out and given to the person or persons importing the same . . .

VI. And for the better preservation of all timber fit for the uses aforesaid; be it further enacted and ordained by the authority aforesaid, That no person or persons within her Majesty's colonies of New Hampshire, the Massachusetts Bay, Rhode Island, and Providence Plantation, the Marraganset Country, or Kings Province, and Connecticut in New England, and New York, and New Jersey, do or shall presume to cut, fell, or destroy any pitch, pine trees, or tar trees, not being within any fence or actual inclosure, under the growth of twelve inches diameter, at three foot from the earth, on the penalty or forfeiture of five pounds for each offence, on proof thereof to be made by one or more credible witnesses on oath, before one or more justice or justices of the peace within or nearest to such place where such offence shall be committed; one moiety of such penalty or forfeiture to be to her Majesty, her heirs or successors, the other moiety to the informer or informers. . . .

11. The Threat of Parliamentary Intervention in the Internal Political Life of the Colonies

A. The Attack on the Private Colonies

WITHIN FIVE years after its creation in 1696, the Board of Trade had decided that effective government of the empire required the resumption of the private colonies by the Crown, and for two decades beginning in March, 1701 it tried to persuade Parliament to pass a bill for that purpose. Because it advocated parliamentary measures, this campaign differed markedly from the earlier movement against the private colonies in the 1680's, which relied exclusively upon the courts, and it revealed the expanded conception of Parliament's jurisdiction over the colonies following the Glorious Revolution. Document 1 below is the Board of Trade's initial indictment of the private colonies of March 26, 1701; Document 2 is the bill "for reuniting to the Crown the Government of Several Colonies and Plantations" introduced into Parliament in the spring of 1702.

1. REPORT OF THE BOARD OF TRADE (1701)

SOURCE: William L. Saunders (ed.), *The Colonial Records of North Carolina* (10 vols., Raleigh, N.C., 1886–90), I, 535–537.

Having formerly on severall occasions humbly represented to your Majesty the state of the Government under Proprietors and Charters in America; and perceiving the irregularities of these Governments dayly to increase, to the prejudice of Trade, and of your Majesties other Plantations in America, as well as of your Majesties Revenue arising from the Customes here, we find ourselves obliged at present humbly to represent to your Majesty;

That those Colonies in general have no ways answered the chief design for which such large Tracts of Land and such Priviledges and Immunities were granted by the Crown.

That they have not conformed themselves to the severall acts of Parliament for regulating Trade and Navigation, to which they ought to pay the same obedience, and submit to the same Restrictions as the other Plantations, which are subject to your Majesties immediate Government, on the contrary in most of these Proprieties and Charter Governments, the Governours have not applyed themselves to your Majesty for your approbation, nor have taken the Oaths required by the acts of Trade, both which Qualifications are made necessary by the late Act for preventing frauds and regulating abuses in the Plantation Trade.

That they have assumed to themselves a power to make Laws contrary and repugnant to the Laws of England, and directly prejudicial to Trade, some of them having refused to send hither such Laws as they had enacted, and others having sent them but very imperfectly.

That diverse of them have denyed appeals to your Majesty in Councill, by which not only the Inhabitants of those Colonies but others your Majesties subjects are deprived of that benefit, enjoyed in the Plantations, under your Majesties immediate Government, and the Parties agrieved are left without remedy from the arbitrary and Illegal proceedings of their Courts.

That these Colonies continue to be the refuge and retreat of Pirates & Illegal Traders, and the receptacle of Goods imported thither from forreign parts contrary to Law: In return of which Commodities those of the growth of these Colonies are likewise contrary to Law exported to Forreign parts; All which is likewise much incouraged by their not admitting appeals as aforesaide.

That by raising and lowering their coin from time to time, to their particular advantage, and to the prejudice of other Colonies, By exempting their Inhabitants from Duties and Customes to which the other Colonies are subject, and by Harbouring of Servants and fugitives, these Governments tend greatly to the undermining the Trade and Welfare of the other Plantations, and seduce and draw away the People thereof; By which Diminution of Hands the rest of the Colonies more beneficial to England do very much suffer.

That these Independent Colonies do turn the Course of Trade to the Promoting and proprogating woolen and other Manufactures proper to England, instead of applying their thoughts and Endeavours to the production of such commodities as are fit to be encouraged in these parts according to the true design and intention of such settlements.

That they do not in general take any due care for their own defence and security against an Enemy, either in Building Forts or providing their Inhabitants with sufficient Armes and Amunition, in case they should be attacked, which is every day more and more to be apprehended, considering how the French power encreases in those parts.

That this cheifly arises from the ill use they make of the powers entrusted to them by their Charters, and the Independency which they pretend to, and that each Government is obliged only to defend its self without any consideration had of their Neighbours, or of the general preservation of the whole.

That many of them have not a regular militia and some (particularly the Colonies of East and West New Jersey) are no otherwise at present than in a state of Anarchy and confusion.

And because the care of these and other great mischiefs in your Majesties Plantations and Colonies aforesaid, and the introducing such an administration of Government and fit regulation of Trade as may put them into a better State of Security and make them duly subservient and usefull to England, does every day become more and more necessary, and that your Majesties frequent Commands to them have not met with due complyance: We humbly conceive it may be expedient that the Charters of the severall Proprietors and others intitling them to absolute Government be reassumed to the Crown and these Colonies put into the same State and dependency as those of your Majesties other Plantations, without prejudice to any man's particular property and freehold. Which being no otherwise so well to be effected as by the Legislative power of this Kingdome. . . .

2. Bill to Reunite the Private Colonies (1702)

Source: William Noel Sainsbury, et al. (eds.), Calendar of State Papers, Colonial Series, America and the West Indies (London, 1860–   ), 1702, 210–211.

Whereas by virtue of several Charters and Letters Patents under the Great Seal of England passed and granted by several of his Majesty's royal Predecessors, as also by his present Majesty and the late Queen Mary of blessed memory, the several Colonies, Provinces and Plantations of the Massachusets Bay, New Hampshire, Rhode Island and Providence plantation, Connecticut in New England, East and West New Jersey, Pennsylvania and the adjacent territories, Maryland, Carolina and the Bahama or Luca Islands in America, have been granted unto several persons, together with the absolute government or authority over his Majesty's subjects in those places, whereby the grantees were not only made Proprietors of the soil and lands comprehended within the said places, but also Lords and Governors thereof; and whereas the severing of such power and authority from the Crown and placing the same in the hands of subjects hath by experience been found prejudicial and repugnant to the trade of this Kingdom and to the welfare of H.M.'s other Plantations in America and to H.M.'s revenue arising from the Customes, by reason of the many irregularities committed by the Governors of these Plantations and by those in authority there under them, by encouraging and countenancing pirates and unlawful traders and otherwise. Be it therefore enacted, by the King's most excellent Majesty, by and with the advice and consent of the Lords Spiritual and Temporal and Commons in Parliament assembled, and by the authority of the same; that all and singular the clauses, matters and things contained in any Charters or Letters Patents heretofore passed under the Great Seal of England by any of H.M.'s royal Predecessors or by his present Majesty and the said late Queen, relating to the government of H.M.'s subjects within the said Plantations, Colonies or places, or any of them, or within any other Plantation, Colony or place in America, whereby any power or authority is granted to any person or persons from the Crown, be and is hereby declared and enacted to be utterly void and of none effect. And it is hereby further declared and enacted that all such power and authority, priviledges and jurisdictions be and are hereby reunited, annexed and vested in his Majesty, his heirs and successors, in right of the Crown of England, to all intents and purposes, as though no such Charters or Letters Patents had been had or made; Provided always that nothing herein contained shall be construed to extend any ways to alter, take away, diminish or abridge the right or title, which any person, persons or bodies politick or corporate have or lawfully may have or claim to any land, tenements or hereditaments or any other matter or thing (authority and government only excepted) by virtue of the said or any other Charter or Letters Patents by any mean assignments or conveyances or otherwise howsoever; Provided also that nothing in this Act contained shall be construed to impower his Majesty, his heirs or successors to govern the said Plantations, Colonies or places or any of them or the inhabitants thereof otherwise than according to the Laws in force in the said Plantations and places respectively, not repugnant to the Laws of England, and such other laws and constitutions as shall from time to time be made by the General Assemblies of the said respective Plantations according to the several and respective priviledges, as at any time heretofore granted to the said several

Plantations and Colonies respectively, by any Charter or Charters or Letters Patents under the Great Seal of England, and according to the usages in H.M.'s other Plantations in America.

B. *The Menace of Parliamentary Taxation*

The growing tendency of imperial officials to think in terms of turning to Parliament for help in enforcing its directives was illustrated in 1711–13 by the repeated threats, inaugurated by the Board of Trade and endorsed by the ministry and Privy Council, of parliamentary action to raise a revenue for the support of the royal administration in New York. The first of these threats was made in a Board of Trade report to the Privy Council on March 1, 1711. This report, reprinted in full below, discusses in detail the considerations that led the Board to propose such a drastic measure.

Source: Grant and Munro (eds.), *Acts of the Privy Council, Colonial*, II, 637–642.

. . . Having laid before Your Majesty such Account as We received from Your Majesty's Governor of New York, of the Settlement of the Palatines, and of their being Imployed in the Production of Naval Stores in that Province, We now beg Leave humbly to Represent to Your Majesty the Difficulties he has met with from the Assembly, in relation to his procuring the Grant of a Revenue There.

The last Act of Assembly whereby a Revenue was Granted to Your Majesty for Defraying the publick Charges of that Government, Expired the 18th of May 1709; The Governor who Arrived There in June 1710, did on the first of September following, in his Speech at his Opening the first Session of Assembly, among other things earnestly Recommend to them, the providing a fitting and necessary Supply for the Service of Your Majesty's Government, And that they would take Care to restore the Publick Credit. In Order whereunto, at the Desire of the Assembly an Estimate of the Yearly Charge of that Government was laid before them, Part of which Estimate they disallow'd, And prepared another Estimate of the Charges of that Government.

On the 25th of October following, the Assembly Voted Two thousand Five Hundred Ounces of Silver, towards Defraying the Governor's necessary Expences for One Year; The Value of which Quantity of Silver he computes at little more than half of what Your Majesty has been pleased to appoint for his Salary; Whereupon he Communicated to them, that Part of Your Majesty's Instructions, whereby he is Impowered to receive to his own Use as Governor Twelve Hundred Pounds Sterling a Year, out of the publick Revenue of that Province, And Added, that he presumed They would not Dispute Your Majesty's Right of appointing a Salary for the Use of Your Governor.

They struck out some Entire Articles in the said Estimate of the Yearly Charge of that Government, And Retrenched Others to less than One half, though some of the Members proposed, That what the Governor Offered, might be further Considered, and one of them having prest it with some Warmth was Thereupon Expell'd the Assembly. Afterwards on the 2nd of November they Voted Twelve Hundred Pounds more, for Defraying the Charge of the Government and for the Security of the Frontiers.

On the 6th of November following a Bill was brought into the Assembly, giving a Power to the Treasurer of that Province, out of the Publick Treasure lying in his hands (unappropriated) to Issue Five Thousand, Six Hundred and sixty seven Ounces and a Half of Silver, for the Use of the Garrison and other the Uses therein particularly mentioned: Which Summ the Governor informs Us was little more than half of what was necessary, and very much less than what has Usually been Allowed for those Services.

To this Bill the Council made an Amendment, by which the Mony was Directed to be issued by Warrant of the Governor, by and with the Advice and Consent of the Councill, Conformable to Your Majesty's Instructions in that behalf, And to former Practice there. The Assembly Disagreed to this Amendment, And there were several Conferences between the Council and Assembly on the Subject Matter of that Amendment, without any good Effect. Whereupon the Governor found himself Obliged on the 25th of the said November last to prorogue the Assembly to the first of March next, in hopes they will Then meet in a better Temper. In the mean time by this Proceeding of the Assembly there is no Provision made for the Payment of the said Governor's Salary, or for Defraying the Other Publick and Necessary Charges of that Government; Except what may Arise from the Two Acts past that Session for setling an Excise on Strong Liquors, and for laying Dutys on the Tonage of Vessells and Slaves; All which 'tis Computed will fall much short of the 'forementioned Services.

The Governor has inform'd Us, of what Reasons some of the Members of the Assembly give for their not providing for the

Support of that Government as formerly, with his Observations upon Such their pretended Reasons. And We further beg Leave humbly to lay the same before Your Majesty.

They pretend that the Expence of that Province on Account of the late intended Expedition against Canada, has so Impoverish'd them, That they are not able to Raise Mony to Answer the Usual Charge of the Government: Upon which the Governor Observes, that the Service of that Expedition was defrayed by a Land-Tax (the greatest part whereof we presume was spent among themselves) whereas the Mony given for the Charge of the Government, was usually Raised by Dutys on Goods Imported and Exported, and on Excise.

Another Reason they give is, That the Misapplication of Revenues formerly Granted, has, as they Alledge, brought a Considerable Debt on the Country.

To Remove that Objection the Governor proposed to several Members of the Assembly, That a Clause might be inserted in the Revenue Bill, to Oblige the Receiver General to be Accomptable to the Assembly as well as to Your Majesty; That such other Clauses might be Added, as would Effectually Restrain the Governor and Councill from loading the Country with further Debts by any Payment to be Issued out of the Revenue.

But 'tis believ'd the true Reasons of this Proceeding of the Assembly, are, First, That in a Great Measure some of the Neighbouring Governments are Exempted from so great a Charge.

As to this, the Governor Observes, That the Province of the Massachusets Bay is at Twenty Thousand Pounds yearly Charge, for the Defence of their ffrontiers, whilst those of New York, are for the most Part Defended and Secured by Your Majesty's Regular Forces There.

Another Reason is, That by Act of Assembly every Assembly man being allowed Six Shillings a day, during the sitting of the Assembly, the better to secure his being Chosen from time to time, he only Considers the saving of the Country's mony, without having any manner of Regard to the necessary Services of the Government.

Lastly, the Governor adds, That of late a Notion has very much prevailed among those People, that Your Majesty has not a Power of Appointing Salaries out of the Revenue Raised by them, and the pretended Right they have Assumed to themselves of Retrenching the Governor's Salary, in the manner beforementioned, is founded on that Notion, which in Our Opinion, should not be Countenanced.

This being a State of the Difficulties the Governor has met with from the Assembly, in relation to his procuring the Grant of a Revenue, as it appears to Us from the Journal of Assembly, and from the Governor's Letters, We beg Leave to Offer to Your Majesty Our humble Opinion,

That Your Majesty's said Governor be Directed to Represent to the Assembly, That it being Your Majesty's Undoubted Prerogative to Constitute a Governor of that Province, with an appointment of such Salary as your Majesty in Your Royal Wisdom, has judged Suitable to the Character, and necessary for the Support and Maintenance of that Government, it has therefore been justly displeasing to Your Majesty, to find they have Refused or Neglected to make the like Sufficient Provision for the 'foresaid purpose, as has been made in the time of Your Majesty's late Governors. And Thereupon that the said Governor be further Directed in the most Effectual manner to Recommend to them the Granting the like Revenue for the Support and Maintenance of that Government, as has Usually been Granted. And the better to induce the Assembly to Comply therein, We humbly Conceive it may be proper to intimate to them, that if they shall persist in refusing or Neglecting to provide for the Necessary Support and Maintenance of that Government under the Administration of Your Majesty's present Governor, in like manner as the same has hitherto been Supported and Maintained, they must Expect, that such their Refusal or Neglect will give a just Occasion to the passing an Act by the Parliament of Great Britain, for Granting to Your Majesty the like Revenue to Arise, and be paid there, for the Support and Maintenance of that Government as has Usually been granted by Act of Assembly for that Service.

Her Majesty in Councill Approving of the said Representation is pleased to Order, as it is hereby Ordered, that the Right Honourable The Lords Commissioners of Trade and Plantations do forthwith draw up Heads of a Bill to be layd before the Parliament of Great Britain for Enacting a Standing Revenue of what has been Usually Allowed within the Province of New York for the Support of the Governor there, and the necessary Expences of the Government, according to former Acts of Assembly: And that they present the same to Her Majesty at this Board, in Order to Her Majesty's further Pleasure Therein.

12. Search for a Viable Imperial System

A. A Just and Well-Disciplined Empire

AMONG THE many English writers who addressed themselves to solving the problems of the empire in the decades immediately following the Glorious Revolution, Charles Davenant, the economist, was probably the most liberal toward the colonies. In his essay "On the Plantation Trade," published in 1698 and reprinted in part below, he set forth the general principles that he thought ought to govern the relationship between the mother country and the colonies, and proposed a series of specific measures to implement them. Like every other English writer on the subject during his generation, he wanted to hold the colonies to a strict dependence upon England. But he also proposed to permit them a generous amount of freedom, and emphasized the desirability of providing efficient and just administration in both England and the colonies and giving as much encouragement as possible to the colonies by catering to their interests whenever they did not conflict with those of the parent state. Also like many other writers, Davenant advocated the consolidation of the continental colonies into a general government, specifically recommending a scheme earlier proposed by William Penn.

SOURCE: Charles Davenant, *Political and Commercial Works* (4 vols., London, 1771), II, 10–11, 29–38, 40–41, 51–55.

Colonies are a strength to their mother kingdom, while they are under good discipline, while they are strictly made to observe the fundamental laws of their original country, and while they are kept dependent on it. But otherwise, they are worse than members lopped from the body politic, being indeed like offensive arms wrested from a nation, to be turned against it as occasion shall serve.

Not that we think the greatness these colonies may arrive at in a natural course, and in the progress of time, can be dangerous to England. To build ships in the way of trade, or for their own defence, can administer no true cause of jealousy. . . .

And, generally speaking, our colonies while they have English blood in their veins, and have relations in England, and while they can get by trading with us, the stronger and greater they grow, the more this crown and kingdom will get by them; and nothing but such an arbitrary power as shall make them desperate, can bring them to rebel. . . .

Our interest in America, generally speaking, may bring an immense profit to this kingdom, if it is well looked after by the government here, but otherwise in all likelihood it will either decline, or come to be a strength that may be turned against us.

If such a scheme of a council of trade . . . be not thought advisable, it is submitted to public consideration, whether the Plantations are not of importance enough to deserve a particular council to be established by the King, for the inspection of affairs thereunto relating, in the following, or some such like method.

1st, That the care of America be made the province of a select number of lords and gentlemen of reputation, both for parts and fortune, and in such a number as will admit of two committees, that so business may be better dispatched.

2dly, That they be authorized under the great seal of England, by the name and stile of Lords Commissioners for the English Plantations in America, to consider and inspect all affairs relating to the Government, Trade, Revenues, Plantations, and further improvement of those countries.

3dly, And no business being well done in this kingdom, where attendance is not recompenced with some advantage, that every commissioner have a salary of £1000. per ann.

4thly, That the respective colonies be required to send a true state of their case to these Lords; as for example, of their situation, extent of territory, numbers of people, produce, revenue, civil policy, with proposals which way to improve every country, to their own and this nation's profit; and all to be registered in the Plantation Office.

This, compared with what enquiries the Lords may themselves make, and informations they may receive at home, may give them such an idea and knowledge of all affairs in America, as it will not be difficult for them to put things into a form and order of government that shall always preserve those countries in their obedience to the crown, and dependence upon this kingdom; and probably, if they are thus made the peculiar care of some body of men, they will be a lasting revenue to the king, an inexhaustible mine of treasure to England in general, and a great means to multiply seamen and encrease our navigation.

Such a constitution will be something like what we call the Council of the Indies in Spain; but here it may be objected, that the Spaniards are not very good patterns to follow in any model or scheme of government; to which it may be answered, that whoever considers the laws, and politic institutions of Spain, will find them as well formed, and contrived with as much skill and wisdom, as in any country perhaps in the world: So that the errors that people is observed to commit from time to time, do not proceed from a wrong and ill projection, but from the negligent, loose, and unsteady executions of their councils.

Xenophon, in that Tract which is published at the end of the First Part of these Discourses, says, "That governments resemble their governors." This maxim of his is certainly right; and from thence it follows, that the welfare of the American colonies will very much depend upon the conduct and behaviour of such as are sent to reside and govern there by the King's authority.

In former times, this part of policy has without doubt been very much neglected, there having generally been put at the head of these affairs abroad, indigent, ignorant, or extravagant persons, of which one sort made a prey, and the others, by their examples, corrupted the manners of the people.

A good general, by the very march and demeanour of a regiment, can make a near guess at the understanding and abilities of the colonel, if he be unskilful and without discipline, every private centinel shall carry the marks of it about him.

The same holds, and much more strongly, in the government of higher matters: It must therefore be of great importance to the state, that he who is to command a country containing many thousand families, should be a man of abilities, experience, dexterity, courage, temper, and virtue; he ought to be endowed with such a general knowledge as may comprehend the nature of the soil where he is, what improvements it is capable of, and what trades will be most advantageous to it. He should be able likewise to look into the genius of the people he is to govern: He should be a man of discipline, sobriety, and justice, for he that is not so in his own person, can never expect order, nor compel others to obey the laws. A people to whom riches and plenty furnish matter for vice and luxury, should be governed by a strict and skilful hand, which may reform their manners, and at the same time both promote and direct their industry.

In all appearance, hardly any thing would more conduce to the good government of these places, than to follow one course which the King of France observes strictly in his Plantations, and it is to give very large appointments to the governors out of his own coffers, not allowing them any perquisites, or to draw any advantages or profit from the inhabitants.

And as care should be taken to keep them obedient to the laws of England, and dependent upon their mother country, so those conditions, privileges, terms, and charters, should be kept sacred and inviolate, by which they were first encouraged, at their great expence, and with the hazard of their lives, to discover, cultivate, and plant remote places, where in truth they labour as well for us as for themselves, for here at last their treasure centers.

The northern colonies are not upon the same foot as those of the south; and having a worse soil to improve, they must find their recompence some other way, which only can be in property and dominion: Upon which score, any innovations in the form of government there, should be cautiously examined, for fear of entering upon measures by which the industry of the inhabitants may be quite discouraged.

It is always unfortunate for a people, either by consent or upon compulsion, to depart from their primitive institutions, and those fundamentals by which they were first united together: Liberty, choice of their own chief magistrates and officers, was the part constituent of the principal societies that have succeeded so well in the northward regions; to appoint them governors from hence, will certainly be for the good of the courtiers here, but whether this course in the event will be advantageous for those Plantations, is not so easy to determine.

But without doubt it must be very prejudicial both to the southward and northern colonies, that many offices and places of trust there should be granted by patent to persons in England, with liberty to execute such employments by deputies, by which means they are generally farmed out to indigent persons, who grind and fleece the people: So that the inhabitants, though many of them are rich, sober, and judicious men, yet they are excluded from offices of trust, except such as are chargeable in the execution, which is inconsistent with all the rules of well governing a country.

They who have visited the north tract of America, and who have observed the several ways and degrees of cultivation, with respect to the quality and quantity of their produce, the economy of the people, and the administration of the respective governments, cannot better express the disproportion throughout, between place and place, than by comparing them with the many principalities and states of Germany, where the Protestant countries are for the most part better peopled, and their towns better kept, than those under Catholic governments: And so it fares with the hans or free towns, as they are called, above those under absolute and arbitrary princes: Where the constitution is freer, and the magistracy more sober, the people are more industrious, and the country improves in proportion.

And had it not been for provinces begun and carried on by people of sobriety, the English empire abroad would be much weaker than it is at present; it having been the unhappiness of some to take their original from another race of planters, vicious, needy, or criminal, who, though a profit to the kingdom by being there, yet by no means in proportion with the other sort. And as licentiousness breaks out much more apparently in such places, so that is not all, for governors (as is said) are too apt to make their advantages of it, who, by indulging such extravagancies, find their own accounts the better; it being plain that the common people are but too ready to exchange their liberties for licentiousness, and to wink at those who will connive at them.

If ever any thing great or good be done for our English colonies, industry must have its due recompence, and that cannot be without encouragement to it, which perhaps is only to be brought about by confirming their liberties, and establishing good discipline among them: That as they see they are a free people in point of government, so they may by discipline be kept free of the mischiefs that follow vice and idleness.

And as great care should be taken in this respect, so without doubt it is advisable that no little emulations or private interests of neighbour governors, nor that the petitions of hungry courtiers at home, should prevail to discourage those particular colonies, who in a few years have raised themselves by their own charge, prudence, and industry, to the wealth and greatness they are now arrived at, without expence to the crown: Upon which account any innovations or breach of their original charters (besides that it seems a breach of the public faith) may peradventure not tend to the King's profit.

In those colonies, which by charter are not governed from hence, as to all dues belonging to the crown revenue, the King has as an immediate influence, by having an officer of his own upon the spot, as in other places.

And the dues of the crown arising from the improvements of the soil, it seems more probable that such improvement should be made by those who have an interest and property in the country, and who work for themselves, than by governors sent from hence, whose most common aim is to grow rich by fleecing the inhabitants; and this property is without doubt the best caution and pledge for their good behaviour, both to the King and to his subjects in those remote parts, who, as it is said, in former times, have been severely handled by transient governors.

The welfare of all countries whatsoever depends upon good government, and without doubt these colonies will flourish, if they are intrusted to honest, discreet, and skilful hands, who will let them perceive they enjoy the rights and liberties of Englishmen, though not in England.

Industry has its first foundation in liberty: They who either are slaves, or who believe their freedoms precarious, can neither succeed in trade nor meliorate a country. We shall not pretend to determine whether the people in the Plantations have a right to all the privileges of English subjects; but the contrary notion is perhaps too much entertained and practised in places which happen to be distant from St. Stephen's chappel. Upon which account it will peradventure be a great security and encouragement to these industrious people, if a declaratory law were made, that Englishmen have right to all the laws of England, while they remain in countries subject to the dominion of this kingdom. But as the arbitrary proceedings and mal-administration of governors should be severely animadverted upon, so frivolous and wrong complaints should be as much discouraged.

And in this place we think ourselves obliged to take notice, that public enquiry ought to be made into the oppressive and scandalous behaviour of some merchants towards the sugar and tobacco planters.

When the matters of America shall come under such a consideration as may produce a settlement, the parties concerned in trade, property, and interest, will be able to instance many particular regulations that may improve the country, and render the traffic more profitable. In the mean while we have offered what has occurred to our observation, to which we shall add some few remarks relating to the trade, government, and civil policy of those countries which are.

1st, That no province should obstruct or clog the passage of any ship, or goods coming from England through it, with any custom or duty; for that it plainly incommodes and discourages the King's subjects, and puts them upon making shift without the use of those goods, and so far hinders the consumption of our English product and manufacture, and thereby hurts trade and navigation; besides, it is unwarrantable by the laws of England.

2dly, That where the navigation act forbids it not, a coast trade from province to province should be allowed there, as it is here from county to county; by which means sloth will be punished with want, as it should always be, and industry will receive its just reward.

3dly, That one province should not protect the fugitives of another for crimes or debts, but that justice should be done according to the constitution of the several provinces.

4thly, It seems necessary to put Newfoundland, now growing considerable, under some government or other regulation as the Plantations are.

5thly, It may be worth the consideration of the state, whether this present peace may not be a proper season to build forts and citadels for security of the principal islands, in case of a future war.

6thly, Care should undoubtedly be taken, not to lay such heavy duties upon the West-India commodities, as may discourage industry, dispeople the islands, and, in process of time, perhaps, make the planters desperate. And here it may not be improper to take notice particularly of the high imposition laid upon refined sugars, imported hither upon a wrong notion of advancing our manufactures, whereas, in truth, it only turns to the account of about 50 families, (for the refiners of England are no more) and is greatly prejudicial, and a bar to the industry of at least 14,000 persons, which are about the number of those who inhabit our islands producing sugar.

7thly, It would very much conduce to the support and prosperity of the Sugar and Tobacco Plantations, to put the African Trade into some better order. So great a part of our foreign business arising from these colonies, they ought undoubtedly to have all due encouragement, and to be plentifully supplied, and at reasonable rates, with Negroes to meliorate and cultivate the land. The labour of these slaves is the principal foundation of our riches there; upon which account, we should take all probable measures to bring them to us at easy terms.

There are three ways of managing the African Trade; by a joint stock, by an open traffic, or by a regulated company; which of these will be the best is not very easy to determine; but in matters of this nature, experience is the surest guide we can have to follow.

And experience has taught us, that this trade has not been governed with good success, by a company with a joint stock. For it is alleged that they have not supplied the planters with such a plenty of Negroes as was requisite; that they forced them to accept of such a sort as they thought fit to bring; that the usual and fair rate should be, one head with another, from 16*l.* to 20*l.* per head, which, by ill supplying the market, they brought to 40*l.* and 45*l.* per head. That in their dealings they took bond and judgment of the planters, with an interest of 10*l.* per cent. executing their securities upon non-payment, by seizing the Plantations with the utmost rigour. And that these courses have almost depopulated the Southern Islands.

It must certainly be prudent in any trade, manufacture or business, to render the first material as cheap as possible; slaves are the first and most necessary material for planting; from whence follows, that all measures should be taken that may produce such a plenty of them, as may be an encouragement to the industrious planter. . . .

The Writer of these papers has seen a scheme for the general government of the Northward Plantations, which seems contrived with very good judgment; upon which account, he thought it not unseasonable to offer the heads of it here to public consideration.

1. That the colonies of Boston, Connecticut, Rhode Island, New York, both the New Jerseys, Pensylvania, Maryland, Virginia and Carolina, may be authorised to meet once a year, and oftner if need require, by their stated and appointed deputies, to debate and resolve of such measures as shall be most advisable, at any time, to take, for their public tranquility and safety.

2. That in order to it, two persons well qualified for understanding, sobriety and substance, be appointed by each province, as their representatives or deputies, which, in the whole, will make the congress to consist of 20 persons.

3. That the King's commissioner for that purpose especially to be appointed, should have the chair, and preside in the said congress.

4. That they should meet as near as conveniently may be to the most central colony, for the ease of the deputies.

5. Since that may, in all probability, be in New York, both because it is near the centre of the colonies, and for that it is a frontier, and the governor in the King's nomination; that governor to be likewise the King's high commissioner during the session, after the manner of Scotland.

6. That their business should be to hear and adjust all matters of complaint or difference between province and province: As 1st, Where persons quit their own province and go to another that they may avoid their just debts, though able to pay them. 2dly, Where offenders fly justice, or justice cannot well be had upon such offenders in the provinces that entertain them. 3dly, To prevent or redress injuries in point of commerce. 4thly, To consider of Ways and Means to support the union and safety of these provinces, against their common enemies: In which congress, the quotas of men and charges will be much easier and more equally allotted and proportioned, than it is possible for any establishment made here to do; for the provinces knowing their own condition and one another's, can debate that matter with more freedom and satisfaction, and better adjust and balance their affairs in all respects for their common safety.

7. That in times of war the King's high commissioner should be general or chief commander of the several quotas, upon service against the common enemy, as shall be thought advisable for the good and benefit of the whole.

This constitution has some resemblance with the court of the Amphictiones, which was a kind of council where the general affairs of Greece were debated; which if they could have preserved in its original purity, and to the first design of it, that country had not been so easy a conquest to the Romans. . . .

Societies of men are held together by the bands of religion and laws; and having said something upon the first of these heads, we shall now proceed to handle the second.

It will without doubt greatly conduce to the welfare of the Plantations, if their laws and politic institutions were revised and considered by disinterested persons, who should have no concern but to form them a constitution by which they may be well and wisely governed.

In order to this, it is submitted to better judgments, Whether a council of trade, or a council of the Indies, or some such like authority to be appointed especially for this purpose, should not inspect all the present laws and politic institutions of these countries, to the end that a true state of this affair may, at a convenient season, be laid before the parliament of England.

And we are humbly of opinion, that if such laws as may be thought prejudicial to them, or hurtful to this kingdom, were abrogated here; and if such of their old laws as shall be judged sound and wholesome; and if such new institutions as may be esteemed necessary for those parts, did receive some sanction from the legislative power of this kingdom, it would make our whole business in America more consistent, and fasten with surer ties those colonies to this nation.

What we propose is thus: That their first model of future government should be framed here; that afterwards they may have power to make for themselves such laws as they shall think needful for their better polity; and these laws thus enacted among them, not to be rescinded but by authority of parliament in England.

And this seems the more necessary, because heretofore many good laws formed there have been abrogated here, upon the false and corrupt suggestions of interested persons; besides, nothing can be more pernicious to a people, than levity in making and rescinding laws.

A model has been offered, in this Discourse, to public consideration, for erecting the 10 provinces or places that lie Northward, into one national assembly, where all things relating to their better government may be transacted.

And it is submitted to better judgments, Whether it would not greatly tend to the welfare and safety of those places, that laws not contrary to the law of England, enacted in such an assembly, should remain in force, till altered by the legislative power of this kingdom.

Without doubt, it would be a great incitement to their industry, and render them more pertinacious in their defence, upon any invasion which may happen, to find themselves a free people and governed by constitutions of their own making. . . .

With good government it is not improbable but that these colonies may become hereafter great nations; upon which account it seems of importance to give them, in their infancy, such politic institutions as may preserve them for many ages in wealth, peace and safety; and in order to this, the nearer they are brought to the model of the English government, will undoubtedly be the better.

And if they have governors from hence, or to be approved of

here, or of their own electing (according to their several charters) and if they are allowed a national assembly, it would give them the perfect enjoyment of our liberties and constitution.

The original institutions and laws of most countries are sound and good; but as vice prevails, they become obsolete and are forgotten; from whence grow those diseases in the body politic that require the ablest physicians.

By how much a government swerves from its first institution, by so much it has a wrong bent; it should therefore be the care of those to whom the rule and direction of these places is committed, to keep them as much as possible to their original institution.

In the model here proposed, the governors will of course be vested with all the powers necessary for the safety and protection of the whole; and those assemblies may have certain rights which will be as well an ease and safeguard to the governors, as beneficial to the people; but if either part invades the other, it must throw the public into dangerous convulsions.

That government is happy where the bounds between the chief power and the people are so wisely laid out and fixed, that no encroachments can be easily apprehended; for the disputes and quarrels concerning these bounds and limits have always been the chief gain and harvest of bad and designing men, and the field in which they exercise those wicked arts that so often embroil a country. . . .

B. "A Free Constitution of Government in the Plantations"

IN CONTRAST to English writers like Davenant, colonials who were concerned about the problems of the empire were inclined to put less emphasis upon the necessity for keeping the colonies dependent than upon protecting their rights and interests from the greed or maladministration of a corrupt governor or the misinformed decisions of officials in Britain. That the chief prerequisite for the establishment of a well-regulated and smoothly functioning empire was "the setling [of] a free Constitution of Government in the Plantations" in which the Crown would "not . . . have a more absolute Power in the Plantations than in England" was argued forcefully by an anonymous Virginian in An Essay upon the Government of the English Plantations on the Continent of America, published in London in 1701 as an answer to Davenant's essay on the plantation trade, and reprinted in part below.

SOURCE: Louis B. Wright (ed.), An Essay upon the Government of the English Plantations on the Continent of America (1701):

An Anonymous Virginian's Proposals for Liberty under the British Crown, with Two Memoranda by William Byrd (San Marino, Calif.: Huntington Library, 1945), pp 15–21, 23–24, 36–41.

As of late many Controversies have arisen in the *English* Nation; so 'tis observable, that the two great Topicks of Trade and Plantations have had their Parts in the Dispute; and indeed it must be confess'd, that (considering the present Circumstances of the World) they are of the greatest importance to all Nations, but more especially the *English*.

Almost all that hath been hitherto written concerning the Plantations hath had a more peculiar Relation of their Trade, and accordingly the several Advocates either for their Freedom, or binding them to a more strict Dependance upon the Crown of *England*, have framed their Arguments so as they thought might best answer those Purposes; from whence it may be very naturally inferr'd, that some By Ends of their own have had a great Influence over many of them, and that private Interest was the great *Diana* for which they contested.

THE DESIGN OF THESE PAPERS

The Design of these Papers is not to treat of the Trade, but the Government of the Plantations; not how to make them great, and rich, by an open free Traffick, but happy, by a Just and Equal Government; that they may enjoy their Obscurity, and the poor way of living which Nature is pleased to afford them out of the Earth, in Peace; and be protected in the Possession thereof, by their lawful Mother *England*.

I am sensible the *English* Plantations may be rendred very serviceable and beneficial to their Mother Kingdom, and I do not in the least doubt she will make the best Advantage of them she can; 'tis what others would do if they were in her place, and therefore I shall not complain of any Hardships in Trade, neither shall it be mentioned but as it comes in the way, in pursuit of the main Design I have laid down.

The Countries under the *English* Government on the Continent of *America* are healthy and fertile, and very well situate both for Pleasure and Profit, especially *Virginia* and *Maryland*, which, as they are the best and most advantagious to the Crown of *England*;

so likewise is the Air and Climate of them most agreeable to the *English* Constitutions of Body, the Land richest, the Rivers most commodious, and naturally the whole Countries far excelling any part of the Continent either on the North or South of them.

The chiefest Thing wanting to make the Inhabitants of these Plantations happy, is a good Constitution of Government; and it seems strange, that so little care hath been heretofore taken of that, since it could not be any Prejudice, but of great Advantage even to *England* it self, as perhaps may appear by what shall be offered hereafter.

'Tis true, many Propositions have been made for regulating the Governments of particular Plantations, several of which are now extant; but being mostly calculated by Persons who seem to be biassed by Interest, Prejudice, Revenge, Ambition, or other private Ends I dare not rely on them: Some there are which I shall make bold to use some Parts of, as I find them for my Purpose.

OBJECTIONS AGAINST THIS DISCOURSE

But before I proceed further, it is necessary to answer some Objections that may be made against my self, and the Work I am going about.

It hath been alledged by some that the Plantations are prejudicial to *England*; but this is already so well answered by Sir *J. Child* in his New Discourse of Trade, from Page 178, to Page 216, by the Author [Charles Davenant] of the *Essay upon Ways and Means*, in his Discourses on the Publick Revenues and the Trade of *England*, Part II. p. 193, to 209. and several other Writings which have been Published, that I cannot think it needful to say any thing more about it.

The Objections I shall take notice of, are these following:

1. It may be objected, that I being an Inhabitant of the Plantations, may probably be too much biassed to their Interest, and therefore am not to be relied on.

2. That the Plantation Governments are already setled well enough; and it may be dangerous to make any great Alterations in them.

3. That it is necessary the King should be more Absolute in the Plantations than he is in *England:* And consequently,

4. That the setling a free Constitution of Government in the Plantations will be prejudicial to the King's Service.

ANSWER TO THOSE OBJECTIONS

In answer to all which, I beg leave to offer the following Considerations.

1. That, let the Author be what he will, the most material Thing to be respected, is the good or evil Tendency of the Work. If his Majesty's Service seems chiefly aimed at, and no private Interest mixed with it, then I hope that Objection is removed: And for my self, I can with a great deal of Truth and Sincerity affirm, that I have not the least Thought or Design of any thing but his Majesty's Interest and Service, and therein of the Good of all his Subjects in general; but whether the Means I shall propose, may be any wise conducive to those Ends, is humbly submitted to those who have the Honour to be intrusted with the Charge of those Affairs.

THE PLANTATION GOVERNMENTS NEVER WELL SETLED

2. If the Governments of the Plantations are already well setled, there needs not any Alteration, (that, I think, every good Man will grant:) But if upon inquiry, it appears, that none of them have ever been well setled; that the present Method of managing them is inconvenient and prejudicial; and that much better Ways may be found: If, I say, these things can be shewn, why should they not be received: If, being considered, they are not approved, they may be rejected, no Alteration will be made, nor any harm done; but rather Good: For my Attempt may set some better Hand to work on the same Subject; and being instructed by others Observations on my Errors, may be more capable to make Amendments: But this, I think, may be safely said, that if any Alterations in the Government of the Plantations are necessary, they may be much more easily done now they are in their Infancy, than hereafter when they grow more populous, and the Evils have taken deeper Root, and are more interwoven with the Laws and Constitutions of the several Colonies.

THE KING OUGHT NOT TO HAVE A MORE ABSOLUTE POWER IN THE PLANTATIONS THAN IN England

3. It may perhaps be said that it is necessary the King should have a more absolute Power in the Plantations than he hath in

England. I know this hath been said, and pretended to be asserted by Argument; and to make it more passable, it hath been framed into a sort of a *Syllogism,* thus: All such *Kingdoms, Principalities, Dominions,* &c. *as are dependent on the Crown of* England, *and are not a Part of the Empire of the King of* England, *are subject to such Laws as the King is pleased to impose on them; But the* English *Plantations in* America *are dependent on the Crown of* England, *and are not part of the Empire of the King of* England: Ergo, *they are subject to such Laws as the King shall please to impose.* Now it is observable, that the main Stress of this Matter depends upon the Distinction between the *Crown of* England, and the *Empire of the King of* England: And if there is no such Distinction (as possibly there may not) the whole falls to Ground: But if there be such a Distinction, then the clear Tendency of the Argument, is to lay the Plantations intirely at the King's Feet, for him to do what he pleases with them; and the Parliament are not at all concerned in the Business, only upon sufferance. This I take to be the clear Consequence of the Argument, which no King ever yet pretended to; and for which the Lords and Commons of *England* are very much obliged to the Inventer.

But tho' the King's Right and Prerogative are pretended in the Argument, there were other Reasons for inventing it; and that will appear, if it be remembered that it was first made use of upon the following Occasion. In former times a certain Gentleman was made Governour of one of the *English* Plantations, and had a large Commission for his Office, which he put in Execution after such a manner, that the People were not able to forbear shewing the highest Resentments of such Usage; and at last had recourse to Arms.

And hereupon to vindicate the Governour's Proceedings, it was thought necessary to start this Argument of the King's absolute Power in the Plantations, thereby to lay the Odium of an ill Governour's wicked Actions upon the King.

By the ancient known Laws of the Land the King's Power is sufficient to make himself a great Prince, and his Subjects a happy People; and those very Men that raise these strange Arguments for Absolute Power do not aim at the King's Service in it: But they know, that if they make the King Absolute, his Lieutenant will be so of course; and that is their chief Design.

Thus the King's Power is pretended to be made great, whilst in reality his Interest is destroyed, and so is the Interest of England too: for these are the true Reasons that many People who are poor and miserable at home, will not come to the Plantations because they know they shall be ill used.

From what is said, I think it appears very plain, that it is not for the Interest or Service either of the King or Kingdom of England, that the Plantations should be under an unlimited Government: the true Interest of England, is to have the Plantations cherished, and the poor People encouraged to come hither, every Man here being of great Value to England, and most of those that come, are not able to do much good at home.

Whatever Power the King hath in the Plantations must be executed by his Lieutenants: and if it should so happen that the King be mistaken in the Man, and send one who would aim more at his own Interest than the King's Service; and by Extortion, Bribery, and other the like Practices (too often complained of in some Places) should so distract the People, that they make Commotions or Insurrections against him: The King cannot possibly know this till it is too late; and then he will be obliged to inflict the severest Punishments upon some of the most considerable Offenders, to the Ruin of them and their Families, who otherwise might have done his Majesty good Service.

Neither is this all; for by such Commotions the Product of one Year at least will be lost in that Colony where they happen, which will be greater Prejudice to England than the best Governour will ever be able to make amends for; the Loss of the Tobacco made in one Year in Virginia, considering the Customs and the Merchants Damage, by their shipping and Stock being unimployed, will amount to at least £500,000 prejudice to the King and Kingdom of England.

I know it will be said, that all this proceeds either from groundless Jealousies of I know not what Dangers to happen, no one knows when; or else, that I am very much prejudiced against some of the present Governours of the Plantations; to which I answer: That it is not to be supposed such things should happen every Day; but since they have been heretofore, it is probable, they may be again, and the Consequence being so very dangerous, the more Reason there is to endeavour the Prevention of them: And for the other Imputation, I can with a great deal of Truth say, that I have the Honour of being known but to two of the King's Governours, and for both of them, I have the most profound Respect and Regard imaginable; nor can I believe that either of them will find fault with me for endeavouring to prevent those male-Administrations in others, of which they will never be guilty themselves.

A Free Constitution of Government
in the Plantations Not Prejudicial
to the King's Service

4. The other Objection to this Work is, That the setling a free Constitution of Government in the Plantations may be prejudicial to the King's Service. To this I answer, That by a free Constitution of Government, I mean, that the Inhabitants of the Plantations may enjoy their Liberties and Estates, and have Justice equally and impartially administred unto them; and that it should not be in the power of any Governour to prevent this. Now by enjoying Liberty, I understand, the Liberty of their Persons being free from Arbitrary, illegal Imprisonments; not that they should have great Liberties of Trade, or any other Liberties or Priviledges, that may be thought prejudicial to the King or Kingdom of *England*; for my Design is not to complain of our Subjection, or any thing of that Nature; but to shew as well as I can, what may be done for the Interest and Service both of *England* and the Plantations.

It is no Advantage to the King, that his Governours should have it in their Power to gripe and squeeze the People in the Plantations, nor is it ever done, for any other Reason, than their own private Gain. I have often heard Complaints made, that the Governours and their Officers and Creatures, have been guilty of ill things to raise Estates for themselves, or to gratify their own Revenge, or some other Passion; but I never heard, that any of the Plantations were oppressed to raise Money for the King's Service, and indeed I think it is past Dispute, that the King's and Plantations Interest is the same, and that those who pretend, the King hath, or ought to have an unlimited Power in the Plantations, are a sort of People, whose Designs make their Interests run counter to that both of the King and Plantations.

Thus having briefly answered those Objections which perhaps may be made to what I shall offer: I proceed to the main Design, which is to shew several things, which I just beg leave to say, I conceive are amiss, and to propose some Methods for redressing those Grievances. . . .

Grievances on Account of Their Laws

The Inconveniences the Plantations labour under, on Account of their Laws, are very many.

It is a great Unhappiness, that no one can tell what is Law, and what is not, in the Plantations; some hold that the Law of *England* is chiefly to be respected, and where that is deficient, the Laws of the several Colonies are to take place; others are of Opinion, that the Laws of the Colonies are to take first place, and that the Law of *England* is of force only where they are silent; others there are, who contend for the Laws of the Colonies, in Conjunction with those that were in force in *England* at the first Settlement of the Colony, and lay down that as the measure of our Obedience, alleging, that we are not bound to observe any late Acts of Parliament made in *England*, except such only where the Reason of the Law is the same here, that it is in *England*; but this leaving too great a Latitude to the Judge; some others hold that no late Acts of the Parliament of *England* do bind the Plantations, but those only, wherein the Plantations are particularly named. Thus are we left in the dark, in one of the most considerable Points of our Rights; and the Case being so doubtful, we are too often obliged to depend upon the Crooked Cord of a Judge's Discretion, in Matters of the greatest Moment and Value.

Of late Years great Doubts have been raised, how far the Legislative Authority is in the Assemblies of the several Colonies; whether they have Power to make certain Acts or Ordinances in the nature of by-Laws only; or, whether they can make Acts of Attainder, Naturalization, for setling or disposing of Titles to Lands within their own Jurisdiction, and other things of the like Nature; and where Necessity requires, make such Acts as best suit the Circumstances and Constitution of the Country, even tho' in some Particulars, they plainly differ from the Laws of *England*.

And as there have been Doubts made concerning the Enacting of Laws with us, so likewise there have been great Controversies concerning the Repeal of Laws made here: The Assemblies have held, that when any Law made by them, and not assented to by the King in *England* is repealed by them; such Repeal doth intirely annul and abrogate, and even (as it were) annihilate the former Law, as if it never had been made, and that it cannot by any means be revived, but by the same Power that at first enacted it, which was the Assembly; but the Governours have held, that tho' the King hath not assented to the first, yet he hath the Liberty of refusing his Assent to the repealing Law, and by Proclamation may repeal that, and then the other is revived of course: This Dispute, and others of the like Nature, ran very high in the late Reigns.

It is also to be observed as a great Defect, that no one of these Colonies on the Continent, have any tolerable Body of Laws; all of them have some sort of Laws or other; but there is not any such thing amongst them all, as a regular Constitution of Government, and good Laws for Directions of the several Officers, and other Persons therein, with suitable Penalties to enforce Obedience to them.

This seems to have been a Fault in the Beginning; for then it was put into bad Hands, and hath been little mended since: One notorious Instance may be given in *Virginia*. This Colony was at first given for the Encouragement of it to a Company of Adventurers, who by Charter from King *James* the first, were constituted a Corporation, and they set up a sort of Government here, the Chief Magistrates whereof were called Governours and Council; and they (I suppose) as the chief Members of the Corporation, constituted the highest Court of Judicature; afterwards this Countrey was taken into the King's Hands, and the same Constitution of Governor and Council remained; and they to this Day continue to be the highest Court of Judicature in the Countrey; tho' we have no Law to establish them as such, neither have they ever had any Commission for that purpose, and till *April* 1699, were never sworn to do Justice, but being made Counsellors, they took their Places as Judges of Course.

From hence it may be observ'd, that no great Stress is to be laid on any Argument against Alterations in the Plantations, barely because Changes may be dangerous, for (it seems) a Regular Settlement hath never yet been made, and therefore 'tis time to be done now. . . .

Grievances with Relation to the Governours

The next concerning Governours is a tender Point, and must be touched with clean Hands; and when I profess that I do not design to expose any particular Person now in Office, I hope Liberty may be allowed me, to remark some Grievances that the Plantations have, and may have Cause to complain of, if they knew where.

And herein I shall but lightly mention some things, part of which at least, perhaps it may be necessary to reform hereafter, not accusing any Person for what is past.

Some Governours either through Weakness or Prejudice, have contributed very much to raise Factions in the Colonies under their Command, by making use of, and encouraging some one particular Sort or Sett of Men, and rejecting all others, and these Favourites being oftentimes of mean Education and base Spirits, cannot bear their good Fortunes, but thinking absolute Command only is their Province, either for private Interest, or to gratifie their Ambition, Revenge, or some other Passion, they hardly ever fail to run all Things into Confusion; and of these Actions by Favourites, Instances are not wanting.

The King's Governours in the Plantations either have, or pretend to have very large Powers within their Provinces, which together with the Trusts reposed in them, of disposing of all Places of Honour and Profit, and of being chief Judges in the Supream Courts of Judicature, (as they are in many Places, if not all) render them so absolute, that it is almost impossible to lay any sort of Restraint upon them.

On the other side, in some of the Proprieties, the Hands of the Government are so feeble, that they cannot protect themselves against the Insolencies of the Common People, which makes them very subject to Anarchy and Confusion.

The chief End of many Governours coming to the Plantations, having been to get Estates for themselves, very unwarrantable Methods have sometimes been made use of to compass those Ends, as by engrossing several Offices into their own Hands, selling them or letting them out at a yearly Rent of such a part of the Profits, and also by Extortion and Presents, (or Bribery) these things have been heretofore, and in ill Times may be done again.

And here I must beg Leave to say, that I am of Opinion, the Court of England hath hitherto gone upon wrong Principles, in appointing Governours of the Plantations; for those Places have been generally given as the last Rewards for past Services, and they expecting nothing after that, were almost necessitated, then to make Provision for their whole Lives, whereby they were in a manner forced upon such Methods (whether good or evil) as would compass those Ends.

Another very considerable difficulty the Plantations lie under from their Governours, is, that there is no way left to represent their evil Treatment to the King; for nothing of that Nature can be done without Money, no Money can be had without an Assembly, and the Governour always hath a Negative in their Proceedings, and not only so, but if he fears any thing of that Nature, he can let alone calling one, or (being called) can dissolve them at pleasure.

KING UNACQUAINTED WITH THE TRUE STATE OF THE PLANTATIONS

But the last and greatest Unhappiness the Plantations labour under, is, that the King and Court of *England* are altogether Strangers to the true State of Affairs in *America*, for that is the true Cause why their Grievances have not been long since redress'd.

The present Establishment of the Lords Commissioners for Trade and Plantations is very necessary and expedient for that Purpose, and perhaps may be rendred much more so, but they being Strangers to the Affairs in these Parts, are too often obliged to depend on the Relation of others who pretend to be better acquainted. Misrepresentations in those Cases may be very dangerous, and cannot well be prevented, there not being as yet any Method setled for them to gain certain Information of the true State of the Plantations.

REMEDIES FOR THE AFOREMENTIONED GRIEVANCES

Hitherto I have taken notice of some of the most material Inconveniencies attending these Plantations: Now I must beg Leave to offer such Remedies to Consideration as with Submission I conceive may prevent the like Grievances for the future. . . .

REMEDIES FOR THE GRIEVANCES RELATING TO THE LAWS

. . . For remedying of the Grievances mentioned under the Head of Laws, I humbly propose,

1. That some Rule be established, to know what Laws the Plantations are to be subject to, and particularly, how far the late Acts of Parliament do affect them, where they are not expressly mentioned.

LEGISLATURE

2. That it be agreed how far the Legislature is in their Assemblies; whether they have Power of Naturalization, Attainders of Treason, Illegitimating of Heirs, cutting off Intails, settling Titles

to Lands, and other things of that nature; and whether they may make Laws disagreable to the Laws of *England*, in such Cases, where the Circumstances of the Places are vastly different, as concerning Plantations, Waste, the Church, &c.

Courts of Judicature

3. That a good Constitution of Courts of Judicature be established in the several Plantations, as shall be most agreeable to their respective Forms of Government, and other Circumstances.

That the Judges of the Supream Courts in every Province hold their Offices *quam diu se bene gesserint*, and that Provision be made to ascertain what shall be adjudged Misbehaviour in them, or at least, that care be taken, that it be not absolutely in the Governour's Breast, to displace any Judge at pleasure, without shewing his Reasons for the same, together with the Judge's Answer thereto.

That the last Resort of Justice may not be to the Chief Governours and Council here, and thence to the King and Council in *England*, as is now practised in most places; but that from the Judges commissionated as aforesaid, an Appeal directly to *England* may be allowed to such People as think themselves injured, in any Sum exceeding the Value of five hundred Pounds *Sterl*.

Lands to be Confirmed by the King

4. That in the King's Colonies, his Majesty would be graciously pleased to confirm all Lands to the several Possessors, (where any privat Persons Interest is not concerned) as was done by King *Charles* the second in his Charter to *Virginia*, of which also Care should be taken, that it be not infringed, as heretofore it hath been.

Tenants of the Proprietors to Be Secured in Their Lands

And that by some Law for that purpose, good and wholsom Provisions be made, for the setling and adjusting the Inhabitants Titles to those Lands they hold of Proprietors, that those People may not be continually obliged to a servile Dependance upon their Landlords, and thereby be sometimes necessitated either to behave themselves disrespectively and disobediently to the Governour, acting by the King's Authority there, or to be in danger of losing their Lands, being forced to pay extravagant Fines for Confirmation of their Titles, or of being some other way liable to suffer under the Proprietors, or their Agents Displeasure. . . .

C. The Preservation of Existing Colonial Privileges

SOME COLONIALS, like the anonymous Virginian whose essay appears above, thought that the constitutions of the colonies ought to be over-hauled in order to guarantee the colonists the same rights and liberties as Englishmen. Others, especially in the charter colonies where the in-habitants already enjoyed wide privileges, wanted the existing system unchanged. This was the point of view of Jeremiah Dummer in A De-fence of the New-England Charters. Written in 1712–13 in opposition to the efforts of the Board of Trade to obtain a bill to vacate the colonial charters, but not published until 1721, this pamphlet argued strongly for the maintenance of the commercial traditions on which the empire had originally been based. Dummer contended that there was a close corre-lation between the amount of freedom a people had on one hand and the extent and rate of their commercial development and capacity to defend themselves on the other. Because the commercial growth of the colonies ultimately benefited Great Britain, he argued, the interests of the mother country could best be served by giving the colonies as much freedom as possible and, especially, by preserving their traditional "Priv-ileges inviolate."

SOURCE: Jeremiah Dummer, A Defence of the New-England Charters (London, 1721), pp. 60–73.

There is one Thing more I have heard often urg'd against the Charter Colonies, and indeed 'tis what one meets with from People of all Conditions and Qualities, tho' with due respect to their better Judgments, I can see neither Reason nor Colour for it. 'Tis said, that their encreasing Numbers and Wealth join'd to their great Distance from Britain will give them an Opportunity in the Course of some Years to throw off their Dependance on the Nation, and declare themselves a free State, if not curb'd in Time by being made entirely subject to the Crown. Whereas in Truth there's no Body tho' but little acquainted with these or any of the Northern Plantations, who does not know and confess, that their Poverty and the declining State of their Trade is so great at present, that there's far more Danger of their sinking, without some extraordinary Support from the Crown, than of their ever revolting from it. So that I may say without being ludicrous, that it would not be more absurd to place two of His Majesty's Beef-Eaters to watch an Infant in the Cradle that it don't rise and cut its Father's Throat, than to guard these weak Infant Colonies to prevent their shaking off the *British* Yoke. Besides, they are so distinct from one another in their Forms of Government, in their Religious Rites, in their Emulation of Trade, and consequently in their Affections, that they can never be suppos'd to unite in so dangerous an Enterprize. It is for this Reason I have often wondered to hear some Great Men profess their Belief of the Feasibleness of it, and the Probability of it's some Time or other actually coming to pass, who yet with the same Breath advise that all the Governments on the Continent be form'd into one, by being brought under one Vice-Roy, and into one Assembly. For surely if we in earnest believ'd that there was or would be hereafter a Disposition in the Provinces to Rebel and declare themselves Independent, it would be good Policy to keep them disunited; because if it were possible they could contrive so wild and rash an Undertaking, yet they would not be hardy enough to put it in Execution, unless they could first strengthen themselves by a Confederacy of all the Parts.

But to return from this short Digression: Our Neighbours of *Holland*, who are allow'd to be a wise State, did not entertain these Jealousies of their Subjects in *India*, when they were a young and growing Plantation, nor do they even now when they are a potent and flourishing People. Had they done so, and in consequence of it restrain'd and check'd them, *Holland* would not at this Day have drawn such immense Riches from that Part of the World, and furnish'd all *Europe* with *Indian* Commodities. And yet what Reason can be assign'd for the Jealousies we entertain of our Colonies, which the *Dutch* have not, and far stronger with respect to their *Batavian* Subjects? If the Distance be urg'd as an Argument, every body knows that *New-England* is but a thousand Leagues from the *British* Shore, but the *Dutch* must run eight Times that Ground from *Amsterdam* before they arrive at *Batavia*. Or if the Number and Power of the Inhabitants should give any Umbrage, this is an Article which with respect to *Batavia* won't admit of the most distant Comparison. The General of that Place maintains a Port superiour to many Sovereign Princes in *Europe*, and has all the King's in *Java* in a manner Tributary to him. He has 3000 standing *European* Troops, not reckoning the Natives; and all the *Dutch* Inhabitants live in that flowing Wealth and Plenty which makes *Batavia* look like the Capital of a Great and Mighty Empire. But do the States of *Holland* look on this their prosperous

Condition with envious or jealous Eyes? Just the reverse; they do every Thing in their Power still to promote and advance it, well knowing their foreign Plantations can't thrive, but they must receive the Benefit of it themselves, and therefore justly esteem the Wealth of their Subjects Abroad as their own Riches. Why then should not *Great-Britain* form the same Judgment, and proceed by the like Measures in regard to her *American* Dominions, from whence she receives the greatest Advantages? It were no difficult Task to prove that *London* has risen out of the Plantations, and not out of *England*. 'Tis to them we owe our vast Fleets of Merchant Ships, and consequently the Increase of our Seamen, and Improvement of our Navigation. 'Tis their Tobacco, Sugar, Fish, Oil, Logwood and other Commodities, which have enabled us to support our Trade in *Europe*, to bring the Ballance of some Countries in our Favour, which would otherwise be against us, and to make the Figure we do at presemt, and have done for near a Century past, in all Parts of the commercial World.

The Mother Kingdom must therefore needs rejoyce in the Prosperity of every one of her Colonies, because it is her own Prosperity. The Fable of the Belly and Members illustrates this Argument. It would be unreasonable for the Belly to grudge the Labour of digesting the Food and dispersing the Blood and Juices to the extream Parts, seeing they return purify'd and exalted in the Circulation. There's a close Analogy between the Natural Body and the Body Politick; as in the one, a Finger can't ake, but the Whole feels it, so in the other the remotest Plantation can't decay, but the Nation must suffer with it.

If it be said that the Charter Colonies are not so valuable as some of the rest, I answer, that the Inhabitants have the more need of their Charters to make them amends; for People must have some Incouragement to sit down on a cold and barren Soil. Yet I have shown before that they are many ways of great Use and Advantage to the Crown; to which I add, that they will be more so than ever in a few Years, to strengthen the *British* Empire in *America* against the formidable Settlement of *Loisiana*, which for some Years past has bin carry'd on by the *French* with great Expence, and with the utmost Vigour and Application. This Country was given by the late *French* King to the *Sieur Croizat*, but is now (as every Body knows) in the famous *Missisippi* Company, who have a Fund of a Hundred Millions of Livres for this very Purpose, and are daily sending over a vast Number of People for Tillage, as well as all sorts of Artificers, with proper Materials for making a Settlement. It is situate on the great River of *Mississippi*, and by help of the superiour Lakes and Rivers, on some of which the *French* have already erected Fortresses, a Communication may be made between *New-France* and the Gulph of *Mexico*, which indeed was the very Scheme of the *French* Court in projecting this Enterprize, as is expresly declar'd in the Preamble to *Croizat's* Patent. 'Tis easy then to see that the *French* will be hereby enabled to draw a Line, and in Time have a Chain of Towns on the Back of all our Colonies from the Borders of *Cape-Breton* to the westermost Part of *Carolina*. And what *Briton* can consider this without being in Pain for the Fate of our Provinces in future Times? Especially since we know that the *Illinois* and other Warlike *Indian* Nations lye near the *French*, and for many Reasons, which it would be too much a Digression to recount here, are devoted to their Interest, and by consequence ready at all Times to joyn their Forces in any Attempt against us.

This being the Case, I think with humble Submission, it is very preposterous to amuse ourselves with vain, imaginary Prospects of what is scarce possible to come to pass, and neglect doing what is absolutely necessary; I mean, the enlarging and supporting our Provinces, that they may be able to defend themselves against being one Day totally extirpated by a Foreign Power. And then I have only to suggest an old approv'd Maxim, *That every Thing is best preserv'd by the same Principles by which it was at first form'd*, and consequently the best Method of encouraging the Charter Colonies is, to preserve their Privileges inviolate, without which they had never bin setled.

Another Proposition I advanced was, That if these Governments should be adjudg'd to have forfeited their Charters back to the Crown, yet it is not the true Interest of the Crown to resume them.

It is a generally receiv'd Opinion, that the People in the Plantations have an Interest distinct from that of the Crown; when it is supposed at the same time, that the Interest of the Governours, they being the King's Representatives, is one with the Crown; and from these Premises it is concluded, that there can't be too much Power given to the Governours or too little to the People. Whereas, with humble Submission, I conceive this to be a very wrong Judgment, and that the Reverse of it is true. The only Interest of the People is to thrive and flourish in their Trade, which is the true Interest of the Crown and Nation, because they reap the Profit of it. When on the other Hand, the View that Governours generally have is private Gain, which being too often acquir'd by discouraging and oppressing Trade, is not only an Interest distinct from that of the Crown, but extreamly prejudicial to it. The Trade of a young Plantation is like a tender Plant, and should be cherish'd with the fondest Care; but if instead of that, it meets with the rough Hand of Oppression, it will soon die. The proper Nursery for this Plant is a free Government, where the Laws are sacred, Property secure, and Justice not only impartially, but expeditiously distributed. For to what purpose shall the Merchant expose his Estate to the Dangers of the Sea, the Enemy, and many more Accidents, if after all he can't save it at Home from Rapine and Violence?

As this is evident, so is it that whatever injures the Trade of the Plantations, must in Proportion affect *Great-Britain*, the source and Center of their Commerce; from whence they have their Manufactures, whither they make their Returns, and where all their Superlucration is lodg'd. The Blow then may strike the Colonies first, but it comes Home at last, and falls heaviest on our selves.

That Governours are apt to abuse their Power and grow rich by Oppression, Experience shows us. We have seen not many Years since, some Governours seiz'd by their injur'd People, and sent Prisoners to *Whitehall*, there to answer for their Offences. Others have fallen Victims on the Spot, not to the Fury of a Faction or a Rabble, but to the Resentment of the whole Body of the People, rising as one Man to revenge their Wrongs. Others, after being recall'd, have bin prosecuted at the *King's-Bench Bar*, pursuant to an Act of Parliament made in the Reign of the late King *William*, whereby it is provided, That Governours shall be impleadable at Home for any Injuries done in their Governments Abroad. We have had more than one flagrant Instance of this very lately, where Governours have bin convicted and censur'd not so properly for oppressing, as for a direct plundering their People, and such other Acts of Mis-rule and lawless Power, as one would not have thought it possible they should have committed if Experience had not shown it to be more than possible.

I don't however intend by what is here said, to reproach our own Nation, as if we were greater Sinners than others, or to reflect on the present Times, as if they were worse than the former. I know that the same Abuses have bin practis'd in every Age as well as this, and in Foreign Colonies as well as our own. The ancient *Romans* were as brave and as vertuous a People as any in the World, and yet their Proconsuls or Governours were very guilty in this respect. Their Corruption was so notorious as to be distinguish'd by the Name of *Crimen Repetundarum*, a Phrase not us'd in any other Meaning, and deriv'd from the Obligation which the *Roman* Senate laid on their Governours to make Restitution. . . .

Indeed it can hardly be expected but these Corruptions must happen, when one considers that few Gentlemen will cross the Seas for a Government, whose Circumstances are not a little streight at Home, and that they know by how slight and uncertain a Tenure they hold their Commissions; from whence they wisely conclude, that no Time is to be lost. And then for the Account to be rendred at Home, that is not thought of at so great a Distance, for *Procul a Jove, procul a Fulmine*.

To enlarge then the Power of Governours, is to give them greater Power to oppress; and to vacate the Charters is to enlarge their Power, the Government in that Case of Course devolving upon them; as we see in those Plantations which never had any Charters, but are immediately dependent on the Crown. There they have, in a manner, the intire Legislative and Executive Powers, or at least so great an Influence on the constituent Parts of the Former, as leaves them little more than Nominal Sharers, serving rather as Screens to the Governour than a Defence to the People. The Militia is absolutely vested in the Governours, which influences all Elections of Representatives: They appoint Judges, Justices, Sheriffs and other Civil Officers with the Consent, it's said indeed, of the Council; but that such Consent voluntary or involuntary will ever be refus'd, seems too much to be expected, if we consider that altho' the Governours do not indeed appoint the Council, yet they recommend proper Persons to the King; and it may be supposed, that a Gentleman who is intrusted with the chief Command of a Province and is actually on the Spot, will be thought the best Judge who are fit to serve, and therefore his Recommendations will almost always prevail. Besides, if there be a Turn to serve, or an Emergency real or imaginary, and any of the Members should be so refractory as not to give into his Measures with an implicit Faith, the Governour can suspend as many of them as he pleases; and when he has reduc'd the board under a Number limited in his Instructions, he can then fill it up to that

Number *instanter* with whom he pleases; and who will they be, may we presume, but such as are passively obedient to his Will? And too many such there are to be found in all Colonies so constituted, who are content to be *sadled* themselves, provided they may *ride* others under the *chief Rider*. I must farther observe, that where there are no Charters, there are Courts of Equity establish'd, in which the Governour is always Chancellor, and for the most part Chief-Justice, and Ordinary at the same time; which puts the Estates, Lives and Liberties of the Inhabitants, saving the Liberty of Appeal at Home, intirely in his Disposal; and even an Appeal in all Cases under a considerable Sum, in all Cases of the ordinary Jurisdiction, and in all Cases Capital, is either disallow'd by his Instructions, or wholly in the Governour's Breast to allow or not.

The Sum of my Argument is, That the Benefit which *Great-Britain* receives from the Plantations, arises from their Commerce: That Oppression is the most opposite Thing in the World to Commerce, and the most destructive Enemy it can have: That Governours have in all Times, and in all Countries, bin too much inclin'd to oppress: And consequently, it cannot be the Interest of the Nation to increase their Power, and lessen the Liberties of the People. I am so sanguine in this Opinion, that I really think it would be for the Service of the Crown and Nation to incorporate those Governments which have no Charters, rather than Disfranchize those that have.

D. *"The Intire Absolute and Immediate Dependancy" of the Colonies*

THE BOARD of Trade's view on how the imperial-colonial relationship ought to be restructured to secure the most effective imperial system could scarcely have been more different from that of Jeremiah Dummer. In its report on the state of the colonies, submitted to the Crown on September 8, 1721, it discussed at length the trade and government of all of the continental colonies and submitted recommendations "for securing, improving and enlarging your Majesty's Dominions in America." Calling for improvements in colonial defenses, better relations with the Indians, and, most important, wholesale political reforms designed "to secure by all possible means the intire absolute and immediate dependancy" of the colonies, only a few of these recommendations were put into effect. But they stand as the most explicit and comprehensive single statement of the Board's conception of colonial problems and how to meet them. The recommendations are reprinted in full below.

SOURCE: Sainsbury, *et al.* (eds.), *Calendar of State Papers, Colonial, 1720–1721*, 408, 440–449.

In obedience to your Majesty's commands, we have prepared the following state of your Majesty's Plantations on the Continent of America; wherein we have distinguished their respective situations, Governments, strengths and trade, and have observed of what importance their commerce is to Great Britain, whereunto having added an account of the French settlements, and of the encroachments they have made in your Majesty's colonies in those parts; we have humbly proposed such methods, as may best prevent the increase of an evil, which, if not timely prevented, may prove destructive to your Majesty's interest; and have likewise offered such considerations, as, in our opinion, may contribute to the improving and enlarging your Majesty's dominions in America. . . .

Considerations for securing, improving and enlarging your Majesty's Dominions in America.

Having laid before your Majesty the state of your Plantations on the Continent, *etc.*, what further remains is, that we should humbly offer to your Majesty's consideration such methods as have occurred to us, for securing improving and enlarging so valuable a possession as that of your Majesty's Dominions in America; which we conceive might most effectually be done: 1st. By taking the necessary precautions to prevent the incroachments of the French, or of any other European nation. 2nd. By cultivating a good understanding with the native Indians. And lastly by putting the Government of the Plantations upon a better foot. In order therefore to secure your Majesty's Colonies from the encoachments of their European neighbours in America; whereof we receive daily complaints from the several governors on the Continent; it will be highly necessary to begin for fortifying ye two extremities to the north and south. This will appear ye more necessary when it shall be considered how much the French have strengthen'd their settlements in the neighbourhood of Nova Scotia and Carolina, whilst your Majesty's subjects either thro' neglect or misfortune, are much weaker in these two provinces, than any other part of America. It has been already observed that there are not above two British families in all Nova Scotia besides the garrison of Annapolis consisting of at present only six companies of 34 men each, but there are still near 3000 French inhabitants remaining in this Province, who contrary to the Treaty of Utrecht refuse to take the Oaths of Allegiance to your Majesty, and in combination with their countrimen at Cape Breton, are daily instigating ye native Indians not only to commit insults upon your Majesty's subjects fishing upon the coast of Nova Scotia, but even to set up a title to the whole Province in opposition to your Majesty's right. The French likewise pretend that only the Peninsula of Accadie (hardly one third part of Nova Scotia) was yielded to the Crown of Great Britain by the Treaty of Utrecht, and notwithstanding this pretence is sufficiently refuted in the former part of this report, by comparing the Charter to Sir William Alexander the first proprietor of Nova Scotia, with the Article of Cession in the Treaty of Utrecht, yet from these unreasonable cavils in time of profound peace and friendship between the two nations may be collected how desirous the French are to make themselves masters of this Province, which they may easily over-run on the first rupture, the same being in a manner already surrounded by their settlements at Cape Breton, Long Island and Quebeck. In our humble opinion therefore no time should be lost in putting of this Province into a better posture of defence; and we humbly beg leave to repeat our proposal for sending of four regiments of foot to Nova Scotia. Without some assistance of this nature it will be in vain to think of settling Nova Scotia; for planters will never fix where they can have no security for their persons or effects; but whenever this main point shall be sufficiently provided for, it is to be hoped so fertile a country will not want inhabitants, all reasonable encouragement however should be given to adventurers to settle there, and in some former reports to your Majesty, we have humbly offer'd it as our opinion that it would be greatly for Your Service that the present inhabitants of Newfoundland should be engaged to quit that place where they drive a trade prejudicial to ye fishery of Great Britain, and settle in Nova Scotia where they may be useful to this kingdom. We shall not trouble your Majesty with the repetition of the particulars mentioned in former parts of this representation concerning the fortifications proposed to be erected on the Coast of Nova Scotia, but shall beg leave in general to observe that bays and harbours shou'd be secured and some forts built in proper places for the protection of your Majesty's subjects fishing upon this coast. In that part of this report relating to the French Settlements we have taken notice that nature has furnished the British Colonies with a barrier which may easily be defended, having cast up a long ridge of mountains between your Majesty's Plantations and the French settlements extending from South Carolina to New York; but there are doubtless several passes over these mountains which ought to be secured as soon as they shall be discovered, and we had the honour not long ago to recommend to your Majesty's approbation a proposal for fortifying the passes on the back of Virginia. In our opinion all possible encouragement should be given to discoveries and undertakings of this nature; for if all the passes over this ridge of mountains are not secured, your Majesty's subjects will be lyable to the insults of the French and of the Indians under their influence, who are very numerous. But altho' these mountains may serve at present for a very good frontier, we should not propose them for the boundary of your Majesty's Empire in America. On the contrary it were to be wished that the British settlements might be extended beyond them and some small forts erected on ye great lakes in proper places by permission of the Indian proprietors; and we would particularly recommend ye building of a fort on the Lake Erie, as hath been proposed by Col. Spotswood your Majesty's Lieut. Governor of Virginia, wherby the French communication from Quebeck to the River Mississippy might be interrupted, a new trade open'd with some of the Indian nations, and more of the natives engaged in your Majesty's intrest.

There will be the same reason for erecting another fort at the falls of Niagara, near the Lake Ontario. Mr. Burnet your Majesty's Governor of New York hath already form'd a scheme for this purpose which we hope he may be able to execute by the consent and assistance of the Seneccees, one of the Five Indian nations dependant on your Majesty, to whom the soil belongs. But because these lakes lye at a very great distance from the settlements already made by your Majesty's subjects, to secure intermediate stages a third fort might be built at the head of the Potomack River which divides Virginia from Maryland, and a fourth at the head of Sasquehana River, which runs thro' Pensylvania into the Bay of Chesapeake. Carolina likewise being the southern frontier of your Majesty's Plantations, and lying much exposed to the incursions both of the French and Spaniards, as well as to ye insults of the Indians; demands your Majesty's immediate assistance and protection. It would be for your Majesty's service, that the heads and emboucheurs of all rivers running thro' this Province should be secured; in our humble opinion, a less force than four regiments of foot will not be sufficient for the protection of your Majesty's subjects there, especially considering how many places will require garrisons; for besides those already mentioned under the head of Carolina, it will be highly necessary that three others should be erected on the Savanah, Catahooche and Hagaloge rivers; for at Palachakolas on the Savanah river the French had formerly a Settlement in the time of Charles the Ninth, and intend to settle there again if not prevented. A fort on Catahooche River would secure a communication with the Bay of Apalatche, and another on Hagaloge River might not only interrupt the communication of ye French settlements, but likewise give your Majesty's subjects an opportunity of gaining the Charokees, a war-like nation and the only Indians of consequence in those parts that have not already made peace with the French. We are very sensible that this proposal will be attended with expence; but we hope it may be fully justify'd by the necessity thereof, for the preservation of the British Colonies in America.

In relation to the Indians. The second particular wherein your Majesty's intrest is highly concerned with respect to the trade and the security of the British Plantations, is that of cultivating a good understanding with the native Indians, as well those inhabiting amongst your Majesty's subjects, as those that border upon your Majesty's Dominions in America; and herein at all times hath consisted the main support of our French neibours who are so truly sensible of what consequence it is to any European nation settling in America to gain the natives to their intrest, that they have spared no pains, no cost nor artifice to attain this desirable end; wherein it must be allowed, that they have succeeded, to ye great prejudice of your Majesty's subjects in those parts, having debauched as hath already been observed, some part of the Five Nations bordering upon New York from their ancient league and dependance on the Crown of Great Britain. For this purpose their missionaries are constantly imploy'd, frequent presents are made to the Sachems or Kings of ye several nations, and incouragement given for intermarriages between the French and natives, whereby their new empire may in time be peopled without draining France of its inhabitants. It was for this reason that in the draught of instructions for the Governor of Nova Scotia, we took the liberty of proposing to your Majesty that proper incouragement should be given to such of your Majesty's subjects as should intermarry with the native Indians; and we conceive it might be for your Majesty's service, that the said instructions should be extended to all the other British Colonies. Your Majesty and your Royal Predecessors have frequently made presents to the Indian chiefs, more particularly to those of the Five Nations; but as the same have always hitherto been a charge upon the civil list, which is generally overburthened, so those presents have not been very regularly or seasonably sent to America, and consequently many opportunities of improving the British intrest in those parts, must have been lost for want of them; for which reason it is to be hoped that more exactness will be had in this particular for the future. It is likewise much to be lamented that our zeal for propagating of the Christian faith in parts beyond the seas, hath not hitherto much enlarged the pale of the British Church amongst those poor infidels, or in any sort contributed to promote the intrest of the State in America. But as it is not so immediately our province to propose anything particular upon this head; we can only wish that the same may be hereafter put upon a better foot. There is however one other method left for gaining the good will of these Indians, which Providence hath put into our hands, and wherein ye French could not possibly rival us if we made a right use of our advantage, and that is the furnishing of them at honest and reasonable prices with the several European commodities they may have occasion for; but even this particular from the unreasonable avarice of our Indian traders, and the want of proper regulations, has turn'd to our detriment, and instead of gaining us friends, has very probably created us many enemies. But as we are intirely of opinion that the Indian trade, if fairly carried on, would greatly contribute to the increase of your Majesty's power and intrest in America; we should humbly propose, that the same may be put under as good regulations as ye nature of the thing will admit; for on the succesful progress of this trade, the inlargement of your Majesty's Dominions in those parts doth almost intirely depend; in as much as all the settlements that may at any time hereafter be made beyond the mountains, or on ye lakes, must necessarily build their hopes of support much more upon ye advantage to be made by the Indian trade, than upon any profits to arise from planting at so great a distance from the sea. This trade then ought by all possible means to be encouraged, it ought to be equally free in all parts to all your Majesty's subjects in America; and all monopolies thereof discouraged, that no one colony or sett of people whatsoever may engross the same to the prejudice of their nei'bours. All your Majesty's

Governors in their respective governments should use their utmost endeavours to prevent the traders from imposing upon the Indians, upon complaint of any injustice done them cause satisfaction to be made, and upon all occasions shew the utmost resentments against the offenders. And that your Majesty's subjects may be the more easily induced to extend this trade as far westward, upon the lakes and rivers behind the mountains as the situation and ability of the respective colonies will permit; forts should be built and garrisons settled in proper places, to protect them. It would likewise be for your Majesty's service that the several Governments of your Majesty's Plantations should endeavor to make treaties and alliances of friendship with as many Indian nations as they can, in which treaties all your Majesty's subjects should be expressly included; all the Indian nations in amity with your Majesty's subjects should, if possible, be reconciled, to each other; and all traders should be instructed to use their endeavors to convince the said Indians, that the English have but one King and one interest. And if any Indian nation in league or friendship with any of your Majesty's Colonies, should make war, plunder or any way molest any other Indian nation in friendship with the same colony, your Majesty's Governor should use all possible endeavours to oblige the said Indians to make satisfaction for their breach of faith to ye party aggrieved. And that all the Governors of your Majesty's Plantations may be informed of the State of every other Government, with respect to the Indians; it will be necessary that every Governor upon his making any treaty with any Indian nation, should immediately communicate the same to all other your Majesty's governors upon the Continent. We are likewise of opinion that it might be convenient to imitate the French in sending home some chiefs of the most considerable clans or nations to whom they take care to shew the glory and splendor of the French nation in Europe; that the said Indians may upon their return instill the greater respect for them amongst their countrymen. All which particulars would in our humble opinion much conduce to the securing of the natives in your Majesty's intrest, and to the enlargement of your frontiers in America.

In relation to the Government of the Plantations. The laws and constitutions of your Majesty's Colonies are copy'd from those of Great Britain, but fall short of them in many particulars; some of which have however from time to time been corrected and amended by your Majesty's instructions to the respective Governors of the different colonies under your Majesty's immediate Government; and they might be rendered still more perfect if your Majesty's commands met with due obedience in the Proprietary and Charter Governments. This is the great obstacle which has hitherto made it impracticable to put the Plantations in general upon a better foot; and therefore we shall beg leave to mention some of those inconveniencies that have arisen from the large powers and privileges subsisting by virtue of several Charters granted by your Majesty's Royal Predecessors, whereby not only the soil but likewise the dominion or government of several colonies is absolutely alienated from the Crown, to certain Proprietors, who far from imploying the said powers and privileges to the use for which they were designed, as we find by former reports from this Board, have frequently refused obedience to such orders as have been given by your Majesty's Royal Predecessors, have broken thro' the laws of Trade and Navigation, made laws of their own contrary to those of Great Britain, given shelter to pirates and outlaws, and refused to contribute to the defence of the nei'bouring Colonies under your Majesty's immediate government, even in cases of the greatest emergency, altho' they would not have been able to subsist themselves without the assistance of their nei'bours. And altho' in justice to some of the Proprietary Governments, it must be allowed, that they are not all equally involved in this charge, yet certain it is that great inconveniencies do arise from so many different forms of governments, and so many different intrests on the Continent of America; nor is it to be expected that either our Indians or European nei'bours, should pay that respect to your Majesty's subjects, which all those who have the happiness to be under your Majesty's protection might otherwise reasonably hope for; until it shall appear, that all the British Colonies in America hold immediately of one Lord, and have but one joint intrest to pursue; for which reason, and many others, we shall first humbly propose that all the Proprietary Governments should be reassumed to the Crown, either by purchase, agreement or otherwise, as conceiving this to be one of those essential points without which your Majesty's Colonies can never be put upon a right footing, it might likewise be further observed upon this head, that some of the Proprietary and Charter Governments have shewn too great an inclination to be independant of their mother Kingdom, and have carried on a trade destructive to that of Great Britain, wherein they might undoubtedly be more effectually restrained if they were all of them under your Majesty's immediate government, and were by proper laws compelled to follow the commands sent them by your Majesty; and it hath ever been the wisdom, not only of Great Britain but likewise of all other States, to secure by all possible means the intire absolute and immediate dependancy of their Colonies. On the other hand, it were but just to consider the planters, whatever governments they may live under, as your Majesty's subjects; and that in all reasonable things not prejudicial to the intrest of Great Britain, they should be favour'd and incouraged, more particularly in the raising of naval stores of all kinds, whereby they may greatly advantage themselves and contribute to render their mother Kingdom absolutely independant of all the Northern Powers, and that their religion, liberties and properties should be inviolably preserved to them. We have already had a very successful proof of what due incouragements produce in the particulars of pitch and tar, which at present are made in as great perfection in your Majesty's Plantations, as in any other part of the world, and in such plenty as will enable us to supply foreign parts, since it hath reduced the common price of those commodities one third of their former cost within the space of a very few years, whereby the importation of pitch and tar from the Baltick is greatly decreased, and much mony saved in the ballance of our trade; nor is it to be doubted but iron, flax, hemp and all sorts of timber, might likewise be had from your Majesty's plantations, with the same success upon sufficient encouragement, whereby the trade and navigation of these Realms would be highly advanced, and the Plantations diverted from the thoughts of setting up manufactures of their own interfering with those of Great Britain, and from carrying on an illegal trade with foreigners; but we shall have an opportunity of explaining ourselves more particularly upon this head, in a separate representation to your Majesty relating to such further premiums as we conceive necessary for promoting so useful a design. Your Majesty's revenues arising from the Quit Rents reserved upon grants of land made by your Majesty and your Royal Predecessors, bear no proportion to the extent of your Majesty's territories in America; for such has been the improvident management in this particular that whole provinces have been granted without any, or upon very small reservations to the Crown, and the Governors of your Majesty's Colonies, who are by their commissions and instructions usually impowered to make grants of lands, have frequently abused their authority herein, by making exorbitant grants to private persons, and the small quit rents that have been reserv'd, have not been so punctually collected and accounted for, as they ought to have been; the registers of such grants being very imperfectly kept, and no due obedience paid to your Majesty's Auditor of the Plantations. There are likewise other abuses practised in the manner of taking up of lands, whereby ye grantees preserve their claim whilst Your Majesty is defrauded of your quit rents, ye lands remain uncultivated, and the industry of the fair planter is discouraged.

To prevent these abuses it may be necessary for your Majesty's service, that the Governors of your Majesty's colonies on the Continent, should, for the future, be restrained from making grants without reservation of the usual quit rents to your Majesty, and from making any grants exceeding 1000 acres to any person in his own, or any other name in trust for him, and that all grants hereafter to be made should be void, unless the land granted, or at least two thirds thereof, be cultivated within a certain term of years to be fixt for that purpose.

That no person should be allow'd to hold any lands for which a patent hath not been actually pass'd, either under the seal of the respective Plantation, or the great Seal of this kingdom, and that all persons petitioning, for the future, to take up lands, should be obliged, upon allowance of such petition, to pass a patent for the same within the space of six years, and pay the usual duties due thereon to Your Majesty; in default whereof the said allowance to be void and the lands to be grantable to any other person. That an exact register be kept of all grants already made or to be made, that the quit rents arising therefrom be duly accounted for to your Majesty's Auditor of the Plantations; and that likewise all mony whatsoever levy'd in your Majesty's name; in any of your Majesty's Colonies be accounted for to the said Auditor; which we the rather mention because some of the northern provinces (particularly that of New York) have of late refused to account with your Majesty's Auditor, for monies raised by their Assemblies; which is a practise detrimental to your Majesty's authority, and tends to ye shaking of that dependency which they owe to your Majesty and to their Mother Kingdom. The preservation of the woods in America, which hath hitherto been much neglected, is another particular of very great consequence to your Majesty's service; in as much as the same might prove an inexhaustible store for the Royal Navy of Great Britain. And altho' several Parliaments have been so sensible of the importance of this article, that laws have been made in England for this purpose; yet the daily complaints from America are a proof how ill these laws are executed, and how little regard is paid to your Majesty's Commission and Instructions to Your Surveyor General of the Woods; which is not so much to be wondered at, considering the present Surveyor only acts by Deputy no ways qualify'd for that employment, altho' so extensive a trust would require the constant attendance of a capable and well experienced officer, and ought not to be left to the management of a deputy.

But the many inconveniencies that arise from the granting of offices in the Plantations to persons acting by Deputy there, may deserve your Majesty's animadversion; and we would humbly propose that no offices in the Plantations may be granted for the future without an express clause in each Patent obliging the grantee to attend and discharge the duty of his office in person. We beg leave further to observe that the laws at present in force for the preservation of your Majesty's woods, are very defective; for the exception therein made whereby liberty is given for the cutting of timber growing upon the lands of several persons, hath given rise to many pretentions for destroying timber fit for the service of the Royal Navy; wherefore we wou'd humbly propose that further provision should be made, by act of Parliament in Great Britain for ascertaining your Majesty's right to the woods and the boundaries thereof. But the most effectual way to put in execution what we have already offered upon this subject to your Majesty's consideration, and to render the several provinces on the Continent of America, from Nova Scotia to South Carolina, mutually subservient to each other's support, will be to put the whole under the Government of one Lord Lieut. or Captain General, from whom all other Governors of particular provinces should receive their orders in all cases for your Majesty's service, and cease to have any command respectively in such province where the said Captain General shall at any time reside; as is at present practised in the Leeward Islands, where each island has a particular Governor, but one General over the whole. The said Captain General should constantly be attended by two or more Councillors deputed from each plantation, he should have a fixed salary sufficient to support the dignity of so important an employment, independent of the pleasure of the inhabitants; and in our humble opinion, ought to be a person of good fortune, distinction and experience. By this means a general contribution of men or mony may be raised, upon the several colonies in proportion to their respective abilities; and the utility of this proposal is so evident, that we shall not trouble your Majesty with any further reasons to inforce the same; but in case your Majesty should be graciously pleased to approve thereof, we shall take a further opportunity of explaining in what manner it may best be executed. But we humbly crave leave to inform your Majesty, that it will be further necessary for your service that whoever presides at this Board, may be particularly and distinctly charged with your Majesty's immediate orders in the dispatch of all matters relating to the Plantations, in such manner as the first Commissioner of the Treasury and Admiralty do now receive and execute your Majesty's Commands, with whom the said Captain General, and all other Governors of your Majesty's Plantations, may correspond. We the rather mention this, because ye present method of despatching business relating to the Plantations, is lyable to much delay and confusion; in as much as there are at present no less than three different ways of proceeding herein, that is to say, by immediate application to your Majesty, by one of your Secretaries of State; by petition to your Majesty in Council, and by representation to your Majesty from this Board; from whence it happens that no one office is thro'ly informed of all matters relating to the Plantations, and sometimes orders are obtained, by surprize, disadvantagious to your Majesty's service; whereas if the business of the Plantations were wholly confined to one office, those inconveniencies would be thereby avoided.

IV

Accommodation, 1721–1748

13. The Eighteenth-Century Empire in Theory

A. The Official Conception of Empire

BY THE middle of the eighteenth century, imperial ideas about what the nature of the relationship between mother country and colonies was and ought to be had been so frequently and fully articulated as to become, at least for the officials who held them, virtually unchallengeable. They infused the reports, letters, and decisions of the Board of Trade, as well as of many lesser officials in colonial administration in both Britain and the colonies. One of the most succinct and eloquent summaries of these ideas appears in "A Short Discourse on the Present State of the Colonies in America, with Respect to the Interest of Great Britain." This essay was written in 1726 and submitted to the Crown in November, 1728 by Sir William Keith, governor of Pennsylvania from 1717 to 1726 and later an earnest, though unsuccessful, placeseeker in London. Although Keith's "Discourse" offered several novel suggestions and reflected the author's personal experiences in the colonies, it repeated all of the views about the colonies conventionally held in imperial circles. No action was taken in response to any of Keith's proposals, but they represented a superb statement of the official conception of empire during the middle decades of the eighteenth century. The "Discourse" is reprinted below without the introduction from the first published edition, which varies from the original manuscript by omitting a paragraph proposing the extension of English stamp duties to the colonies by act of Parliament.

SOURCE: Sir William Keith, A Collection of Papers and Other Tracts, Written Occasionally on Various Subjects (London, 1740), pp. 168–184.

ON A PROVINCIAL DEPENDANT GOVERNMENT

When either by Conquest or Increase of People, foreign Provinces are possessed, and Colonies planted abroad, it is convenient, and often necessary, to substitute little dependant provincial Governments, whose People being infranchised, and made Partakers of the Liberties and Privileges belonging to the original Mother State, are justly bound by its Laws, and become subservient to its Interests, as the true End of their Incorporation.

Every Act of a dependant Provincial Government therefore ought to terminate in the Advantage of the Mother State, unto whom it owes its Being, and by whom it is protected in all its valuable Privileges: Hence it follows, that all advantageous Projects, or commercial Gains in any Colony, which are truly prejudicial to, and inconsistent with the Interest of the Mother State, must be understood to be illegal, and the Practice of them unwarrantable, because they contradict the End for which the Colony had a Being, and are incompatible with the Terms on which the People claim both Privilege and Protection.

ON A BRITISH COLONY IN AMERICA

Were these Things rightly understood among the Inhabitants of the British Colonies in America, there would be less Occasion for such Instructions and strict Prohibitions as are daily sent from England to regulate their Conduct in many Points; the very nature of the Thing would be sufficient to direct their Choice in cultivating such Parts of Industry and Commerce only, as would bring some Advantage to the Interest and Trade of Great Britain. They would soon find by Experience, that this was the solid and true Foundation whereon to build a real Interest in their Mother Country, and the certain Means of acquiring Riches without Envy.

On the other hand, where the Government of a Provincial Colony is well regulated, and all its Business and Commerce truly adapted to the proper End and Design of the first Settlement, such a Province, like a choice Branch springing from the main Root, ought to be carefully nourished, and its just Interests well guarded. No little partial Project, or Party Gain, should be suffered to affect it; but rather it ought to be considered, and weighed in the general Ballance of the whole State, as an useful and profitable Member, for such is the End of all Colonies; and if this Use cannot be made of them, it would be much better for the State to be without them.

ON THE ADVANTAGES ARISING TO BRITAIN FROM THE TRADE OF THE COLONIES

It has ever been the Maxim of all polite Nations, to regulate their Government to the best Advantage of their trading Interest: wherefore it may be helpful to take a short View of the principal Benefits arising to Great Britain from the Trade of the Colonies.

1.   The Colonies take off and consume above one sixth Part of the Woollen Manufactures exported from Britain, which is the chief Staple of England, and main Support of the landed Interest.

2. They take off and consume more than double that Value in Linen and Callicoes, which is either the Product of *Britain* and *Ireland*, or partly the profitable Returns made for that Product carried to foreign Countries.

3. The Luxury of the Colonies, which increases daily, consumes great Quantities of *English* manufactured Silk, Haberdashery, Houshold Furniture, and Trinkets of all Sorts; also a very considerable Value in *East-India* Goods.

4. A great Revenue is raised to the Crown of *Britain* by Returns made in the Produce of the Plantations, especially in Tobacco, which at the same time helps *England* to bring nearer to a Ballance their unprofitable Trade with *France*.

5. Those Colonies promote the Interest and Trade of *Britain*, by a vast Increase of Shipping and Seamen, which enables them to carry great Quantities of Fish to *Spain, Portugal, Leghorn, &c.* Furs, Logwood, and Rice to *Holland*, whereby they help *Great Britain* considerably in the Ballance of Trade with those Countries.

6. If reasonably encouraged, the Colonies are now in a Condition to furnish *Britain* with as much of the following Commodities as it can demand, *viz.* Masting for the Navy, and all Sorts of Timber, Hemp, Flax, Pitch, Tar, Oil, Rosin, Copper Oar, with Pig and Bar Iron, by Means whereof the Ballance of Trade to *Russia* and the *Baltick* may be very much reduced in Favour of *Great Britain*.

7. The Profits arising to all those Colonies by Trade is return'd in Bullion or other useful Effects to *Great Britain*, where the superfluous Cash, and other Riches acquired in *America* must center, which is not one of the least Securities that *Britain* has to keep the Colonies always in due Subjection.

8. The Colonies upon the Main are the Granaries of *America*, and a necessary Support to the Sugar Plantations in the *West-Indies*, which could not subsist without them.

By this short View of the Trade in general we may plainly understand, that those Colonies can be very beneficially employed both for *Great Britain* and themselves, without interfering with any of the staple Manufactures in *England*; and considering the Bulk and End of their whole Traffick, it were Pity that any material Branch of it should be depress'd, on Account of private and particular Interests, which, in Comparison with these, cannot justly be esteem'd a national Concern; for if the Trade of the Colonies be regulated to the Advantage of *Britain*, there is nothing more certain, than that the Discouragement of any material Branch for the Sake of any Company, or private Interest, would be a Loss to the Nation. But in order to set this Point yet in a clearer Light, we will proceed to consider some of the most obvious Regulations on the *American* Trade, for rendering the Colonies truly serviceable to *Great Britain*.

REGULATIONS ON THE PLANTATION TRADE

1. That all the Product in the Colonies, for which the Manufacture and Trade of *Britain* has a constant Demand, be enumerated among the Goods which by Law must be first transported to *Britain*, before they can be carried to any other Market.

2. That every valuable Merchandize to be found in the *English* Colonies, and but rarely any where else, and for which there is a constant Demand in *Europe*, shall also be enumerated, in order to assist *Great Britain* in the Ballance of Trade with other Countries.

3. That all Kinds of Woollen Manufactures for which the Colonies have a Demand, shall continue to be brought from *Britain* only, and Linens from *Great Britain* and *Ireland*.

4. All other *European* Commodities to be carried to the Colonies, (Salt excepted) Entry thereof to be first made in *Britain*, before they can be transported to any of the *English* Colonies.

5. The Colonies to be absolutely restrained in their several Governments from laying any Manner of Duties on Shiping or Trade from *Europe*, or upon *European* Goods transported from one Colony to another.

6. That the Acts of Parliament relating to the Trade and Government of the Colonies, be revised and collected into one distinct Body of Laws, for the Use of the Plantations, and such as Trade with them.

Supposing these Things to be done, it will evidently follow, that the more extensive the Trade of the Colonies is, the greater will be the Advantages accruing to *Great Britain* therefrom; and consequently, that the Enlargement of the Colonies, and the Increase of their People, would still be an Addition to the national Strength. All smaller Improvements therefore pretended unto, and set up by lesser Societies for private Gain in *Great Britain*, or elsewhere, although they might have a just Pretence to bring some Sort of a publick Benefit along with them, yet if they shall appear to be hurtful unto the much greater, and more national Concern of those useful trading Colonies, they ought in Justice to the Publick to be neglected in Favour of them; it being an unalterable Maxim, that a lesser publick Good must give place to a greater; and that it is of more Moment to maintain a greater, than a lesser Number of Subjects, well employed to the Advantage of any State.

On the Legislative Power

From what has been said of the Nature of Colonies, and the Restriction that ought to be laid on their Trade, it is plain that none of the *English* Plantations in *America* can with any Reason or good Sense pretend to claim an absolute legislative Power within themselves; so that let their several Constitutions be founded on antient Charters, Royal Patents, Custom by Prescription, or what other legal Authority you please; yet still they cannot be possessed of any rightful Capacity to contradict, or evade the true Intent and Force of any Act of Parliament, wherewith the Wisdom of *Great Britain* may think fit to affect them from Time to Time. In discoursing therefore on their legislative Powers, improperly so called, we are to consider them only as so many Incorporations at a Distance, invested with an Ability of making temporary By-Laws for themselves, agreeable to their respective Situations and Climates, but no ways interfering with the legal Prerogative of the Crown, or the true legislative Power of the Mother State.

If the Governors, and General Assemblies of the several Colonies, would be pleased to consider themselves in this Light, one would think it is impossible they could be so weak as to fancy, that they represented the King, Lords, and Commons of *Great Britain*, within their little Districts; and indeed their useless, or rather hurtful and inconsistent Constitution of a negative Council in all the King's Provincial Governments, has, it is believed, contributed to lead them into this Mistake; for as long as the King has reserved to himself in his Privy Council, the Consideration of, and a Negative upon, all their Laws, the Method of appointing a few of the richest, and proudest Men in a small Colony, as an upper House, with a Negative on the Proceedings of the King's Lieutenant-Governor, and the People's Representatives, seems not only to cramp the natural Liberty of the Subject there, but also the King's just Power and Prerogative; for it often happens, that very reason-

able and good Bills, sometimes proposed for the Benefit of the
Crown, by the Wisdom of a good Governor, and at other times
offer'd by the People's Representatives, in Behalf of their Constituents, have been lost, and the enacting of such made impracticable, by the Obstinacy of a Majority in the Council, only because
such Bills did not square with their particular private Interest and
Gain, or with the Views which they form to themselves, by
assuming an imaginary Dignity and Rank, above all the rest of the
King's Subjects in the Province: And as to the Security, which it is
pretended either the Crown, or a Proprietary, may have by such a
negative Council, it is in Fact quite otherwise; since that Caution
would be much better secured, if this Council was only a Council
of State to advise with the Governor, and be constant Witnesses of
all publick Transactions; for it cannot be thought that an Officer,
who is not only under Oaths and Bonds, but answerable by Law for
his Misconduct, and removeable at Pleasure, would, in the Face of
Witnesses so appointed, contradict a rational Advice, thereby
subjecting himself to grievous Penalties and Losses. Neither is it to
be supposed, that these Men, if they had only the Privilege of
advising, would oppose such good Bills, or other reasonable Propositions, as they well knew they had no Power to reject; but while
they find themselves possess'd of a peremptory Negative, without
being in any Sort accountable for their Opinions, it is easy to
imagine how such a Power may be used on many Occasions, to serve
their private Interest and Views in Trade, as well as to indulge
the too natural Propensity which Mankind have, especially abroad,
to rule over and oppress their poor Neighbours: Besides, an artful and corrupt Governor will find Means, by Preferments &c. so
to influence a negative Council, that knowing themselves to be
under no Bonds, or any other valuable Penalty, to answer the Party
aggrieved by their Opinions, they may, without Risque, proceed in
such a Manner, as to screen the Governor in many Things, which
otherwise he would be personally, and singly bound to account for
in a legal and just Way.

If then a Council of State, only to advise with the Governor,
shall appear in all Emergencies and Cases that can be proposed to
be equally useful, and not attended with the Inconsistencies,
Obstructions, and Disadvantages of a negative Council, the one
seems to be much preferable to the other, and more agreeable to
that Liberty, and just Equality, which is established by the common Law among *Englishmen*; and consequently less productive of

those Grievances and Complaints, which have been so frequent hitherto from the Plantations.

At first View it will appear natural enough for an *Englishman*, who has tasted the Sweetness of that Freedom, which may be enjoyed under the happy Constitution of a King, Lords, and Commons in *Great Britain*, to imagine that a third Part should be form'd in the little Governments of the Plantations, in Imitation of a House of Lords; but if we rightly consider it, that Part of the Constitution is already most properly, and fully supply'd, by the Lords of his Majesty's Privy Council; besides, let us suppose, that instead of a House of Lords in *Britain*, the like Number of select Commoners were invested with a Power to sit apart, and to put a Negative on the Proceedings of a House of Commons, consisting of three times the Number of Persons of equal Rank, representing all the Commons of *Great Britain* in Parliament; the Inconsistency and Unreasonableness of the Thing presently obtrudes itself on our Minds; and yet such is the very Case of the Negative which is now practised by the Councils in *America*.

On the Civil Jurisdiction

Next to the legislative Power we shall proceed to consider the civil Jurisdiction in the Plantations, which by their own Acts is branched out into so many Forms, almost in every Colony, that it is scarce practicable to reduce them under such Heads in a short Discourse, as to make it intelligible to those who are unacquainted with the Affairs of *America*.

It is generally acknowledg'd in all the Plantations, that the Subject is intitled by Birth-right to the Benefit of the common Law of *England*; but then as the common Law has been altered from Time to Time, and restricted by Statutes, it is a Question in many of the *American* Courts of Judicature, whether any of the *English* Statutes, which do not particularly mention the Plantations, can be of Force there, until they be brought over by some Act of Assembly in that Colony, where they are pleaded: And this creates such Confusion, that according to the Art and Influence of the Lawyers and Attornies before Judges, who by their Education are for the most Part but indifferently qualified for that Service, they sometimes allow the Force of particular Statutes, and at other times reject the whole, especially if the Bench is inclinable to be partial, which too frequently happens in those new and unsettled Countries. And as Mens Liberties and Properties in any Country chiefly depend on an impartial and equal Administration of Justice, this is one of the most material Grievances which the Subjects in *America* have just Cause to complain of; but while for the Want of Schools and other proper Instruction in the Principles of moral Virtue, their People are not so well qualified even to serve upon Juries, and much less to act upon a Bench of Judicature, it seems impracticable to provide a Remedy, until a sufficient Revenue be found out amongst them to support the Charge of sending Judges from *England* to take their Circuits by Turns in the several Colonies on the Main, which, if it be thought worthy of Consideration, will appear neither to be improper nor impracticable; and until something of that Nature can be done, all other Attempts to rectify their Courts of Law will be fruitless.

Courts of Chancery, which are known to be necessary in many Cases, to correct the Severity of Common Law, seem to subsist there on a most precarious Foot; for it does not appear that there is a proper and legal Authority to hold such a Court in any of the Colonies; nevertheless, by Custom, every where some kind of Chancery is to be found in one Form or other; so that when a rich Man designs to contest any thing in Dispute with his poor Neighbour, if he can contrive to bring him into Chancery, he is sure the Matter will rarely, or never be brought to Issue, which on many Occasions proves an intolerable Oppression; wherefore it is hoped, that so high a Jurisdiction, issuing immediately from the Crown, will in due Time be put on a more regular and certain Establishment in the Plantations.

On the Military Strengh

A militia in an arbitrary and tyrannical Government may possibly be of some Service to the governing Power; but we learn from Experience, that in a free Country it is of little Use. The People in the Plantations are so few in Proportion to the Lands they possess, that Servants being scarce, and Slaves so excessively dear, the Men are generally under a Necessity to work hard themselves, in order to provide the common Necessaries of Life for their Families; so that they cannot spare a Day's Time without great Loss to their Interest; wherefore a Militia there would become more burthensome to the poor People, than it can be in any Part of *Europe*. Besides, it may be question'd how far it would consist with good

Policy, to accustom all the able Men in the Colonies to be well exercised in Arms; it seems at present to be more adviseable, to keep up a small regular Force in each Province, which on Occasion might be readily augmented; so that in Case of a War, or Rebellion, the whole of the regular Troops on the Continent, might without Loss of Time be united or distributed at Pleasure; and if, as has been said before, a suitable Revenue abroad can be raised for the Defence and support of the Plantations, it would be no difficult Matter, both to form and execute a proper Scheme for that Purpose.

On Taxes

Land is so plenty, and to be had so very cheap in *America*, that there is no such Thing as Tenants to be found in that Country; for every Man is a Landlord in Fee of what he possesses, and only pays a small Quit, or Ground Rent to the Lord of the Soil; and this makes it impracticable to find an Assembly of such Freeholders in any of the Colonies, who will consent to lay any Tax upon Lands; nor indeed is it to be expected they should voluntarily agree to raise any Revenue among themselves, except what is absolutely necessary for erecting and supporting Court Houses, Bridges, Highways, and other needful Expences of their Civil Government, which is commonly levied upon Stock, an Excise on foreign Liquors retailed, or a small Poll Tax. And the Publick there is generally in Debt, because they are extreamly jealous of Attempts upon their Liberties; and apprehensive, that if at any Time their publick Treasury was rich, it might prove too great a Temptation for an artful Governor, perhaps in Concert with their own Representatives, to divide the Spoil amongst them.

On Their Independency

It must be allowed that a Share of personal Interest or Self-Love influences in some Degree every Man's Affections, and gives a natural Impulse to all our Actions; and although this is most perceptible in Trade or Commercial Affairs, yet there is not any other Transaction in Life that passes without it. And as it is with Men in this Case, so we find it has ever been with all States or Bodies Politick, as long as they continue independant one upon another. The wisdom of the Crown of *Britain* therefore, by keeping its Colonies in such a Situation is very much to be applauded; for while they continue so, it is morally impossible that any dangerous Union can be form'd among them, because their Interests in Trade, and all Manner of Business, being intirely separated by their Independancy on each other, every Advantage that is lost or neglected by one Colony, is immediately picked up by another; and the Emulation that continually subsists between them in all Manner of Intercourse and Traffick, is ever productive of Envies, Jealousies, and Cares, how to gain upon each other's Conduct in Government or Trade, every one thereby endeavouring to magnify their Pretensions to the Favour of the Crown, by becoming more useful than their Neighbours to the Interest of *Great Britain*.

On the Management of Plantation Affairs

But to render the Colonies still more considerable to *Britain*, and the Management of their Affairs much more easy to the King and his Ministers at home, it would be convenient to appoint particular Officers in *England*, only for the Dispatch of Business belonging to the Plantations; for often Persons who come from *America* on purpose either to complain, or to support their own just Rights, are at a Loss how, or where to apply: This Uncertainty does not only fatigue the Ministers, but frequently terminates in the Destruction of the Party, by his being referr'd from Office to Office, until both his Money and Patience be quite worn out. Such Things in Time may cool People's Affections, and give them too mean an Opinion of the Justice of their Mother Country, which ought carefully to be prevented; for where there is Liberty, the Inhabitants will certainly expect Right, and still have an Eye towards obtaining it one Way or other.

It may be considered therefore how far it would be serviceable to put all the Crown's Civil Officers in the Plantations of what kind soever, under the Direction of the Board of Trade, from whom they might receive their several Deputations or Appointments; and to whom they ought to be accountable, both for their Receipts and Management: And if a particular Secretary was appointed for the Plantation Affairs only, or if the first Lord Commissioner of that Board was permitted to have daily Access to the King, in order to receive his Majesty's Commands in all Business relating to the Plantations, the Subject's Application would then be reduced into so narrow a Compass, and the Board of Trade would always be so perfectly acquainted with the King's Pleasure, that great Dispatch might be given, even to those distant Matters, without taking up too much of the Minister's Time, and interfering with other (perhaps more important) Business. The People of the Colonies would be pleased to find themselves thus equally regarded, without giving one any undue Preference to another; and all the Rents, Customs, Revenues, and other Profits in any Manner arising from the Plantations, would then center in one Place, where another proper Member of the same Board might be appointed Treasurer of that particular Revenue, to answer all such Orders as should be issued from Time to Time for the Plantation Service. And as the Revenues from *America* would in all Probability be increasing daily, it may reasonably be expected, that the Expence of paying the Board of Trade, and other Officers wholly employ'd in Plantation Affairs, which is now born by the Civil List, would then more properly arise, and be discharged out of the *American* Fund; and the Overplus remaining would in Time become a most useful Stock, for purchasing of Proprietary Lands, erecting Forts, and extending the present Settlements as far as the great Lakes, or may be applied to such other Uses as his Majesty shall think proper for that Purpose.

Conclusion

When we do but cast an Eye on the vast Tract of Land, and immense Riches which the *Spanish* Nation have in little more than one Century very oddly acquired in *America*; insomuch, that the simple Privilege of trading with them, on very high Terms, is become a Prize worth contending for among the greatest Powers in *Europe*. Surely we must on due Reflection acknowledge, that the Preservation and Enlargement of the *English* Settlements in those Parts, is of the last Consequence to the Trade, Interest, and Strength of *Great Britain*. And moreover, considering how that the last Resort of Justice in the Plantations is solely lodged in the King's sacred Person, with the Advisement of his Majesty's Privy Council, exclusive of *Westminster-Hall*, or any other Judicature. The Brightening of this Jewel in the Crown, may not perhaps be thought unworthy the Care of the present happy Reign, to which the Improvement, and future Security of so large a Part of the *British* Dominions, the Advancement of Trade, and universally supporting the glorious Cause of Liberty, seem to be reserved by the peculiar Hand of Providence.

14. The Eighteenth-Century Empire in Operation

A. *The Arguments Against the Enforcement of "Long Established Maxims"*

ONE OF THE main reasons that no attempt was made to implement plans like those of Keith was that the theories on which they were based contrasted so sharply with actual conditions in the colonies that even their advocates realized they could never be enforced without a massive effort on the part of the imperial government. There were a few officials, in fact, who thought them so completely out of date as to be entirely inappropriate to the situation in the mid-eighteenth-century colonies. One such man was Sir William Gooch, who as lieutenant governor and chief representative of the Crown in Virginia from 1727 to 1749 was one of the two or three most successful royal governors during the eighteenth century. Like his model, First Minister Sir Robert Walpole, Gooch was a pragmatic and hardheaded administrator, who preferred to work within the existing political framework unencumbered by unnecessary ideological considerations. In the following document—a close answer to Keith's "Discourse," which was sent by the Board of Trade to some of the governors for their comments—Gooch explained why he thought the "long established Maxims in the Government of the Plantations" recommended by Keith were entirely "Visionary" and of no "benefit to the Crown or real Advantage to Great Britain."

SOURCE: Thomas H. Wynne (ed.), *History of the Dividing Line and Other Tracts from the Papers of William Byrd* (2 vols., Richmond, Va., 1866), II, 228–248.

As the Introduction to our Author's Scheme must necessarily convey to every Reader the most exalted Idea of his Majesty's Incomparable Vertues; So the Subsequent Sheets will I hope appear with such a Face of Truth, as to create in every loyal Breast a just resentment against the Malignity of a writer who has taken the Liberty to abuse so much goodness by partial & unjust Representations of a Faithfull & obedient People; which no other View than by infusing grounless Jealousies of their Conduct, to procure for himself an Employment in the Management of that imaginary Revenue, which he proposes to raise by the Duties of Stamps on Paper and Parchment.

To vindicate his Majesty's good Subjects in the Plantations from the unjust Aspersions of this Author; to point out the particulars wherein he wou'd impose long established Maxims in the Government of the Plantations, as the effect of his own Twelve Years observations; and to shew the impracticableness of this Scheme, full of Various & contradictory Windings, is the design of the following Remarks, which shall be prosecuted in the same Order & Method he has been pleased to range them, that the World may the better observe the Labyrinth this Projector is leading us into.

On a Provincial Dependant Government

The Description he has given of a Provincial Dependant Government, so far as it concerns the American Plantations, which were first Seated by English Men, & not subdued by Conquest, may be fully understood, and the Dependancy of the Plantations on the Mother State is clearly asserted in the 5th Section of the Act for Encouraging Trade made in the Fifteenth Year of the Reign of King Charles the Second; that this Author with all the Pains and Trouble he has been at, has really found out nothing in his long & accurate Observations in America, but what every one knew whose concern & Business it was, long before he was born. Nor do his Majesty's Ministers entrusted with the Care of the Plantations, nor do the Inhabitants of the several Provinces themselves need now to be put in mind of the Dependance the Plantations have on Great Britain; since every valuable Branch of the American Trade is secured by Law from the Danger of being diverted into any other Channel. If therefore this writer instead of laying down General Positions, which no Man ever denied, concerning the Original design of settling Colonies abroad, had pointed out the particular Provinces in which any Advantageous Projects are set on Foot prejudicial with, & inconsistent to the Mother State, he had done much better Service to the Publick, and more Justice to the Plantations, than by leaving Mankind at Liberty to charge all of them with Practices innumerable & incompatible with the Terms on which the People Claim both Priviledges & Protection.

On a British Colony in America

Here the Author charges the Inhabitants of the British Colonies in general with not understanding the true End & design of their Settlement in America, and what they owe to their Mother Country; and endeavours to prove his Charge by the Instructions & Strict Prohibitions, which in many Points are daily sent from England to regulate their Conduct, In answer to this it may be fairly urged, that as the People in the Plantations always have and ever will pay a due Obedience to all Laws made in England for regulating their Conduct, and all other Orders and Instructions which the Crown thinks fit to transmit for their better Government, so it is no such great Wonder, as the Writer wou'd make it, if some amongst them remember that as English Men, they have a Natural Liberty of pursuing what may promote their own benefit in such Matters as are not prohibited by Former Laws and Instructions, We see the same thing done in England by many Private Persons, notwithstanding all the Care of his Majesty's Officers; but that the collective Body of the People in any of the British Colonies in America have combined to thwart the Interest of the Mother State, as seems to be under this Head insinuated is a gross misrepresentation, an extravagant Conceit framed in his own Brain. It is indeed true that Instructions & strict Prohibitions are sent into America, & are frequently evaded where crafty and designing Men have had the Dexterity to lead the well meaning Inhabitants into Schemes as much prejudicial to their own Interest as that of Great Britain of which the Author can give a very remarkable Instance in the Case of the Paper Bills struck in Pensylvania, but this ought not to be charged on the Plantations in General,

If our Author had been so ingenuous as not to have thought himself safest by being in the dark, he might have distinguished by his Wise Observations those Provinces whose Commerce and Government are truly adapted to the Proper End and Design of their First Settlement; and pointed out those other Plantations which Great Britain had so much better be without; for then on the one Hand, he had deserved the thanks of those, who ought not only to have been thus treated by him, but carefully nourished by their Mother Country; And on the other hand he had given the disobedient and ill disposed Provinces opportunity to set themselves Right in their Sovereign's Opinion.

But while he is intent in turning Topsy Turvy long established Constitutions in Colonies well regulated in point of Government and Trade, nor with, but against Reason; I shall be content to leave it to every impartial Reader to Consider whether the Inhabitants of the Plantations have not reason to fear his ill meaning towards them & that no Government will be allowed to be well regulated but what is the Ofpring of his own Invention, which how consistent it is with the Trading Interest will appear hereafter.

On the Advantages arising to Great Britain from the Trade of the Colonies

This contains a pretty just enumeration of all the Advantages accruing to Great Britain from the Plantation Trade; And his Arguments for obviating any discouragements this Trade may receive for the Sake of any Private Interest, are no doubt most true, and Conclusive, This is a Priviledge of Writing every honest Man may lay claim to, and gives the Reader Encouragement to hope, that for the future he shall be on better Terms with the Writer, but also in the next Paragraph, after having made use of the best Means for his Information he again follows the Dictates of his own Conscience & Understanding.

For by Regulations in the Plantation Trade 'tis first to be remembered that all the Regulations mentioned by this Author as such as have been Established long since, either by Acts of Parliament or the Kings imediate Authority, except the Fourth and last, and these require some Animadversions. Under the Fourth Regulation he seems to exclude the Plantations from the Liberty they enjoy by the Acts of Trade of Importing Provisions from Ireland, & Wine from the Maderas and Azores, and will allow only salt to be brought directly to the Plantations without First being entered in England. But as these are necessary for the Plantations, and no way Interfere with the Trade of Great Britain; it is to be hoped that the same Liberty will be still continued, and if 'tis thought an Indulgence, that some of the Plantations at least deserve it. The last Regulation mention'd by our Author is the Collecting the Acts of Parliament relating to the Plantations into one distinct Body; and this may be said to be all his own, for who does not know that the present Secretary to the Commissioners of the Customs some Years ago made very exact Collection of all the Laws relating to Trade which any concerned in the Plantations may easily purchase, and many have before this Author discovered the usefulness thereof, so that 'tis not of such mighty Importance as to give occasion for an immediate Address to his Majesty.

On the Legislative Power

Under this head the Author has couched an invidious Insinuation as if the Assembly in the Plantations pretended to an Absolute Legislative Power within themselves, & thereby presumed to contradict and Evade the Intent and force of the Acts of Parliament of their Mother Country, than which nothing can be more false and unjust, And 'tis hoped that the Lords Commissioners of Trade (under whose Consideration 'tis said this wonderfull Performance lys) will have the goodness to Vindicate his Majestys Subjects of the Plantations from so foul an Aspersion which might otherwise render the best of Subjects (I speak only of some Colonies) very justly to be suspected of their Sovereign. But had this Authors Observations been conceived under a more Auspicious Planet, it wou'd have been needless for me to tell the Reader, that not any of the Plantation Assemblies ever pretended to contradict the Acts with which the Parliament of Great Britain have thought fit to affect them, well knowing that the Authority which they derive from the Crown expressly prohibits all such Endeavours, nor are they Ignorant of it that all Laws contrived by them, and tending to that purpose wou'd be vain and ineffectual; Since by the Statute of the 7th & 8th of King William all such Laws as are repugnant to the Acts of Parliament therein mention'd or to any other Law thereafter to be made in England relating to the Plantations are declar'd Null and Void. But yet with this Author's Leave, the People of the Plantations conceive they are possessed of a Legislative Power, properly so called, by Virtue of their Charters, & the Royal Grants, which enable Governors with the Advice of the Council and Assemblies to make Laws and Ordinances, for the good Government of their Respective Provinces; under this Restriction, that such Laws be conformable to the Statutes of England; and this Power the Plantation Assemblies have exercised from their first Institution to this time; not as so many petty Corporations at a Distance, but as Communities deriving their Authority from the Crown. Thus they have in the respective Provinces established Laws for regulating Proceedings in their Courts of Justice; they have settled Titles to Lands, and declared Slaves to be real Estate; and have made many other necessary Rules for securing the Properties of the Subject agreeable to the particular Circumstances of the several Colonies; which are far different from the Nature of Temporary By Laws made by little Corporatio:s. And it is the great comfort of the Inhabitants in the Plantations that these very Laws of theirs have been from time to time approved of by those Ministers of the Crown, set apart for that Purpose, who have had as much at heart the legal Prerogative of the King, and the true Interest of the Mother State, and as much Capacity to Judge of both, as this Writer can pretend to with all his Twelve Years remarks.

But the Author resolving to go thro' Stitch when sticking at Foundations, proceeds to reprehend the weakness of the Governors and General Assemblies in the several Colonies, who fancy that they Represent the King Lords and Commons of Great Britain; but this is a weakness to which the Author himself was once Subject, and as such might well have Spared charging it on others, who to be sure had a much better Title to fancy themselves the King's Representatives. However the Governors of the Plantations undoubtedly are now much obliged to him for setting them right in this particular; for indeed it has been hitherto a general received Opinion that a Governor having the Chief Command of a Province by the Kings immediate Commission; did in that Capacity represent the Person of his Royal Master; And we have heard of a Governor in a certain Province who took it mortally ill to be told, he was not the King's Representative, tho' at the same time he acted under the Authority of an old Woman, the Proprietor. But 'tis to be hoped that such weakness will not hereafter prevail among such Governors. Then as to the Assemblies fancying themselves to Represent Lords and Commons, it would be an unpardonable weakness shou'd they pretend to it, but this Writer willfully I fear, mistakes an Endeavour to imitate so great an Example in the Manner of Proceedings in a Legislative Capacity (a weakness very pardonable) for a Vanity of assuming this Power, which wou'd be wholly inexcusible, but it is an undoubted Truth, that the making a Law by the Governor, Council and Representatives of the People in the Original Establishment of the Plantations in General [is] founded on their Charters and other Royal Grants, and has never been complained of, either by the People themselves, or centured by those Lords to whom the Crown has committed the inspection of the Plantations.

Those who are Strangers to everything may fancy what they please, by the Strength of which our Author proceeds to a Negative Council as he calls it, and this Negative Council consists of a few of the richest and proudest Men in each Colony, here he is happier than perhaps he thinks of, for there may possibly be one Man more in the World which thinks as he does. But pray Sir are the Richest Men in a Country for that Reason the least fit to share in the Legislature, or are they less Capable of Consulting the general Interest of Community in which they live, or less concern'd for securing the Liberties and Properties of a Free People? And as to the Just Power and Prerogative of the Crown, can they be more safely trusted in the Hands of the People's Representatives, than in that of a Council who owe the Rank they hold to the Kings Favour, and are removable at his Pleasure? But, I had almost forgot, it seems these Rich Councellors are proud too, and therefore unfit to be entrusted with any Power of Legislation; Surely this Ingenious Author might without Twelve Years Observation have found out that there are many Men not very Rich that have an equal Share of Pride with the most wealthy, And supposing that the Council of the several Plantations were modelled according to his Scheme, and all the Rich Men excluded, cou'd he imagine that their Successors wou'd be more Capable of Serving the King, and promoting the true Interest of the Colonies, than those they succeed? or will they be less liable to the Vanity of assuming to themselves an imaginary Dignity & Rank above the rest of the King's Subjects? These are very uncommon Observations nor cou'd I have believed them to have been the Author's own, had he not extravagantly insisted upon them beyond all Sence & beyond all Truth. For he gos on and tell us that these Councellors are to be only a Council of State to advise the Governors, Risum teneatis, Amice, and be Solemn Witnesses of all Publick Transactions, and a most notable security they must needs proves, when the Author owns that an Artfull corrupt Governor will find Means by preferment, &C, so to influence a Council, rich and proud too, that they shall skreen a Governor in many things, which otherwise he must be personally bound to account for in a just and Legal Way.

May not then this new modelled Council of State from which all Rich Men it seems are to be excluded be as liable to the like Influence as the Councils now Establish't, and may not their necessitys rather dispose them to be bribed by Preferments into sinfull Compliances, than those whose Estates set them above such a Temptation? And may not these New Fashion'd Councellors have as great a natural propensity to Rule over & Oppress their poor Neighbours? Undoubtedly they may! Nay are Subject to the like Temptations and passions with other Men, and perhaps more, since 'tis probable they may meet some Occasions to indulge such Passions, for being no further usefull in a Government than to look on while the Governor and his lower House of Assembly are transacting the Publick Affairs of the Colony; besides, they may soon fall under the ridicule and contempt of their Fellow-Subjects, and by that be lead to make revengefull, Returns expecially when a corrupt Governor may find it for his Interest to join in the Oppression.

But while the Councils in the Kings Provincial Governments are as liable to be removed as the Governors themselves, and that if any of them should obstinately oppose any Law prepared in the Assembly for the Publick Good, or the Interest of the Crown, a good and watchful Governor wou'd find means to take from them the power of doing further Mischeif, there is no Danger to the Crown or Mother State in preserving the present Constitution. And as to the Proprietary Governments, seeing those Proprietors themselves from their own personal knowledge, or from the Recommendation of their Lieutenant Governors, have the Nomination of the Council in their Respective Provinces, and have thought fit to entrust such Council with a Share in the Legislature as a necessary Part of the Constitution, it wou'd be hard to deny them this Check on their Deputies, when the People themselves of the several Provinces have never complain'd of any Inconvenience from this Establishment.

On the Civil Jurisdiction

However unintelligible the Civil Jurisdiction in the Plantations may be to some who are altogether unacquainted with American Affairs; Yet if by Civil Jurisdiction it be understood the Administration of Justice in the Courts of Law, I will venture to pronounce that the practice of those Courts is exactly suited to the Circumstances of the Respective Governments, and as near as possible it can be, conformable to the Laws and Customs of England. It is hoped the common Law of England will still be acknowledged as the Birth-right of every Subject in the Plantations; and as to the English Statutes which do not particularly mention the Plantations, tho' made since the Settlement thereof, there was never any disputes in the Courts of Judicature whether they were binding on the Subjects of the Plantations, because the Resolutions of the Judges in England have determin'd that they are not, If any such partial Judges are to be found in the Plantations, who allow the Force of the English Statutes in one Case, and reject the same in another, the Governors are much to blame for continuing such Judges: And admitting there may be some such in the Inferior Courts, yet while the Supreme Courts in each Province are filled with Men of Integrity, good Sence (for the Truth will out in spite of our Author) and a Competent knowledge in the Laws (tho' they are not all of them profund Lawyers) the Subject will not be much injured, thro' the Ignorance of Inferior Magistrates. That the People in the Plantations are so destitute of proper Instructions in Principles of Moral Vertue, as to unqualify them even to serve upon Juries, much less to set upon a Bench of Judicature, is an Aspersion no less severe than untrue. Many of the Natives have had their Education in England, and others born and brought up there are now become Inhabitants, and without any reflection upon this Author it may very easily be made appear that there are Numbers in the Plantations that understand the Principles and Practice of Moral Vertue as well as himself (especially if paying a Man's Just Debts be reckoned a Moral Vertue) & such as the People would as readily chuse to be tried by either as Judge or Jury; But as this noise about the Civil Jurisdiction, as he calls it, is only design'd to forward his Scheme of a Revenue, for which some use must be found out, & as one is the maintainnance of Judges to be sent from England to take their Circuits by turns thro' all the Provinces on the Main (which no doubt would prove a very extraordinary means to expedite Justice, as Four of 1500 Miles being but a meer Trifle) with a very wanton Pen, he at once disqualifies all the Inhabitants in America, from serving as Judge or Juror. This Argument if there be any thing in it, equally proves that they also ought to be sent from England, for what can his Judges do, if there is not a Jury to be had that understands the Principles of Moral Virtue. It is therefore humbly hoped his Majesty will be graciously pleased to continue the Courts of Justice under the present Establishment, until the People themselves find it inconvenient, or are provided with some better means to support the charge of other Judges than what this Schemist has yet contrived. He next proceeds to consider the Courts of Chancery, and says, there does not appear to him a proper & legal Authority to hold such a Court in any of the Colonies; but herein he is again much mistaken and shou'd have taken Care to inform himself a little better, because 'tis very certain that in many of the Colonies, Courts of Chancery are establish't by Acts of their Assemblies pursuant to their Authority derived from the Crown; and in the others, the Governors take themselves to be sufficiently Authorized to Act as Chancellors, by having the Custody of the great Seal of their Province committed to them, but whether this Gentleman had a legal Authority to set himself up for the Chancellor of the Province of Pensylvania, or whether in that Capacity he acted with due regard to the speedy Execution of Justice as he ought is a question he can best resolve. For in most of the Colonies it is certain the Proceedings in Chancery are remarkably expeditious, and the Author would be very much put to it to give One single Instance of any Suit depending in the Plantation Chancerys half so long as they commonly do in England.

On the Military Strengh

Here the Writer advanceth a Parodox, which is not Easily to be reconciled to Common Sence: A Militia, says he, in a Tyrannical & Arbitrary Government may possibly be of some Service to the Governing Power; But we learn from Experience that in a free Country it is of little use, and therefore, he proposes in the Room of the Militia the Establishment of a standing Army in each Province; Now let any one consider but the Nature of the Militia in the British Plantations, and then reflect whether that or a standing Force be most consistent with the Safety of those Colonies; The Militia of the Colonies consists of all the Free Men able to bear Arms, under the Command of Persons chosen from among the People of the best Familys and Fortunes; or in the words of his Majesty's Instructions "they are listed under good Officers" commissioned by the respective Governors; therefore, Reader now Judge, whether these Men are fit Tools for an Arbitrary & Tyrannical Government; or whether they are more likely to join with the Governing Powers! And having something to lose, may therefore be more ready to be apply'd to evil Purposes, if any such were to be feared under his Majesty's most happy Reign.

The Reason this Writer gives for laying aside the Militia, are these Two; first an Ease to the poor Labourers and Planters; secondly, the Danger of exercising & training the Inhabitants in the Exercise of Arms.

As, to the First, there is no Free Man in the Plantations but what may without Loss attend the usual Musters appointed by the several Laws of the Colonies; These Exercises if well regulated and contrived (as I know a Province where they now are) are rather a diversion than a Trouble, and will always be better born by the People, than to see themselves deprived of the necessary Means for their Defence, whenever there shall be occasion to make use

thereof; and the Author's Compassion for the Industrious La-
bourer will rather be found the greatest Cruelty, when 'tis considered that by the Use of Arms, he exposes their Throats to be cut
by their Slaves, or a worse & more dangerous Enemy the Shoals of
Convicts which are readily transported to the Plantations, and
being dispersed thro' a large Extent of Land can scarce be kept in
Obedience, but by the Terror of a Militia ready to Supress them, if
they shou'd dare to Form any Combinations against their Masters.

As to the Second, it is most unjust in the Author to insinuate
such a groundless Jealousy of the Plantations, as if any danger
cou'd accrue to Great Britain by accustoming their Inhabitants to
the Exercise of Arms. He has himself under this very head shewed
that no danger can arise thereby, where he acknowledges that the
Labouring People are under a necessity to work hard to provide the
common Necessarys of Life For their Families, and if so, how can
these People find time to plot and Contrive against the Government which the King is pleased to set over them! And as to the
rich Men he confesses that all the Superfluous Cash & other Riches
acquired in America must Center in Great Britain; and what better
Security can they be bound in for their Obedience? Where is the
Danger then from their bearing Arms? Or how can it be thought
inconsistent with good Policy to continue the Militia in the Establishment it now is, when all the Plantations intirely depend upon
Britain for a supply of necessaries, and when it is well known their
Riches are deposited. If the Subject in America were to take up
Arms; as this writer wou'd insinuate, what Enemy are they to
attack? It can hardly be imagined that they will fall upon one
another; because they are like to be small gainers by the Adventure;
And as to their Mother Country, it is very certain, that such
attempt wou'd entirely destroy their Trade upon which their daily
& necessary Subsistence depends. So that the Author's sly insinuation about the Plantation Militia, must appear to all considering
Men, to be without any Sort of Foundation, and calculated only to
make his Scheme of Stamp Duties appear more necessary; for what
else can be imagined from his proposal of keeping up a small regular standing Force in each Province, since it is evident from the
Situation of the Plantations on the Continent, that a small standing force wou'd be of little Service to the Protection of any Province whatever, either in Case of War or Rebellion. And if this
standing Force shou'd be so numerous as to be serviceable in either
of them, the Author will find it a more difficult Matter to form and

execute a proper Scheme for raising a suitable Revenue to support it. The Extent of the British Dominions along the Sea Coast of the Continent is at least 1500 Miles, in which are many Bays, Rivers & Harbours, where an Enemy may land without danger or disturbance from this small standing Force propos'd to be kept up; and then how difficult it will be to join Troops so dispersed, may be easily Judged from the Number of Rivers, Creeks, and unpassable Morasses, which are so frequently met with, and will be always found in their Marches. And the same may be said as to the difficulty of defending the Frontiers of the Plantations towards the Land where the French are settled along the back of these Plantations, besides many Numerous Nations of Indians ready to join them against whose Incursions a small standing Force in each Province will prove but a slender Security. This part of the Project being so very ridiculous and stuffed with such Apparent Contradictions to Reason and Common Sence, I shall dismiss it and go on to the Authors next Head.

On Taxes

And here the Writer complains that Land is so plenty and Cheap in America that there is no Tenant to be found, nor an Assembly that will consent to lay a Land Tax, and indeed it is difficult to say which way they shou'd, for if Lands be of no Value, how can this Tax be proportioned or levied, or what Revenue, can at all be raised from that which is of no worth? But the Author might have added, that tho' the Lands being of no certain Value are not Taxed, yet the People are sufficiently Taxed in most Places in the Produce of their Labours upon those Lands, besides their being burdened with a Poll-tax, and other Duties; and if by these they can defray the necessary Expences of the Civil Government, there seems no great Occasion to blame them for not having useless Sums in their Treasury, without charging this Parsimony on the Jealousy of their Liberties, or the Rapine of an Artfull Governor, joined with the fraudulent Combinations of their own Representatives; for no instance can be given of such a Confederacy; tho' this Gentleman may perhaps know a Governor who got into his Clutches £2000 of the Superfluous Treasure of a certain Province, but was too Artfull to let the Peoples Representatives share a Farthing of it with Him; a shrew'd Specimen of that self Love with which the Writer introduces the following Article.

On Their Independancy

In which there is nothing new or worthy of Consideration, except a clear Demonstration which is no ways inconsistent with good Policy to allow the People of the Plantations the use of Arms, since the Emulation amongst the independant Governments, if at last it seems only which of them shall best recommend themselves by being most usefull to the Interest of Great Britain; an Emulation which ought never to be discouraged by any unnecessary Taxes and other hardships, and decide the Controversy in favour of a truly Meritorious People, who ought to be left to that defence with which they are best pleased.

On the Management of Plantation Affairs
in England

The People of the Plantations have ever acquiesced in whatever Method the Crown has thought fit to direct them in their Applications to the Throne in all Matters relating to their Particular Affairs; And if by this Gentleman's endeavours, or otherwise, a more speedy and easy Means of Address shall be appointed, they will receive the favour with the gratitude that becomes them; But if the Appointment of all the Civil Officers in the Plantations of what kind soever, and their several Commissions for those Employments are immediately to be granted by the Lords of Trade or by any other Hands in England, it is very easy to foresee, what a confusion must unavoidably follow such a new Regulation. For it must be remembered that many of the Offices are of so little Profit, that they are scarce worth applying for, especially at such a distance and Paying Extraordinary Fees, of the Commissions; besides it may well be thought worthy of Consideration, how despicable the Governor of a Province must be when stript of the Power of disposing of the few places that fall within his Government, and how little serviceable to the Crown when deprived of the only means of rewarding Merit and creating and [exerting] Influence. If by obliging these Officers to Account with the Lords of Trade, or their Treasurer, for their Receipts of all the Revenues of the Plantations, be meant, that the several Duties and Revenues, which are now raised for the Support of the Respective Governments shou'd be remitted to this Treasurer; then it will follow that all Sallaries to those Officers must also be paid there, and what an unnecessary

Trouble this may create both to that Honourable Board, and to the Officers themselves need not be particularized. But if the Author's meaning be, as indeed it is hard to guess what he means, that only the Revenue he now Projects shou'd be under the Management of Officers immediately appointed by and accountable to the Lords of Trade and their Treasurer, tho' the People of the Plantations must be greatly affected by such a Tax; it will undoubtedly be a Comfort to the respective Governors to be exempted from any Share in the Management thereof, since thereby they will be acquitted from any Imputation of concealment or Fraud, when the produce of this Revenue is found to fall far short of the mighty Expectation this Projector builds his Scheme upon. Which leads us to consider the last head of this ingenious Project.

OF A REVENUE IN AMERICA

And here the Author confesses that all that has been said hitherto will signifie very little unless such a Revenue can be raised to support the needfull Expence. This then is the Basis of the whole Scheme. And for which all that has been offered by him was written for if no such Revenue can be raised, there will be then no Employment for him, and what Pity will it be that such an Artfull Projector shou'd at last be left in the Lurch, who has with Twelve Years painfull Observations made such mighty discoveries in the Plantation Trade as, bating some few particulars, were found out and well known long before he set his Foot in America. However, a Revenue it seems must be raised, or else all these fine Improvements must come to Nothing, And therefore he humbly submits it, whether the Duties of Stamps upon Paper & Parchment may not with good reason be extended by Act of Parliament to all the American Plantations. Now to understand the reason for extending this Duty to America, it may not be improper to consider, what may probably be the produce of this Duty to answer the use for which it is intended. As to the Duties on Parchment there is so little of that used at least on the Continent of America, that the Projector will hardly find a Man that will farm it at 100£ a Year; for seeing all Deeds and Conveyances are in the Plantations put on Record, People are in little concern whether the Originals are preserved or not, and therefore few Persons are at the Expence of engrossing such Conveyances on Parchment. Then as to the Stamps on Paper on which it is supposed all the Proceedings in the

Court of Judicature are written, and all bonds and other Writings Obligatory; besides the great inequality between the Numbers of People and the Riches of England, and that of the Plantations, and consequently a great disproportion in the Number of Law Suits, with the summary way of Proceeding of all small Causes in the latter; and if to this it be considered, that in the Management of this Duty many Officers must necessarily be employed in so large a Circuit as the American Plantations, it is much to be doubted whether this Duty will amount to much more than the Charge of Management; And it is humbly submitted whether it be at all reasonable to burden the useful People of the Plantations with such a Duty, for the sake of maintaining a Number of useless Officers. But as neither the Projector of this Duty, nor any other Person can form any certain computation of what it may produce. It seems very preposterous for him to build on such a Slight Foundation, those mighty Superstructures of maintaining Judges in all the Provinces, a standing Force in each, erecting Forts, paying the Board of Trade, and all other Officers employed in the Plantation Affairs. For as all Commissions and other Instruments which pass under the great Seal and pay the highest Duties are to be excluded out of the Computation of this Revenue, so there are many Writs, Processes, and other Instruments at Law which are charged with this Duty in England, that are unknown in most of the Plantations; as are also Presentations, Institutions and Inductions to Eclesiastical Benefices, and many other Publick Instruments, which bring in large Sums there. But there is one insuperable difficulty in the collection of this Duty which must not be omitted, and that is the want of Coin (which this Writer might well have remember'd) wherewith to discharge it. In New England, New York, the Jerseys, Pensilvania, and both the Carolinas there is a Paper Currency in which all Publick Taxes and Fees are paid, and in which the Bulk of their Commerce is carried on, and as this Paper Money bears a different Value in each several Province, and in all of them a great disproportion from Sterling Money, so in the Tobacco Plantations of Virginia and Maryland for want of Coin the Publick dues and Officers Fees are paid in Tobacco. It will therefore be almost impracticable to raise this Duty with that Equality which the Wisdom of the Parliament ever observes in Taxing the Subjects. But supposing this difficulty cou'd be surmounted, by allowing the Plantations to pay this Tax as they do other Duties, how can this Revenue be remitted to the Treasury of the Board of Trade? Will he accept of the Paper Bills of Credit, or of the Tobacco of Virginia or Maryland? For tho' there are many People in America ready enough to part with their own Paper Money, and to allow a considerable [sum] for Bills of Exchange payable in London; Yet I believe the Author of this Extraordinary Scheme would be hard put to it to find one man of Credit in the Plantations, to give Sterling Money in England for those Paper Bills; especially for any such Sum as the Author supposes this Duty to raise; and it is very apparent that the worthy Author did not think so far at his Entrance on to this Scheme, or in the finishing of it Artfully concealed it, being unwilling to start a difficulty which must overthrow his whole Design, for, to borrow an elegant expression from him, which upon another Occasion he makes use of, "The Inconsistency of the Thing dos presently obtrude itself upon our Minds." But it may possibly be alledged this Fund is at present supposed to raise no more than will maintain the Itenerant Judges and pay the Soldiers. It is true the Itenerant Judges such as the Writer proposes need be under no concern for the Payment of their Salaries in Paper-Money or in Tobacco, seeing they are in Turns to travel through all these Provinces in the Discharge of their Duty, if their allowances are not very large they will find Opportunities enough in their Circuits to spend all they receive without puzzling their Brains about remitting it for England. But the Case of the Soldiers of the standing Army is really to be pitied, if ever they shou'd be commanded to march out of their respective Provinces to a general Rendevzous in another, for the Pay they receive in One Province, will not purchase them (were there Publick Houses as there are none) one Pot of Ale in another, nor is it possible to encamp them, or Canton them, in such a Manner upon a March, as may in some Degree relieve them either from Hunger or Thirst. In this Sence only the Independancy of the several Provinces, if they upon any Account deserved to be suspected, is highly to be applauded, but the Reader will prevent me enlarging on this Head, and therefore I shall finish my Answer to this Article with only adding, that many Bills very rarely pass beyond the Limits of the Country where they are Coin'd, and that I fear our Authors standing Army will be fitter to disband than fight, whenever there shall be occasion to draw them together to oppose an Enemy. From what has been offered in Answer to this Discourse, it is hoped that the Right Honourable the Lords Commissioners for Trade and Plantations, to whom the consideration thereof is Submitted, will have little regard to the Visionary Scheme of our Author seeing what he has now advanced tends to no kind of benefit to the Crown, or real Advantage to Great Britain, but of most pernicious Consequence to the Plantations in General, and that their Lordships will interpose to preserve to the loyal Subjects of his Majesty's Plantations, the same Share of Royal Favours which they now happily enjoy; that their Lordships will have the Goodness to discourage all Projects tending to Subvert that Establishment under which the Plantations have so long been happily Governed, in fine that they will be pleased, to oppose this Vain Scheme of extending the Stamp Duties to the American Plantations, which can only prove an intollerable burden to the poor Inhabitants, without any real advantage to our most Gracious Sovereign, or the British Nation.

B. The Aversion to Extremes

ANOTHER VERY important reason that proposals like those of Keith were never seriously pursued by the Walpole government was the determination of Walpole and other Whig leaders to avoid extreme measures that might lead to major political problems. This attitude is clearly revealed below in the two letters, one official and the other private, written by the Duke of Newcastle to Governor William Burnet of Massachusetts on June 26, 1729. They relate to the long struggle to persuade the Massachusetts House of Representatives to settle a permanent salary upon the royal governor.

SOURCE: Sainsbury, et al. (eds.), Calendar of State Papers, Colonial, 1728–1729, 412–414.

OFFICIAL LETTER

The late proceedings of the House of Representatives, in relation to the settling a fix'd salary on you as Governor of the Massachusets Bay, having undergone a thorough examination, and the report of the Lords of the Committee thereupon having received H.M. approbation in Council; I herewith transmit to you, by Her Majesty's command, the inclosed copy thereof, that you may be duly informed of what has past here upon that head, and that you may make such further use of it, as you shall judge most proper for H.M. service. You will observe, that the Agents for the Representatives have been duly heard, not only by the Lords Commissioners for Trade, but likewise by the Lords of the Committee, who are both of opinion, that the salary of £1000 sterling per annum ought to be settled on you during the whole time of your Government; and there is too much reason to think, that the main drift of the Assembly, in refusing to comply with what has been so frequently and so strongly recommended to them, is to throw off their dependance on the Crown; which proceeding can in no wise be justified by their Charter, and never will be allowed of by His Majesty. This obstinacy of theirs has produced the final determination of laying the whole matter before the Parliament, which had certainly been done this last Session, if it had not been prorogued before the report was made to Her Majesty; However, it will be delay'd no longer than till the first meeting of the Parliament in the winter, and if the further steps that shall be then taken in this affair, should not be so agreeable to the House of Representatives as they could wish, they must consider, that it is entirely owing to themselves. As to your particular, I am glad to find, that your conduct is so throughly justified and approved and that no consideration could prevail with you to give up this Article of your Instructions.

Private Letter

By my other letter, and the copy of the Order in Council inclosed in it, you will plainly see, it is the intention of the Crown, that the affair of settling a salary on you should be laid before the Parliament at their first meeting, as it undoubtedly will, unless the House of Representatives take care to prevent it in time by complying with what is expected of them. However it were to be wished the bringing things to that extremity might be avoided; and as it happens luckily for them, that they have so long an intervall of time to consider better of it, and to prevent any further ill consequences, perhaps they may be willing to improve this opportunity. And therefore I write this particular letter to you, by H.M. command, that you may endeavour to bring them to a better temper, and to make them sensible, that their laying hold of this occasion to comply with what is here thought so just and reasonable, will be the only means of recommending them to H.M. favour and protection, and of promoting the true interest of the Province; and that if they slip this opportunity, it will be too late for them to expect any other. You will observe that tho' you were by your former instructions to insist on the salary being settled not only on yourself, but likewise on all future Governors, you are now left at liberty to accept it for yourself only, provided it be settled during the whole time of your Government; wherefore since the Crown has thought fit to recede in this particular, their refusing to comply with what is now proposed, will be the more inexcusable. Her Majesty depends upon your skill and prudence in making a proper use of these hints, in order to dispose the Assembly to pay a due obedience to H.M. commands; but whatever you do of that kind, is to come as from yourself in your private capacity, and not to let it look like any new overture to them on the part of the Crown, as if it were not really intended to lay the matter before the Parliament. But in case of a voluntary compliance on their part in the first place, and that it be done in due time before the meeting of the Parliament, you may then let them know that you will represent it as a mark of their duty to H.M., and use your best endeavours, that a stop may be put to any Parliamentary enquiry.

15. The Interplay of Interests

A. The Coalescence of Colonial and British Interests

IN THE inevitable conflict of interests which occurred in the British Empire, colonial groups could hope for success only when their objectives either did not interfere with the interests of any British group or actually coalesced with those of a powerful British lobby. An example of the second situation was the successful combination of Carolina rice growers with British rice traders in 1730 to persuade Parliament to pass a law permitting the direct export of rice from Carolina to southern Europe. Their campaign for this law in Parliament may be followed in the following excerpts from the journals and debates of the House of Commons on February 26 and March 17.

SOURCE: Leo F. Stock (ed.), *Proceedings and Debates of the British Parliament Respecting North America* (5 vols., Washington, D.C.: Carnegie Institution, 1924–41), IV, 57, 60–62.

Feb. 26.   A petiton of several merchants, factors, and traders to Carolina, in behalf of themselves, and others, was presented to the House, and read; setting forth, that, before Carolina rice was made an enumerated commodity, it was shipped directly to Spain and Portugal, but, since, the petitioners are obliged to import it into Great Britain; so that, before the market abroad can be supplied with it, it is frequently spoiled (being a grain of a tender nature) by the length of time, necessarily taken up by two voyages, neither can it arrive, before the markets abroad are supplied by the Genoese, and Leghornese, and other foreign nations; and, as the bringing it into England first occasions a double expence, and makes it dearer at market, and arrives there after Lent, when there is the greatest demand for it, so there is very little sold in those countries, who consume as much, as all Europe beside, but the trade is in the hands of foreigners, to the detriment of the English merchants, and planters: and praying, that rice, of the growth of his Majesty's plantations in America, may be taken from among the enumerated commodities, so far, as that they may be permitted to transport it to the Spanish West Indies, Spain, and Portugal, without touching first in Great Britain.

Ordered, that the said petition be referred to the consideration of a committee; and that they do examine the matter thereof, and report the same, with their opinion thereupon, to the House. . . .

Mar. 17. Mr. Burrell reported from the committee, to whom the petition of several merchants, factors, and traders to Carolina, in behalf of themselves, and others, and also the petition of several merchants, trading to Spain, Portugal, etc., on behalf of themselves, and others, and also the petition of several merchants of the city of Bristol, on the behalf of themselves, and others, were referred; that the committee had examined the matter of the said petitions, and had directed him to report the same, as it appeared to them, to the House: and he read the report in his place, and afterwards delivered it in at the clerk's table; where the same was read, and is, as follows; *viz.*

That the committee (pursuant to the order of the House, dated the 26th day of February last) proceeded to examine the matter of the petitions; and, to prove the allegations thereof, witnesses were called; *viz.*

Mr. *Wragg* and Mr. *Geo. Brailsford*, merchants; who, being examined, said, that, before rice, of the growth of Carolina, was made an enumerated commodity, the inhabitants thereof used to ship off considerable quantities to Spain and Portugal, which occasioned a large consumption of it, and encouraged the enlargement of the plantations; but, since the enumeration, being obliged to import it into Great Britain, and likewise before the markets in Spain and Portugal can be supplied, it is often spoiled, being subject to weavels and worms, which alter the colour, and make it of less value, when it comes to those markets.

And they further said, that the importing of rice from the said plantation into Great Britain first occasions a double expence of freight, and other charges, which makes it dearer, and is the occasion of their arrival in those parts after Lent is over, which is the season of the greatest demand for that commodity; so that now there is very little sold in those countries (except when the crops of rice, or corn, fail in the Levant) who consume as much, as all Europe besides; but they are chiefly supplied by foreigners, to the great detriment of English merchants, factors, and planters.

And the same witnesses also said, that, if the enumeration was taken off, the inhabitants of Carolina would be able to vend 18 or 20,000 barrels of rice more per annum, each barrel weighing upwards of three hundred weight, the produce of which would be fifty thousand pounds advantage to the balance of the trade of Great Britain.

And the House being moved, that the twelfth section of the act, made in the third and fourth years of the reign of the late Queen Anne, intituled, An act for granting to her Majesty a further subsidy on wines and merchandizes imported, whereby rice, of the growth of the English plantations in America, is made an enumerated commodity, might be read;

The said clause was read.

Ordered, that leave be given to bring in a bill, to repeal so much of the act, made in the third and fourth years of the reign of the late Queen Anne, intituled, An act for granting to her Majesty a further subsidy on wines and merchandize imported, as prohibits the importation of rice directly from the British plantations in America, to any port in Europe, southward of Cape Finisterre; and that Mr. Burrell and Sir Abraham Elton do prepare, and bring in, the same.

B. The Predominance of British Interests

WHENEVER COLONIAL interests clashed directly with British interests, colonial interests invariably came out second best. An illustration of this process, which may be seen in the two documents below, was the successful effort of British hatmakers in 1732 to secure parliamentary legislation intended to curtail a potentially competitive hat industry growing up in the northern continental colonies. The first document is a summary of the petition of the hatmakers, presented to the House of Commons on February 17, 1732; and the second is the act passed by Parliament in response to that petition the following June 1.

1. THE PETITION OF THE BRITISH HATMAKERS

SOURCE: Stock (ed.), Proceedings and Debates of the British Parliaments, IV, 132–133.

Feb. 17. A petition of the master, wardens, and assistants, of the Company of Feltmakers, London, in behalf of themselves, and all the hatmakers of Great Britain, was presented to the House, and read; complaining, that the inhabitants of the plantations in America, being supplied with beaver skins at less expence, than the petitioners, have been induced to set up a manufacture of hats, and are thereby enabled, not only to supply the foreign markets, but even to send over hats to Great Britain, to the great prejudice of the petitioners, and the manufacture of this kingdom: and therefore praying, that the House will take the premises into consideration, and provide some remedy, to prevent the inhabitants of the said plantations from exporting any hats, of the manufacture of the said plantations, to any place whatsoever; which will increase the customs and navigation of this kingdom, and set to work great numbers of poor families here, and enable the petitioners to revive the said declining trade; and that the petitioners may have such relief in the premises, as to the House shall seem meet.

2. THE HAT ACT OF 1732

SOURCE: Pickering (ed.), *Statutes at Large*, XVI, 304–305, 307–308.

WHEREAS *the art and mystery of making hats in Great Britain hath arrived to great perfection, and considerable quantities of hats manufactured in this kingdom have heretofore been exported to his Majesty's plantations or colonies in* America, *who have been wholly supplied with hats from Great Britain; and whereas great quantities of hats have of late years been made, and the said manufacture is daily increasing in the British plantations in* America, *and is from thence exported to foreign markets, which were heretofore supplied from Great Britain, and the hat-makers in the said plantations take many apprentices for very small terms, to the discouragement of the said trade, and debasing the said manufacture: wherefore for preventing the said ill practices for the future, and for promoting and encouraging the trade of making hats in Great Britain,* be it enacted by the King's most excellent majesty, by and with the advice and consent of the lords spiritual and temporal and commons in this present parliament assembled, and by the authority of the same, That from and after the twenty ninth day of *September* in the year of our Lord one thousand seven hundred and thirty two, no hats or felts whatsoever, dyed or undyed, finished or unfinished, shall be shipt, loaden or put on board any ship or vessel in any place or parts within any of the *British* plantations, upon any pretence whatsoever, by any person or persons whatsoever, and also that no hats or felts, either dyed or undyed, finished or unfinished, shall be loaden upon any horse, cart or other carriage, to the intent or purpose to be exported, transported, shipped off, carried or conveyed out of any of the said *British* plantations to any other of the *British* plantations, or to any other place whatsoever, by any person or persons whatsoever. . . .

VI . . . That if any action, bill, plaint or information, shall be commenced or prosecuted against any person for what he shall do in pursuance of this act, such person so sued shall and may file common bail or enter into a common appearance, and plead the general issue, not guilty, and, upon issue joined, may give this act and the special matter in evidence; and if the plaintiff or prosecutor shall become nonsuit, or suffer discontinuance, or if a verdict pass against him, or if upon demurrer judgment pass against him, the defendant shall recover treble costs, and damages.

VII. And it is hereby further enacted by the authority aforesaid, That no person residing in any of his Majesty's plantations in *America* shall, from and after the said twenty ninth day of *September* one thousand seven hundred and thirty two, make or cause to be made, any felt or hat of or with any wool or stuff whatsoever, unless he shall have first served as an apprentice in the trade or art of felt-making during the space of seven years at the least; neither shall any felt-maker or hat-maker in any of the said plantations imploy, retain or set to work, in the said art or trade, any person as a journeyman or hired servant, other than such as shall have lawfully served an apprenticeship in the said trade for the space of seven years. . . .

IX. Provided always, That nothing in this act contained shall extend to charge any person or persons lawfully exercising the said art, with any penalty or forfeiture for setting or using his or their own son or sons to the making or working hats or felts in his or their own house or houses, so as every such son or sons be bound by indenture of apprenticeship, for the term of seven years at the least, which term shall not be to expire before he shall be of the full age of twenty one years . . .

X. Provided also, and be it enacted by the authority aforesaid, That every felt-maker residing in the said plantations, who at the beginning of this present session of parliament was a maker or worker of hats or felts, and being an housholder, and likewise all such as were at the beginning of this present session apprentices, covenant servants, or journeymen in the same art or mystery of felt-making so as such apprentices serve or make up their respective apprenticeships, shall and may continue and exercise the trade or art of making hats and felts in the said plantations, although the same persons were not bound apprentices to the same art for the term of seven years. . .

C. The Political Power of British Trading Interests

THE FACT that powerful British trading interests were so formidable that colonials could not successfully compete with them even when they had the backing of the administration was revealed in the excise controversy of 1733. In an attempt to secure redress of some longstanding grievances against the British merchants who handled their tobacco, Virginians cooperated with Sir Robert Walpole in his famous excise scheme, which was defeated by opposition elements led by the tobacco traders. The debate over this measure may be followed in the excerpts below from the proceedings in the House of Commons for March 14–16 and April 4–5, 1733.

SOURCE: Stock (ed.), Proceedings and Debates of the British Parliaments, IV, 197–199, 201, 204–206.

Mar. 14.   The order of the day, for the House to resolve itself into a committee of the whole House, to consider of the most proper methods for the better security and improvement of the duties and revenues already charged upon, and payable from, tobacco and wines, was read. . . .

Then the House resolved itself into the said committee. . . .

Ordered, that the report be received to-morrow morning, being Friday. . . .

Mar. 14-15.   Sir Robert Walpole: . . . In discussing this subject, it will be necessary first to advert to the condition of our planters of tobacco in America. If they are to be believed, they are reduced to the utmost extremity, even almost to a state of despair, by the many frauds that have been committed in that trade, and by the ill usage they have sustained from their factors and correspondents in England, who from being their servants, are become their tyrants. These unfortunate people have sent home many representations of the bad state of their affairs; they have lately deputed a gentleman with a remonstrance, setting forth their grievances, and praying for some speedy relief: this they may obtain by means of the scheme I intend now to propose; but I believe it is from that alone they can expect any relief. . . .

Mr. Alderman Perry . . . Permit me now to take some notice of the tobacco-planters, and of the hardships they are laid under by their tobacco-factors, who are, it seems, now become their lords and masters. I am sure none of them ever thought of complaining, till they were put upon it by letters and applications from hence. There are hardships in all trades, which men must necessarily submit to, or give up their business; but every man, that understands the tobacco-trade, must see that the hardships the factors labour under, are by much the most numerous and the most grievous; and if this scheme should take effect, they will become so grievous, that no man would be able to continue in the trade; by this the planters would be utterly undone, and the trade quite lost to this nation; for it will be impossible for them to manage their plantations, or to send their produce to Britain, without having some considerable merchants settled here, to send ships to receive the same in America, to receive and dispose of it after it is landed here, and to supply them with ready money till their tobacco can be brought to a proper market. As to the remonstrance, mentioned by the honourable gentleman to have been lately sent over by the tobacco-planters, I know it was obtained by letters sent from hence, and I believe many of those who joined in it, now heartily repent of what they have done; it was drawn up in a form of a petition to this House, and was designed to have been presented, but it seems the promoters of it have thought better of the matter: however, that it was obtained in the unfair manner I have represented, I am now ready to prove to the conviction of the whole world.

This then being the case, as the scheme now proposed to us cannot be supposed to be of any great benefit to the public revenue, as it will be so far from being an advantage to the fair trader, or to the honest planter, that it may probably ruin both, and entirely destroy our tobacco trade; though I, and all honest men, and I defy that honourable gentleman, I defy the whole world to reproach me with one unfair practice in the whole course of my life, I say, though I and all honest men wish from our hearts that frauds may be prevented in this, as well as in every other branch of the public revenue, yet I cannot give my assent to a proposition that may be of so dangerous consequence; a proposition which I look upon to be inconsistent with our constitution; I am convinced it would prove a most fatal stroke to the liberties of my country, which will, I doubt not, be made plainly appear by other gentlemen of much greater abilities than mine: and to every man who has a regard for his country, or for the people he represents, this last must be a sufficient reason for being against it, even though it were otherwise the most beneficial scheme that had ever been proposed. . . .

Mar. 16. Sir Thomas Robinson: . . . As this bill [to levy an excise] appears to me to be attended with certain advantages to the tobacco trade . . . I beg leave to ask a few questions of those who are conversant in trade. . . .

Were not the charges in the bills of sale from the factor to his planter a very great hardship on the latter? According to all those I have seen, they never amounted to less than 25 per cent, and oftener to much more, on the whole neat produce returned to the planter for his tobacco. I do not mean to accuse the factor of taking an extravagant or unjust gain on this head: but what I think we are now contending to remove, is the pretence for and the foundation of these charges, which have been so greatly detrimental to that trade, and so great a hardship on the Virginia and Maryland planters, who now send you a merchandize that proves to this nation, by the great quantities re-exported to foreign markets, a very beneficial branch of your commerce; and if something be not now done in their behalf, I am told from very good hands, we shall run the risque of losing this staple of tobacco: then it will be too late to consider what methods are best for collecting the duties on it; and therefore, were there no other motive for this bill, this consideration alone would weigh greatly with me, to make a trial, at least, of the method now proposed for giving relief to so considerable a part of our American colonies. . . .

If then this scheme be found to be no real detriment to the fair merchant, and a certain benefit to the planters, I believe in another particular it will be a demonstrable advantage to the public, I mean an improvement of the revenue. . . .

Apr. 4. Alderman Perry undertook it to make it appear that the utmost which can possibly be recovered by this bill is £20,000; the frauds (said he) can be but upon 800 hogsheads of tobacco, the duty of which is not £12,000. . . .

Another argument for this bill is the ease of the planter with respect to the abuses put on him by his factors here. It had been more candid, before this was made out, not to have publicly exposed characters to the world unheard, by sending pamphlets under the postmaster's covers gratis, to all the great cities to inflame the subjects against them as rogues and cheats; it had been more candid to have heard the merchants on this affair, and it had been fit that Sir John Randolph, the planters' agent, had been called before us, and questioned on the subject of the representation he is said to bring over, wherein we are so strongly charged, and I hope we shall yet call for him, for I shall ask him many questions. By the way, I desire to know how he came not to present his representation to this House as it is addressed, but chose to print it and make it an appeal to the people. In that paper he pretends the factors make an oppressive gain, but I assert that when all the fees of officers, the advance of our money and long credit we give to retailers is deducted, we do not get sixpence on a hogshead we sell for them.

If this bill passes, if I continue in the same mind I am, I will quit my trade, as every honest man will do, for if I should offer at a seat in Parliament, is it possible I can act an independent part? No, Sir, this bill will subject me to arbitrary power, and my vote must be at the will of the minister. . . .

I own there may be men found who are of over-grown fortunes, and able to pay down the duty, and when you have turned out of the trades a number of fair and reputable merchants who have less wealth but more regard to their fellow subjects, these richer men may take it up, but then the trade will be monopolized into a very few hands, and the planter will be enslaved to them. Sir, I speak against my own interest in urging this; for though I have not a very great fortune, because my grandfather and father who with me have followed this trade for 70 years, left me their own example to content myself with a fair and honest gain, rather than to make haste to be rich, yet my fortune is perhaps good enough for me to commence one of these monopolizers; but I scorn the thought, and shall choose to sit down and leave off business rather than increase what I have by extortion and the oppression of my fellow traders.

Another argument against this bill is the timing of it, for the merchants have at this very time 70 ships abroad, sent before this scheme was known, all sailed before the Parliament sat; these must bring vast damage to the merchant, because their bargains and agreements are settled upon the account foot, which if this bill passes ought to be upon another foot, so that this is absolutely robbing us of so much. I said it before, and I say it again, the representation from Virginia was framed and cooked up here; not only the president, Mr. [Robert] Carter, now dead, repented the signing it, as he wrote me himself, but most of the planters have repented it, too, being sensible that if you subject their tobacco to excise laws, you will reduce them to a worse condition than they were in before. . . .

Apr. 5. A motion being made, and the question proposed, that such a number of copies, of the bill for repealing several duties, and an impost, now payable on tobacco of the British plantations; and for granting an inland duty in lieu thereof, be printed, as shall be sufficient for the use of the members of the House.

And the previous question being put, that that question be now put; the House divided.

The noes go forth.

Tellers for the yeas, Mr. Perrot, Mr. York: 112.

Tellers for the noes, Mr. Selwyn, Mr. Orlebar: 128.

So it passed in the negative.

D. The Preference for West Indian Interests

WHEN THE interests of rival colonial groups clashed, there was a strong tendency among people in power in Britain to favor those of the agricultural staple colonies, and especially of the West Indian sugar colonies, over those of the northern continental colonies, despite the fact that by the middle decades of the eighteenth century, the northern colonies were becoming economically more important to the home islands because of their rising consumption of British manufactures. The preference for the West Indies was revealed during the years 1731-33, when West Indian planters tried to persuade Parliament to act to discourage merchants from the continental colonies from trading with foreign sugar islands instead of the British West Indies. The debate over this issue lasted for three years and may be followed in the selections from the proceedings in the House of Commons printed as Document 1 below. Document 2 is an excerpt from the Molasses Act, which was eventually enacted on May 17, 1733, over the protests of the northern colonies.

1. DEBATES OVER THE MOLASSES ACT

SOURCE: Stock (ed.), *Proceedings and Debates of the British Parliaments*, IV, 93–94, 123–126, 184–187.

1731

Mar. 22. Sir John Rushout reported from the committee, to whom the petition of several merchants, planters, and others, trading to, and interested in, his Majesty's sugar colonies in America, in behalf of themselves, and many others, was referred; that the committee had examined the matter of the said petition, and had directed him to report the same, as it appeared to them, to the House: and he read the report in his place, and afterwards delivered it in at the clerk's table; where the same was read, and is, as followeth; viz.

That the committee (pursuant to the order of the House) proceeded to examine the matter of the said petition; and, to prove the allegations thereof, witnesses were called; viz.

Mr. Jonathan Sisson; who said, that, since the treaty of Utrecht, a considerable trade has been carried on between New England, and other English northern colonies, and the French sugar colonies, especially at Martinque; and that horses, lumber, flour, and other goods, are sent by the people of the northern colonies, and sold to the French, in exchange for molasses, and rum, particularly molasses (of which the French make great advantage, which being formerly of so little use to them, that they gave it to their horses and hogs) by means of which trade they have been enabled to enlarge their plantations, and have cut down their woods, to gain more ground, being now supplied with lumber, and other plantation necessaries, from our northern colonies; whereby the French are greatly enriched, and the British sugar colonies impoverished; and this has caused the necessaries, particularly lumber, for the plantations, to be very dear in the English colonies, who can take off all the horses, and lumber, they carry to Martinique: the French can't be supplied with those necessaries from any other place, by reason of the navigation of Canada being so very difficult, and dangerous: the northern colonies may be supplied with molasses, and rum, from the English sugar colonies, at reasonable prices; for rum was sold the last year at 12 d. per gallon, Barbado's money, which is £28 per cent. difference between that and English money.

He further said, that the French at Martinique freight English ships from thence with rum and molasses on their own accounts, and send the same to Boston, to their factors or agents there, the produce whereof is laid out in the building of vessels, and, when built, the factors, agents, or builder, before they make a bill of sale to the right owner, take an oath before the governor there, that they are not the property of foreigners, and that they are the true owners thereof; upon which they obtain a register in their own names, and the oath taken, that they are not for foreign service, is by these means evaded; and those ships, and chiefly the small ones, are manned with English and Irish sailors, hired by the French, and, as they have occasion, carry molasses and rum to the northern colonies, as well as to Cape Briton, from whence those goods are carried in the New England coasting vessels to Boston, and there disposed of, as before-mentioned. He added, that considerable sums of money were carried by those ships from Barbados, and our other sugar islands, to Martinique, in order to procure a more quick dispatch to be given to their loading of sugars and molasses, for which no more than £1 per cent. duty is paid, for the produce of the French islands, on exportation; and that little else is carried to Boston, besides molasses and rum; but, if a stop could be put to this trade, a great advantage would accrue to the English sugar settlements: some of our planters have already removed to New York, and others are going, which, in a great measure, is owing to this trade: formerly the profits, ariseing to the planter from rum and molasses at Barbados, was about one-third of the value of the produce of the plantation, and generally paid more than the charge of such plantation. . . .

1732

Jan. 26.   Ordered, that leave be given to bring in a bill, for the better securing and encouraging the trade of his Majesty's sugar colonies in America; and that Mr. Winnington and the Lord Malpas do prepare, and bring in, the same.

Jan. 28.   Mr. Winnington presented to the House (according to order) a bill, for the better securing and encouraging the trade of his Majesty's sugar colonies in America; and the same was received, and read the first time.

Resolved, that the bill be read a second time.

Ordered, that the said bill be printed.

Jan. 28.   Mr. Perry, member for London, said, that this bill was of such a nature, that all our colonies in America are some way or another concerned therein; that it was of the utmost consequence to the trade and navigation of this kingdom, and therefore ought to be maturely considered, not only within doors, but likewise by all those without doors who understand any thing of trade, and have a regard for the prosperity and welfare of their native country; and that all such might have an opportunity of giving their sentiments upon this occasion, he moved, that the bill might be printed. This motion being seconded and agreed to by the House, the bill was accordingly ordered to be printed.

Mr. Winnington spoke next;

Sir: As this bill is of very great consequence to the trade of this nation in general, and to the well-being of our settlements, either upon the continent or in the islands of America, we ought to consider the particular trade and produce of every one of our settlements; and therefore, that we may have as much insight into this matter as possible, I move, that the representations sent over from our several colonies, and laid before the honourable the Commissioners of trade and plantations, may be laid before this House, before we go upon the second reading of the bill. Mr. Winnington was supported by

Col. Bladen, who spoke as follows:

Sir: There have been several representations sent over to his Majesty from our settlements in the West-Indies, which representations have been referred to the board of trade to be considered by them, and for them to report their opinion upon the matter therein contained to his Majesty: some of them we have already considered, and have given our opinion upon them; but there are others that we have not as yet had time so thoroughly to consider as to be able to give any opinion upon them; however, Sir, in these last we shall make all imaginable dispatch, and shall be ready to lay them before the House as soon as possible.

Mr. Perry spoke again.

Sir: As this is an affair of so great consequence, we ought not to be in any hurry about passing the bill; we must wait till we have all those materials, which are necessary for giving us a full information in the affair before us. There is particularly in the bill, as now brought in, a clause about lumber, which in my opinion will do more harm to the trade of most of our colonies, and consequently to the trade of this nation, than all the other clauses can do good; but I shall have another opportunity, I hope, of giving my sentiments fully upon this head, and therefore I shall not trouble the House with them at this time.

Mr. Sandys said,

Sir: This bill was last session of parliament a long time before this House; there is no clause in the bill now brought in, but what was in the former, and every one of them was then fully considered and particularly examined into. The committee, that was appointed last session of parliament for drawing up the bill, were no less than three months about it; in which time they certainly had under their consideration every thing, that could possibly be thought of for giving them any light into the affair. I believe there is no gentleman in this House, but what is persuaded that some measures ought to be taken, and speedily taken too, for giving an encouragement to our sugar-colonies, so as to enable them to carry on a trade, at least, upon an equal footing with their rivals in the sugar-trade. The only reason of the bill's not passing, which was brought in last session of parliament, was that they had not had time in the other House to consider the affair so fully as they thought was necessary; I have been informed, that some of the members of the other House even complained, that it was hard that we did not allow them three weeks to consider of an affair, that we had been above three months in examining into. As the bill now before us contains nothing but what was in the former bill, which was so fully considered as to pass through this House, I am therefore of opinion, that there is no occasion to make any delay in the passing of this bill, or to wait for any farther information in the affair; for I am persuaded we can receive none, but what has been already laid before this House, and fully considered in the passing of the former bill.

Mr. Oglethorpe spoke next.

Sir: In all cases that come before this House, where there seems to be a clashing of interests between one part of the country and another, or between one set of people and another, we ought to have no regard to the particular interest of any country or set of people; the good of the whole is what we ought only to have under our consideration: our colonies are all a part of our own dominions; the people in every one of them are our own people, and we ought to shew an equal respect to all.

I remember, Sir, that there was once a petition presented to this House by one county, complaining, that they were very much injured in their trade, as to the sale of beans, by another; and therefore they modestly prayed, that the other county should be prohibited to sell any beans.

Such things may happen, I hope it is not so at present, but in the case, before us, if it should appear, that all our plantations, upon the continent of America, are against that which is desired by the sugar colonies, we are to presume, at least, that the granting thereof will be a prejudice to the trade or particular interests of our continent settlements; and, surely, Sir, the danger of hurting so considerable a part of our dominions, a part so extensive as to reach from the 34th to the 46th degree of northern latitude, will at least make us incline to be extremely cautious in what we are going about.

I shall be as ready as any man, to give all possible relief and encouragement to our sugar colonies; but if the relief or encouragement asked for appear to be an injury to the whole, or if it appears that it will do more harm to the other parts of our dominions than it can do good to them, we must refuse it; we must think of some other methods for putting them upon an equal footing with those, who are their rivals in any particular branch of trade.

We may form some judgment, Sir, from the appearances that were before us last session of parliament: but we may form a much more distinct judgment of things from what may be brought before us now. Some of those, concerned here for our settlements upon the continent, seemed last year to be indifferent; they seemed in some manner to give the affair up, I believe without any good authority from their constituents; but now the colonies themselves have had an opportunity to consider the affair then before us, and to send over their thoughts upon the subject in a proper and authentic manner; their true and real sentiments will best appear from the representations they have sent over; and till these are laid before us, we cannot give our opinions, either as to their inclinations, or as to the weight of the objections that they may make.

I must say, Sir, to the honour of the gentlemen concerned in the Board of Trade, that they are as exact and as diligent in all the matters which fall under their province as any board in England; they have much more business than most others, and their business will be daily increasing, in proportion as our colonies increase in riches and in power. It is already one of the most useful boards we have, and as long as the same good conduct is pursued, it will always be of great benefit and advantage to the trade of the British dominions. . . .

1733

The resolution being . . . amended, it was agreed to without any division; and then Mr. Winnington stood up again, and moved, that a duty of 4 s. per hundred weight, sterling money, be laid on all foreign sugars and paneels, imported into any of his Majesty's colonies or plantations in America. This was agreed to without any opposition.

Then colonel Bladen made the two following motions, viz. 1. "That a duty of 6 d. per gallon, sterling money, be laid on all foreign molasses and syrups imported into any of his Majesty's colonies or plantations in America: and 2. That a duty of 9 d. per gallon, sterling money, be laid on all foreign rum imported into any of his Majesty's colonies or plantations in America." Hereupon,

Sir John Barnard, in opposition thereto, said, that as the trade then stood between our northern colonies and the French sugar islands, it appeared, that our colonies bought molasses of them at a very low price, and distilled them into rum, by which they provided themselves at a small charge with the rum that was necessary for them in their trade with the Indians, and in their fishing trade; they had, it was true, most of the materials for making this rum from the French; but then the manufacture was all their own, and thereby a great many of our subjects in that part of the world were employed and maintained: that by laying such an high duty on French molasses, we should lay them under a necessity of manufacturing it themselves; so that our subjects would lose all that employment, and instead of buying molasses in their natural dress from the French, as they did formerly, they would be obliged to purchase the same molasses manufactured into rum, whereby the French sugar islands would take of them at least three times the money they took formerly: that as molasses was a bulky commodity, it would not be easy to run them into any of our northern colonies, so that the French would be laid under an absolutely necessity of manufacturing them into rum, and when manufactured into rum, it would be easy to carry that rum, and sell it in a smuggling way to our fishing vessels at sea, and even to run it into every one of our colonies on the continent of America: that the sea coasts belonging to us in that part of the world were of such a vast extent, and so many little harbours and creeks to be every where met with, the roads so little frequented, and the towns so open, that it would be impossible to prevent the running of French rum on shore, or the conveying it from one town to another after it is landed. No, not even if we should send thither the whole army of excise officers which we have here at home; the sending them thither, might indeed, add a good deal to our happiness in this country, but all of them together could be of no service for such a purpose in that country: that as to the laying a duty both on foreign rum and molasses, he would not be altogether against it, but then it ought to be only a small duty, for the sake of giving an advantage to our own sugar colonies in that respect, not such an high duty as was in a manner equal to a prohibition; for that was really granting a monopoly to our sugar islands, with respect to a commodity that is absolutely necessary for our northern colonies, both in their fishing trade and in their trade with the native Indians; and as the French were our rivals likewise in both those trades, we were about giving them a certain advantage as to these trades, and that without doing them any harm as to their sugar-trade; for if they sold sugar and rum cheaper than our colonies did, they would have vend enough for all they could make; they would have a stolen market for it in the British dominions, and an open market in all other parts of the world.

Colonel Bladen answered, that he had often heard our army of excise-officers set in a very terrible light, and represented as of the most dangerous consequence to the liberties of the nation, but now he heard it urged that this whole army would not be able to reduce our northern-colonies; and he was sure, if they were not, there was no fear of their being able to reduce this nation: but without sending any of that army to America, he hoped there would be no such thing as smuggling in that part of the world; it was to prevent such a pernicious practice, that he proposed only laying a duty on foreign rum; he did not propose a prohibition, and the duty he had proposed was no higher, than what was absolutely necessary for putting our own sugar-islands on an equal foot with the French.

Sir John Barnard replied, that he had said, that our whole army of excisemen would not be able to prevent the running of French rum in that country; he did not talk of reducing the country, he had not so much as mentioned the word, but he believed it would be much easier to reduce the country, than to prevent the running of French rum in it, in case what was then proposed should take effect: that if the gentleman really meant to prevent running, he was very unfortunate in what he had proposed, for he had proposed the only method that could be thought on, for setting up and encouraging the smuggling-trade; which was that of laying on a high duty, equal to, if not above, the first price of the commodity upon which it was laid. Then the question being put, the three foregoing motions were severally agreed to without any division.

After this, the two following motions were agreed to without any opposition, 1. "That all the Duties charged on the importation of all sugars and paneels of the growth, product and manufacture of his Majesty's Colonies and Plantations in America, into Great Britain, be drawn back on exportation of the same." 2. "That a drawback or allowance of 2 s. per hundred weight on all sugars, refined in and exported from Great Britain, be paid on the exportation thereof, over and above all drawbacks or bounties now payable thereon." This last resolution was seconded by

Sir John Barnard, who said, that he would agree to that as well as the other resolution with all his heart, for that the two last were the only resolutions they had come to, which, in his opinion, would be of any real use to our sugar-colonies; and particularly the last resolution he was glad to see moved, because he hoped it would make them think of some other things relating to our trade, which stood in need of some such redress from Parliament: that there were several foreign materials imported into this kingdom, liable to duties on importation, which duties were drawn back, if the materials were again exported in the same shape; but if manufactured and made more valuable by the labour of our own people, neither the merchant nor the manufacturer could draw back the duties, even though they should afterwards export the same, and could shew that this manufacture was made of materials that had paid a duty on importation; and would have had a drawback on exportation, if they had been carried out rough as they were brought in: that this was a scandalous oversight when these duties were first imposed, but it was much more scandalous that in so long a time this oversight had never been amended: that there were several examples of this oversight could be given, but he would then only mention the duties on foreign hemp, flax, cordage, etc., which were drawn back if the goods should be exported in the same condition they were imported: but if these very goods should, by the labour and industry of our own people, be manufactured into cables, ropes, and other tackle for shipping, and then exported, the exporter could not have any drawback: that this was a great loss to that branch of our trade, which was a very considerable branch, but would be much more considerable if it were not for this hardship it laboured under. . . .

2. THE MOLASSES ACT OF 1733

SOURCE: Pickering (ed.), Statutes at Large, XVI, 374.

WHEREAS the welfare and prosperity of your Majesty's sugar colonies in America are of the greatest consequence and importance to the trade, navigation and strength of this kingdom: and whereas the planters of the said sugar colonies have of late years fallen under such great discouragements, that they are unable to improve or carry on the sugar trade upon an equal footing with the foreign sugar colonies, without some advantage and relief be given to them from Great Britain: for remedy whereof, and for the good and welfare of your Majesty's subjects, we your Majesty's most dutiful and loyal subjects, the commons of *Great Britain* assembled in parliament have given and granted unto your Majesty the several and respective rates and duties herein after mentioned, and in such manner and form as is herein after expressed; and do most humbly beseech your Majesty that it may be enacted, and be it enacted by the King's most excellent majesty, by and with the advice and consent of the lords spiritual and temporal and commons in this present parliament assembled, and by the authority of the same, That from and after the twenty fifth day of *December* one thousand seven hundred and thirty three, there shall be raised, levied, collected and paid, unto and for the use of his Majesty, his heirs and successors, upon all rum or spirits of the produce or manufacture of any of the colonies or plantations in *America*, not in the possession or under the dominion of his Majesty, his heirs and successors, which at any time or times within or during the continuance of this act, shall be imported or brought into any of the colonies or plantations in *America*, which now are or hereafter may be in the possession or under the dominion of his Majesty, his heirs or successors, the sum of nine pence, money of *Great Britain*, to be paid according to the proportion and value of five shillings and six pence the ounce in silver, for every gallon thereof, and after that rate for any greater or lesser quantity; and upon all molasses or syrups of such foreign produce or manufacture as aforesaid, which shall be imported or brought into any of the said colonies or plantations of or belonging to his Majesty, the sum of six pence of like money for every gallon thereof, and after that rate for any greater or lesser quantity; and upon all sugars and paneles of such foreign growth, produce or manufacture as aforesaid, which shall be imported into any of the said colonies or plantations of or belonging to his Majesty, a duty after the rate of five shillings of like money, for every hundred weight *Avoirdupoize*, of the said sugar and paneles, and after that rate for a greater or lesser quantity. . . .

16. The Dynamics of Internal Colonial Politics

A. The Fear of Executive Power

THE FEAR of prerogative and executive power that had been so manifest among members of Parliament during the seventeenth century continued to animate colonial legislators long after it had ceased to be of major importance in England. Why this fear persisted and how it shaped the perceptions of colonial politicians are revealed especially clearly in the two selections below. Document 1 is an excerpt from the editor's preface to The Groans of Jamaica, a pamphlet written anonymously and published in London in 1714 complaining of the behavior of Lord Archibald Hamilton, governor of Jamaica. Document 2 is a portion of an address by the New York Lower House to Governor George Clinton on July 14, 1749.

1. THE ABSENCE OF EFFECTIVE PROTECTION
AGAINST A DESPOTIC GOVERNOR

SOURCE: *The Groans of Jamaica, Express'd in a Letter from a Gentleman Residing there, to his Friend in London* (London, 1714), iv–viii.

I must own, it has, oftner than once, been the Subject of my Admiration, as well as Contemplation, how it should come to pass, that in all the Revolutions of State, and Changes of the Ministry, which have happened here, these Sixty Years past, and upwards, ever since the happy Restoration of King Charles IId. so great an Accession to the Power, Riches and Glory of this Kingdom, as are undoubtedly the several Colonies which compose the *British* Empire in *America*, should (even in the most noted Periods of that Time, for either Peace or War) lye still so much neglected, under such a precarious Government and grievous Administration, as they have, for the most part, labour'd under, both before and since the late signal Revolution; tho' of late Years (as far as I can learn) still worse and worse.

'Tis true, the present Ministry have had their Heads so much imployed about the weightiest Affairs of State, at home, and in settling the general Peace of *Europe*; that it may, very justly, be supposed, they have not had Time enough, as yet, to look so far Abroad, as to have taken immediate Cognizance of the several

Constitutions, present Circumstances, and particular Grievances of the *British* West India Plantations. But, 'tis hoped that, in due Time, these may likewise fall under their serious Consideration.

I know some designing and wicked People have been, and still are, at no small Pains to inculcate into the Minds of all Persons in Authority, whom they have the Opportunity of conversing or corresponding with, very mean Notions and Sentiments of the Births, Education, Manners, Principles, and other Qualities of the Inhabitants of those Plantations; and, under such disadvantagious Characters, their several Oppressors have, from Time to Time, endeavour'd to misrepresent them here, as a turbulent, factious, and uneasie People, never to be pleased, under any Government whatsoever.

To which it may very justly be replied, That, upon an impartial Examination and Tryal, it would manifestly appear, that all the Contentions and Animosities, which, at any time, happen between the Governour and Inhabitants of any of the *West-India* Plantations, have (generally speaking, and particularly as to *Jamaica*) had their first Rise, from some grievous and intolerable Acts of Oppression, in the Administration: And therefore 'tis not to be much wonder'd at, if such should produce some Repinings, Heart burnings and Discontents, among a People otherways very peaceably disposed; when the wisest of Men found from his own Experience, and left it to us, as a certain Aphorism, recorded in Scripture, that *Oppression maketh even a wise Man mad.*

It cannot be denied, but that, in peopling those Plantations, many Persons of obscure births and very different Characters went, or were, from time to time, sent and transported thither, as Occasion required: But 'tis as true, that some thousands of Persons of very creditable Families, good Education, and loyal Principles, went thither likewise; some through the Narrowness of their Circumstances; some to avoid the Miseries of the Civil War at home; and others to improve such paternal or acquired Fortunes and Estates, as they thought convenient to carry along with them, at the time.

The present Inhabitants are generally Her Majesty's natural born Subjects; Natives either of *England, Scotland,* or *Ireland,* or born of such, in the Plantations: Many of them are Gentlemen of very liberal Education, some even at Universities: And such having, by their own, or their Forefathers Industry, acquired the Property and Possession of very considerable Plantations and

Estates, and being desirous and willing to enjoy the same com-
fortably, and to live peaceably, as good and dutiful Subjects, cannot but grudge extremely to find, that (as particularly in *Jamaica*)
profound Ignorance, accompanied with vast Impudence in some, a
stupid, blind, indolent and implicite Acquiescence in others, and a
crafty, active, knavish Genius, blended with Lewdness, Atheism
and Irreligion in a third sort; and all varnished over, with a servile,
fawning, seeming Obsequiousness, should be the Chief, if not the
only, recommending Qualities, to entitle even the worst of Men,
tho' sprung up as suddenly, in one Night's time, as Mushrooms out
of a Dunghill, to a Go——r's Favour; while, at the same time, Men
of Virtue, Merit and Capacity, are not only discouraged, insulted,
and oppressed, but also revil'd, belied and ridicul'd, to an intolerable Degree, with Buffoonry, Impudence and Nonsense: to the
great Encouragement of Vice and Immorality, in those Parts.

Could we reasonably suppose, and be assured of a constant Succession of wise, judicious, just, good and pious Princes on the
Throne, like Her present Majesty; and of such like Governors, in
all Provinces and far distant Plantations, and that these again
would, in their Choice of all subordinate Judges, Magistrates and
other Officers, regulate themselves by the most apparent Proofs of
the Vertue, Merit and Capacity of the several Candidates, for
Offices of Trust and Profit: I believe all good Men would join with
me in Opinion, That, of all the several Forms of Government on
Earth, an unlimited absolute Government would undoubtedly be
the best, on many Accounts; but the Experience the World has
had of the lamentable Weakness of some Princes and Rulers, of all
Degrees; and of the extravagant Passions and insatiable Avarice,
Ambition, Lust, and Revenge of some others; has so fully demon-
strated the Vanity and Folly of such a fruitless and chimerical
Supposition, that the Wisdom of our Ancestors found it necessary
to tie up even the best of our Princes, as well as the bad, by good
and wholesome Laws.

The Consideration whereof makes it still so much more the
Subject of my Wonder; that a Governor of any Colony of Her
Majesty's Free-born Subjects, in the *West-Indies*, so far distant
from the Seat of Redress, either by Appeals, or otherwise, should
be vested with a Power to govern, in a more absolute and unlimited
manner there, than even the Queen her self can, according to Law,
or ever did attempt to exercise in *Great Britain*.

The Governor of *Jamaica* (e.g.) is not only CAPTAIN GEN-ERAL, and Commander in Chief of that Island, and other the Territories thereunto belonging, and likewise CHANCELLOR, and Vice-Admiral thereof; but has also the sole Power of nominating, appointing, continuing, turning out, and putting in again, at Pleasure, as often and whensoever he will, all and every one of the Judges of all the other Courts of Judicature, throughout the said Island; and likewise the Power of calling, continuing, adjourning, proroguing, dissolving, and issuing new Writs, for succeeding Assemblies, at Pleasure, without any manner of Limitation, as to time or otherways: by Means whereof, the Free-holders have been frequently plagued, harrassed and disappointed, in their own private Affairs, by Elections and long Sessions, to little good Purpose, at times very unseasonable for the Planting-Interest; and as frequently prorogued or dissolved again, whenever they could not be prevail'd upon, to comply implicitely with the arbitrary Dictates, and injurious Measures of some few designing Persons, whose constant Plot is to enrich themselves, by enslaving the Inhabitants.

The Governor is likewise, in effect (tho' not nominally) BISHOP of *Jamaica*: For, he's vested with the sole Power of nominating, appointing, and collating Ministers in all and every one of the Parishes of that Island; (which are 17 in Number) has also the granting of all Letters of Administration, all Probates of Wills and Testaments, all Licences for Marriages, and Licences for permitting School-Masters to teach; the naming and appointing Guardians for absent Orphans: And, in short, is sole Judge of all Matters relating to the Consistorial or Ecclesiastick Law there:

Now, how such an universal Knowledge, Experience and Judgment, both of Men and Things, as seems necessary to accomplish any Man, for the Discharge of so universal and unlimited a Trust, in so many different Capacities as aforesaid, should (without immediate Inspiration) be acquired, by a Person who was never, any way, noted for the Brightness of his natural Parts, and who had not the Advantage of any other Education, but what he had between the Stem and Stern of a Ship, eversince he was sent a young Youth to Sea, in or about the Year 1687, is (I must own) above my Comprehension. And yet (which adds still to the Miseries of that Island) all the Commissions, Commands, Orders, Injunctions, Directions, Judgments, and Decrees of this same Despotick Go——r, (or rather of his Triumvirate Tutors) are incomparably less liable to be reversed, than the Decrees of the most knowing as well as the most learned and judicious Lord High Chancellor of *Great Britain.*

For. 1st. There can be no Appeal from the said Go——r's Judgment, unless the *Subjectum Controversia* be of the Value of £. 500 at the least. 2dly. None can come off that Island, on any pretence whatsoever, without the Governor's express Leave in writing, under his Hand; which is sometimes not to be obtain'd, but by giving very extravagant Bail, far beyond the Value of the Subject-Matter in Debate; and frequently not, at all, on any account. And 3dly, Even when an Appeal reacheth hither, it cannot be try'd any where, but before the Queen in Council: And the said Governor happening to be born of a great Family, (tho' he be the very Refuse and worthless Dregs thereof) his noble Relations, Allies, and their Friends here, may possibly be so far prepossessed, by a natural Byass (how imperceptible soever to themselves) in his Favour, and for supporting whatever is said to be for his Power, Interest and Credit (tho', much more properly, for that of his scandalous Tutors) that 'tis ten to one, but a poor Appellant, after all his Trouble, Pains and Expence, may come off, with the weeping Cross, at last. . . .

The melancholly Consideration of all which, as well as of the large Joint-Stock-Purse, raised from the Produce of Prize-Goods, Escheated Estates, and other Spoils of the Oppressed, which that nimble, crafty, and Jesuitical V——n (Mr. R——by) has ready at Command (as being absolute Plenipotentiary here, for the Go——r and his scandalous Faction) and likewise of the amazing Reception, Countenance and Protection he has likewise hitherto met with, makes many injur'd and oppress'd Persons in *Jamaica*, who otherwise would be Appellants, sit down tamely, and bear with their Miseries, as well as they can, for the time; rather than attempt swimming against the Stream, while they see the Torrent of their Despotick Go——r's Fury, as well as that of his Tutors and Tools, run with so impetuous and irresistible a Force, as at present; notwithstanding the manifest Bent of the Generality of the Inhabitants Inclinations against them.

2. THE CASE AGAINST LONG-TERM SALARIES FOR GOVERNORS

SOURCE: *Votes and Proceedings of the General Assembly of the Colony of New-York, June 27, 1749 to August 4, 1749* (New York, 1749), pp. 14–17.

May it please your Excellency,

We His Majesty's most dutiful and loyal Subjects, the General Assembly of the Colony of *New-York,* now attend your Excellency with our Answer to your Excellency's Message of the 12th Instant; and if the Parts thereof appear to be somewhat incoherent, it must be imputed to too close a Pursuit of your Excellency's Method in that Message.

Your Excellency begins with charging us, with renewing Differences in every new Session, tho' after every Prorogation you had spoke to us as if no such Differences had existed in a former Session. Any one who reads, and considers your Excellency's Manner of expressing this, would naturally conclude, that these Differences had long subsisted; that there had been several new Sessions, in every of which the General Assembly had taken Occasion to renew the former Differences, and that on the contrary, your Excellency had studied to avoid them. You well know, *Sir,* that this is the very first Session since the Dispute between your Excellency and the present General Assembly arose; which had its Rise from your Excellency's Demand of a five Years Support, by your Speech of the 14th of *October* last; and whether your Excellency has not given Occasion for the Continuance of that Dispute, by your Speech at the Opening of the present Session (the only One we have had since the Determination of that wherein this Dispute was first started) we leave every impartial Reader to judge. . . .

We are very sensible, that it is the Usage of the Parliament of *Great-Britain,* in raising of Money for the publick Service, only to appropriate the several Sums to the general Uses for which they are intended, and leave the particular Application or Disposition thereof to his Majesty; But we beg Leave to observe to your Excellency, that we conceive there is a vast Difference between the Condition of those his Majesty's happy Subjects, who live under his immediate Government in the Kingdom of *Great Britain,* and these whose unhappy Lot it is, by the great Distance they are from him, to be under the Command of Governors of Provinces.

Our most gracious Sovereign neither has, nor can have, any Interest separate from his People; he cannot injure them without injuring himself; and therefore it is, that the great Representative of the Nation repose such an entire Confidence in him, as to leave the particular Disposition of all publick Monies solely to him: If any Misapplication happens, it must be entirely owing to subordinate Officers, who may be call'd to an Account, and punished (as they often have been) by the Parliament, for their Mismanagement: But the Case of his Majesty's Subjects in the Plantations is vastly different: They have Governors sent to them, generally entire Strangers to the People they are sent to govern; they seldom have any Estates in the Colonies where they are appointed Governors, and consequently their Interest is entirely distinct and different from that of the People; and therefore it is, that they seldom regard the Welfare of the People, otherwise than as they can make it subservient to their own particular Interest; and as they know the Time of their Continuance in their Governments to be uncertain, all Methods are used, and all Engines set to work, to raise Estates to themselves: And therefore, should the publick Monies be left to their Disposition, what can be expected, but the grossest Misapplication under various Pretences, which will never be wanting! This has often been actually the Case in this Colony; and when such Misapplications happen, there are no Means of Redress: The Governors cannot be called to an Account by the Representatives of the People; and as to any Security which might be expected in the Council, it is generally obviated, by their being intimidated by sudden and peremptory Suspensions. In this Situation of Things, we are fully persuaded, that our most gracious Sovereign (whose distinguishing Character it is, to be equally careful of all his faithful and loyal Subjects, how distant soever from his Royal Presence) will not condemn the General Assembly, for taking Care that the Money given by them, be duly applied to the respective Uses for which they give it; and we are well informed, that the Right Honourable the Lords Commissioners for Trade and Plantations, have on a former Occasion, declared, That they thought it very reasonable to oblige the Assembly as much as possible at all Times, to dispose of Money by them granted, in such Manner as they desire.

And on this Head, we must declare to your Excellency, that we cannot answer it to our Constituents, to pass any Bill for raising Money on them, and leave it to be disposed of at the Will and Pleasure of a Governor; and this we hope your Excellency will accept for a categorical Answer.

Your Excellency, towards the Conclusion of your Message, intimates, that you have now done all that is in your Power, to put an End to the unhappy Differences which have so long subsisted, to the Prejudice of the People we represent. If your Excellency means, that you have done it by this Message, we must declare, that tho' we have considered every Part with the utmost Attention, we are not able to discover that it has any Tendency that Way: Such a Motion would be received by us with the greatest Pleasure; as we are far from having any Inclination, that there shou'd be any other Contest between the several Branches of the Legislature, than which should contribute most to the real Service of his Majesty, in the Welfare of this his loyal Colony. And we now declare to your Excellency, that we are heartily willing to provide an honourable Support for his Majesty's Government in this Colony, in the Manner wherein it has been done ever since your Excellency came to the Administration.

We are extremely griev'd, that we are obliged to remain here with great Expence to our Constituents, and Inconvenience to our own private Affairs, without any Prospect of serving the Publick: But at the same Time, we take Leave to assure your Excellency, that no Inconvenience, how great soever, to which our own Persons or private Affairs may be expos'd, by Means of our being kept here, shall ever prevail upon us to abandon the true Interest of our Country.

By Order of the General Assembly,

DAVID JONES, *Speaker*

B. The Imperatives of Institutional Cooperation

IN A FEW colonies, the judicious behavior of the governors and an unusually stable social and political situation mitigated the traditional suspicion of the executive among legislators and led to an emphasis upon cooperation between branches in pursuit of the common good. The conditions making such cooperation possible and the benefits thought to make it desirable may be seen in the two speeches of Sir John Randolph printed below. The first was made to the Virginia House of Burgesses on August 24, 1734, on the occasion of Randolph's first election as its speaker; and the second, on August 6, 1736, following his second election and presentation to Governor William Gooch.

SOURCE: Henry R. McIlwaine and John P. Kennedy (eds.), *Journals of the House of Burgesses of Virginia* (13 vols., Richmond, Va.: Virginia State Library, 1906–15), *1727–1740*, 175–176, 241–242.

I

GENTLEMEN [of the House of Burgesses]

I come now to experience all the Degrees of your Favor and
Kindness to me; and it will not become me to pretend any Unwill-
ingness to accept what you think me worthy of: Tho' I know, after
Gentlemen have emploied all their Interest to be elected into this
Office, they usually represent themselves absolutely incapable of
discharging the Duties of it. But if this be done without a Consciousness of the Truth of what they say, or any Design to depart
from the Right of their Election, it must either be a false Appearance of Modesty, or a blind Compliance with a Custom, that
perhaps, in the beginning, was founded upon Truth and Reason,
but by Time, like many others, becomes only an Abuse of Words;
which I cannot follow: And I the rather avoid it, because I intend,
upon no Occasion, to give you any Instance of the least Insincerity,
which I think not only very useless, but the most vicious Thing in
the World. Therefore, I must own, I do with a particular Pleasure
embrace the Opportunity you have given me, of employing my
small Talents, which appear to you in a much better Light than
they deserve, still in your service; and I thank you for this additional Instance of your Confidence in me, in bestowing your
greatest Trust upon me. But as to my fitness to serve you, Time
and your own Experience will best determine it; so it may be
needless to raise your Expectations about it: Only thus much I will
assure you, that all the Advantages I may have received from a long
Experience of the Methods of this House, shall be improved for
the Advancement of your Reputation, and the Public Good; and I
will not imagine, that the Pageantry and Formalities of this Office,
are any Part of the Honors of it, which I know must proceed from a
Labor and Diligence to prevent any Imputation upon your Proceedings and Resolutions. To this I am bound, not only by the
Duty I owe to you, but by my own Interest; since nothing can
happen amiss here, that will not be reflected on me, perhaps in
more than my due Proportion, while the Weight of my own failings will lie wholly on my self, and perhaps of some that may be
only imaginary: For as, on the one Hand, it is not the easiest Thing
in public Debates, so to hold in one's own Temper, as to avoid all

just Occasions of Reproach; so on the other, it is one of the hardest, to place what is done justly and laudably in such a View as will be acceptable to every Body. The Prejudices with which we imbibe all of our own Opinions, which are generally impressed upon us too hastily, are often the Occasion of great Injustice in this Particular: And the Partiality of Mankind is such, that they cannot cordially approve what is done by those who do not concur with all their Sentiments; but are apt to charge the contrary Side with Ignorance, Obstinacy, or perhaps Corruption. Yet tho' this be very common, every Body is ready to condemn it as one of the great Weaknesses of Human Nature; which is most evidently true from this, that both Sides, in every Opposition, of which one must certainly be in the wrong, entertain the same Rancour and Animosity against each other, from an imaginary Excellence of their own Modes of Thinking. But I have abundant Reason to hope, from my Experience of the Candor and Good-will of this House towards me, that I shall be exempted from any unkind Censures of this Sort; and indeed, seeing we have the Happiness, which seems almost peculiar to our selves, of being under none of the Perturbations which we see every where else arising from the different Views and Designs of Factions and Parties, and have yet no Footsteps of Corruption among us, instead of raising any Heat or Intemperance in our Debates, which are always unnecessary, we should look upon all Differences among us to proceed from the Doubtfulness of Expedients that shall be proposed for the Common Good: And upon that Account, the Minority should submit calmly and chearfully to what the Majority determines, 'til Time and Experience shall either convince, or furnish them with more forcible Arguments against it. Then we shall hear one another patiently, put the Weight of every Man's Reason in the Ballance against our own, and at last form a Judgment upon the whole matter; which, if not the wisest, yet, resulting from the Integrity of our own Principles, will be honest and commendable. But if we come, by our Resentments and Impatience of being out voted, or by our Affections, to consider Men more than the Matter, we shall be sure to be always in the wrong, because what we do from Considerations without us, can have no good Foundation; and we must lose all the Advantages of Reasoning and Argument. And, however Mankind may be provoked, by being thwarted with the Sentiments of other Men, a Variety of Opinions is not only absolutely necessary to our Natures, but is likewise of all Things the most useful;

since if all Men were of one Mind, there would be no Need of Councils; no Subject for Learning and Eloquence; the Mind would want its proper Exercise, and without it, like the Body, would lose its natural Strength, from a Habit of Sloth and Idleness. Truth itself will receive an Addition of Strength by being opposed, and can never be in Danger of suffering by the Test of Argument.

These being Notions by which we should be directed, in discharging the Trust the People have reposed in us, if we would establish them in our Practice, we should then attain the true Dignity of our Representation; and I flatter myself, from your accustomed Prudence and Moderation, every Gentleman here will consider what it is to represent the People of any Country.

But indeed, I know I must make the worst Figure myself, if I shall be found unable to perform what it will be my Duty to dictate to others; if I shall endeavour to make the established Rules of your Proceedings subservient to my own Fancies and Humours, or Interests; or shall bring into this Chair a Restlesness and Impatience about Points that may be carried against my Sentiments; or shall pretend to any Authority of swaying any Member in his Opinion; I say, then I shall deserve to have no Influence upon your Proceedings; but do not doubt, nay I hope, you will mortify me with the utmost of your Contempt for the Inconsistence of my Theory and Practice. And if I shall happen to succeed better, I will pretend to no other Praise, but that of not having deceived the Expectations of so many worthy Gentlemen, who have continued to heap upon me such a Series of Favors, which so long as I retain the Memory of any Thing, I must look upon as the chief Foundation of the Credit and Reputation of my Life.

II

[August 6, 1736]

[SIR,]

I humbly thank you for this your favourable Opinion; which I don't pretend to deserve, but will use it as a proper Admonition, whereby I ought to regulate my Conduct in the Exercise of the Office you are now pleas'd to confirm me in; which I do not intend to magnify to the Degree some have done, feeling we are no more than the Representative Body of a Colony, naturally and justly dependent upon the Mother Kingdom, whose Power is circumscribed by very narrow Bounds; and whose Influence is of small Extent. All we pretend to, is to be of some Importance to Those who send us hither, and to have some Share in their Protection, and the Security of their Lives, Liberties, and Properties.

The Planters, who sustain'd the Heat and Burthen of the first Settlement of this Plantation, were miserably harrassed by the Government, in the Form it was then established, which had an unnatural Power of Ruling by Martial Law, and Constitutions passed by a Council in England, without the Consent of the People, which were no better: This made the Name of Virginia so infamous, that we see the Impressions of those Times, hardly yet worn out in other Countries, especially among the Vulgar: And such have been in all Ages, and for ever must continue to be, the Effects of an Arbitrary Despotic Power; of which the Company in London, in whom all Dominion and Property was then lodged, were so sensible, that they resolved to establish another Form of Government more agreeable and suitable to the Temper and Genius of the English Nation. And accordingly, in July, 1621, pass'd a Charter under their Common Seal, which was founded upon Powers before granted by Charters under the Great Seal of England; whereby they ordered and declared, That for preventing Injustice and Oppression for the Future; and for advancing the Strength and Prosperity of the Colony, there should be Two Supreme Councils; One to be called, The Council of State, consisting of the Governor, and certain Councillors, particularly named, to serve as a Council of Advice to the Governor; the other to be called by the Governor, Yearly, consisting of the Council of State, and Two Burgesses to be chosen by the Inhabitants of every Town, Hundred, or other Plantation; to be called, The General Assembly: And to have free Power to treat, consult, and conclude, of all Things concerning the Public Weal; and to enact such Laws for the Behoof of the Colony, and the good Government thereof, as from Time to Time should appear necessary or requisite: Commanding them to imitate and follow the Policy, Form of Government, Laws, Customs, Manner of Trial, and other Administration of Justice used in England; and providing that no Orders of their General Court should bind the Colony, unless ratified in the General Assemblies, This is the Original of our Constitution, confirmed by King James the First, by King Charles the First, upon his Accession to the Throne, and by all the Crown'd Heads of England, and Great-Britain, successively upon the Appointment of every new Governor, with very little Alteration. Under it, we are grown to whatever we now have to boast of. And from hence, the House of Burgesses do derive diverse Privileges, which they have long enjoy'd, and claim as their undoubted Right. Freedom of Speech is the very Essence of their Being, because, without it, nothing could be thoroly debated, nor could they be look'd upon as a Council; an Exemption from Arrests, confirm'd by a Positive Law, otherwise their Counsels and Debates might be frequently interrupted, and their Body diminished by the Loss of its Members; a Protection for their Estates, to prevent all Occasions to withdraw them from the necessary Duty of their Attendance; a Power over their own Members, that they may be answerable to no other Jurisdiction for any Thing done in the House; and a sole Right of determining all Questions concerning their own Elections, lest contrary Judgments, in the Courts of Law, might thwart or destroy Theirs.

All these, I say, besides others which spring out of them, are incident to the Nature and Constitution of our Body; and I am commanded by the House, to offer a Petition in their Behalf, that You will be pleas'd to discountenance all Attempts that may be offer'd against them, and assist us with Your Authority in supporting and maintaining them against all Insults whatsoever: And Lastly, I must beg Your Favour to my self, that You will not construe my Actions with too much Severity, nor impute my particular Errors and Failings to the House.

To which the Governor answer'd;

The House of Burgesses may always depend upon my Care to support them in their antient Rights and Privileges.

And then Mr. Speaker went on:

We have long experienced Your Love and Good Will to the People of this Country; and observe with what Readiness you exert it upon all Occasions.

The Art of Governing Well, is thought to be the most abstruse, as well as the usefulest Science in the World; and when It is learnt to some Degree of Perfection, it is very difficult to put it in Practice, being often opposed by the Pride and Interest of the Person that governs. But You have shew'd how easy it is to give universal Satisfaction to the People under Your Government: You have met them, and heard their Grievances in frequent Assemblies, and have had the Pleasure of seeing none of them proceed from Your Administration: You have not been intoxicated with the Power committed to You by His Majesty; but have used it, like a faithful Trustee, for the Public Good, and with proper Cautions: Raised no Debates about what it might be able to do of itself; but, on all important Occasions, have suffer'd it to unite with that of the other Parts of the Legislature: You never propose Matters, without supposing Your Opinion subject to the Examination of Others; nor strove to make other Mens Reason blindly and implicitly obedient to Yours; but have always calmly acquiesced in the Contrary Opinion: And Lastly, You have extirpated all Factions from among us, by discountenancing Public Animosities; and plainly prov'd, that none can arise, or be lasting, but from the Countenance and Encouragement of a Governor. . . .

I do not mention these Things, for the Sake of enlarging my Periods, nor for Flattery, nor for conciliating Favour: For if I know my self at all, I have none of the Arts of the first, nor the Address that is necessary for the other. And I hope, I shall never be one of those, who bestow their Commendations upon all Men alike; upon those who deserve it, as well as those who do not.

Permit me then, Sir, to beseech You to go on in the same steady Course: Finish the Character You have been almost Nine Years establishing; Let it remain unblemished, and a Pattern to those who shall come after You; Make us the Envy of the King's other Plantations; and put those Governors out of Countenance, who make Tyranny their Glory; and tho' they know their Master's Will, fancy it a Dishonour to perform it.

C. The Perils of Corruption

In MASSACHUSETTS, beginning with the administration of Governor William Shirley in the 1740's and in a few other colonies later, the governors obtained enough informal powers through the relatively extensive patronage available to them to enable them to influence the colonial lower houses much as Sir Robert Walpole manipulated the House of Commons during his long tenure as First Minister. In such situations, opposition groups in the colonies began to talk less about the dangers of prerogative and, employing the rhetoric of the opposition to Walpole in Britain, more about the perils of the people's representatives being corrupted by the executive and his adherents. The dangers that might derive from legislators thus corrupted, and the steps necessary to prevent them from materializing, were discussed in the following anonymous election pamphlet published in Massachusetts in 1742.

Source: A Letter to the Freeholders and Other Inhabitants of this
Province, Qualified to Vote for Representatives in the Ensuing
Election (Boston [?], 1742).

MY DEAR COUNTRYMEN,

If we did but duly consider the great Trust we repose in those who
we send to represent us in the General Court, (for it is no less than
our Lives, Estates and Liberties, Religious and Civil, and that of
our Posterity) we should not make so light a Matter of it, as we too
too often do, and be so indifferent about it.

A vertuous Prince generally makes a vertuous Court, and a
vertuous Legislature will exceedingly contribute, and is one of the
best Means to make a vertuous People; and till we are so, we have
little Reason to expect to be a happy People.—We are a professing
People, and are favoured with the Enjoyment of very valuable
Privileges, Religious and Civil, for which our brave Ancestors made
this Settlement; it should therefore be our greatest Care to hand
down to Posterity those most invaluable Privileges, as unincum-
ber'd as possible.

It is cruel and inhumane, and therefore unjust, to give away our
Estates from our Children, which they have a natural Right to
(except for very extraordinary Reasons) but I conceive it to be
much more so, to give away their Liberties and Privileges, the least
whereof, once given up, is exceeding difficult (if possible) ever to
be recovered again; and however small and triffling it may seem to
be, it's very unsafe parting with it, and the Value of it is never so
well known, as when we are deprived of it; and I can't help thinking those to be really the truest and best Subjects to their Prince,
who are most tenacious of their just and lawful Liberties.

You may observe in the English Prints by the last Ships from
London, what a Spirit of Liberty and Love for the Publick Weal,
and Credit of the Nation, breaths in the good People of those large
Cities of London, Westminster and York, for publick Justice
against any (tho' ever so great Men) who shall sacrifice the publick
Welfare of the Nation, to their private Avarice and Gain, and
against too great a Number of Placemen and Pensioners sitting in
Parliament.

And will not such a noble Publick Spirit, fire us with an honest
Zeal in this Part of the World, to look about us, and inquire, if
there have been any such among us, who have been influenced by

Posts of Honour and Profit, to vote, and act too much, as Men in Power would have them? And if there have been such, to prevent it as much as may be for the future, by chusing such Men only as are least likely to be influenced thereby?

I esteem it a great Happiness, that we have not a great many Posts of Profit among us; and wish we may be always so happy on that Account: For it often happens in many Parts of the World, that some of the most worthless Men enjoy them; and it's likely such Men, who will do any dirty Work, that a Man of Virtue would be ashamed of, will enjoy them.

You all know that our Legislature is made up of Governour, Council, and Representatives, who are, or should be, dependant on each other: For no Law can be made without the Consent of each Part of the Legislature, and that Form of Government was, I suppose, designed to maintain a Ballance of Power, and it is to be hoped no Part of it will ever give up any of that Share, which of Right belongs to it; for if they should, what will become of the Ballance? And we all know there is no great Danger from one particular Quarter. Now let us consider seriously, that in Case the Governour should by any Means get to be independant on the other two Branches, what Mischiefs might possibly, nay, very probably, ensue; and the late Hon. House of Representatives say, and I think very justly, "That to be independent and arbitrary are the same Things in Civil Policy"; and what can possibly make a Governour more independent and arbitrary, than a fixed or large Salary? And what can be more certain, than that the Representative Body of this People are better Judges of the Abilities and Circumstances of their Constituents, than the Governour can possibly be? And will any Freeholder vote for such a Person to represent him and his Posterity, who, he shall have Reason to think, or fear, may be tempted to give up so valuable a Part of their Rights, as their being Judges of their own Abilities, in such an Affair, which has been so long defended (and at great Expence) by our Representatives, as from the Date of our Charter? I hope there will be very few, if any such among us, especially at this Time, when the Fees of the Officers, (if they follow the Example of the new Clerk of the Superior Court) are raised *Three Hundred per Cent*, i.e. Four Times to what they were a Twelvemonth past. And your Estates by the last Supply Bill, are depreciated near *Thirty per Cent*; for please to remember the Possessor of one of these new Tenor Bills must pay *Twenty six Shillings* and *Eight Pence* for an

Ounce of Silver, and is not to receive his Silver so soon as the Time fixed for the Redemption of the first new Tenor Bills (which may now not improperly be called middle Tenor Bills) so that the Difference of Interest on Account of the more distant Period for the Exchange added to *Six Shillings* and *Eight Pence* (because the Possessor of the middle Tenor Bills is to have an Ounce of Silver for *Twenty Shillings*) will sink near Thirty *per Cent.* of every Man's Estate. Upon this great Fall of every Man's private Stock, the Officer instead of sharing with his Brethren in the common Calamity, rises *Three Hundred per Cent.* in his Demand. In short, if this should go on, notwithstanding the golden Dream of *being happily arrived at a new Era of Justice*, we shall soon find to our Cost, that the Profits of the Officers will be immense, when compared with the People's sinking Estate, the Consequence of which must be, the compleat Conquest of Prerogative over Liberty.

Therefore I would hope, and humbly advise every Elector, when he comes to vote, that he would ask himself a few such Questions as these, and as his Honour and Conscience shall direct him, so let him vote accordingly.

1st. *Question.* Whether the Religious Privileges of this Country, which were the Causes of its Settlement, are not worth preserving, and do not in a great Measure (under GOD) depend upon the flourishing State of the College? And therefore whether it is not the incumbent Duty of every Elector, to vote for such to represent him, who will be very careful in the Choice of Councellors (who make a great Part of the Board of Overseers of the College) that they be such as are for making no Inroads either upon the Government or Rights of that Society?

2dly. Whether the Men of the best Knowledge, Reason and Vertue, as well as Estates, are not more likely to serve us in the General Court, and less liable to be tempted from their Trusts, with Posts of Honour and Profit, than Men of different Characters?

3dly. Whether you ought to vote for a Man to represent you there, that you would not trust with your Estate, or who is not noted for an honest just Man in his Dealings with his Neighbour?

4thly. Whether you really think you do Justice to your Country to vote for one who you have Reason to think will not only vote for augmenting or settling the Salary himself, but use his Interest to persuade others to do so also? And I suppose it will not be difficult (by Inquiry) to know, what Set of Men (if there were any such) were inclined and voted that Way in the late House.

I believe it is allowed by every Body, that we never needed more the wisest and best Men among us, to represent us there, than at present, as the Recruiting Officers have, and I suppose continue to inlist indented Servants. This is a Burthen which falls heavy upon Artificers and Mechanicks in the Maritime Towns, for whose Benefit the Salutary Law to prevent Masters of Vessels carrying off Servants, was undoubtedly enacted; and every Interposition of the Magistrate for releasing any Servant from his Commitment upon that Law, is a violent and arbitrary Suspension of the Law, which is a Crime of a more atrocious Nature than People are aware. However, Justice to distinguished Merit demands, that honourable Mention be made of the faithful Behaviour of A——l W——y, Esq; late one of His Majesty's Justices of the Peace for the County of *Suffolk*, as a Justice of the Peace. This upright Gentleman well knowing that the Law of the Land was the only Rule to guide him in the Discharge of his Office, did, upon proper Application made, issue his Warrant to apprehend a Runaway Servant, who had inlisted with the Recruiting Officer: In this he is justified by the Original, Fundamental and Irrepealable Law of Government, the Security of Property; by the Law of this Province, and the Example of Lord Chief Justice *Raymond* . . .

If every Elector will act conscientiously and uprightly in their ensuing Elections, we may hope to have a wise House of Representatives, who will also chuse such Gentlemen to sit at the Council Table, who will, in the Discharge of the other Parts of their high Trust as Councellors, be actuated by the same good Principles which influence them considered as a Branch of the Legislature. They will therefore in the Discharge of their Trust as Overseers of the College be very careful of that Society, upon whose Prosperity the Churches of this Land (under GOD) have so great a Dependance, agreable to the pious Design of our Forefathers in that happy Foundation: And in the Discharge of that Part of their Duty which relates to the Appointment of Civil Officers, they will be upon their Guard, and not consent to the Appointment of an unqualified Person to an executive Office in the Government, nor to the Removal of any Judge, unless he has been guilty of Malfeazance in his Office; and then we may hope for a Blessing on their

Publick Councils. "Where impious Men bear Sway, the Post of Honour is a private Station."

P.S. You may observe by the Prints from *England*, that it's very common for Cities, Corporations, &c. to give their Representatives Instructions in any extraordinary Cases, and I have been well informed (tho' I live at some Distance from *Boston*, and my Circumstances will not allow me to go often there, and I have not been lately there to make particular Enquiry) that the Town of *Boston* have often given their Representatives Instructions in extraordinary Cases, and particularly in Governour Burnett's Time, when he insisted so much on a fixed Salary, by no Means to consent to, but to use their Endeavours against fixing a Salary, &c.

D. The Dangers of Legislative Power

FOR MEN *in the royal administration, the lower houses with their constant grasping for power seemed to be the primary sources of danger in the polity. To avoid these dangers, they appealed to colonial legislators to be careful to preserve a proper and equal balance among the branches of government according to the prevailing theory about the British constitution. The essay "Observations on the Balance of Power in Government," written in 1744–45 by Caldwallader Colden, long-time royal official in New York, is a superb statement of this political position and the arguments that lay behind it.*

SOURCE: *The Letters and Papers of Cadwallader Colden* (9 vols., New York: New-York Historical Society, 1918–37), IX, 251–257.

It is the great Happiness of the People of the Province of New York that the Government is form'd as near as may be upon the same Plan with that of our Mother Country. Our Constitution of Government is nearly the same with that which the People of England value so much that they have at all times cheerfully hazarded their lives and fortunes in the support of it and to reduce it to its primitive form whenever it has by any Artifice or by the Misfortunes of the Times been altered. And therefor it seems evident to me that it is most prudent in us to keep as near as possible to that plan which our Mother Country has for so many ages experienced to be best and which has been preserved at such vast expence of Blood and Treasure.

This Constitution consists in a proper Ballance between the

Monarchical Aristocraticall and Democratical forms of Government of which our Constitution is compounded and when ever the Ballance is altered by an overbearing power in any of these three parts of our Constitution the Constitution it self is so far altered and such Alteration has been allwise accompanied with many Disturbances and often with Civil Wars and Revolutions of the State.

Immediately after the Conquest by William the 1st The Monarchy had too great a Weight in the Scale and the Democracy very litle. The Commons then seem to have had litle or no Authority and consequently could not be of any use in reducing the Constitution to its proper Ballance. The Barons then were the only Check upon the Regal Authority and the Reducing the Regal Authority to its proper bounds was the Occasion of the Civil War with the Barons In which they had so much success that they brought the overweight on their side.

The Ballance being again destroyed by the overweight in the Aristocratical part of our Constitution Many Mischiefs and Civil Wars etc. ensued from the overpower and ambition of the Barons. However they never were able entirely to destroy the Constitution.

To lessen their Power the Kings endeavoured from time to time to increase the Power of the Commons in Opposition to the Barons till at last Henry the 7th an Artfull Prince prevailed so far with the assistance of the Commons in crushing the Power of the Barons that the state has never been since his time in any Danger from the over power of the Aristocraticall part of our Government.

But as the Design of Henry the 7th was not to bring the Constitution to its proper Ballance by establishing and reducing each of the Constituent parts to its proper degree and share of Power but to strenthen and augment the Power of the Crown and to weaken the Power of the Aristocracy or Barons. The Power of the Crown became so great under Henry the 8th that if the Succession had not fallen into the hands first of a Minor and afterwards into two females and lastly into the hands of a weak timid prince it is probable our Constitution would have been at an end and an absolute Monarchy had succeeded.

The Barons under Charles the 1st found themselves in no condition to withstand the power of the Crown and therefor they in order to reduce the Constitution to its proper Ballance threw all the weight into the side of the Commons in opposition to the Crown and this was don so inconsiderately that the Ballance turned so far on the side of the Commons that the whole Constitution was thereby overturned and thereby first Anarchy and afterwards Tyranny and absolute Monarchy Introduced.

From what appears from our own History and I believe from the History of all Nations a Mixed Government runs more risk from too Great a Power in the Monarchical part or Democratical than from the Aristocratical and indeed more danger from an over power in the Democratical than from that of the Monarchical because People are allwise Jealous of the Monarchy but fond of every thing that encreases the Democracy. This has been so well observed by all ambitious cunning men that by means of increasing the Democraticall powers they have allwise at last been able to establish the Tyranny at which they aimed. The Instances are so many in History that it is needless to mention any.

In the Constitution of the Government of New York the Governor, The Council and General Assembly have powers in Imitation of the King, Lords, and Commons so far as the very great odds in Circumstances will admit. I have no thoughts of making observation from the History of this Country to show what have been the Consequences of an Over bearing power in any of the Parts of our Constitution. Our History is not so well established as to serve as a Basis for such an enquiry. It can go so litle away beyond our present times and so many will be found Interested in the Relation of Facts, that it will not be easy to agree on the Truth and few will be Indifferent enough as to draw consequences with a view only to discover Truth. For which reason I shall only make some General Observations and put some hypothetical Queries without supposing them to have any other Foundation than in the Imagination of the Inquirer and leave the application to the Judgement or Humour of the Reader.

It is not in the Power of a Governor without Force without money (which he can only obtain of an Assembly) without Friends or any Natural Interest in a Country to alter the Constitution of this Government or exert Arbitrary Powers without the Concurrence of the Council and Assembly or without the Concurrence of an Assembly at least. The Council in this Province can never be an Over Match for any one of the other two parts of our Constitution much less to be able to with stand both together. For it never can be in the Power of the Council to assume Powers inconsistent with the Constitution or Misapply their Legal Powers in Opposition to a Governor while he has the Power of Suspending and the Council must in every Act of Power make use of his Authority to put it in Execution. And without an Assembly they can have no money to support any Design.

The Council can form no Design to lessen a Governor's legal Authority with view to encrease their own Power for without his Concurrence they can exert no Power besides that of their Negative in passing of Laws.

It cannot seem probable that the Council consisting of Men of Estates and Families in this Country will ever join with a Governor to lessen the Liberties and Privileges of the People of this Province when it is considered that any Power any one of the Council can hope to obtain thereby is so far from being hereditary and to descend to his Posterity that he can only enjoy it himself at the will and pleasure of Another upon such Precarious terms that let him have what confidence he pleases in a present Governor he can never think himself secure in that of an unknown successor. I say it can never be supposed that the whole council or a Majority of them can be so abandoned to all sense and honesty as to concur with a Governor in any Measures which tend to the Destruction of the Liberty or Wealth or Prosperity of the Country in consideration of any particular advantages it may be in the Power of a Government of New York to give them.

I think it can with no appearance of any probability be supposed that An Assembly will ever enter into any Measures with a Governor to increase his Power to the Prejudice of the People. But it may be askt,

1. Whether it can be probable that an Assembly would be willing to encrease their own power to the Prejudice of our Constitution.

2. Whether they would be willing (in the direct breach of our Constitution) to have the Nomination of all officers.

3. Whether the Naming all the officers in the Support Bill and annexing Sallaries to their names contrary to the usage of Parliament and the Usage in this Province till very lately be not with design to introduce such claim and to make every officer dependent on their humour solely.

4. Whether their obtaining such favour would not be a weakening of our Government with respect to the other parts of our Constitution that the others cannot exert their Authority or do their Duty or put the Laws in Execution in opposition to the Humour of an Assembly or of the People.

5. Whether Assemblymen be generally so wise prudent and Virtuous that they never mistake the Interest of the Country, can never be misled either through Humour Ignorance or want of Probity to the prejudice of the Country and to the Indangering of its safety and that in cases where litle or no time may be allowed to correct the Mistake by better information and by removing the prevailing humour.

6. Whether this would not weaken the hands of the Administration so far that the officers might neglect or refuse to do their Duty in hopes of impunity by the favour of Powerfull or Popular men in an Assembly and that in cases where the Safety or Defence of the Province may be immediately concerned.

7. Whether the hands of the Government or administration must not be weakened to the greatest degree by alienating the affections of the People from them and lessening that Esteem without which it is impossible that any regard can be had to their orders. When the Publick Acts of the Government insinuate that the Governor and Council are not to be trusted with the smallest sum by a general application but that every Article of Expence or Charge must have its particular sum allotted to it and that in cases where it is scarcely possible that a true Estimate of the charge can be made before hand or what money sudden Emergencies may require.

8. Whether the Open refusing to put the Southeast Bastion of the Fort in sufficient repair where the King's Garrison is placed carry with it an insinuation that the Forts cannot be safely trusted in any hands but in theirs.

9. Whether does not their directing in every article as to the Fortifications their Nominating the Chief Gunner agreeing with him for his Reward and for the Reward of the under Gunners show that they are desirous to have the Command of all the Forts and be not an actual taking of the Command of the Fortifications into their hands.

10. Whether the known Characters of the Governor and the Members of the Council be such as to deserve such Mistrust. That the Character of Assembly men on the Contrary in respect to their knowledge and Integrity is so well established that they ought to have no check to their Resolutions nor want no assistance in their Deliberations And Particularly that they generally understand the Art of Fortification so well that they are the most proper persons to

direct the whole and every minute Article in the Fortifying the City and every part of the Province.

11. Whether the Assembly men be generally so clear sighted and of such penetration that it cannot be in the Power of Disaffected persons, Private Spies, or Ennemies to put them upon such measures as must lead into Confusion and prevent the necessary means for the Defence and safety of the Province.

12. Whether the Publick money be most likely to be carefully and frugally managed when the publick money is put into the hands of Assembly mens Relations and Friends or into the hands of such as have no affinity or Relation with or to Assembly and which of the two are assembly men most likely to call to a strict account.

13. Whether are they most likely to call to Account when the Managers of the Publick Money are appointed by the Governor and Council or when they are appointed by themselves.

14. Are there any many or no Instances where the Distribution of the publick money has been put into the hands of the Relations of Assembly men and no account ever given in where the Assembly have not only neglected but refused to call them to an account.

15. Would it not be very usefull to have an account stated of all the Neglects of the Publick Funds and misapplications of the Publick Money occasioned by the Governors and Members of the Council and also an Account of all the like Neglects and Misapplication by Assembly men That the Country may see the great odds.

16. And would it not be very much for the Honour of Assembly men to order their Treasurer to state such an Account for the thirty years last past that is since the time they have had a Treasurer of their own nomination who is certainly enabled to make out such account since all publick moneys have passed through his hands.

17. Whether the Usage now fallen into of giving Assembly men the Nomination of all officers civil and Military in their respective Counties be not destructive of Good Government and of his Majesties Authority in this Province.

18. Whether they have not made use of this indulgence in order to influence Judgements in the Courts of Justice where they have had lawsuits depending with their Neighbours by getting Justices and Sheriffs appointed to serve that particular turn.

19. Will not this in the end be destructive of all Government

for men only submit to Government in order to be protected in their Lives Liberties and Rights. Must it not bring the Meanest and Worst of men into the Administration and thereby bring the Administration into Contempt, Produce Confusion, Anarchy, and the greatest Mischiefs.

20. Whether Our Mother Country may not think it necessary to abridge us of our Privileges and put us under a more Despotick Government if the Conduct of Assembly men give them any Jealousy of an Inclination in the People here to free themselves of that Dependence on their Mother Country which it is thought proper they should have or if that Conduct give a Jealousy that it is abused to the prejudice of good Government and an equal Distribution of Justice.

V

Reform, 1748–1763

17. The Crisis of Imperial Authority

A. *The Undermining of Colonial Constitutions by the Lower Houses*

As THE authority of the lower houses in all but a few colonies increased during the long period of accommodation from the rise of Walpole until the end of King George's War in 1748, royal governors complained vigorously to imperial authorities about their political and constitutional impotence and stressed the urgency of strong measures by the home government to keep the colonies dependent upon the mother country. In the following letter to the Board of Trade of October 10, 1748, Governor James Glen of South Carolina explained how far the Commons House of Assembly in that colony had extended its power, how little effective authority the governor actually possessed, and how ominous the situation appeared for the future of royal authority in the colonies if reforms were not speedily undertaken.

SOURCE: James Glen to Board of Trade, October 10, 1748, Colonial Office Papers, Class 5, Public Record Office, London, Vol. 372, ff. 80–87. Transcripts of Crown-copyright records in the Public Record Office appear by permission of the Controller of H.M. Stationery Office.

MY LORDS:

. . . there are other things that would add to the hapiness of this Province perhaps I might say of America in general and would make us more beneficial to our Mother Country and preserve our Dependance upon the Crown, That is, If our Constitution were modelled, or at least newly promulged, for by a long loose administration it seems to be quite forgotten, and the whole frame of Government unhinged, the political balance in which consists the strength and beauty of the British Constitution, being here entirely overturned, and all the Weights that should trim and poise it being by different Laws thrown into the Scale of the People; These evils appeared to me to be too bigg for correction during the War, and in the situation that I represented the Country about two Years ago, But my fidelity to His Majesty, makes me now lay them before Your Lordships, as well as my concern for the People, for I shall ever be of opinion, that they hurt themselves by weakening the power of the Crown, and that every deviation from the Constitution of the Mother Country, is dangerous.

I shall lay before your Lordships a few instances. Almost all the Places of either profit or trust are disposed of by the General Assembly, The Treasurer, the Person that receives and pays away all the Public money raised for his Majesty, is named by them, and cannot be displaced but by them, the present and last were most unexceptionable Men, but the one before, by making Partys in the Assembly, keept himself in 'till he broke with great Sums of the Public money in his Hands; besides the Treasurer, they appoint the Commissary, the Indian Commissioner, the Comptroller of the dutys imposed by Law upon Goods imported, the Powder Receiver, (etc.).

I must also observe to your Lordships, that much of the executive part of the Government and of Administration, is by various Laws lodged in different setts of Commissioners, Thus we have Commissioners of the Market, of the Workhouse, of the Pilots, of Fortifications, and so on, without number; Nor have they stopped at civil Posts only, but all Ecclesiastical Preferments are in the disposal, or election of the People, Though by the King's Instructions to His Governor, the Power of collating to all Livings of which His Majesty is Patron, is invested in him, and the King is evidently Patron of all the Parishes in the Province, for the Land upon which the Churches are built, is the King's, and they have been built with money raised for his use, and the Stipends or Salarys of the Ministers (except what is paid them from Home by the Society for propagating the Gospell) arises from taxes imposed for the use of His Majesty; But here the Ministers leave their charges, and new ones are introduced in their room without the knowledge or the least notice taken of the Governor; perhaps it is owing to this that the Governor, though supream Magistrate in the Province under His Majesty, and the Representative here, is not prayed for in any Parish in the Province. This is the single instance in America where it is not done, and what makes it the more absurd, is, that the Assembly is constantly prayed for, during their sittings.

All the above Officers and most of the Commissioners are named by the General Assembly, and are answerable and accountable to them only, and let their ignorance and mistakes be never so gross, let their neglects and mismanagements be never so flagrant, A Governor has no power either to reprove them or remove them; and indeed it were to little purpose to tell them, he is displeased with them, when he cannot displace them, Thus by little and little, the People have got the whole administration into their Hands, and the Crown is by various Laws despoiled of its principal flowers and brightest Jewells. No wonder if a Governor be not cloathed with Authority, when he is stripped naked of Power, and when he can neither reward the Virtuous and Deserving, nor Displace and Punish those that offend, it must be difficult for him to keep Government in order. God Almighty in his moral Government of the World, is pleased to make use of both love and fear, of promises and also of threatenings.

It were no difficult matter to trace to their source these mistakes; and to shew how the People have been misled into such conceits and how pernicious such practices are, but, I hope, I may be excused if I pass over in silence the failings of former Governors, lest I should be thought to mention them as a foil to my own Administration; but I am to sensible of my own imperfections to attempt that. One or two instances may be necessary. I find a Message from one of my Predecessors to the Assembly to the following purpose:

"Mr. Speaker and Gentlemen, My Self and His Majesty's Council are informed, that Fort Johnstone is in a ruinous condition, We therefore desire that you may give directions to repair it."

Your Lordships will observe that this Message was not to raise money for that service, but to take the direction and ordering of the Work; such Messages tend to mislead Assemblys into a belief that they are to have the sole direction of every thing, and a Governor will not be listened to, that shall afterwards tell them, that all Castles, Forts, etc. are the King's and that they cannot be erected, repaired or demolished without proper Authority. The consequence of Assembly's intermeddling with such matters is otherwise bad and mischievous to the Public, for Sums of Money are often thrown away to little purpose; Some Years ago Two Assembly Men were by vote empowered to make a Fort at Port Royal, and for that end received about Eleven Hundred Pounds Sterling of the Public Money. It is injudiciously situated, monstrously constructed, and made of Oyster Shells and is called a Fort; but a Garden fence is as strong, It is really worse than nothing for it may tempt ignorant People to take shelter in it in case of an Enemy, and it will certainly prove a snare to those that do, whereas in case they are not able to make a stand, they may have a chance to escape, if they betake themselves to the Woods.

These things weaken the King's Prerogative, they are also hurtful to the People themselves, and it is easie to mention other matters that are prejudicial to the Mother Country, During the low price of our own Produce and the extravagant rates that British Manufactures sold for, it was impossible for me to dissuade the Inhabitants from working up Cloaths for the wear of their Familys any other way than by convincing them that it was hurtful to themselves, and that the same Lands employed in raising Indico and the other produce of the Province would purchase these Goods better and cheaper than they could make them; and unless We encouraged Vessels to bring in these manufactures, our Produce would lye upon our Hands, but it was difficult to instill this into them after a contrary doctrine had been inculcated, and after rewards had been given of the Public money as premiums for the best cloaths made here for Sale.

Many of the above evils may be corrected if a Council will strengthen a Governor's Stands, and give a due attendance, but as they live many of them at such a great distance, it is difficult for them to do it and therefore I pray, that Your Lordships will be pleased to recommend James Graeme Esq. who resides in Charles Town to succeed Mr. Hammerton who has been now absent near Five Years, this I hope, will appear the more necessary, when I assure Your Lordships, that Mr. Hammerton wrote to Mr. Graeme some time ago, that the only thing that prevented his being named when Mr. Beaufand and Mr. Fenwick were appointed was because he was recommended by the Governor; Mr. Graeme is a Gentleman well acquainted with the Constitution, for supporting the King's Prerogative and Government, and is not of the levelling principles that prevail too much here. In former Letters I have observed to your Lordships that before my arrival the Council had entered a Resolution in their Journalls as an Upper House (though I know of nothing to warrant that name) that they would enter upon no Assembly business whatever in the Presence of the Governor or Commander in Chief, I told them that this could not be warranted from the practice of any other Province in America, and that it was contrary to the British Constitution, for that the King's Throne in the House of Peers was not placed there as an ornament to the Room, but because he had a right to be there, and Lord

Coke sayes, that the Parliament is composed of two Houses, the King and House of Lords makes one House, and the House of Commons is the other, and therefore as the Governor is the King's Representative in the Province, he had a right to be present; with these and some other arguments, I obtained for the Governor the priviledge of being present, but he is not to speak one word not even to tell them that he has an Instruction relative to any business that they may be upon; many errors relating to the Council as a Council, have Laws and Customes to support them, for example, The Governor is restrained by His Commission and Instructions from calling an Assembly or granting any of His Majesty's Lands and many other things, but by the advice of the Council; the meaning seems mighty plain, that the executive part is in the Governor, but that he cannot do these things without their advice, but it has been otherwise understood here, for the Council must sign the election Writts as well as the Governor; and all applications and Petitions for Land are addressed to the Governor and to the Honorable Council, so that the Governor in Council is always interpreted to mean the Governor and the Council.

From the Council the transition is easie and natural to the Assembly; and here many things need a reformation also; In the first place, the election of Members is by ballot, which they vainly say, is an improvement upon their Mother Country; it is indeed different from the method in their Mother Country, and therefore, I think, they should not be indulged in it, for the closer they confine themselves to the Customes at Home the safer they will be, and if the greatest and wisest Men have said in former times, We will not alter the Laws of England, much less should a Colony be heard to say, that she has improved upon the Constitution, But indeed I am far from thinking it an improvement, and therefore out of tenderness to the People, I wish, it were altered as it may defeat the very end that they propose by it, the freedome of elections; for as it is at present managed any Person who attends the ballotting Box may, with a very little slight of Hand, give the election to whom he pleases, I am not insensible, that some great Men have recommended this practice in all popular elections, but with great deference to them, I cannot be of that opinion, because I think it has a tendency to destroy that noble generous openess that is the characteristick of an Englishman, and to introduce a Vile Venetian Juggle and Cunning, and I should be sorry to see the Americans famous for wiles and deceit as the Africans were in former ages; The Number of Members is Forty Five, but without any rule of proportion that I know of, some Places send Five, some Four, three, two and one, and some though equally entitled with any other, are allowed to send none; for example the Township of Orangeburgh, where many foreigners have settled, has petitioned the General Assembly two several times, that they may have the power of sending Representatives, but they have not been able to prevail; this they complain of as a Violation of the Publick faith, for they say, that they were promised the same priviledges with other Subjects, and they think themselves entitled to them, both by the King's Instructions to the Governor, they having above a Hundred House Holders in the Township; and also, as they pay their full proportion of Taxes with others, and indeed since they do bear the burden, I think they should share the benefit equally with others; and besides the having Representatives in Assembly, every Place or Township when it is, as they call it, erected into a Parish, has a Minister paid by the Public, whereas the poor People are without either Minister or Schoolmaster; The Custome of constituting the Members by Acts of Assembly is an evident encroachment upon the Prerogative of the Crown, and perhaps it would be more conformable to His Majesty's Instructions, if every Place in the Province that has been in use to send Members to the Assembly for a certain Number of Years (ten Years, for example) were directed to send two Members and every other Place, or Township that is within His Majesty's Instructions, so far as to have a Hundred House holders, were made a Parish, with the Power of sending one Member only 'till such time as they had also been respectively settled or in use to send Members (for a like number of Years) and from that period might send two, the Assembly would then be more equally constituted, and there would still be a Number sufficient; But the greatest evil, and what is productive of numberless ill consequences, is, that no less than Nineteen are absolutely required to be present to constitute a House, without which Number they cannot even send for an absent Member, or do the smallest act, except to adjourn; This creates many obstructions and delays; I have seen Seventeen and Eighteen attending and adjourning themselves from day to day for a week together, and at length, it has been thought proper to prorogue them for a Month or two, but at the expiration of that time, the same inconveniencys have occurred; so that it has been necessary to dissolve them, though they could not properly be said ever to have had a being, if therefore a fourth or a third part of the whole Number might make a House, I am persuaded that Jealousy would prevent any of the Members from being absent, and Business would then no longer be protracted, but finished with chearfulness and dispatch; at present, a Party of Pleasure made by a few of the Members renders it often impossible for the rest to enter upon Business, and sometimes I Have seen a Party made to go out of Town purposely to break the House as they call it (well knowing that nothing could be transacted in their absence) and in this manner to prevent the Success of what they could not otherwise oppose. Many People here of the best Sense are of opinion that a much less Number than Nineteen would be of great Service, but it is not possible to inspire the Majority with resolution enough to make the alteration. . . .

JAMES GLEN

B. Early Blueprint for Reform

IN RESPONSE to appeals from Glen and other governors and to a series of severe political disturbances in the colonies in the late 1740's and early 1750's, the rejuvenated Board of Trade under the leadership of its new president, the Earl of Halifax, diligently tried after 1748 to find ways to remedy the situation. In the document printed below, the Board explained its general objectives and made a series of specific recommendations. These revealed that its assumptions about the relationship of the colonies to the mother country had not changed much since its previous efforts at reform during the first decades of the century. Entitled "Some Considerations relating to the present Condition of the plantations; with Proposals for a better Regulation of them," the document is undated, but it was probably prepared sometime in 1748 or 1749 shortly after Halifax came to the Board.

SOURCE: Colonial Office Papers, Class 5, Public Record Office, London, Vol. 5, ff. 313–318. Transcripts of Crown-copyright records in the Public Record Office appear by permission of the Controller of H.M. Stationery Office.

The British Empire in America is of that large Extent, already settled so many Leagues backwards from the Coast; daily encreasing and emproving, by the Numbers yearly born there, and by new Settlers from Europe, that it is become of the utmost Consequence to regulate them, that they may be usefull to, and not rival in Power and Trade their Mother Kingdom.

It therefore requires the utmost Application and Attention of the Administration and Legislature, if it be not too late, to look into the several Constitutions of the plantations in America, and so to regulate them that they may answer the End of Settlements, and deserve the Protection given to them from hence: For unless some Care be taken, the People born there, are too apt to imbibe Notions of Indepen[denc]y of their Mother Kingdom.

All Nations who have foreign Settlements, govern them by their own Laws: And although such Settlements may be allowed to make some particular Laws, or Ordinances, Yet such particular Laws, can never be understood to be of any Force, nor ought they to be allowed of, if inconsistent with the Interest of the Kingdom, upon which they are dependent.

The British Settlements have almost all been made by private Adventurers, and are all now under the Direction of the Crown, except those who have particular Priviledges granted to them by Charters or Patents from the Crown: And as it may not have been thought, at the first Settlement of these Plantations, that they would ever become of the Consequence that they now are, many Priviledges have been given, as an Encouragement to new Settlers, without any Imagination, that from thence, such Settlements would have established a Sort of Independency of their Mother Kingdom, as some of them, are inclinable to do, and as the others too probably may, by Reason of their great Encrease of Inhabitants, and their being thereby enabled to furnish themselves by their own Labour and Industry, with great Part of the Manufactures, that are now sent them from hence.

The Consequence of these Considerations, is such, as not to admit any Delay in the timely Prevention thereof, by putting them under such Regulations both at home, and abroad, as may answer the End: At Home, by a proper Inspection into their Conduct, and Abroad, by giveing them proper Encouragement, to send to this Kingdom, such Ore and other Productions, as may be wrought up here; for which they will have a Return, in our own Manufactures. By these Means they will be prevented from applying themselves to manufacturing; For should they once begin to feel the Sweets, and numbers should be engaged therein, It will be next to an Impossibility, to put a Stop to the Pursuit of it; especially considering, that in the Plantations, they are free from the Duties and

Taxes upon the Materials, used with the Manufactures here at home; Which, with many other Incidents, would soon make this an Equivalent to the Difference in the Price of Labour there and here.

But it is necessary to revise the Constitutions of the Settlements abroad, and to regulate them, before any Law can be expected to be of Service there: And any Law without a coercive Power to inforce the same, will be of little Consequence in any Colony, unless that Colony be made to acknowledge a Dependence on the Mother Kingdom.

It may indeed be objected, that the Powers claimed by some of these Settlements, being Grants from the Crown, are not revokeable: But to this, it is answered that by a Law passed here in 1720, many Grants of Incorporation were vacated, under the Description of *Non user and Abuser.* And it's a known Maxim in Law, that if by Virtue of any Grant from the Crown, a much greater Quantity of Land, or greater Powers, are claimed, than could be intended thereby to have been conveyed, the Crown is said to have been deceived, and such Grant, thereby becomes revokeable. Much more strong, is this Argument with regard to the Plantations in America, for it can never be supposed, that any Powers or Priviledges, granted only to encourage Settlements in America, by the Crown, were ever intended to discharge any Part of it's People, from their Allegiance and Dependence, and yet retain a Right of being protected by the Crown. Nor can it be imagined, that this happy regulated Monarchy, should ever intend to establish such little independent Commonwealths; in some of which the Governors, who are chosen annually by the People, give no Security for the due Observance of the Laws of Trade and Navigation, or even take the Oaths of Allegiance, that we know of; From which it is but too easy to judge, what Effect, any other Laws here, without a coercive Power, would have among them.

The general Benefit of the whole, must always take place, of any particular Advantage; And if any particular Advantage, granted at first, to any of these Colonies, shall be found of ill Consequence, to their Mother Kingdom, It ought to be abolished, or amended: But nothing is hereby intended to alter, or take away any private Property or Possession, but only so to regulate the Powers of Government in the Plantations, as to retain and establish their Dependence upon this Kingdom, according to the original Intention of the Crown.

If what has been said, is thought reasonable, the most effectual Way to obtain the End proposed, is to lose no Time in undertaking what shall be found necessary for that purpose, that the Plantations may deserve the Protection they receive from hence, by acknowledging their Dependence, and by proper Encouragements, bring induced, not to manufacture any Production that may be prejudicial to the Trade of this Kingdom.

In order to obtain these good Ends, nothing seems more necessary, than to make all Applications at home, upon this Subject, easy and free from Trouble; As has been in some Measure, mentioned in our General Report upon the State of the Continent, in the Year 1719; the many Offices, that People who have Applications to make, have to go through, deterring them from takeing any Step.

In the Infancy of these Settlements, the little Business attending them, might have easily been dispatched, in any Office where the Application was made; But at present, it requires the constant Application and Attendance of Persons versed in the History of them, to superintend the several Alterations that happen therein. This, from the Constitution of the Board of Trade, seems to have been their intended Business; the other Offices, by reason of the many Affaires that pass under their general Cognizance, not having time, minutely to examine, the many different Transactions, that must necessarily happen, in so many different Settlements abroad: For this Reason the Board of Trade was originally established and was always looked upon, as a Committee from the Council for this purpose: Merchants with regard to Trade; And Others with regard to the Plantations, did then know where to make their Application; And every Return from that Office, being directly to the King in Council, no Person was prevented makeing his Application, from any Fear of Delay. This Practice has for some time been laid aside, and Persons, with regard to Trade and Plantations, do now originally apply to the Crown; from thence they are referred to a Committee of Council, and from thence to the Board of Trade, who make their Report to the Committee, and they to the King in Council; So that many Persons are deterred makeing any Application at all, rather than have the Trouble of attending so many different Offices. Whereas, was the Board of Trade, the sole Office of Correspondence with the Plantations, and wherein all Matters relating thereto, were to be discussed for his Majesty's Information, Business would more readily be transacted, and that Board being answerable for the Execution of such Powers as were contained in their Commission, would expedite every Matter under their Consideration, as it arose; And thereby prevent any Person from attempting what might tend to the Prejudice of this Kingdom, by their Expectation of it's not being, for a long time examined into, from the unavoidable Delays of the different Offices, every Business, now must go through.

This seems the proper Method to put the Plantation Affaires at home, under: And in order to prevent any Partiality abroad, it were to be wished that all Governors, and other Officers, were obliged to enter into Sufficient Security, before their executing their Office, not to receive any Salary or Perquisite during their holding any such Office, but by His Majesty's Appointment; For which purpose there would be, more than a sufficient Revenue there.

With regard to the Laws of the Plantations: When any of them are laid before the King in Council, the King should have the Power of making any proper Alteration in them, as in practiced in such Laws, as are sent from Ireland: And no Law whatsoever should be in Force in the Plantations, till they had obtained the Assent of the Crown; but such only as were to raise Mony for the current Service of the Year, and even not them, if not comformable to the King's Instructions.

And lastly, every Governor should give Security, for his due Observance of the Acts relating to Trade and Navigation, and of his Instructions.

18. The Inauguration of Reform

A. Restricting the Colonial Iron Industry

To ENCOURAGE an old and steadily growing colonial iron industry in the middle colonies to produce raw iron for shipment to Britain rather than finished iron products for use in the colonies, Parliament passed the Iron Act on April 12, 1750. This measure, which came only after a long and bitter contest between British manufacturers of finished iron and producers of raw iron, meant a defeat of the former, who wanted to prohibit all iron manufacturing in the colonies. It was, therefore, also a significant concession to colonial ironmakers, who produced mostly raw iron. A continuation of the old policy of trying to channel colonial industries into activities that would not clash with the interests of important groups in Britain, the enactment of this measure coincided with the growing determination in imperial circles to take a tougher line with the colonies after 1748.

SOURCE: Pickering (ed.), Statutes at Large, XX, 97, 99–101.

WHEREAS the importation of bar iron from his Majesty's colonies in America, into the port of London, and the importation of pig iron from the said colonies, into any port of Great Britain, and the manufacture of such bar and pig iron in Great Britain, will be a great advantage not only to the said colonies, but also to this kingdom, by furnishing the manufacturers of iron with a supply of that useful and necessary commodity, and by means thereof large sums of money, now annually paid for iron to foreigners, will be saved to this kingdom, and a greater quantity of the woollen, and other manufactures of Great Britain, will be exported to America, in exchange for such iron so imported; be it therefore enacted by the King's most excellent Majesty, by and with the advice and consent of the lords spiritual and temporal, and commons, in this present parliament assembled, and by the authority of the same, That from and after the twenty fourth day of June, one thousand seven hundred and fifty, the several and respective subsidies, customs, impositions, rates, and duties, now payable on pig iron, made in and imported from his Majesty's colonies in America, into any port of Great Britain, shall cease, determine, and be no longer paid; and that from and after the said twenty fourth day of June, no subsidy, custom, imposition, rate, or duty whatsoever, shall be payable upon bar iron made in and imported from the said colonies into the port of London; any law, statute, or usage to the contrary thereof in any wise notwithstanding. . . .

IX. And, that pig and bar iron made in his Majesty's colonies in America may be further manufactured in this kingdom, be it further enacted by the authority aforesaid, That from and after the twenty fourth day of June, one thousand seven hundred and fifty, no mill or other engine for slitting or rolling of iron, or any plateing-forge to work with a tilt hammer, or any furnace for making steel, shall be erected, or after such erection, continued, in any of his Majesty's colonies in America; and if any person or persons shall erect, or cause to be erected, or after such erection, continue, or cause to be continued, in any of the said colonies, any such mill, engine, forge, or furnace, every person or persons so offending, shall, for every such mill, engine, forge, or furnace, forfeit the sum of two hundred pounds of lawful money of Great Britain.

X. And it is hereby further enacted by the authority aforesaid, That every such mill, engine, forge, or furnace, so erected or con-tinued, contrary to the directions of this act, shall be deemed a common nuisance; and that every governor, lieutenant governor, or commander in chief of any of his Majesty's colonies in America, where any such mill, engine, forge, or furnace, shall be erected or continued, shall, upon information to him made and given, upon the oath of any two or more credible witnesses, that any such mill, engine, forge, or furnace, hath been so erected or continued (which oath such governor, lieutenant governor, or commander in chief, is hereby authorized and required to administer) order and cause every such mill, engine, forge, or furnace, to be abated within the space of thirty days next after such information given and made as aforesaid; and if any governor, lieutenant governor, or commander in chief, shall neglect or refuse so to do, within the time herein before limited for that purpose, every such governor, lieutenant governor, or commander in chief, so offending, shall, for every such offence, forfeit the sum of five hundred pounds of lawful money of Great Britain, and shall from thenceforth be disabled to hold or enjoy any office of trust or profit under his Majesty, his heirs or successors. . . .

XV. And be it further enacted by the authority aforesaid, That from and after the said twenty fourth day of June, every governor or lieutenant governor, or commander in chief of any of his Majesty's colonies in America, shall forthwith transmit to the commissioners for trade and plantations, a certificate under his hand and seal of office, containing a particular account of every mill or engine for slitting and rolling of iron; and every plateing forge to work with a tilt hammer; and every furnace for making steel, at the time of the commencement of this act, erected in his colony; expressing also in the said certificate such of them as are used, and the name or names of the proprietor or proprietors of each such mill, engine, forge and furnace, and the place where each such mill, engine, forge, and furnace is erected, and the number of engines, forges, and furnaces in the said colony; and if any governor, lieutenant governor, or commander in chief, shall neglect or refuse so to do within six months after the said twenty fourth day of June, every such governor, lieutenant governor, or commander in chief so offending, shall be subject to such penalties and forfeitures, as any governor, or lieutenant governor of any of the said colonies is liable to for any offence committed against this act, to be recovered in like manner, as is by this act directed for the same. . . .

B. Prohibiting Legal Tender Paper Currency

ONE OF THE thorniest and most persistent problems confronting imperial authorities from the time of Queen Anne's War up to the Declaration of Independence was what to do about the legal tender emissions of paper money made, at one time or another, by all of the colonies. The colonists justified these emissions on the grounds that specie was so scarce they had no other way either to obtain enough of a circulating medium to meet the demands of internal trade or to raise money quickly in an emergency. Because even the best regulated of these currencies depreciated somewhat and some of them precipitously, British merchants always feared that colonials would attempt to pay their sterling debts in depreciated paper at face value, and they repeatedly tried to persuade the imperial government to restrict such issues. The ineffectiveness of prohibitory instructions of 1720 and 1740 caused the merchants to clamor for parliamentary measures, and in 1744 and 1749 prohibitory bills were considered but not passed. In 1751, however, Parliament finally did pass the Currency Act, which prohibited further legal tender issues and required the retirement of all old issues in the New England colonies, but did not affect the colonies from New York south. Document A below contains excerpts from some of the hearings held by the House of Commons on March 12 and May 22, 1751, prior to passing the Currency Act, the most important portions of which are included in Document 2.

1. Proceedings in the House of Commons

Source: Stock (ed.), *Proceedings and Debates of the British Parliaments*, V, 464–467, 506–507.

Mar. 12. Sir William Calvert reported from the committee, to whom the petition of the merchants of London, trading to his Majesty's colony of Rhode Island, whose names are thereunto subscribed, in behalf of themselves, and of many of the most considerable of the inhabitants of the said colony, was referred; that the committee had examined the matter of the said petition; and had directed him to report the same, as it appeared to them, together with the resolutions of the committee thereupon, to the House: and he read the report in his place; and afterwards delivered it in at the clerk's table: where the same was read; and is as followeth; *viz.*

To prove the allegations of the said petition. . . .

Alexander Grant Esquire, being examined, said, that the exchange between England and Rhode Island is now from £1,050 to £1,100 Rhode Island currency, for £100 sterling in England; and by the sinking of the value of the currency so much, the creditors of the said colony, and all persons who reside therein, whose effects or estate have consisted in money, or bills of publick credit, have been greatly defrauded:

That what affects the exchange between Great Britain and any one of the four colonies, will affect the exchange of all the rest:

That, in his opinion, it is not possible to prevent the introducing Rhode Island bills in the other three colonies, nor to prevent the government of Rhode Island making fresh emission of bills, without an act of Parliament:

That he knows many persons, possessed of large effects in the said colony, who designed to come to England to live, but were prevented by the depreciating the value of their money, by the increase of bills of credit; and have been thereby rendered incapable of paying their debts here:

That no general tax has been levied, for paying off or sinking the bills of treasury, for upwards of 20 years past, which ought to have been done, except one in 1744, for £10,000 their currency, which is less now than £1,000 sterling.

Then he laid before your committee a Journal of the Proceedings of the General Assembly of the Colony of Rhode Island; which was transmitted to him, with a petition to his Majesty, from the most considerable merchants, and persons of great estates, in the said colony; in which is an account or state of the paper currency of the colony of Rhode Island, etc.; which, upon comparing it with the account or state to the petition annexed, they agreed in every particular.

Your committee observing, that in the said account £176,964 6s 10¼d. is said to be paid in, and burnt, at several times, Mr. Grant said, that that was mostly paid with money received from England, granted upon account of the Canada expedition:

That in the said Journal are several petitions, dated June 13th, 1750, and third Monday in August 1750, signed by a great number of persons, to the general assembly, against emitting any more bills of credit; and in the said Journal is also a resolution of the house of deputies of the said colony, dated August 24th, 1750, that the sum of £50,000 in bills of publick credit, of a new tenor, be emitted by this colony, to be let out upon loan; and a bill was ordered to be prepared for that purpose; which £50,000 is equal in value to £400,-000 bills of credit, of the old tenor.

Then the Journal of the House, of the 25th of April 1740 (that an humble address be presented to his Majesty, humbly to desire him that he will be graciously pleased to require and command the respective governors of his colonies and plantations in America, punctually and effectually to observe his Majesty's royal instructions, not to give assent to, or to pass, any acts, whereby bills of credit may be issued in lieu of money, without a clause be inserted in such act, declaring that the same shall not take effect, until the said act shall be approved by his Majesty), was read: in pursuance of which address, a letter from the Lords Commissioners for Trade and Plantations, approved by an order of their Excellencies the Lords Justices, in Council, dated 14 August 1740, was, with a copy of the said address, sent to the governor and company of Rhode Island, signifying to them, that by the said address they might perceive how much the House of Commons apprehend the commerce of Great Britain to have been affected by the large and frequent emissions of paper currency, in his Majesty's colonies in America, in which Rhode Island has had too large a share; and that his Majesty, in pursuance of the said address, had sent circular instructions to the several colonies more immediately under his government, not to pass any more bills for the issuing of paper money, without a clause inserted therein, to suspend the execution till his Majesty's pleasure should be signified thereupon; and admonishing and advising them to pay all due regard to his Majesty's intentions, and to the sense of the House of Commons, upon this occasion.

Then the Journal of the House, of the 29th of May 1749 (that an humble address be presented to his Majesty, that he will be graciously pleased to give directions, that there be laid before this House, in the next session of Parliament, an account of the tenor and amount of all the bills of credit which have been created and issued in the several British colonies and plantations in America, as well those under proprietors and charters, as under his Majesty's immediate commission and government, that shall be then outstanding, distinguishing the amount of the same in each colony or plantation, and the respective times when such bills, so outstanding, were issued, with the amount of the said bills in money of Great Britain, both at the times when such bills were issued, and at the time of preparing the said accounts, and also the times fixed for the calling in, sinking, and discharging, such bills, and the funds appropriated for that purpose), was also read: in pursuance of which address, his Grace the Duke of Bedford, one of his Majesty's Principal Secretaries of State, on the 19th July 1749, wrote a letter to the governor and company of Rhode Island, signifying the said address to them, and his Majesty's pleasure thereon, that they should order the accounts, mentioned in the said address, to be transmitted to him, in order to their being laid before the Parliament; which account was transmitted to his Grace accordingly; and being produced to your committee, and compared with the account or state of the paper currency of the said colony, to the petition annexed, it agreed therewith.

Upon the whole, your committee came to the following resolutions:

Resolved, that it appears to this committee, that the value of silver, in the colony of Rhode Island, hath, between the years 1742 and 1749, varied from 28s. or thereabouts (the value in 1742) in [to] 60s. per ounce, or thereabouts (the value in 1749); and that in 1742 the exchange between England and Rhode Island was from £500 to £550 Rhode Island currency, for £100 sterling, and in the year 1749 the exchange was from £1,050 to £1,100 Rhode Island currency, for £100 sterling in England.

Resolved, that in the four governments of New England; viz. the Massachusetts Bay, New Hampshire, Rhode Island, and Connecti-

cut, the bills of credit issued in one government have a promis-
cuous currency in the other three governments; and experience has
shewn it to be impracticable to prevent the introduction of bills of
credit issued in one government, into the other three, without an
act of the Parliament of Great Britain.

Resolved, that the great rise in the value of silver, and in the
exchange, occasioned by the repeated emissions of paper bills of
credit (particularly in Rhode Island) hath been the means of defrauding the creditors, in all the four governments, of great part of
their property; and, by introducing confusion into dealings, hath
proved a great discouragement to the trade of these kingdoms.

Resolved, that, notwithstanding repeated notices of the sense of
this House, the said colony of Rhode Island, on the 3d of August
last, passed a vote for emitting of £50,000 in bills of publick credit,
of a new tenor, equal to £400,000 currency, to be let out upon loan,
in contempt and defiance of the authority of his Majesty, and this
House, contrary to the representations and remonstrances of many
of their own inhabitants, to the further depreciation of their currency, and the defrauding of the creditors of all the four colonies.

Resolved, that it is the opinion of this committee, that, in order
to remedy the growing inconveniencies of paper currency, the bills
of credit in his Majesty's colonies or plantations of Rhode Island,
and Providence plantations, Connecticut, the Massachusetts Bay,
and New Hampshire, in America, be regulated and restrained.

The said resolutions, being severally read a second time, were,
upon the question severally put thereupon, agreed to by the House.

Ordered, that leave be given to bring in a bill, pursuant to the
said resolutions: and that Sir William Calvert, Mr. Bayntun, Mr.
Beckford, and Mr. Alderman Baker, do prepare, and bring in, the
same. . . .

May 22. The order of the day being read, for receiving the report from the committee of the whole House, to whom the bill to
regulate and restrain paper bills of credit, in his Majesty's colonies
or plantations of Rhode Island, and Providence plantations, Connecticut, the Massachusets Bay, and New Hampshire, in America,
and to prevent the same being legal tenders, in payment of money,
was committed;

A petition of Robert Charles Esquire, agent for his Majesty's
colony of New York, in America, was presented to the House, and
read; setting forth, that the said colony, and several others of his

Majesty's colonies on the continent of America, have enjoyed, for many years past, and do now enjoy, the benefit of a paper credit, rendered absolutely necessary, from the want of gold and silver sufficient for the trade and circumstances of such colonies; which paper credit being established by laws, some whereof have had the royal sanction, and declared a legal tender (except in some particular cases) in discharge of all debts and demands within the said colonies, has excited industry, has proved a necessary and useful medium of trade, has enabled the said colonies to provide for the defence of wide extended frontiers, without almost any charge to this kingdom, and has furnished the means of seconding the views, and promoting the measures, of this their mother-country; and that the said colonies, lying contiguous, have with each other mutual traffick, and many reciprocal engagements, from which such connections must and do arise, that any remarkable alteration in one colony becomes soon felt in another; any inconvenience brought upon one, soon communicates itself to the others; and thus, what affects New England may affect New York: and alleging, that the said bill depending in the House, should the same pass into a law, will essentially alter the nature and quality of the paper credit of America, to the grievous hurt of individuals, the disappointment of publick service, and confusion in all manner of dealings; and that to allow a future paper credit, for services that must be carried on, and for purposes absolutely necessary, and at the same time to declare, that it shall be no legal tender, effectually destroys the liberty it seems to give; seeing it is scarcely to be imagined that any one will receive that for money, which he is sensible another may refuse to receive, as money, from him; and that the said bill is, in many other respects, ill calculated for the interest of America, or the preferable one, that of this kingdom: and therefore praying, that the petitioner, in behalf of the said colony of New York, the most considerable one upon that continent, may be heard against the said bill; or that the House may give such other relief in the premises, as to the House shall appear just and equitable. . . .

2. The Currency Act of 1751

Source: Pickering (ed.), *Statutes at Large*, XX, 306–309.

Whereas the act of parliament made in the sixth year of her late majesty Queen Anne, intituled, An act for ascertaining the rate of foreign coins in her Majesty's plantations in America, hath been entirely frustrated in his Majesty's said colonies of Rhode Island and Providence plantations, Connecticut, the Massachusets Bay, and New Hampshire in America, by their creating and issuing, from time to time, great quantities of paper bills of credit, by virtue of acts of assembly, orders, resolutions or votes, made or passed by their respective assemblies, and making legal the tender of such bills of credit in payment for debts, dues and demands; which bills of credit have, for many years past, been depreciating in their value, by means whereof all debts of late years have been paid and satisfied with a much less value than was contracted for, which hath been a great discouragement and prejudice to the trade and commerce of his Majesty's subjects, by occasioning confusion in dealings, and lessening of credit in those parts; therefore, for the more effectual preventing and remedying of the said inconveniencies, may it please your most excellent Majesty, that it may be enacted; and be it enacted by the King's most excellent majesty, by and with the advice and consent of the lords spiritual and temporal and commons in this present parliament assembled, and by the authority of the same, That from and after the twenty ninth day of September one thousand seven hundred and fifty one, it shall not be lawful for the governor, council or assembly for the time being, or any of them, or for the lieutenant governor, or person presiding or acting as governor or commander in chief, for the time being, within all or any of the aforesaid colonies or plantations of Rhode Island, and Providence plantations, Connecticut, the Massachusets Bay, and New Hampshire, to make or pass, or give his or their assent to the making or passing of any act, order, resolution, or vote, within any of the said colonies or plantations, whereby any paper bills or bills of credit, of any kind or denomination whatsoever, shall be created or issued under any pretence whatsoever; or whereby the time limited, or the provision made for the calling in, sinking or discharging of such paper bills, or bills of credit, as are already subsisting and passing in payment, within any of the said colonies or plantations, shall be protracted or postponed; or whereby any of them shall be depreciated in value, or whereby the same shall be ordered or allowed to be re-issued, or to obtain a new and further currency; and that all such acts, orders, resolutions or votes, which shall or may be passed or made, after the said twenty ninth day of September one thousand seven hundred and fifty one, within all or any of the said colonies or plantations, shall be, and are hereby declared to be null and void, and of no force or effect whatsoever.

II. And be it further enacted by the authority aforesaid, That all such paper bills, or bills of credit, as are now subsisting, and passing in payments, . . . shall be duly and punctually called in, sunk and discharged, according to the tenor of and within the periods limited by the respective acts, orders, votes or resolutions, for creating and issuing, or continuing the same. . . .

III. Provided nevertheless, That nothing in this act contained shall extend, or be construed to extend, to restrain any governor or governors, council or assembly . . . from making or passing any act or acts of assembly in any of the said colonies or plantations, for the creating and issuing of such paper bills, or bills of credit, in lieu of, and for securing such reasonable sum or sums of money, as shall be requisite for the current service of the year. . . .

IV. Provided also, That nothing herein contained shall extend, or be construed to extend to restrain any governor or governors, council or assembly . . . from making or passing any act or acts of assembly, in any of the said colonies or plantations, for creating and issuing such paper bills, or bills of credit, in lieu of and for securing such reasonable sum or sums of money as shall, at any time hereafter, be necessary or expedient upon sudden and extraordinary emergencies of government, in case of war or invasion. . . .

VII. And be it further enacted by the authority aforesaid, That from and after the twenty-ninth day of September one thousand seven hundred and fifty-one, no paper currency, or bills of credit, of any kind or denomination, which may be made, created or issued in any of the said colonies or plantations, pursuant to the provisions herein before made in this act, shall be a legal tender in payment of any private bargains, contracts, debts, dues or demands whatsoever, within the said colonies or plantations, or any of them.

VIII. Provided, That nothing herein contained shall extend, or be construed to extend to make any of the bills now subsisting in any of the said colonies a legal tender.

IX. And be it further enacted by the authority aforesaid, That if any governor or commander in chief for the time being, in all or any of his Majesty's said colonies or plantations, whether commissioned by his Majesty, or elected by the people, shall, from and after the said twenty ninth day of September one thousand seven hundred and fifty one, give his assent to any act of assembly, order, resolution or vote, for the emission or issuing of any paper bills, or bills of credit, of any kind or denomination whatsoever; or for prolonging the time limited for calling in and sinking any such paper bills, or bills of credit, as are now subsisting and passing in payment; or for re-issuing or depreciating the same, contrary to the true intent and meaning of this act; such act, order, resolution or vote, shall be *ipso facto* null and void, and such governor or commander in chief shall be immediately dismissed from his government, and for ever after rendered incapable of any publick office or place of trust.

C. Extending the Authority of the Board of Trade

THE INABILITY *of the Board of Trade to gain support for many of its proposals for dealing with colonial problems during the early years of the Halifax regime led Halifax to insist that the authority of the Board be extended, so that colonial governors would be directly responsible to it. Halifax won approval for this action in early 1752, and the following circular instruction, dated April 14, 1752, informed all royal governors of the change. Representing the achievement of one of the longstanding objectives of the Board, it marked the first time since the Board's creation in 1696 that it had actually been given original jurisdiction over any part of colonial administration.*

SOURCE: Labaree (ed.), *Royal Instructions to British Colonial Governors*, II, 748–749.

Whereas the governors of such of our colonies and plantations in America as are more immediately under our government are, in particular cases as well as in general, directed and required by our instructions to transmit unto us by one of our principal secretaries of state and to our Commissioners for Trade and Plantations accounts from time to time of all their proceedings and of the condition of affairs within their respective governments; and whereas it doth appear to us that it will tend to the benefit of our said colonies and plantations, the ease and convenience of our subjects, and the greater regularity and dispatch of business if the correspondence be confined to and pass through but one channel; it is therefore our express will and pleasure that in all cases wherein by our instructions you are directed to transmit any particular or general accounts of your proceedings or of matters relative to the affairs of our province under your government, you do for the future transmit the same to our Commissioners for Trade and Plantations only, in order that they may be laid before us. Provided, nevertheless, and it is our express will and pleasure that whenever any occasions shall happen within our said province under your government of such a nature and importance as may require our more immediate direction by one of our principal secretaries of state, and also upon all occasions and in all affairs whereon you may receive our orders by one of our principal secretaries of state, you shall in all such cases transmit to our said secretary only an account of all such occurrences and of your proceedings relative to such orders.

D. *The Attack on the Power of the Lower Houses*

WITH ITS *enlarged powers, the Board of Trade set out to strengthen imperial authority in the colonies. It concentrated especially upon reducing the power of the lower houses of assembly. The character and objectives of this effort—which was largely unsuccessful—may be surmised from the following instruction, issued on August 10, 1753, to Sir Danvers Osborne, newly appointed governor of New York.*

SOURCE: Labaree (ed.), *Royal Instructions to British Colonial Governors*, I, 190–193.

Whereas it hath been represented to us that great disputes and animosities have for some time past subsisted amongst the several branches of the legislature of our province of New York, that the peace and tranquillity of the said province has been disturbed, order and government subverted, the course of justice obstructed, and our royal prerogative and authority trampled upon and invaded in a most unwarrantable and illegal manner; and whereas the assembly of our said province have not only refused to comply with the powers and directions which we have thought it expedient to give by our commission and instructions to our governor of the said province with respect to money raised for the supply and support of government, but have also in open violation of our said commission and instructions assumed to themselves, in the laws which they have annually or occasionally passed, the disposal of public money, the nomination of all officers of government, the direction of the militia and of such other troops as have been raised for our service, and many other executive parts of government, which by our said commission and instructions we have thought proper to reserve, and which by law belong to our governor only; and whereas it likewise appears that some of our council of our said province,

not regarding the duty and allegiance they owe us and the trust we
have reposed in them, have joined and concurred with the assembly in these unwarrantable measures; we therefore, being extremely sensible how much all such animosities and divisions
amongst the different branches of the legislature and the unwarrantable proceedings which have attended the same must affect
and prove destructive of the peace and security of our said province, lessen and impair that due authority which by right belongs
to us in the government thereof, and thereby alienate the hearts
and affections of our loving subjects, and being determined, at the
same time that we do protect all our loving subjects in the lawful
enjoyment of their rights and privileges, not to permit our own
authority and prerogative to be in any degree violated or unduly
lessened by any enroachments whatever; it is our express will and
pleasure and you are hereby strictly enjoined and required forthwith upon your arrival to use your best endeavors in the most
prudent manner to quiet the minds of our loving subjects and
reconcile the unhappy differences subsisting amongst them, and
having called the council and assembly of our said province together, you are to signify to them in the strongest and most solemn
manner our high displeasure for their neglect of and the contempt
they have shown to our royal commission and instructions, by
passing laws of so extraordinary a nature and by such their unwarrantable proceedings, and that we do strictly charge and enjoin
them for the future to pay to our said commission and instructions
due obedience, receding from all unjustifiable encroachments upon
our legal authority and prerogative and demeaning themselves in
their respective stations with a due regard thereto, and to the
peace, security, and prosperity of the province. And whereas nothing can more effectually tend to reëstablish good order and government within our said province and promote its future peace and
prosperity than the having a permanent revenue settled by law
upon a solid foundation for defraying the necessary charges of
government, for want of which great inconvenience and prejudice
have hitherto arisen to our service and to the affairs of our said
province; it is therefore our further will and pleasure that you do in
the strongest manner recommend to the assembly in our name
without delay to consider of a proper law to be passed for this
purpose, taking care that such law shall be indefinite and without
limitation, and that provision be made therein for the salary
allowed by us to our captain general and governor in chief of our

said province, and likewise for competent salaries to all judges, justices, and other necessary officers and ministers of government, and for repairing the fortifications and erecting such new ones as the security and safety of the province may require, for making annual presents to the Indians, and for the expense attending the same, and in general for all such other charges of government as may be fixed and ascertained. It is nevertheless our will and pleasure, and you are hereby empowered, after the passing of such law as aforesaid, to give your assent to any temporary law or laws for defraying the expenses of temporary service, provided always that the said law or laws do expire and have their full effect when the services for which such law or laws were passed shall cease and be determined, and that they be consistent with our royal prerogative and our commission and instructions to you. And it is our further will and pleasure that all money raised for the supply and support of government or upon emergencies for a temporary service, as aforesaid, shall be disposed of and applied to the service only for which it was raised, by warrant from you by and with the advice and consent of the council of our said province and not otherwise, but the assembly may nevertheless be permitted from time to time to view and examine the accounts of money disposed of by virtue of laws made by them, which you are to signify to them as there shall be occasion. And it is our further will and pleasure that if any of the members of our council or any officer holding or enjoying any place of trust or profit within our said government shall in any manner whatever give his or their assent to or in any ways advise or concur with the assembly in passing any act or vote whereby our royal prerogative may be lessened or impaired, or whereby any money shall be raised or disposed of for the public service contrary to or inconsistent with the method prescribed by these our instructions to you, you shall forthwith remove or suspend such councillor or other officer so offending, giving to our Commissioners for Trade and Plantations an immediate account thereof, in order to be laid before us.

E. Recommendation for Colonial Union

THE BOARD also moved to strengthen the defenses of the colonies and to increase their military effectiveness. On August 9, 1754, on the eve of the French and Indian War, it presented a plan for this purpose to the Crown. The covering letter submitted with this plan, explaining its general goals and the considerations behind it, is reprinted below. One of the central features of the plan was a military union of the colonies under a general commander-in-chief, who could cooperate with an intercolonial assembly composed of a commissioner from each colony with power to apportion military expenses among the colonies according to their size and wealth. Of special interest is the Board's opinion that the scheme could be carried into effect only by "an interposition of the Authority of Parliament"—one of many instances of the Board's growing predisposition to call for the intervention of Parliament in colonial matters.

SOURCE: O'Callaghan and Fernow (eds.), *Documents Relating to the Colonial History of the State of New-York,* VI, 901–903.

May it please Your Majesty.

In obedience to Your Majesty's commands signified to us by Sir Thomas Robinson, one of Your Majesty's Principal Secretaries of State in his letter dated the 14th of June last, we have prepared and herewith humbly beg leave to lay before Your Majesty the draught of a Plan or Project of General Concert to be entred into by Your Majesty's Several Colonies upon the Continent of North America for their mutual and common defence, and to prevent or remove any encroachments upon Your Majesty's Dominions.

This Plan consists of three distinct parts or propositions, vizt

1st That a certain and permanent method be established for maintaining such Forts as are already built upon their Frontiers, or may be further necessary to be built for supporting proper garrisons in such forts, for defraying the expence of the usual and necessary presents to the Indians & other contingent charges, and for establishing & subsisting Commissarys in such of the Forts as shall appear to be necessary for the management of Indian services.

2[d] That upon any attack or invasion upon any of Your Majesty's Colonies, provision may be made for raising such a number of troops over and above those upon the ordinary Establishment, as may be necessary to oppose and repel such invasion or attack.

3. That the command of all the Forts & Garrisons and of all Forces raised upon emergencies & the sole direction of Indian Affairs be placed in the hands of some one single person, Commander in Chief, to be appointed by Your Majesty, who is to be authorized to draw upon the Treasurer or other proper Officer of each Colony for such sums of money as shall be necessary, as well for the ordinary as extraordinary service, according to the Quota settled for each Colony.

The two first points are proposed to be established by the mutual consent and agreement of the Colonies themselves, to be finally ratified and confirmed by Your Majesty; it appearing to us that this method might be liable to the least objection and perhaps the speediest in point of execution.

With regard to the manner in which the Colonies are to proceed in deliberating upon and settling such parts of it as depend upon them, the view and object of the measure and the general plan of it is precisely stated to them, the points upon which they are to deliberate, and for which provision is to be made on their part, the method of proceeding in settling those points, and of finally ratifying and confirming them when settled, are ascertained as the preliminaries upon which they are to proceed.

The necessity of this Union and the security and advantages which will arise to the Colonies from it, are so apparent, that we hope no difficulty will occur on their part. If however it should be found upon trial that this measure should be defeated by any of the Colonies either refusing or neglecting to enter into a consideration of the points referred to their deliberation; or, after they are settled, by refusing to raise such supplies as are proposed by this plan to be the fund for the execution of it: We see no other method that can be taken, but that of an application for an interposition of the Authority of Parliament.

The execution of the third and last Proposition of this plan, so far as regards the power which the Commander in Chief will have over the Forts & Garrisons, and over all troops raised in the Colonies and in the management of Indian Services, depends singly upon Your Majesty; who may, as we humbly apprehend, legally and by virtue of your own authority, invest any person your Majesty shall think proper, with such power. In order however to the proper and effectual exercise of this power it is proposed that it should be agreed and settled by the Colonies, that he should be authorized under certain regulations and restrictions to draw upon the Treasurer or other proper officer of each Colony for such sums as shall be settled to be paid by them for the ordinary as well as the extraordinary service. We shall not take up Your Majesty's time in entring into any arguments to prove the propriety and necessity of an appointment of this kind, as we humbly apprehend it will evidently appear to Your Majesty, that circumstanced as the Colonies are, divided into separate and distinct Provinces, having little or no connexion with or dependence upon each other, neither this nor any other plan of Union could be effectual, unless the command of the Forts and troops and the management of Indian affairs and services should be put under one general direction.

These are the principal observations which have occurred to us as necessary to be submitted to Your Majesty upon this Plan; to which however Your Majesty will permit us to add, that as it is proposed that in order to settle the several Points, the Commissioners nominated by the Colonies should meet at such time and place as Your Majesty should appoint; we humbly submit it to Your Majesty whether it may not be adviseable that the City of New York should be the place of meeting, as being the most central & therefore the most convenient in point of situation.

Upon the whole however we must observe to Your Majesty that from the delay which must necessarily attend the execution of any new plan for an Union of the Colonies, it cannot be made to answer the purpose of a present exigency. Whatever circumstances therefore of danger or exigency may subsist at this time, such danger must be guarded against and such exigency provided for, by an application of such means of strength and force as can be procured in the most expeditious and effectual manner under the direction of some proper person to be appointed by Your Majesty[s] Commander in Chief of all Your Majesties Forts and Garrisons in North America and of all Forces raised therein or sent thither, and likewise Commissary General for Indian Affairs; which, for the reasons we have already given, appears to us to be absolutely necessary and expedient for your Majesty's service

All which is most humbly submitted

> DUNK HALIFAX
> JAMS GRENVILLE
> FRAN: FANE
> ANDW STONE
> JAMS OSWALD
> RICHd EDGCUMBE
> THOS PELHAM.

F. The Intervention of Parliament

THE INCREASING conviction that Parliament should handle difficult colonial problems led on May 23, 1757, to the following resolutions by the House of Commons upon the conduct of the Jamaica Lower House.

Later interpreted as a declaration "that the Colonies have no Constitu-
tion, But that the Mode of Government in each of them depends upon
the Good Pleasures of the King as expressed in his Commission and
Instructions to his Governor," these resolutions are of the utmost signi-
ficance because they mark the intervention of Parliament for the first
time in the domestic political affairs of a colony.

SOURCE: *Journals of the House of Commons,* XXVII, 910–911.

Resolved . . . That the Resolution of the Assembly of the Island of Jamaica, contained in the Minutes of the said Assembly, of
the 29th Day of October 1753, in the Words following; *viz.* "Resolved, That it is the inherent and undoubted Right of the Representatives of the People to raise and apply Monies for the Service
and Exigencies of Government, and to appoint such Person or
Persons for the receiving and issuing thereof, as they shall think
proper; which Rights this House hath exerted, and will always
exert, in such manner as they shall judge most conducive to the
Service of his Majesty, and the Interest of his People"; so far as the
same imports a Claim of Right in the said Assembly to raise and
apply public Money, without the Consent of the Governor and
Council, is illegal, repugnant to the Terms of his Majesty's Commission to his Governor of the said Island, and derogatory of the
Rights of the Crown and People of Great Britain.

Resolved . . . That the Claim, in the said Resolution, of a
Right in the Assembly to appoint such Person or Persons for the
receiving and issuing of public Money, as the said Assembly shall
think proper, is illegal, repugnant to the Terms of his Majesty's
Commission to his Governor of the said Island, and derogatory of
the Rights of the Crown of Great Britain.

Resolved . . . That the Six last Resolutions of the Assembly of
Jamaica, of the 29th Day of October 1753, proceed upon a manifest Misapprehension of his Majesty's Instruction to his Governor,
requiring him not to give his Assent to any Bill of an unusual or
extraordinary Nature and Importance, wherein his Majesty's Prerogative, or Property of his Subjects, may be prejudiced, or the Trade
or Shipping of this Kingdom any-ways affected, unless there be a
Clause inserted, suspending the Execution of such Bill, until his
Majesty's Pleasure shall be known; and that such Instruction is just
and necessary, and no Alteration of the Constitution of that
Island, nor any-ways derogatory to the Rights of his Subjects there.

G. The Failures of the Navigation System

DURING THE Seven Years' War, the ineffectiveness of the navigation system became especially obvious as reports drifted into Britain of colonial trading with the enemy islands in the West Indies. At the request of the Board of Trade, the Commissioners of the Customs prepared the following remarks on May 10, 1759, identifying the major areas of difficulty and making it clear that wholesale reforms would be necessary to stop most of the common violations of the system.

SOURCE: Customs Commissioners to Treasury, May 10, 1759, Treasury Papers, Class 1, Public Record Office, London, Vol. 392, ff. 38–39. Transcripts of Crown-copyright records in the Public Record Office appear by permission of the controller of H.M. Stationery Office.

May it Please Your Lordships

Mr. Pownall, Secretary to the Lords Commissioners for Trade and Plantations, having, in his Letter of the 24th February last, transmitted Copies of several Letters, and Representations, which have been made to their Lordships, as far back as the year 1739, relating to great Difficulties, and Doubts, which are therein mentioned to have occurred, in the execution of the Acts of Trade, and to the many illegal and improper practices which have been set up to evade their force, and effect, to the great prejudice of the Commerce of this Country, and of His Majesty's Revenue of Customs and Duties: We have considered all the said Letters and Representations, and compared them with all the Papers in Our Office relative to these points, which Papers, though they have a retrospect of near twenty years, are not found adequate to the Information the Board of Trade are now desirous of receiving on this subject; nevertheless, We beg leave to lay before your Lordships such general Observations, as have occurred to Us, on this Occasion, Your Lordships having been already apprized of this Matter by Our Secretary's Letter of the 6th of March last, inclosing Copy of the abovementioned Letter from the Board of Trade.

As We humbly presume, it cannot be intended, that We should enter into a Minute detail of the conduct of the Officers of the Customs, in the Plantations, for twenty Years past, or that We should trouble your Lordships with an Account of the repeated Directions, which have been given them, from time to time, for the due execution of their Duty, We beg leave to consider the Papers before mentioned as principally confined, to the three following points Vizt.:

1st. The illicit Importation of Rum and Molasses from the French Islands into the British Northern Colonies.

2dly. The Importation of Goods from different parts of Europe (particularly Holland, and Hamburgh) into North America, and the carrying Enumerated Goods from thence to the said places, and others in Europe, contrary to Law, where by all such Imports and Exports are restrained to Great Britain only.

3dly. The pernicious practice of supplying the French Colonies and plantations with provisions from his Majesty's Colonies, or from Ireland.

With respect to the first of these three points, it must occur to your Lordships that so long as the high Duty on Foreign Rum, Sugar, and Molasses, imposed by the Act of 6th of his present Majesty, (and then intended, We apprehend, as a Prohibition) continues, the running of those Goods into his Majesty's Northern Colonies will be unavoidable, notwithstanding all the Orders that have been given, or may be given, to prevent it; and yet it is extremely difficult to foresee, how far it may be expedient to attempt to remedy this Evil by an alteration of this Law, which was passed, at the request of the British Planters, as an Encouragement to their Trade.

As to the second point, so far as the same relates to the Importation of European Goods into North America, We are to observe, that the great extent of the Coast very much favours the running thereof, before the Masters make their Reports at the Custom house; upon their arrival there a strict Examination of their Clearances is the only cheque upon this practice, and no endeavours have been wanting in this Board to oblige the Officers of the Customs to attend thereto. With respect to Enumerated Goods exported from the Northern Colonies, in case the Ships that clear out, from thence for Great Britain, will be guilty of Frauds and deviation, by carrying their Goods to other Places in Europe than Great Britain; it is impossible, for the Officers of the Customs, in the Plantations, to prevent it; The Bonds given for the legal discharge of the Cargoes may indeed be put in Suit, if proper Certificates of such discharge be not produced within Eighteen Months, but these prosecutions must be carried on in the ordinary course of proceedings in the Colonies, where, it is apprehended, that Verdicts, upon points of this Nature, are not so impartial, as in England.

With respect to the third point, We must confess to your Lordships, that, as, in North America opportunities are so easy of supplying the French with provisions, and the distance from hence is so great, We despair, by the means of the Officers of the Revenue, of putting any effectual stop thereto, especially, as We find, that the same practice is carried on directly, or indirectly, at so much hazard and expence, even from Ireland, where the Laws are so much less liable to abuse, than under proprietary Governments in North America. . . .

S. Mead
J. Evelyn
R. Cavendish
Edward Hooper
C. Amyand
H. Pelham

19. To Preserve the Benefits of Empire

A. Subordination and Liberty

How FAR THE general sentiment that the imperial government had to undertake comprehensive measures in order to keep the colonies dependent had penetrated into the consciousness of the British political nation was indicated by the appearance of a number of tracts and essays in the 1750's and early 1760's recommending the reorganization of the empire upon more rational grounds. All of the writers of these essays agreed that the colonists should retain a large amount of liberty, but the prevailing sentiment was that their liberties should be constricted to make them consistent with the proper subordination of colonies to their mother country. One of the best statements of this position was that by Malachy Postlethwayt, the economist. It is reprinted below from Dissertation XVII of his Britain's Commercial Interest Explained and Improved (London, 1757).

SOURCE: Malachy Postlethwayt, *Britain's Commercial Interest Explained and Improved* (2 vols., London, 1757), I, 461–474.

The reader will please to remark, that, from the connection we have endeavoured to preserve in this series of animadversion, our great aim tends towards such a union amongst all his Majesty's dominions, as will promote the mutual strength and vigor, as well as the mutual prosperity of them all; for the happy general union that we would cement, is no less constitutional than commercial, and such also as may the least interfere with the particular interest of each other, but advance that of the whole.

In relation to the constitution of our continent colonies in America, it is certain, that as things have been many years conducted, the proprietory and charter-governments, being different from the regal ones, have occasioned many disorders and abuses, that have proved no less detrimental to themselves than to the mother-state. That such abuses and disorders are the necessary and unavoidable consequences of such their constitution; I will not presume to say: I am rather inclined to believe, that these governments might as well have subsisted without these abuses, provided a due regard had been constantly paid to the royal command and instructions given, from time to time, to these colonies.

The unwarrantable constructions which some of the colonies

have put on the charters granted them by the crown, are altogether inconsistent with that dependence . . . which they owe to their mother-country; for although these charters entitle them to make bye-laws for the better ordering their own domestic affairs; yet they do not, nor cannot entitle them to make laws which may obstruct either the trade of this kingdom, or lay restraints and difficulties on the neighbouring colonies: for, as the being and power of those colonies flow from the crown, under certain restrictions, particularly in not passing any laws inconsistent with the constitution and laws of this kingdom; so the expediency of such laws are only to be judged of by His Majesty, or the legislature, as it is conceived these colonies cannot be proper judges in their own case.

Yet to such excess have they proceeded in some of the charter-governments, namely, in Rhode Island and Connecticut, as to enact laws, that no law shall take effect in their colonies, unless it is first enacted into a law by them; and some of them have made themselves judges of the expediency of their own laws, by not transmitting them to their mother-country for examination and sanction. For it is the crown and the grand legislative power of Great Britain that must remain the eternal supreme judge of what laws are, or are not fit and expedient to be passed, in its dependent colonies. For the system of government in America must be regulated by the mother-government system; and the want of attending to this in the first American frame of government, has occasioned disputes in the colonies, unspeakably detrimental to the security of these colonies, as well as the rights and properties, and the regal prerogative.

It is neither for the interest of the crown, or the whole legislative power of England, to prejudice the colonies; the common interest of the nation dictates their right to all due encouragement: but it is to be considered, that there is a public benefit as well as a private one to be regarded; and that all advantages arising from the colonies to this kingdom consist in their mutual dependance, and that their seperate interests would clash with each other, if they shall be permitted to exercise any power, which may be contrary to the true interest of the mother-state, or of his Majesty's other colonies dependent thereon.

His Majesty's orders, and instructions, are intended as the sole guide and measure of the conduct of those governours of colonies that are more immediately dependant on the crown. But has not experience shewn, that where there are no penalties inflicted on disregard thereof, the end of government in distant colonies cannot be attained? If there be no certain regulation established, whereby the measures of the government may be effectually executed, under colourable pretences, will not this open a door to detrimental encroachments upon the crown, and acts of oppression upon the subject?

If the instructions of the crown be such, that the occasional circumstances of affairs in the colonies put the governors under a necessity of deviating from such instructions, is not that a sufficient reason why governors should represent their difficulties properly to the crown, and propose remedies as emergencies may require? But can it be consistent with that interesting dependency that all colonies must have on their mother-state, to depart from the royal or the legislative order of the state? Since the evil consequent on a little temporary delay, cannot be put in competition with that train of evils, which must arise from the violating those salutary connective regulations made for the general good government of the colonies, and safety of the subject? Has not the winking at such violation been productive of general destruction upon the whole, not less than violent rapine and oppression on individuals? Does not such deviation from the royal and legislative orders open a door for all fraud and encroachment, as well upon the subject as upon the crown?

Although there appears great wisdom in the framing the constitution of our colonies, especially, at the time when they were first settled; yet time and experience have shewn that there are still many things wanting to render the system complete: there seems a necessity, an indispensable necessity for the aid of the legislature in establishing the said constitutions by law, with penalties on such, who should presume to deviate therefrom. The best of laws are no more than a dead letter without they are duly executed. And what danger could arise from hence, either relative to the prerogative of the crown, or the safety of the subject?

The strengthening the hands of the crown, so as to guard against encroachments, cannot impede the due course of public business; the governors of our colonies being obliged to have all public concerns of the colonies registered in the journals of council, cannot obstruct the business of the crown. Those being timely transmitted to our council of trade at home, will occasion all things necessary to be laid occasionally before the parliament; and what is requisite to be done, will be duly and timely enforced by the authority of law.

And will not this regular intercourse of business between the grand legislative power and the colonies give such strength and vigor to the latter, that they can never obtain without it? Has not a want of this proved one apparent, though gradual cause, of the present calamities under which our plantations labour?

The actions of the wisest men are formed agreeable to their informations. What may appear extremely wise and prudent, and in all respects well calculated to guard the crown from surprise, and the subject from injury, may yet have a different tendency, as it relates to our distant settlements; for without unity of design; without mutual relation between the systems observed abroad, and at home, and a uniform and inviolable course of proceedings between both, it will be impossible to prevent the affairs of America from running into confusion, or free the crown and the parliament from surprise. Nor can this, we humbly apprehend, be ever effectually prevented in any other manner than by the aid of parliament, in establishing an invariable rule of constant and timely intercourse, in relation to the transactions of the colony-councils abroad, and our board of trade at home.—It is impossible for the sovereign, or for those employed in the administration, to protect his Majesty's subjects abroad, otherwise than inviolably maintaining this uniform correspondence, in order to inflict penalties on such as shall act contrary to their duty, and regulate all colony-laws according to the eternal standard of a reciprocal interest between them and those of their parent kingdom—Without such a steddy method of proceeding, the crown cannot protect and extend our trade and commerce, or in other respects exercise its prerogatives.

For want of this, it may be useful to hint some of the methods which have been taken by several of our governors in our plantations to evade His Majesty's instructions, and to conceal acts of oppression.—Such governors do many acts of government without the advice or privity of their council, and, therefore, no records in the journals of their council appear thereof—At other times, the acts of council, have, by a governor's influence, been imperfectly recorded, and in some cases wholly omitted—When this precaution has not been used, and petitions of complaint have been preferred to his Majesty against them, they have, under frivolous pretences, kept back the records, and not duly transmitted them to England.

Such governors also have too often formed party and factious connections in assemblies, and past by-laws for the emission of paper-currency, and other laws, suited to their private interests, without suspending clauses to give the injured an opportunity to lay their grievances before the crown, previous to the carrying such detrimental laws into execution. Is it not notorious too, that such governors have dispossessed the crown-grantees of their lands, without legal trial or process? Have they not in more colonies than one issued blank patents or grants for lands, and afterwards affixed the seal of the colony thereto, and put them into private hands to be disposed of? Have not these detestable practises introduced the utmost confusion in some of the colonies? For when blank patents or grants are so issued, is it not in the power of such who hold them, by antedating the same, to claim the property of others? Will not this occasion such mixture of claims, and such confusion in property, as to put it out of the power of courts of law to determine the right of the subject? Must not these practices occasion every thing of this kind to be arbitrarily decided by acts of power and violence?

Acts of violence exercised in His Majesty's colonies, can scarce gain credit from those who enjoy the blessing of a regular government at home. Let those who have the power to redress pry into the complaints repeatedly made against his majesty's governors, and other officers employed in our colonies, and the proof sent home to support them, and they will find evidence enough of what has been only hinted; and they will find also that these grievances have been occasioned by want of a well-regulated system for the conduct of public affairs between Britain and her American colonies. Is it to be admired that these practises have sowed the seeds of confusion in our plantations, and given the enemies those advantages over us, which we at present experience? Have not these arbitrary and illegal proceedings been productive of these convulsions, which at different periods of time have happened in several of our colonies? Have not these things made the people uneasy in their situation, and caused them to think themselves unhappy under the best of governments and the best of kings? And have not such treatment often prompted them to act in opposition to His Majesty's measures, or to whatever else may have been wisely proposed for the benefit of the public?

England hath many difficulties to encounter in relation to the government of its colonies, particularly, as we have observed, its charter-governments; yet these, we humbly conceive, might easily be redressed by the aid of parliament. For it seems to be full time, at present, for the wisdom of the nation to determine upon such a union in government and constitution of every part of its dominions as may tend to strengthen the whole British empire; for although she has hitherto maintained her power, with variety of dominions annexed, that have acted independently of her, as it were, though supported by her; yet this policy does not seem capable of much longer upholding her, against enemies, who govern every part of their dominions by one and the same steddy principle of union; by the same interesting laws, and regulations, the due execution of all which, is vigorously, and orderly enforced.

The frontiers of our colonies in North-America are large, naked, and open, there being scarce any forts or garrisons to defend them for near two thousand miles. The dwellings of the inhabitants are scattering at a distance from one another; and it is very difficult, if not almost impossible, for the number of our colonies independent on each other, by reason of their different sorts of governments, views, and interests, so to unite their military strength amongst themselves as to make head against the united military strength of the enemy. For, several of these governments pretending to, or enjoying some extraordinary privileges, which the favour of the crown formerly granted them, exclusive of others, if their assistance has been demanded or implored by any of their distressed neighbours and fellow subjects, when attacked by the enemy, in the very heart of their settlements; have they not scandalously affected delays, insisted on ridiculous niceties and punctilios, started unreasonable objections, and made extravagant demands, or other frivolous pretences, purposely to elude their reasonable demands? And have they not by an inactive stupidity or indolence, appeared insensible to their distressed situation, and regardless of the common danger, because they felt not the immediate effect of it? Has not their own security been precarious at the same time, since what happens to one colony today, may reach another adjacent one tomorrow? Will a wise man stand with his arms folded, when his neighbour's house is on fire? Yet has not this been the conduct of our North-American colonies towards each other, for want of their being under due regulations by our parliamentary laws to inforce obedience to the instructions and the commands of the crown?

Things being come to extremities, it becomes every true friend to his country now to speak out. Does not the experience of many years dictate and inforce the necessity of a substantial remedy to these absurdities and shameful injuries? Does it consist with the wisdom of this nation to permit these things longer to prevail without redress? Let every patriot suggest his remedy; and let the great representative make the best use of them all.

Let all the colonies appertaining to the crown of Great Britain on the continent of America be united under a legal, regular and firm establishment, settled and determined by the wisdom of a British legislature, aided by the best information that can be obtained: after which, why should not a lord lieutenant-general be constituted and appointed, by the crown of England as supreme governor over these colonies, to act in subordination to the voice of a British parliament? It may also be further humbly proposed, that two deputies shall be annually elected by the council and assembly of each province; who might be in the nature of a great council, or general convention of the estates of the colonies; and, who by the order, consent, and approbation, of the lord-lieutenant, or governor-general, shall meet together, consult and advise for the good of the whole, settle and appoint particular quotas, or proportions of money, men, provisions, &c. that each respective government shall be obliged to raise for the mutual defence and safety, or for the invasion of the enemy, when needful: and in all these cases the lord-lieutenant-general might have a negative voice, but not the power to enact any thing as a law with their concurrence, or that of the majority of them: all which shall be subject to the controul of the parent legislature.

The quota, or proportion, that may be allotted, and charged on each colony, may nevertheless, be levied and raised by its own assembly, in such a manner as they shall judge most easy and convenient, and as the circumstances of their affairs will, at certain junctures, admit.

Other jurisdictions, powers, and authorities, respecting the honour of His Majesty, the interest of the plantations, and the liberty and property of the proprietors, traders, planters, and inhabitants in them, may be invested in, and cognizable by, the above said lord-lieutenant-general, and grand convention of the estates, according to the laws of England. These suggestions being only general are humbly submitted for the more knowing to amend, digest, and perfect.

A coalition, or union, something of this nature, tempered, with moderation and judgment, and a general encouragement given to the labour, industry, and good management of all sorts and conditions of persons inhabiting, or interested in the several colonies above-mentioned, will, in all probability, lay a lasting foundation for dominion, strength, and commerce and revive the present sinking state of the British empire; and thereby, with other co-adjutorial measures, render it once more the envy and the admiration of its neighbouring enemies.

Let us revive the consideration of our ancestors, and grow wise by their misfortunes. Had the ancient Britons been happily united amongst themselves, the Romans had never become their masters; while they fought in separate bodies, we well know, the whole island was subdued: so, if the English colonies in America were wisely consolidated into one body, and happily united in one common interest, according to the general principles we have adopted throughout this treatise; if their united forces were framed to act in concert for the common safety, and their commercial councils regulated for their general prosperity; would not such political concord and harmony establish invincible strength and power, while the contrary must prove their absolute ruin and destruction? . . .

B. Liberty and Subordination

A SCHEME FOR colonial reconstruction based upon principles far more congenial to the colonials than the recommendations of Postlethwayt was proposed by Thomas Pownall, a former governor of Massachusetts with considerable knowledge of and interest in the colonies, in his analysis of The Administration of the Colonies. This major treatise on colonial administration was published first in 1764, and reprinted in several new and expanded editions during the decade before the Declaration of Independence. Like Postlethwayt, Pownall thought that the administration of the empire needed to be overhauled. But he insisted that colonial, as well as imperial ideas about the relationship between the colonies and the mother country should be taken into account, and that all reform measures should be compatible with the "true [commercial] spirit from whence . . . [the empire] arose." It is significant, however, that Pownall, the most liberal toward the colonies of all of the British writers on imperial problems of his generation, was as firm as Postlethwayt in demanding that the complete subordination of the colonial governments to the imperial government had to be maintained.

SOURCE: Thomas Pownall, The Administration of the Colonies (London, 1764), pp. 22–39, 128–131.

. . . I will proceed, confining myself solely to the matters of the colonies; to review some points that deserve, and will require, the consideration of government, if it ever means to profit of, and lead the great Atlantic and American interest which it has acquired, and to unite it to its dominion.

Before entering into these matters, I do not think it would be impertinent just to mark the idea of colonies, and their special circumstances, which makes it a measure in commercial governments, to establish, cultivate, and maintain them.

The view of trade in general, as well as of manufactures in particular, terminates in securing an extensive and permanent vent; or to speak more precisely, (in the same manner as shop-keeping does) in having many and good customers: the wisdom, therefore, of a trading nation, is to gain, and to create, as many as possible. Those whom we gain in foreign trade, we possess under restrictions and difficulties, and may lose in the rivalship of commerce: those that a trading nation can create within itself, it deals with under its own regulations, and makes its own, and cannot lose. In the establishing colonies, a nation creates people whose labour, being applied to new objects of produce and manufacture, open new channels of commerce, by which they not only live in ease and affluence within themselves, but, while they are labouring under and for the mother country, (for there all their external profits center) become an increasing nation, of appropriated and good customers to the mother country. These not only increase our manufactures, encrease our exports, but extend our commerce; and if duly administered, extend the nation, its powers, and its dominions, to wherever these people extend their settlements. This is, therefore, an interest which is, and ought to be dear to the mother country: this is an object that deserves the best care and attention of government: and the people, who through various hardships, disasters, and disappointments; through various difficulties and almost ruinous expences, have wrought up this interest to such an important object, merit every protection, grace, encouragement, and privilege, that are in the power of the mother country to grant.

It becomes the duty of the mother country to nourish and cultivate, to protect and govern the colonies—which nurture and government should precisely direct its care and influence to two essential points. 1st, That all the profits of the produce and manufactures of these colonies center in the mother country: and 2dly, That the colonies continue to be the sole and special proper customers of the mother country. It is on this *valuable consideration*, (as Mr. Dummer, in his prudent and spirited defence of the colonies says) they have a right to the grants, charters, privileges and protection which they receive; and also on the other hand, it is from these grants, charters, privileges and protection given to them, that the mother country has an exclusive right to the external profits of their labour, and to their custom. To these two points, collateral with the interests, rights and welfare of the colonies, every measure of administration, every law of trade should tend: I say collateral, because, rightly understood, these two points are mutually coeval and coincident with the interests, rights and welfare of the colonies.

It has been often suggested, that care should be taken in the administration of the plantations; lest, in some future time, these colonies should become independent of the mother country. But perhaps it may be proper on this occasion, nay, it is justice to say it, that if, by becoming independent is meant a revolt, nothing is further from their nature, their interest, their thoughts. If a defection from the alliance of the mother country be suggested, it ought to be, and can be truly said, that their spirit abhors the sense of such; their attachment to the protestant successions in the house of Hanover will ever stand unshaken; and nothing can eradicate from their hearts their natural, almost mechanical, affection to Great Britain, which they conceive under no other sense, nor call by any other name, than that of *home*. Besides, the merchants are, and must ever be, in great measure allied with those of Great Britain: their very support consists in this alliance. The liberty and religion of the British colonies are incompatible with either French or Spanish government; and they know full well, that they could hope for neither liberty nor protection under a Dutch one; no circumstances of trade could tempt them thus to certain ruin. Any such suggestion, therefore, is a false and unjust aspersion on their principles and affections; and can arise from nothing but an intire ignorance of their circumstances. Yet again, on the other hand, while they remain under the support and protection of the government of the mother country; while they profit of the beneficial part of its trade; while their attachment to the present royal family stands firm, and their alliance with the mother country is inviolate, it may be worth while to inquire, whether they may not become and act independent of the *government and laws* of the mother country:—and if any such symptoms should be found, either in their government, courts, or trade, perhaps it may be thought high time, even now, to inquire how far these colonies are or are not

arrived, at this time, at an independency of the government of the
mother country:—and if any measure of such independency,
formed upon precedents unknown to the government of the
mother country at the time they were form'd, should be insisted
on, when the government of the mother country was found to be
so weak or distracted at home, or so deeply engaged abroad in
Europe, as not to be able to attend to, and assert its right in
America, with its own people:—perhaps it may be thought, that no
time should be lost to remedy or redress these deviations—if any
such be found; or to remove all jealousies arising from the idea of
them, if none such really exist.

If the colonies are to be possessed, as of right, and governed by
the crown, as domains of the crown, by such charters, commissions,
instructions, &c. as the crown shall, from time to time, grant or
issue; then a revision of these charters, commissions, instructions,
so as to establish the rights of the crown, and the privileges of the
people, as thereby created, is all that is necessary. But while the
crown may, perhaps justly and of right, *in theory*, consider these
lands, and the plantations thereon, as its domains, and as of special
right properly belonging to it; not incorporated and of common
right with the dominions and realm of Great Britain: in consequence of which theory, special rights of the crown are there established; and from which theory, the special modification under
which the people possess their privileges is derived.—While this is
the idea on one hand, the people on the other say, that they could
not forfeit, nor lose the common rights and privileges of Englishmen, by adventuring under various disasters and difficulties; under
heavy expences, and every hazard, to settle these vast countries, to
engage in untried channels of labour, thereby increasing the nation's commerce, and extending its dominions; but that they must
carry with them, where-ever they go, the right of being governed
only by the laws of the realm; only by laws made with their own
consent:—that they must ever retain with them the right of not
being taxed without their own consent, or that of their representatives; and therefore, as it were by nature divided off from the share
of the general representation of the nation, they do not hold, by
tenor of charter or temporary grant, in a commission, but by an
inherent, essential right, the right of representation and legislature,
with all its powers and privileges, as possessed in England. It is,
therefore, that the people do, and ever will, until this matter be
settled, exercise these rights and privileges after the precedents

formed here in England, and perhaps carried, in the application, even further, than they ever were in England; and not under the restriction of commissions and instructions: and it is therefore also, in matters where laws, made since their establishment, do not extend to them by special proviso, that they claim the right of directing themselves by their own laws. While these totally different ideas of the principles, whereon the government and the people found their claims and rights, remain unsettled and undetermined, there can be nothing but discordant jarring, and perpetual obstruction in the exercise of them;—there can be no government, properly so called, but merely the predominancy of one faction or the other, acting under the mask of the forms of government. This is the short and precise abstract of the long and perplexed history of the governments and administrations of the colonies, under the various shapes with which their quarrels have vexed themselves, and teized government at home.

If this idea of the crown's right to govern these as domains be just, and be as right in fact, as it is supposed to be in theory, let it be settled and fixed by some due and sufficient authority, what it is, and how far it extends. But this is not all; let it be so established, that where it ought, it may actually, and in practice, be carried into execution also. If this right be doubted; or if, being allowed, it finds itself in such circumstances as not to be able to carry its powers into execution, it will then become an object of government, to see that these colonies be governed, and their affairs administered some other way. There is no doubt in the theory of our constitution of the king's right, in time of war and array, to exercise martial law: and yet in practice it has been found right, (and would not otherwise be permitted) that this martial law should be confirmed by parliament.

If, therefore, the several points wherein the crown, or its governors acting under its instructions, differ with the people be considered, and it be once determined what, in order to maintain the subordination of the government of the colonies to the government of Great Britain, is necessary to be done,—the mode of doing that will be easily settled. If it be a point determined, that it lies wholly with the crown to fix and actuate this order of government—the crown will duly avail itself of that power, with which it is entrusted, to enforce its administration. But if it be found that, however this may lie with the crown as of right, yet the crown is not in power to establish this right,—it will of course call in aid the power of the legislature, to confirm and establish it. But if, finally, it should appear, that these colonies, as corporations within the dominions of Great Britain, are included within the imperium of the realm of the same,—it will then of right become the duty of legislature to interpose in the case; to regulate and define their rights and privileges; to establish and order their administration; and to direct the channels of their commerce. Tho' the first of these measures should be, in strict justice, the crown's right—yet the second is the only next practicable one: and altho' the second, as such, may most likely be adopted—yet the third is the only wise and sure measure. In the second case, the crown, having formed its several general instructions for the several governments, according to their various charters, grants, and proprietaries, will order the same, in those points which it cannot influence and determine by the effect of its own negative, to be laid before parliament, to be considered and confirmed by the legislature, in the same manner as are the rules for governing the army. In the third case, the crown will order its ministry to lay before parliament the rights and powers of the crown; the rights, privileges and claims of the people; with a general state of the colonies, their interest and operations, as related to the crown, as related to the mother country, as related to foreign powers and interests, and to the colonies of foreign powers, as related to the laws and government of the mother country;— perhaps pointing out some general plan of government, judicatory, revenue and commerce, as may become, what I hinted at in the beginning of this paper—a leading measure to the forming Great Britain, with all its Atlantic and American possessions, into one great commercial dominion. In the one case, the instructions of the crown, either some general form of such, or the special ones given to each governor, on each fresh nomination, will be confirm'd by parliament, as the rules and orders for governing the army are. In the other, a general bill of rights, and establishment of government and commerce on a great plan of union, will be settled and en-acted: the governments of the several colonies, on the continent and in the islands, will be considered as so many corporations, holding their lands in common soccage, according to the manor of East Greenwich, united to the realm; so that, for every power, which they exercise or possess, they will depend on the government of Great Britain; so that, in every movement, they may be held, each within its proper sphere, and be drawn and connected to this center: and as forming a one system, they will be so connected in

their various orbs and subordination of orders, as to be capable of
receiving and communicating, from the first mover (the government of Great Britain) any political motion, in the direction in
which it is given. Great Britain, as the center of this system, must
be the center of attraction, to which these colonies, in the administration of every power of their government, in the exercise of
their judicial powers, and the execution of their laws, and in every
operation of their trade, must tend. They will be so framed, in
their natural and political interests; in the rights, privileges, and
protection they enjoy; in the powers of trade, which they actuate,
under the predominating general commerce of the nation, that
they will remain under the constant influence of the attraction of
this center; and cannot move, but that every direction of such
movement will converge to the same. At the same time that they
all conspire in this one center, they must be guarded against
having, or forming, any principle of coherence with each other
above that, whereby they cohere in this center; having no other
principle of intercommunication between each other, than that by
which they are in joint communion with Great Britain as the
common center of all. At the same time that they are, each in their
respective parts and subordinations, so framed, as to be actuated by
this first mover,—they should always remain incapable of any
coherence, or of so comspiring amongst themselves, as to create
any other equal force, which might recoil back on this first mover:
nor is it more necessary to preserve the several governments subordinate within their respective orbs, than it is essential to the
preservation of the empire to keep them disconnected and independent of each other: they certainly are so at present; the different manner in which they are settled, the different modes under
which they live, the different forms of charters, grants and frame of
government they possess, the various principles of repulsion,—that
these create the different interests which they actuate, the religious
interests by which they are actuated, the rivalship and jealousies
which arise from hence, and the impracticability, if not the impossibility of reconciling and accommodating these incompatible ideas
and claims, will keep them for ever so. And nothing but a tamper-
ing activity of wrongheaded inexperience misled to be meddling,
can ever do any mischief here. The provinces and colonies are
under the best form as to this point, which they can be. They are
under the best frame and disposition for the government of the
mother country (duly applied) to take place. And as there cannot

be a more just, so there cannot be a wiser measure than to leave them all in the free and full possession of their several rights and privileges, as by grant, charter, or commission given, and in the full exercise thereof, so far, and no further, than as derived therefrom. If, upon a revision, there be found any, and perhaps some one such at least, may be found, who have grossly and intentionally transgressed these bounds, such should be an exception to this rule, and be made an example also to others.

Under the guidance therefore of these principles—that the final external profits of the labour and produce of colonies should center in the mother country,—that the colonists are the appropriated special customers of the mother country,—that the colonies, in their government and trade, should be all united in communion with, and subordination to the government of the mother country, but ever disconnected and independent of each other by any other communion than what centers here:—Under the guidance of these principles, with a temper and spirit which remember that these are our own people, our brethren, faithful, good and beneficial subjects, and free-born Englishmen, or by adoption, possessing all the right of freedom:—Under the guidance of these principles, and with this temper and spirit of government,—let a revision be made of the general and several governments of the colonies, of their laws and courts of justice, of their trade, and the general British laws of trade, in their several relations in which they stand to the mother country, to the government of the mother country, to foreign countries, and the colonies of foreign countries, to one another; and then let those measures be taken, which, upon such a review, shall appear necessary; and all which government can do, or ought to do at present, will be done.

Upon such review it will appear, under this first general head, in various instances, that the two great points which the colonists labour to establish, is the exercise of their several rights and privileges, as founded in the rights of an Englishman; and secondly, as what they suppose to be a necessary measure in a subordinate government, the keeping in their own hands the command of the revenue, and the pay of the officers of government, as a security for their conduct towards them.

Under the first head come all the disputes about the King's instructions, and the governor's power.

The King's commission to his governor, which grants the power of government, and directs the calling of a legislature, and the establishing courts, at the same time that it fixes the governor's power, according to the several powers and directions granted and appointed by the commission and instructions, adds, "and by such *further powers, instructions,* and authorities, as shall, at any time hereafter be granted or appointed you, under our signet or sign manual, or by our order in our privy council." It should here seem, that the same power which framed the commission, with this clause in it, could also issue its *future orders and instructions* in consequence thereof: but the people of the colonies say, that the inhabitants of the colonies are entitled to all the privileges of Englishmen; that they have a right to participate in the legislative power; and that no commands of the crown, by orders in council, instructions, or letters from Secretaries of State, are binding upon them, further than they please to acquiesce under such, and conform *their own actions* thereto; that they hold this right of legislature, not derived from the grace and will of the crown, and depending on the commission which continues at the will of the crown; that this right is inherent and essential to the community, as a community of Englishmen: and that therefore they must have all the rights, privileges, and full and free exercise of their own will and liberty in making laws, which are necessary thereto,—uncontrouled by any power of the crown, or of the governor, as derived therefrom; and, that the clause in the commission, directing the governor to call together a legislature by his writs, is declarative and not creative; and therefore he is directed to act conformably to a right actually already existing in the people, &c.

Just, as this reasoning may be, and right, as it may be, that the assembly, in its legislative capacity, as one branch, should be independent of the governor as another branch in the legislature,—yet sure, so long as these governments are subordinate to the government of the mother country, even the legislature cannot act independent of it, nor of that part of it which the constitution has determined is to govern these colonies. I do not here enter into the discussion of this point; I only endeavour fairly to state it, as I think, it is a matter which ought to be settled some way or other, and ought no longer to remain in contention, that the several matters which stand in instruction, and in dispute in consequence of it, may be finally placed upon their right grounds; in the doing of which it must come under consideration, how far the crown has or has not a right to direct or restrict the legislature of the colonies,—or if the crown has not this power, what department of government has, and how it ought to be exercised;—or whether in fact or deed, the people of the colonies, having every right to the full powers of government, and *to a whole legislative power*, are under this claim entitled in the powers of legislature and the administration of government, to use and exercise in conformity to the laws of Great Britain, the same, full, free, independent, unrestrained power and legislative will in their several corporations, and under the King's commission and their respective charters, as the government and legislature of Great Britain holds by its constitution, and under the great charter. . . .

I have not gone into the thorough examination of these subjects above-mentioned, nor have I pointed out, in all their consequences, the effects that this or that state of them would have. I have only pointed them out as worthy the attention of government; and, I am sure, whenever government takes them under consideration, they will be better understood than any explanation of mine can make them.

Were some such arrangements taken for a revision and further establishment of the laws of trade, upon the principle of extending the British general commerce, by encouraging the trade of the colonies, in subordination to, and in coincidence therewith, the trade of the colonies would be administered by that true spirit from whence it rose, and by which it acts; and the true application of the benefits which arise to a mother country from its colonies would be made. Under this spirit of administration, the government, as I said above, could not be too watchful to carry its laws of trade into effectual execution. Some of the laws of trade direct the prosecution and punishment of the breach of them to take its course in the courts of vice-admiralty. And it has been thought, by a very great practitioner, that if the laws of trade were regulated, on a practicable application of them to the state of the colony trade, that every breach of them should be prosecuted in the same way, by an Advocate appointed to each court from Great Britain, with a proper salary, who should be directed and impowered to prosecute in that court, not only every trader that was an offender, but also every officer of the customs, who thro' neglect, collusion, oppression, or any other breach of his trust, became such: but I own, was it not for the precedent established already by some of the laws of trade, I should doubt the consistency of this measure with the general principle of liberty, as establish ¹ in the trials by a jury in the common law courts.—Under the present state of those laws, and that trade, whatever be the course of prosecution, there is great danger that any severity of execution, which should prove effectual in the cases of the importation into the colonies of foreign European and East India goods, might force the Americans to trade for their imports, upon terms, on which the trade could not support itself, and might become in the event a means to bring on the necessity of these Americans manufacturing for themselves. Nothing does at present, with that active and acute people, prevent their going into manufactures, but the proportionate dearness of labour, as referred to the terms on which they can import; but encrease the price of their imports to a certain degree, let the extent of their settlements, either by policy from home, or invasion of Indians abroad be confined, and let their foreign trade and navigation be, in some measure, suppressed;—their money-currency limited within too narrow bounds, by a total prohibition of paper-money; —this proportion of the price of labour, considering the length of the winters, when no labour can be done without doors, and considering how many hands will be taken from navigation and settlements, together with the want of money, the means of purchasing, will much sooner cease to be an object of objection to manufacturing there, than is commonly apprehended. And if the colonies, under any future state of administration which they see unequal to the management of their affairs, once come to feel their own strength in this way, their independence on government, at least on the administration of government, will not be an event so remote as our leaders may think, which yet nothing but such false policy can bring on. For, on the contrary, put their governments and laws on a true and constitutional basis, regulate their money, their revenue, and their trade, and do not check their settlements, they must ever depend on the trade of the mother country for their supplies, they will never establish manufactures, their hands being elsewhere employed, and the merchants being always able to import such on terms that must ruin the manufacturers, unable to subsist without, or to unite against the mother country; they must always remain subordinate to it, in all the transactions of their commerce, in all the operation of their laws, in every act of their governments;—and to repeat what I have already said, as they will thus become conscientiously in each individual, so will they constitutionally, in their respective governments, subordinate, attached, and obedient to the mother country, and to the supreme government thereof;—and the several colonies, no longer considered as demesnes of the crown, mere appendages to the realm, will thus become, united therein, members and parts of the realm, as essential parts of a one organized whole, *the commercial dominion of Great Britain*. The taking leading measures to the forming of which, ought, at this juncture, to be the great object of government.